The Woman Who Could Not Forget

The Woman Who Could Not Forget

IRIS CHANG BEFORE AND BEYOND
The Rape of Nanking

Ying-Ying Chang

PEGASUS BOOKS
NEW YORK

THE WOMAN WHO COULD NOT FORGET

Pegasus Books LLC
80 Broad Street, 5th Floor
New York, NY 10004

Copyright © 2011 by Ying-Ying Chang

Introduction copyright © 2011 by Richard Rhodes

First Pegasus Books trade paperback edition 2011

Interior design by Maria Fernandez

Library of Congress Cataloging-in-Publication Data is available.

ISBN: 978-1-60598-172-7

10 9 8 7 6 5 4 3 2 1

Printed in the United States of America
Distributed by W. W. Norton & Company

To my husband, Shau-Jin, for his patience, support, and love

and

To Christopher, so he will know his mother

CONTENTS

IRIS CHANG:
AN INTRODUCTION

by Richard Rhodes

T his book celebrates the life of a remarkable young woman. It was a life cut short by early death, but it is no less worthy of celebration because of that fact. "Any man's death diminishes me," the English poet and cleric John Donne wrote in his most celebrated meditation, ". . . because I am involved in mankind." Any woman's death as well, but every man and woman's *life* increases us, because every human life is an expression of the nearly limitless possibilities of human invention, compassion—of human love. Even those whom we consider evil, those who perpetrate evil acts, reveal human possibilities, however much we tremble to know them.

Iris Chang found her first full voice as a writer, and her purpose as a young Chinese-American, exhuming the horrors of the Japanese massacre of Chinese civilians in Nanking in December 1937 and January 1938. I have written about other horrors—the early "bullet holocaust" of the Jews of Poland and the Soviet Union following the German invasion of those countries in 1939 and 1941, the atomic bombings of the Japanese cities of Hiroshima and Nagasaki—and know how painful the work of reading documents and interviewing witnesses and survivors can be. Secondary trauma is a hazard of such a project. As did Iris, I experienced nightmares and mild depression, which I took for a sign that I was entering, if only distantly and safely, into the experience of the victims I was writing about.

I know why I chose to explore such terrible events. I don't know why Iris did, but I suspect her deepest purpose was to embody the compassion she felt for the victims, and her outrage at the perpetrators, in careful, thoughtful witness. She was as well indignant that the Nanking Massacre had been half-forgotten in the West and minimized, if not actually denied, by the Japanese government. Her cultural background helped her to frame her perspective on this complicated history. So did her equal facility in Mandarin and in English.

But to mention only her best-known work is to leave out another rich part of Iris's life: her life as a person—as a child, a daughter, a young adult, a wife, and a mother. In the course of our lives from birth to death we fill multiple roles. None is complete without the other; each complements the other. Whatever your religious beliefs, at minimum those we have lost survive in our memory of them. In this memoir Iris's mother, Ying-Ying Chang, shares her memories of that other part of Iris's life, the part that was private. Writing it, Ying-Ying tells us, helped her work through her grief at her daughter's death. For those who knew Iris only or primarily through her books, learning more about her life enlarges our sense of who she was and how she came to her celebrated work.

I met Iris only once, and knew her otherwise through her work and through correspondence, but what an afternoon that meeting was! I had not yet moved to California; I was visiting San Francisco on a book tour. Iris and I had previously been in touch, probably on the grim subject of massacres, and I had invited her to join me for lunch. We did, at the hotel where I was staying in downtown San Francisco, on a quiet day that I recall as a Sunday. Iris's first appearances must have always been surprising. Certainly I was surprised (and delighted) by her remarkable presentation: she was tall, striking, articulate, intense.

We lingered at table for something like three hours. The restaurant emptied out; the table was cleared; the waiters probably changed shifts. We compared notes about writing. We complained about our publishers, as all professional writers do when their readers probably expect them to be discussing more literary matters (but writing is almost always financially a thin string and worrisome). Iris was troubled about the attacks on her book. I remember wondering if she was concerned unnecessarily—the attacks she described seemed so unlikely in America at the turn of the millennium. I see from this memoir that she was not. There was reason for her concern, attacks that continue online to this day. When Iris was alive they were direct and personal—and from her perspective, threatening.

I had a chance to know Iris personally. Now that I also know her parents, I see where her intelligence and her courage came from. In this brave memoir you will meet a unique young woman and her family and share in the celebration of a life. When the loss of someone dear to us or of some public personage such as a writer or artist moves us, the French anthropologist Claude Lévi-Strauss once wrote, "we suffer much the same sense of irreparable privation that we should experience were *Rosa centifolia* [i.e., the rose species] to become extinct and its scent to disappear forever." Memoir can't bring Iris Chang back, but it can at least allow us to experience her presence again. It was always a vivid presence, full of the courage of her convictions, full of life.

—*Richard Rhodes*

FOREWORD

"The Power of One" was the credo Iris stood by and often shared with her audience and fans through her rigorous writings and hundreds of speeches from coast to coast during her meteoric and yet brilliant career.

That was one of the reasons for which Iris was so driven and dedicated to certain causes in her life, devoted her complete energy and every waking moment to think, strategize, promote, strive, evaluate, and then retry in order to make a difference, more often than not, as a lone ranger with *"The Power of One"*!

She was also a great team player. For the years since Iris walked into our lives in the heart of Silicon Valley, specifically in a community center in the City of Cupertino in California, during an international conference in December 1994, that slender and photogenic young woman with a ponytail as many have seen in the docudrama film, *"Iris Chang: The Rape of Nanking,"* constantly talked and wrote to us (the most active members of the Global Alliance for Preserving the History of WWII in Asia—a North America-based community group), shared with us her meticulously gathered, documented, and researched historic facts, and took part in related academic activities in the U.S. and Canada. She never failed to stay in touch wherever she was, whether at home or in a hotel room miles and miles away from the nearest airports. The crisp sound of her keyboard strokes over the phone, documenting every word that we exchanged, is still reverberating in the back of my mind to this day. Hundreds and thousands of her e-mails to many, years before the majority of Americans discovered the word "Internet," certainly qualify her as a great communicator and a fellow "cyber warrior" of mine. The bulk of this book is based on the huge e-mail archive that her mother, also an outstanding and meticulous scholar, has kept over the years.

Evolved from shy to shine. As she rose to become an international bestseller author for her book exposing the horrific history of Japan's unprecedented rampage in eight weeks in 1937 and 1938—massacre of hundreds of thousands of civilians, raping women and girls of all ages, looting and burning down China's defenseless ancient capital, Nanking, Iris quickly transformed herself from a seemingly nerdy bookworm and prolific journalist into a top-notch public speaker at all occasions, including in the presence of the president of the United States and the first lady at a *Renaissance Weekend*. It used to take her all day to prepare for a fifteen-to-twenty-minute presentation when *"The Rape of Nanking"* was published in December 1997. A year later, a memorable moment took place on MacNeil-Lehrer's *PBS Newshour* program—Iris turned a stuttering Japanese ambassador to the United States, Kunihiko Saito, into jelly in less than thirty seconds in a live televised debate.

Message to all the Japanese right-wingers: "Iris was neither an agent of the Chinese government nor an American spy as you have absurdly suggested, just an agent of change"!

All-around human-rights champion. While most people are familiar with her exceptional writing, Iris however wasn't just passionate about certain subjects with her relentless advocacy—such as her pursuit of justice for those who were brutally victimized or murdered in Asia and the Pacific theater by the Imperial Japanese war machine during WWII. She also held deep and unwavering conviction to civil rights and human rights at home and abroad.

For example, Iris was extremely disturbed by the widespread Muslim-bashing in the country immediately after the 9/11 terrorist attacks and George W. Bush's unjust invasion of Iraq. She took part in a TV cable public forum along with Jewish and Arabic activists who shared her serious concerns even though Iris was at the time intensely involved in her vast book research and numerous speeches at universities and national television/radio stations. Her gloomy face reflected her profound feeling for those victimized by racial prejudice and hatred as she discussed how history sadly repeated itself in America and elsewhere—from the past discrimination against immigrants (Irish, Jews, Chinese, etc.), to the unconstitutional internment of Americans of Japanese descent, to the modern-day bashing of ethnic minorities.

Spoke from her heart and soul. It is also interesting to note that her writing style rankles some who have criticized her as a historian with bias and rage. Well, Iris inked the words that virtually placed herself in the shoes of her subjects as if she were in the room or courtyard with them as the victims faced their suffering and ultimate doom. Iris was a perfectionist and always held true and faithful to historical facts, but she presented her findings in a very dramatic, often unpleasant, way that some would rather choose to reject than accept how any human being could become absolutely devilish, given certain circumstance.

Caring and responsive at all times. It's human nature that we are all corruptible by power, wealth, and fame. Iris, however, never let fame shear her humanity and good next-door-girl nature. Yearly after her passing, her readers, mostly strangers, have spoken of the e-mails or phone calls that they received from Iris in response to their random questions. Many high-school and college students were inspired by her personal messages. A number of her fellow authors, including some well-known bestseller writers, also have expressed their gratitude for her generous contributions of either review or unreserved assistance to help publish their work.

Not without fear! Her admirers praise Iris as a fearless crusader. That is only partially true, though. Iris was a fighter. That's for sure. But she incessantly lived on edge and in fear of unpredictable harm to herself and her family rising from the constant threats from rogue history deniers. She did not ever let the fear overcome her determination to pursue justice, though. This young woman somehow harnessed the ultimate courage of a spirited soldier to charge forward nevertheless.

An insightful book. This memoir was written from a loving mother's perspective in chronicling Iris's life and career, many of her joyful moments, love of life and literacy, deepest fear, courage, and her succumbing to the weight of depression in the end. Readers will learn facts that were previously unknown to most of us, the ups and downs in the life of a small-town girl from the Midwest who became a bigger-than-life star in modern American literacy. With Iris's firm belief: "anyone can do it," we should and must follow her steps to strive for greatness.

Public service. Despite the social taboo in discussing mental illness and the excruciating recount of Iris's final journey through depression and a nervous breakdown, Ying-Ying has painstakingly documented all turns of events, day by day and sometimes hour by hour. It is to inform readers how and what might have happened to an apparently outgoing and all-around healthy woman psychologically. She has thoroughly recorded what Iris went through and how the family dealt with the difficult situation, from the sudden news of Iris's breakdown during a research trip, through months of treatment with their desperate attempt to learn and cope with something totally unknown to the family members as often happening to others caught up in comparable circumstance. She has documented the diagnoses, their interactions with doctors, and various medicines used.

In addition, Ying-Ying has also included in the epilogue the findings and valuable references from her follow-up studies after Iris passed away. Her intent is to offer this book about mental illness, related treatments, choices of medicine, and precautionary measures as a public service so others would hopefully be benefitted from taking appropriate preemptive actions to prevent similar tragedies in the future.

One must understand how hard it was for Ying-Ying to go through her recollection, relive her nightmare once again, and spend several years to compile and document the relevant information. It was very honorable on her part to do so. This is a great gift to the public. It is done to honor the memory of her beloved daughter, Iris Chang.

—*Ignatius Y. Ding*

The Woman Who Could
Not Forget

1

The Shock

I want to forget that day. But I never will.

It was Tuesday, November 9, 2004. The phone rang at 8:30 A.M. Our son-in-law, Brett Douglas, told us that our daughter, Iris, had slipped out of their home during the night. Her white 1999 Oldsmobile Alero was not in the garage.

We rushed to their townhouse, just a two-minute walk from our own home. A San Jose police officer had already been there, talked to Brett, and left. Brett showed us a printed note he had found next to Iris's computer. It was addressed to Brett; my husband, Shau-Jin; Iris's brother, Mike; and me. She had printed out the note at 1:44 A.M. It read, in part:

> *Dear Brett, Mom, Dad and Mike:*
>
> *For the last few weeks, I have been struggling with my decision as to whether I should live or die.*
>
> *As I mentioned to Brett, when you believe you have a future, you think in terms of generations and years; when you do not, you live not just by the day—but by the minute.*

You don't want someone who will live out the rest of her days as a
mere shell of her former self. . . . I had considered running away, but I
will never be able to escape from myself and my thoughts.
  I am doing this because I am too weak to withstand the years of pain
and agony ahead. Each breath is becoming difficult for me to take. . . .
The anxiety can be compared to drowning in an open sea. I know that my
actions will transfer some of this pain to others, indeed those who love me
the most. Please forgive me. Forgive me because I cannot forgive myself.
  Love, Iris

My heart was pounding in my chest so loudly, I could hear it. I could barely breathe. I told Shau-Jin and Brett we needed to go find her, to bring her back.

In the past few weeks, Iris had often talked about how she didn't want to live any longer. She had been severely depressed since she'd returned from Louisville, Kentucky, where she had gone to interview American POWs of World War II for a book on the Bataan Death March. Before she went to Kentucky on August 12, she had barely slept for four straight nights and had eaten almost nothing. Soon after arriving in Louisville, she'd had what seemed to be a nervous breakdown in her hotel room. Shau-Jin and I had jumped on a flight and brought her back to San Jose, where she had seen three psychiatrists for depression and taken antipsychotic drugs and an antidepressant. In October, Iris's two-year-old son, Christopher, went to live with Brett's parents in Illinois.

My husband and I couldn't understand how Iris's life had unraveled so quickly. That spring, she had gone on a whirlwind five-week trip to promote her latest book, *The Chinese in America*. Before Iris had left for the book tour, she'd seemed perfectly fine. When she returned home in early May, she became apprehensive and preoccupied, believing someone wanted to harm her. After she had the breakdown, three months later, her paranoia had worsened.

On October 28, after I discovered an application to own a gun and a firearms safety manual in her purse, I found out she had visited a gun shop in east San Jose. When I confronted her, she realized I was watching her closely and became distant. She didn't return my phone calls or answer my e-mails. I brought flowers and food to her doorstep, but she didn't even allow me to come into her home or get near her.

Now she had left a suicide note and disappeared. But I still held out hope. Maybe she had changed her mind about killing herself and would soon come home—as she had in September, when she had checked into a local hotel for the day but returned that evening. I had never really been a religious person, but as my knees shook and my hands trembled, I started to pray.

Shau-Jin and I returned home and got ready to leave. But we soon realized that it would be impossible to find her without a plan.

"What are we going to do?" Shau-Jin asked me in desperation.

"I don't know," I said, my voice shaking. "Let me check with the police."

I called the San Jose Police Department with the case number Brett had given us and asked whether the police had any news about Iris. One officer told me that the police had already put her name and her car's license plate number into the missing-persons database.

"No new information," he told me, assuring me that police would inform us of any developments right away.

I was so desperate, I called the Police Department every half hour or so. I always got the same answer.

"What do you think Iris will do?" I asked Shau-Jin.

He didn't answer. He was as scared as I was.

I decided to share the news with all our close relatives. First I called my son, Michael. He was the only other person who really knew what was going on with his sister. Michael was a software engineer for a Silicon Valley company, and his office was close to our home. Unfortunately, Michael was in New York on business. I reached him on his cell phone and he listened in stunned silence, quickly deciding to fly back home as soon as possible.

I also called my older brother, Cheng-Cheng, in nearby Palo Alto, my younger brother, Bing, in New Jersey and my younger sister, Ging-Ging, in Maryland. In the meantime, Shau-Jin called his two brothers, Shau-Yen in New Jersey and Frank in Los Angeles, in hopes that they could offer guidance. They were all in shock, because Iris had prohibited us from telling anyone, even close relatives, about her nervous breakdown. None of my siblings even knew Iris had been depressed. They tried to calm me down, saying that Iris would certainly change her mind about taking her life and return home soon. But they offered no concrete ideas of what I should do.

Each of them soon called me back and asked me details about Iris's recent struggle with depression. Repeating the details over and over left me exhausted.

It was ironic that one of the worst days in my life up until that point, September 21, 2004, had given me hope. That was the day that Iris went missing for several hours. At the time, Brett was out of town and we were taking care of her.

When she didn't return home by late afternoon as promised, we reported her missing to the police. At the time, she was taking a new antipsychotic drug called Abilify, plus the antidepressant Celexa. She had experienced side effects from the drugs: shoulder and leg pain, drowsiness, and agitation.

Against my wishes, she had insisted on driving herself to the library that morning. When she returned home at about 8 P.M., she told us that she had checked into a Crowne Plaza Hotel close to where we live. She said she had become so sleepy after shopping that she had gone to the hotel and fallen asleep for several hours. We were extremely relieved, of course.

So I thought that maybe she had checked into a hotel again. I opened the Yellow Pages with shaking hands and called the Crowne Plaza and other major hotels in the area, asking whether they had a guest named Iris Chang or Iris Douglas, her married name. They didn't.

I then looked up the phone numbers of spas in the seaside city of Santa Cruz and in the forested mountains west of San Jose. Iris liked getting massages and had often gone with Brett and her friends to spas there. But spa employees told me they didn't have any guests named Iris, or anyone who matched her description. Still, I had some hope that she'd registered under a different name.

My brain was fried, my body trembling. I kept calling Brett to ask if he had any new information. He didn't. Brett had informed his parents in Illinois about her disappearance and was busy searching Iris's home office for clues and sending all the information he could to the missing-persons detective assigned to Iris's case.

As Shau-Jin kept pacing back and forth in the family room, I suddenly envisioned Iris browsing in a bookstore, one of her favorite things to do since she was a child. I systematically called several big bookstores in the area. I asked them whether they had seen a thin, tall Asian woman with long black hair in the store. Again, no luck.

I called Iris's cell phone but, as usual, it was turned off. I also wrote her an e-mail, pleading with her to come home. I assumed she would be checking her e-mail periodically, even if she was hiding somewhere.

By late afternoon, my throat was dry and coarse from talking on the phone. I was drained and devastated, and the police continued to tell us that there was nothing new. I told Shau-Jin that we needed to go look for her car, even though I figured the chances of finding her were slim. Still, I told Shau-Jin, we needed to search for her. I couldn't just sit at home and do nothing.

Shau-Jin drove up and down the rows of cars in the parking lots of several nearby hotels and places she liked to shop, as I scanned all the cars and license plate numbers. I was in a different world, oblivious to all the people around me. I concentrated only on scanning the parked cars and their license plates. But Iris's car was not there.

My heart was still pulsating with anxiety, and my hope faded as twilight turned into darkness. Under the dim yellow lights in the parking lot of the Crowne Plaza Hotel, we circled the lot one more time. Finally, we gave up and drove home.

I felt as if I were on the edge of a cliff, about to fall down into a deep valley below. I became even more frightened as I peered out the windows of our townhouse into the night sky. If she had driven to a strange place, she could had been robbed or even killed by someone in the street because she was so mentally vulnerable. It had been eighteen hours since she'd printed out the note, and no one could tell us where she was.

At about 8 P.M., I called Iris's most recent psychiatrist and told him that Iris had disappeared and left a suicide note. He asked me to read the note to him.

Previously, the psychiatrist had always thought I was a neurotic mother and too protective of Iris. He hadn't believed Iris was suicidal until we informed him that Iris was browsing suicide Web sites. But Iris never disclosed her innermost feelings to him.

I once asked Iris what she talked about during her therapy sessions. She said she and the psychiatrist spent a lot of time talking about the philosophy of life. It seemed too abstract to me. I worried that she wasn't getting the help she needed.

Now the psychiatrist was telling us that Brett, Shau-Jin, and I should go to the Golden Gate Bridge, one of the most popular places in the world to commit suicide, because Iris had mentioned "drowning in an open sea" in her suicide note. Hearing his words, I felt my spine dripping with cold sweat. He urged us to drive to the bridge and check out the parking lots. But Shau-Jin and I were already exhausted physically and emotionally after a day of fruitless searching. We did not have the energy to drive to San Francisco.

But I was able to find the phone number of the Golden Gate Bridge Patrol. I gave an officer Iris's car license plate number and description of what she looked like. For the next few hours, I was in constant contact with the officer. He was patient and kind.

Eventually, however, he told us that no one who looked like Iris was near the bridge, and her car wasn't there either.

A creepy thought engulfed me: if Iris had driven her car over a cliff and plunged into the ocean, we might *never* find her.

I also thought about how she had talked in recent weeks about "escaping." What if she had driven to some remote place and planned to hide there indefinitely? "O, Iris, please come home," I shouted to myself in desperation.

I can't recall when I fell asleep that night. I just remember the frightening sound of a ringing telephone piercing the quiet darkness. It was Brett. He said he was coming to our home with a police officer. I looked at the clock on the wall. It was nearly midnight.

We opened the door. Brett and a plainclothes officer came in. Both looked solemn.

"I'm sorry to inform you that Iris is dead," the officer said. "She shot herself early this morning and her body was found in her car, near Los Gatos."

I felt as if I'd been caught in a violent storm. The thunder was deafening. The lightning blinded me. The earth seemed to shake.

Shau-Jin and I collapsed onto the carpet of our living room, and I found myself falling into an endless black tunnel. I heard my voice echoing:

"Iris, Iris, how could you kill yourself? How could you desert Christopher, me, and your father?

"How could you do such a thing to me?

"How can I live the rest of my life without you?"

But I would have to. All I have now are decades of memories—some haunting, but most filled with love.

Iris Chang was the author of a 1998 *New York Times* best seller, and when she died she was only thirty-six years old.

Her bestselling book, *The Rape of Nanking: The Forgotten Holocaust of World War II*, published in 1997, on the sixtieth anniversary of the massacre, examines one of the most tragic chapters of World War II: the slaughter, gang rape, and torture of hundreds of thousands of Chinese civilians by Japanese soldiers in the former capital of China. The book made a huge impact on the global redress movement regarding the Imperial Japanese war crimes in Asia during World War II.

Her death shocked the world. No one believed a best-selling author, a young, beautiful rising star like Iris Chang, would kill herself. Her death was headline news in almost all the major newspapers throughout the world. The news was also immediately broadcast over radio and TV stations. The shockwave hit Chinese Diaspora communities hard, all over the globe.

On November 19, 2004, six hundred people showed up on short notice to her funeral in Los Altos, California. The chapel at Gate of Haven cemetery was too small for such a huge number of people; mourners overflowed onto the lawn outside the chapel. Many of them were Iris's friends and supporters, but most were strangers and admirers. Letters, telegrams, and flowers of condolence poured in from all corners of the world.

During the funeral, James Bradley, the best-selling author of *Flags of Our Father* and *Flyboys*, addressed his eulogy to Iris's two years old son. He said, in part (the complete text of the Eulogy is located in the Appendix),

> *Christopher, your mother was Iris Chang. . . . Five years before you were born, I was struggling in my effort to write a book about the six flag-raisers in the photo.*
>
> *For two years I had tried to find a publisher. Twenty-seven publishers wrote me rejection letters. . . .*
>
> Flags of Our Father *became a* New York Times *#1 best seller. Twenty-seven publishers had said 'No.' Your mother had said 'Do it. . . .'*
>
> *(She) touched millions and will be remembered on all continents in countless ways. Here is just one of them. . . .*
>
> *And later—when you make that difficult but rewarding inner journey to discover your unique mission in the universe—when you*

find your personal truth—I hope you will acknowledge the example of your valiant mother who once fearlessly told truth to the world.

Perhaps you will write an acknowledgement to her, a thank-you like I once did.

A thank-you that begins with two bright and hopeful words.

Those two beautiful words: Iris Chang.

Michael Honda, of the California House of Representatives, made a tribute to Iris in the form of the Congressional Record in the 108th Congress. He stated that "Iris will be remembered for her work and service to the community. . . . Our community has lost a role model and close friend; the world has lost one of its finest and most passionate advocates of social and historical justice."

In Iris's obituary in the *New York Times*, Iris's agent, Susan Rabiner, said "*The Rape of Nanking* spent ten weeks on the *New York Times* 'Best Seller' list, and close to half a million copies have been sold," and "The book drew wide international attention."

In the *Los Angeles Times*, the obituary read, "The late historian Stephen Ambrose said Chang was 'maybe the best young historian we've got, because she understands that to communicate history, you've got to tell the story in an interesting way.'"

George Will, the *Washington Post* columnist, praised Iris in his 1998 article, saying "Something beautiful, an act of justice, is occurring in America today. . . . Because of Chang's book, the second rape of Nanking is ending." And reporter Richard Rongstad eulogized her with these words: "Iris Chang lit a flame and passed it to others and we should not allow that flame to be extinguished."

Of course, most of the descriptions of Iris were of her public persona.

Her book, since its publication seven years before, had created a firestorm in Japan. Right-wing groups in Japan had attacked her book in an attempt to cover up and whitewash their stained history.

Because of the unusual circumstances surrounding her death, there has been much speculation in the media. Many of these conjectures were wide of the mark, because Iris had always been a very private person. Most people only knew the Iris they saw on TV and in the papers, but not her true self.

Who was Iris Chang? What was her family background, her cultural heritage? How did she decide to become a writer, what motivated her to write the book *The Rape of Nanking*, what was her ambition, her American Dream, the reason for her suicide and whether her death could have been prevented? These are some of the questions I try to answer in this book.

The main purpose of this book is to give the world a full and accurate picture of Iris's life and the environment in which she grew up. The readers will learn how this young author was able to accomplish her life's goal of fighting for historical truth and social justice. Iris was a woman who could not forget the sufferings of those who had perished as a result of wartime atrocities. She was single-handedly and unflinchingly fighting for justice for those who had been otherwise forgotton by history. The reader will also learn—for the first time—the tragic circumstances surrounding the last few months of her life.

There has been much speculation and a spate of rumors in the media about Iris's mental condition. Without the authors knowing anything of her private life, most of the news on the Internet and even a book that was published about her mental state were purely speculations. Only family members knew what actually happened to Iris in those final days. The rumors about Iris's mental state are an injustice to her. I could not let the true story of her life be left untold.

This book will dispel many of these myths and will present Iris Chang—her trials and tribulations, her successes and failures, her love and joys, her sadness and pain—in short, Iris Chang as only we, her family, knew her. This biographical memoir is something that I had to do for Iris. And it's something I think Iris would have wanted me to do.

The Birth

The apple and cherry trees were in full blossom on the campus of the Institute for Advanced Study in Princeton, New Jersey. Baby Iris was lying in a brand-new stroller under the pink quilt my mother had just mailed her. I looked at her tiny little face; she was so peaceful in her deep slumber. It was mid-April 1968, two weeks after she'd been born.

Iris was born at Princeton Hospital in Princeton, New Jersey on March 28, 1968. At the time, my husband, Shau-Jin, was doing his postdoctoral work at the Institute for Advanced Study at Princeton, and I was doing my own postdoc at the Department of Biology at Princeton University just down the road. We were both freshly graduated from Harvard University, where we'd received our PhD's, he in physics and I in biochemistry.

The Institute for Advanced Study at Princeton is a one-of-a-kind place, a haven for theoretical physicists and mathematicians. Albert Einstein was one of its first faculty members and spent the last twenty-two years of his life there. It is a unique place because postdocs from colleges and universities throughout the world come for pure research and do not have to teach. There are no students, only faculty and postdocs. The Institute encourages and supports the original and speculative thinking that produces advances in knowledge. After five years as a graduate student, Shau-Jin was able to devote all of his time to doing what he found most interesting in his field—theoretical high-energy particle physics.

In the summer of 1967, we lived in the on-site housing project of the Institute. The place was unbelievably beautiful. It was a completely furnished one-bedroom apartment. The living room was spacious, with big wide windows, and the furniture provided was very contemporary and artistic. Huge pine and flowering trees, such as cherry and crab apple, surrounded the house, which had acres of grassy lawn. It was something of a culture shock after five years of graduate-student life in Boston.

I started working at Professor John T. Bonner's laboratory in the Department of Biology in the fall of 1967. Dr. Bonner is a world-famous authority on slime mold. My research was on the biochemical aspect of the attractant of the amoeba at the early stage of slime mold. Just before I arrived, the laboratory had identified the chemical identity of the attractant. It was a very exciting time. Dr. Bonner wanted me to find out why the extracellular concentration of the attractant of amoeba was so low. I was able to identify an enzyme that degraded the attractant very quickly. I worked very hard to get it done. I became pregnant shortly after we arrived at Princeton, and I needed to produce some results quickly, because this was my first postdoctoral job. Before I quit my job at the end of January 1968 due to my pregnancy, I was able to finish the experimental part of my research. The work was subsequently published in the journal *Science*, a combination of hard work and a little bit of luck.

My pregnancy made me feel awful in the mornings. Iris was overdue and was eventually born two weeks past her due date, and I was anxious the whole time. When I finally arrived at the OB unit of Princeton Hospital, I had been in labor for over fourteen hours. Iris was born at 1:12 P.M. on Thursday, March 28, 1968. I was exhausted but happy. Looking at her little face, I was in awe. At her birth, Iris did not have much hair, and her face was plump and pink, but I already thought she was the most beautiful baby ever.

⁓◦⊙◦⁓

We had decided on "Iris" as her English name and "Shun-Ru" as her Chinese name before she was born. At the time, there was no easy test to determine the gender before a baby was born, so we prepared a name for each possible sex, which took weeks of thinking. Both of us felt Iris was a good name for a baby girl; Shau-Jin especially did, as he loved Greek mythology. According to Greek mythology, Iris was a goddess of the rainbow who carried messages between heaven and earth and trailed a rainbow behind her as she passed. Greek scholars thus suggested that Iris and her rainbow represented a brief union of the earth and sky. At the same time, the word "iris" is also a vital component of our eyes for seeing the world—though, at the time, we did not realize it was also the name of a flower. Her Chinese name was my idea. Shun-Ru in Chinese is an adjective to describe something pure and innocent. The names in some ways reflect her life, which we never anticipated at the time.

The Institute's housing department was very kind—after they heard that we had a newborn, they let us move to a bigger housing unit, which had two bedrooms. They also gave us a brand-new baby crib. Indeed, the Institute knew how to provide a loving and nurturing environment for intellectuals and scholars.

With no relatives around, Shau-Jin and I raised Iris completely by Dr. Spock's famous book. Iris had a very small appetite. From the very beginning, she would only take a few ounces of formula at each feeding, and I always wondered whether she'd had enough. Being a scientist, I faithfully recorded her amount of intake at each feeding. At the end of each day, I would add up the total ounces of formula Iris had had. My friends laughed at me for being so systematic and analytical.

For many months after Iris was born, Shau-Jin was very happy and jubilant. When he got home from work, he would ask to hold her and feed her; he even changed her diaper. I did not realize how happy he was until one of his physicist colleagues told me that Shau-Jin had been continuously smiling at work since the time Iris was born.

The colleague said "I have not seen him close his mouth since then. Does he smile while he's sleeping?"

Although we were very happy with this new addition to our lives, the outside world was in chaos. Not only was there war in Vietnam, but, just a week after Iris was born, Martin Luther King, Jr. was assassinated on April 4, 1968 in Memphis, Tennessee. The whole country plunged into shock. Violence broke out in major cities across the nation, from Los Angeles to New York. Holding Iris in my arms, I could not breathe as I watched the burning and looting on TV. My heart sank as I wondered what kind of world Iris would grow up in. When that week's issue of *Newsweek* arrived, the magazine's front cover was of King lying in his coffin, with an old lady crying over his body. I told Shau-Jin I would save this issue for Iris, so that when she grew up she would learn what had been happening in the world at the time of her birth.

Then on June 5, when Iris was only two months old, Robert Kennedy was assassinated in Los Angeles. Again, the whole country went into shock. It reminded me of the day John F. Kennedy had assassinated in Dallas in 1963. Shau-Jin and I had then been graduate students at Harvard. We had been in the U.S. only one year at that time, having just arrived from Taiwan. The whole country had been in mourning. Now, however, in addition to the sadness, I felt anger. As I embraced Iris close to my chest and fed her, I looked into her eyes and murmured to myself: how can I protect you from this senseless world?

I still have that issue of *Newsweek* from April 15, 1968, but the cover and the paper have turned yellow. Iris has been dead for six years at this writing, and the United States is trapped in another "Vietnam."

I was quite uncertain at this time whether I should stay home as a full-time mom or return to work. On the one hand, I wished to stay home and take care of the baby, and believed, as my own mother told me, that no one was a better caretaker than the mother herself. On the other hand, I had just received my doctoral degree, and I really loved my work. Besides, from the very beginning, my dream was to become a scientist, and I wished to contribute what I had learned to society. After six months at home as a full-time mother, my continuous internal debating and struggling had made me miserable. Seeing me so unhappy, Shau-Jin encouraged me to go back to work. He said he believed that an unhappy mom at home would be worse than a happy working mom. I therefore landed a part-time postdoctoral research job in the lab of Professor Jacque Fresco in the Department of Chemistry at Princeton. I started working three days a week in the fall of 1968, when Iris was six months old.

In the 1960s, the majority of women stayed at home once they had children. There were not many childcare facilities or support groups for professional women, or working-mother models I could follow. I managed to work part-time for a year, but it was not without physical and mental challenges.

When I went to the lab to work after dropping Iris with her sitter, I could not stop thinking about what was happening to her. Had she stopped crying? What was the sitter doing with her if she continued to cry? These thoughts were excruciating. Sometimes, I could not concentrate on work, as I wondered whether I had made the right choice.

One way to solve the problem was to persuade my mother in Taiwan to come help. My mother was very willing and happy to do so. She spent about three months with us, but after three months my father back in Taiwan was unhappy and lonely. My mother returned home.

Yet I learned so much from my mother during those three months. First of all, my mother told me that Iris stopped crying once she saw me leave for work. She said "As soon as your car disappeared from the driveway, she turned to me, smiling with her tears still in her eyes."

As a biologist, I've always been interested in child development and fascinated by the biochemical basis of brain function. Although Shau-Jin is a physicist, he too is very interested in many biological phenomena. We often discussed at the dinner table how to bring up Iris using the best available knowledge. For example, we had read an article in one of the child-behavior magazines indicating that it's essential for normal brain development for children to go through the crawling stage. Before Iris could walk, we let her crawl all over our living room.

Shau-Jin was especially eager to expand Iris's brain function. He bought two three-dimensional wooden puzzles, one a sphere and one a cube, and put them in front of her when she was only a few months old. Since Iris seemed to have no interest in them other than putting them in her mouth, Shau-Jin started to play with the toys himself. It took *him*, a physicist, several hours to figure out the puzzles, as well how to put them back to their original shape after taking them apart. After that, these puzzles went onto Shau-Jin's office desk to test his graduate students' IQ!

When Iris was born, Shau-Jin and I agreed that we should teach Iris both English and Chinese. There are several advantages to speaking two or more languages. We knew for learning languages, it was better to start in a child's early years. It was natural for us teach her Chinese in addition to English, because Shau-Jin and I speak Chinese at home. At the beginning, we were not so sure about teaching two languages at the same time. Some of our Chinese friends told us that if we let our children learn both Chinese and English, they would get confused. They said that life in the U.S. for Chinese immigrants was hard, and they strongly urged us to teach the next generation only perfect English for survival. However, a visiting professor from Holland in the Bonner lab where I was working assured me otherwise. He told me that in Holland every child learned several languages when they were little without difficulty. He added that children who learned several languages were smarter than those who learned only one language. I therefore did a little research and found that indeed new language centers could be formed in the brain when children were introduced to multiple languages early on. With this knowledge at hand, we determined to teach Iris both languages. We would speak Chinese at home but English outside of the home.

In 1969, Shau-Jin was offered the position of assistant professor in the Department of Physics at the University of Illinois at Urbana-Champaign. So, in the summer of 1969, we ended our two-year stay in Princeton. But just before our move to Illinois, Shau-Jin was invited to a physics conference in Trieste, Italy. We were eager to take this opportunity to visit Europe.

We spent two weeks of June in Europe while Iris was only fifteen months old. My friends thought it would be too stressful to bring such a young toddler to foreign countries, but we managed. We brought with us dozens of disposable diapers and an infant back carrier, and we took turns carrying Iris on our back. We saw the Castle of Miramare in Trieste, the St. Marcus Square in Venice, the Vienna woods, and the River Danube. It was an unforgettable experience, walking through the magnificent Vienna parks that surround the summer palace, Schönbrunn. We were young and did not have any problems carrying a twenty-pound child. A photo shows the three of us sitting on top of a stone rail in a memorial overlooking the palace and the city of Vienna. Shau-Jin and I are holding Iris on our lap. We are all smiling and looking into the future with the brightest hope that our daughter will be a Chinese Phoenix.*

---

* In the Chinese culture, people wish for their sons become a "Dragon" and their daughters a "Phoenix" (Feng Huang). The Chinese Phoenix is an ancient colorful bird of grace and high virtue. When paired with a dragon, a phoenix symbolizes the Empress, and a dragon represents the Emperor. These also are the symbols signifying the highest achievement one can reach.

Childhood

W hen Iris was less than a year and a half old, we made the move to the University of Illinois at Urbana-Champaign where Shau-Jin had accepted the teaching position. But he was also going to attend a physics workshop in Boulder, Colorado in August, before the start of the school year.

On August 2, 1969, we hopped into our first new car, a green Dodge Dart, and headed west. We bought the car from a dealer located on the border of New Jersey and Pennsylvania for $2,400. Because we did not have much money, we bought a basic car with no extras, such as automatic shift or air conditioning.

First, we drove to Urbana to visit the university campus and look for living quarters for the fall. We found a new duplex, of which we rented one part, and bought some second-hand furniture. After these arrangements were made, we continued our journey to Colorado. We drove through the contrasting landscapes of the cornfields of Iowa and Nebraska, to the beautiful Rockies of Colorado. Once in Boulder,

Shau-Jin met all his physicist friends again, like a summer camp reunion. During the day, Shau-Jin was doing physics and I ran errands with Iris. In the evenings, Shau-Jin would have his friends come to our home for an informal gathering. On the weekends, we would often hike on the nearby trails with Iris in a carrier on our backs. We took turns carrying her. We explored many of the nearby state parks and, of course, Rocky Mountain National Park was the most impressive of all. I secretly wished that we could live in this beautiful part of the country for the rest of our lives.

After the workshop in Boulder was over, we began our drive back to Urbana. Iris, who was seventeen months old at the time, did not feel well. When we were about halfway home, she developed a high fever and, unfortunately, our new car's lack of air conditioning didn't help. It was the end of August, and the temperature in the car was unbearably hot. We decided to drive the rest of the way during the night while it was cool, and stay in an air-conditioned motel during the day. That evening, we stopped at a small town near Omaha. It was too late to see a doctor that evening, but we were able to consult one on the phone. Without seeing Iris, all he could say was to keep her temperature down, something we were already desperately trying to do.

I was so worried about Iris's condition that I wanted to get back to Urbana as soon as possible. She was fussing and crying with the fever, and I was trying to soothe her as best I could, but all I could do was to watch over her helplessly. At that moment, I suddenly realized how my parents must have felt more than thirty years ago when my brothers, sisters, and myself were ill during those difficult war years in China when we were growing up. My thoughts flashed back to the 1930s and 1940s in China as Shau-Jin drove through Iowa on that dark, moonless night in August.

⁂

I was born in Chungking (now Chongqing), China in 1940. Chungking was the wartime capital of China during the eight-year-long War of

Resistance against Japan, *Kang Ri zhanzheng*. Nineteen forty was a year of great suffering for the Chinese people. It was just one year before the Japanese bombed Pearl Harbor, which brought the United States into the war in Asia. China had been fighting Japan alone since 1931, when Japan had invaded Manchuria.

My parents escaped from Nanking in 1937 and retreated with a vast number of refugees, first to Wuhan on the Yangtze River, and then by train to Hengshan, a small town near one of the major north-south railroads. We stopped at Hengshan because my mother was in the last month of her pregnancy. She was carrying my elder brother, Cheng-Cheng, who was born in 1938, six days after the Chinese New Year.

In 1940, the Japanese Army had occupied a good portion of northern, eastern, and southern China, and now they started to bomb the southwestern provinces. Since it was the capital, Chungking was one of the prime targets. Japanese airplanes dropped bombs on Chunking day and night, hoping to bomb China into submission. According to my parents, the air raids went from once a day to twice a day. Once the air raid sirens sounded, everyone dropped whatever they were doing and ran into the bomb shelters. At the time, China did not have sufficient airpower to defend her skies. Groups of twenty to fifty Japanese bombers would frequently appear over Chungking's skies and drop bombs at will. Thousands of civilians were killed, their homes, schools, and hospitals destroyed. In later years, my parents described to us the many horrors they witnessed after the bombings. There were always numerous fires. Whole blocks of houses were destroyed. My father saw charred bodies everywhere and smelled the stench of burning flesh. My mother saw a severely burned woman holding the charred body of her child whom she had tried to save, but she herself was burned in the process. There were many other scenes of horror that my parents could not forget, such as a hand hanging from a tree, or part of a leg dangling on an electrical wire, grotesque reminders of the bomb explosions.

A few weeks before I was due, my father registered my mother in Chungking Central Hospital, located by the Yangtze River. He thought that since the hospital looked sturdy and well built, my mother would be safe there. Several days later, the Japanese bombed the hospital, and a part of it was destroyed. Fortunately, my mother was moved into the hospital bomb shelter just in time.

To avoid the constant bombing, my father arranged to have our family moved to a village in the mountains where there were many natural caves that served as bomb shelters. In those times, living was extremely difficult. There was a severe shortage of supplies—medical supplies in particular—and daily necessities were now luxuries. The Japanese had bombed and cut off our supply routes. All available resources were used to support the war effort.

During that time, I was sick with amoebic dysentery due to eating contaminated food and drinking unsanitary water. My parents told me that I had a high fever and bloody diarrhea. Nowadays it's easy to cure such illness with modern medicine, but at that time and in those conditions it could lead to death. My father desperately ran from drugstore to drugstore in Chungking trying to find the needed medicine. Miraculously, he found it in a small store on a small side street of Chungking, and I was saved.

On that dark moonless night, our car speeding through the lonely cornfields of Iowa, I touched Iris's forehead and truly understood the love of parents for their child. It was a sacrifice, an unconditional love. I could now identify with these feelings and was fully touched.

<hr>

After we arrived in Urbana, near Labor Day 1969, we moved into our rented duplex. The house was located in the west of Champaign. Urbana-Champaign is a twin city and Champaign is west of Urbana. (The major campus of the University of Illinois is in Urbana.)

Once we settled down, I started to look for a job. I had applied to the Department of Biochemistry. After two months of waiting, Professor

Lowell Hager called me and said that he could hire me on a part-time basis, which, given my situation, was ideal. So I started working as a research associate in November, when Iris was nineteen months old.

I was actively looking for a baby-sitter, and, to my good luck, I was introduced to a student's wife, Mrs. Hsu, who had a son about Iris's age. In the morning, we brought Iris to Mrs. Hsu's home, and at the end of the day we picked her up. Iris cried the first several times we dropped her off, but gradually she got used to the routine and played with Mrs. Hsu's son very well. To me, this was a big relief. Mrs. Hsu was a nice lady and a good mother. She was very kind to Iris.

One day, I told her that I'd noticed that Iris liked to frown and did not smile as she had before. I asked her why.

She said, "Have you smiled yourself lately?"

That one question enlightened me. Indeed, Shau-Jin and I had been troubled by a number of issues in our departments, and we were actually unhappy at the time. Mrs. Hsu encouraged me to relax and enjoy my life. From that day on, I often looked at myself in the mirror and practiced smiling. What a difference it made to my appearance when I smiled! What showed on my face was what Iris would see. She would imitate and use everything she saw as a model.

Shau-Jin and I were already thinking about having a second child. I found out that I was pregnant again in February 1970. Life was really busy. Shau-Jin was active in teaching and research and had published a number of papers. My time was equally busy in the laboratory doing my research, taking care of Iris, and doing household chores. Cooking and shopping consumed the majority of my time when I was not in the laboratory. I had no outside help—in fact, we could not afford to hire any outside help, because the amount I paid the sitter had already taken a big bite out of our salaries.

In March 1970, my mother in Taiwan became seriously ill, and in April I was sick too. The pregnancy, the research, and a small child to take care of made me physically and mentally exhausted. I was badly in need of rest, and I also needed to visit my mother in Taiwan. After six months on the job, I decided to quit. I was determined to be a devoted mother and to concentrate on raising Iris and on awaiting the arrival of our second child.

Iris seemed very happy when I decided to stay home with her, and it was a happy time for me too. I even bought a sewing machine and made simple dresses for Iris and myself. When we wore the dresses, made of the same fabric and from the same pattern, it caught people's eyes in the street. They commented that we were a lovely pair, mother and daughter. By now, Iris had become a beautiful, energetic little girl. She was very active and loved to talk to me in Chinese.

Urbana-Champaign is a mid-sized college town, 140 miles south of Chicago. The University is the center of the town. It seemed that everyone in town was in some way associated with the university. I had a good time socializing with Shau-Jin's colleagues and their wives. We also found a big group of Chinese-American faculty in town. Everyone was nice to us newcomers. We met a number of good-hearted people who showed us around the town. This kind of sincerity, honesty, and down-to-earth quality exhibited by the people of this Midwest college town had been missing in the big cities where we'd lived before. This is probably one of the reasons we lived there for many happy years.

On September 24, 1970, Michael was born. It took several months for Iris to adjust to the idea that she now had a baby brother. Iris was fascinated with him, but I think her feelings were mixed. She had been the center of the attention in the family, and now my attention was split between her and Michael.

By the time Michael was six months old and Iris was three years old, I felt that Iris needed to play with other children in her own age group. We decided to send her to a nearby preschool for two or three days a week.

When the summer of 1971 arrived, Shau-Jin took the whole family with him to visit the Fermi National Accelerator Laboratory near

Chicago for a month, and then we drove to Aspen, Colorado, where a physics conference and workshop was taking place. We spent a month in the high country of the Rocky Mountains. In Chinese, there is a saying: "Hearing it a hundred times is not worth as much as seeing it once." That was our philosophy. We took our children to as many places as we could.

In the spring of 1971, we found a small old house with a big fenced back yard at 1101 Broadmoor Drive, in south-central Champaign. This was the first house we'd ever owned. Shau-Jin started a vegetable garden and planted tomatoes, beans, Chinese leeks, and other varieties. We also erected a gym set for Iris and Michael. In the middle of the back yard stood a big maple tree. Iris usually spent her time playing under the tree and on the swings. She loved the swings and spent long hours on the gym set. She and Michael also played with water toys in a big round plastic bathtub on the back porch. Summer was hot in Champaign, and the big fenced-in yard with trees and grass was ideal for the children.

Despite the pastoral setting, 1971 was a difficult time in our lives. Shau-Jin worked extremely hard, and the Physics Department liked him very much. He had many papers published in prestigious physics journals and was considered one of the leading physicists in his field. He was also rated by his students as an excellent teacher. This was quite an honor for an immigrant such as Shau-Jin, whose native language was not English. The department promoted him to associate professor with tenure after only two years. But unfortunately, at that time the University of Illinois froze the whole university budget, according to the Illinois state government policy, due to a state budget deficiency. That year there were no salary increases for the entire university. Shau-Jin got promoted in rank, but without the commensurate increase in salary. We had a new mortgage to pay, and the house needed remodeling. We now had a family of four, with two young children. We were feeling the pinch financially, and it became necessary for me to go back to work.

In the fall of 1971, I returned to Dr. Hager's lab in the Department of Biochemistry at the University of Illinois. I had been away from the lab since the spring of 1970; but in the interval that I wasn't working, I attended the department seminars once in a while, when there were interesting speakers coming to campus. I reminded myself constantly that I should keep up in my field so I would not be out of date.

We sent Iris to a Montessori preschool, which was located just across the street from our house. It was very convenient for me to walk her there in the morning before I went to work. This was one of the reasons we bought that particular house.

Iris seemed unhappy in the Montessori preschool. She started to suck her fingers excessively. She frequently woke up in the middle of the night. I learned that, for Iris, a new house and a new school, plus our own hectic lives, made her emotionally insecure. She had nightmares at night, and she needed to be reminded of our love for her. I learned at this very early time that Iris was a sensitive child. What happened around her seemed to affect her more than ordinary kids. I also learned that I would have to deal with her feelings in a more special and tender way.

—❧—

In 1972, my parents immigrated to the U.S. and lived in New York City. Iris and Michael could finally meet their grandparents in person. Although my mother had visited us in 1968 when Iris was just a few months old, Iris had no memory of her. Iris and Michael knew of their grandparents in Taiwan, but meeting them in person would be a very different experience.

An opportunity came for Shau-Jin to visit the Brookhaven National Lab in Long Island, New York in the summer of 1972, very close to my parents in New York City.

My parents lived in a part of a rental house where my brother had helped them settle down temporarily. My father was seventy-three years old at the time, and my mother was fifty-eight. This was the last stop of their long life's journey. They had grown up in China, lived through both the Sino-Japanese War and the civil war between the Nationalists and Communists, and finally settled down in Taiwan. They had never thought they would come to the U.S. to retire, despite the fact that their five children were all here.

When we visited my parents in the summer of 1972, they had just arrived a few months before and were having difficulties adapting to their new lives. This was especially true for my father, who continuously complained that he had bad headaches due to the trans-Pacific and transcontinental flight. It took him a long time to correct his jetlag. My mother was overjoyed to see Iris and Michael, though. She had raised five children and had loved children all her life. Iris was her first granddaughter, and, as mentioned above, she had taken care of her in Princeton for several months when Iris was just a few months old. Therefore, she had a special place in her heart for Iris. My mother was a very good cook, and the first thing she did when we visited was to go to the kitchen to fix some good food for all of us. She derived much enjoyment from watching others eat her food, which for her was an expression of love as well as nourishment.

Iris was impressed with the books my father had brought over from Taiwan, now crammed in box after box in the bedroom. I told Iris that her grandpa was a great writer who had read and written many books.

Grandpa was taking every opportunity to lecture Iris and Michael. He didn't miss a chance, even with a bad headache, to tell them that they should not forget Chinese culture and that they should learn to speak and read Chinese as well. I was sure Michael did not understand what he was talking about, and I saw him sneak away. Iris was curious, however. She listened but later asked me why grandpa spoke so loud. Smiling to myself, I was sure both of them secretly agreed that they liked grandma, with her yummy food, better.

My father at one point asked me to come to his side. He specifically instructed me that I should remember to teach Iris and Michael

Chinese. The way he spoke to me, he seemed to think that we would not see each other again. He was wrong: he lived into his nineties. But on that day when we first saw each other since I'd left home for the U.S. ten years earlier, he said "You came to America to learn Western modern technologies. You should know that China has a five-thousand-year-old history. As for philosophy and ethics, the West needs to learn from us!"

My father was a very proud man. He was loyal to his old country and a fervent admirer of Chinese culture. He always reminded me of the beauty of Chinese literature and philosophy. He wanted me not to forget our Chinese roots, no matter where we went. He told me, emphatically, "You should be very proud to be Chinese!"

⚬⚬⚬

In the spring of 1972, Shau-Jin was awarded a Sloan Fellowship. This gave him the opportunity to relinquish his teaching duties. He decided to visit the Institute for Advanced Study at Princeton again in the fall of 1972 for one academic year. His plan was that after the end of the Institute visit, he would go to Europe to visit CERN, a center for European nuclear research based in Geneva. So when we came back from the Brookhaven National Lab at the end of the summer of 1972, we sublet our Champaign house for one year and left for Princeton.

As for me, I still waged a constant struggle in my mind between career and family, as so many women have done and continue to today. I wanted both to have a successful career and to raise a happy family.

After Michael was born, I had stayed at home raising children without working for a year, but I just could not help feeling bored and frustrated even though I loved Michael and Iris with all my heart. So I had gone back to work, but then felt frustrated for different reasons. The baby-sitter was not as competent as I had hoped, and when I got home millions of house chores were waiting for me. I was physically exhausted. The break I was about to take in 1972 at Princeton would give me a chance to think and reflect and ask myself what was really the most important thing in my life.

When we moved to Princeton, I got a chance to be a full-time mom again. Maybe due to the beautiful scenery in this attractive small town in New Jersey, things would improve. I was very happy to be back in Princeton.

Iris was almost five years old; her birthday was coming. I always envied the full-time housewives who could take time to make good meals for the entire family and bake some cookies or a nice cake. I thought I should do something for Iris's birthday party. I happened to see a picture of a beautiful gingerbread house in one of the home or women's magazines. This is it, I told myself.

I told Iris I was going to make a gingerbread house for her fifth birthday and would invite her little friends to come over and enjoy it. Iris was very excited. The day before her birthday, she watched me in the kitchen. She also served as a self-appointed guard to prevent Michael from taking the M&M candies that we were going to use for the decoration of the gingerbread house. Since I was not working, and I was no longer rushed or nagging at them, both Iris and Michael seemed very happy and behaved amiably. There was a peaceful atmosphere in the house, the kind of peace that had not been in our home for a long time.

We first baked a full sheet of gingerbread and then cut it into the size of the walls and the roof according to the recipe. We used powdered sugar mixed with a little water to serve as glue to put the house together. Also, we baked several gingerbread men hand in hand, and put them standing in front of the house to serve as a fence. Using red-and-white candy canes, chocolate chip cookies, and colorful M & Ms, we decorated the front door, the roof, and the chimney. Finally, a beautiful gingerbread house appeared. Iris was very excited, overwhelmed by the beauty, and suggested that we should not eat it, or at least let it stand there for a while after the party.

When the party finally came, all the little girls and boys adored the gingerbread house. They surrounded it and pointed to the décor and exclaimed how beautiful it was. All the kids announced with admiration how lucky Iris was. I could see that she was the center of the attention. She was very pleased, and her eyes were locked on the gingerbread house the whole time with a streak of pride on her face. I was pretty proud myself!

The year in Princeton was a happy time, especially because we were already familiar with the Institute and the surrounding town. Most of the visitors at the Institute were scholars from foreign countries in the fields of mathematics, physics, history, and economics. We met families from Germany, Switzerland, France, Greece, Czechoslovakia, Ireland, and more. A person did have the opportunity to broaden his worldview in this setting. The interesting thing was that the children of most of those visitors could not speak English well, so you did have a sense that being bilingual or multilingual was an advantage for children. This confirmed our earlier belief that teaching both Chinese and English to our children would reap benefits for them in their later lives.

At the time, I was ready to start teaching Iris to read and saw an article on how to encourage children to read. It suggested that parents could write the name of an object on an index card and attach the card to the object. Therefore, the inside of our house was full of index cards attached to, for example, chair, table, lamp, sofa, cup, and so forth. Our friends could not believe that we were so devoted and had a fun time teasing us. They remarked, "Ah! Are you trying to produce an Einstein?!" Indeed, we lived on Einstein Drive, and all the roads in the Institute were named after famous physicists or mathematicians, so perhaps we did have "Einstein" on the brain!

Iris was attending the preschool located in the housing complex of the Institute. The teacher was a very kind lady. In class, she encouraged the children to express themselves. Iris was still very shy and did not speak much at school. The teacher was particularly nice to Iris, trying to help bring her out of her shell, and she told me that Iris loved to read. She suggested that maybe we could lead her to talk about the story in a book we read together, which would help her move on to talking about other things.

One day, Iris seemed to want to tell me a story, and I suggested we write it down. In the house we had piles of used computer printouts, which we gave to the children so they could write and draw on them. Iris started out by drawing pictures with colorful markers about the story. On each page, I then helped her write down the words she dictated to me. It was a "catch a robber" story. After we finished the story, I made it into book form by stapling the pages together. On the front page we wrote "The Story by Iris Chang." She took the book to the school the next day and showed it to her teacher. When I picked her up, the teacher told me that she had let Iris read the story to the class. It was a big success. This was probably Iris's first book and certainly her first "book reading."

Princeton was just under an hour away from New York City. During weekends, we often took the two children to New York to visit my parents. My sister Ling-Ling had come to the U.S. before my parents had, and she also lived in New York City. Ling-Ling was four years older than I, and had been a news reporter in Taiwan. Like our father, she was also a writer and a poet and had published several books. Iris was impressed. I wondered: did she secretly want to be a writer, too?

When the term at Princeton ended in the spring of 1973, we prepared to leave for Europe for the summer. Shau-Jin was going to visit CERN in Geneva, but I had a bigger plan: I wanted to take this opportunity to tour as many European countries as possible.

During that summer, before we even reached Geneva, we toured London, Amsterdam, Belgium, and Paris. By the time we got to Paris, the two children were tired of the gypsy lifestyle and refused to see any more museums or historical buildings.

Finally we reached Geneva, where Shau-Jin would be working at CERN for the next several months. We lived in a high-rise building near the Geneva airport. During the day, Iris attended a nearby pre-school called La Rond, where both French and English were spoken. We took the opportunity, since we had been already in Geneva, to visit the nearby cities in Switzerland and neighboring countries. At the end of our four months in Europe, everyone seemed to have had enough castles, cathedrals, museums, fountains, and sculptures for a lifetime, and all were longing to go home.

⚬⚭⚬

When we returned to the U.S., Iris attended kindergarten at Bottenfield School near our house in Champaign, Illinois. Michael went to the Montessori school across the street, the same one Iris had attended.

One day, Iris came home from school with a note from her kinder-garten teacher. It was a letter that said that Iris had speech problems; the teacher asked our permission to send her to speech therapy class every morning for a half hour before regular school hours.

Our first reaction was: "Speech therapy? Impossible!"

Later, after we talked to the teacher, we realized that Iris was very shy at school and did not talk at all in class discussions. This was totally in contrast to the way she was at home. Iris talked a *lot* at home, more than average children. She talked endlessly to me, describing what had happened in school in every detail. We agreed to let Iris go to the special speech class every morning. We also took her teacher's advice: inviting her friends to come to our house to play, to enhance her social skills. Before long, she was very active in school and had made a number of good friends in her class. Years later, when we watched Iris speaking eloquently on television interviews, I told our friends the story: that when Iris was a little girl, she had been shy and did not like to talk in school. No one believed it.

⚬⚭⚬

Once we came home from Europe in the fall of 1973, Shau-Jin and I firmly believed that we needed to teach both children not just to speak Chinese, but to read and write it as well. At home, we spoke Chinese and enforced it by answering the children in Chinese even though they spoke to us in English. It was hard to enforce the rule sometimes, because Iris and Michael spoke to each other in English. By the time Iris enrolled in kindergarten, I was seriously thinking about establishing a Chinese class so Iris could learn written Chinese in an organized setting.

At the time, there were not many Chinese-Americans in Urbana-Champaign. The number of Chinese children was so few that to form a Chinese class was not possible without recruiting. To gather enough students was even harder due to the fact that some Chinese families believed that learning Chinese at such a young age would slow down their learning of English. Nevertheless, with my persuasion and that of others, a Chinese class was established later in the fall of 1973. On Saturday mornings, about ten children were gathered in a classroom on the University of Illinois campus.

The children attending this class could not watch Saturday-morning cartoons on TV and had to get up early, like they did on school days. They did have lots of complaints. When Iris asked why she had to go to Chinese class on weekends, we told her that knowing one more language was to her advantage in a world that was becoming smaller. We also ensured her if she could master Chinese, at least she could work in the UN as a translator in the future, if there were no other opportunities for her. Already quite precocious, this answer seemed to satisfy her.

We struggled through many years for this Chinese class, until both our children had graduated from elementary school. In teaching Chinese, we decided we should teach children the traditional Chinese characters (as opposed to the simplified ones used by the People's Republic of China), but decided to use the PRC's Pinying phonetic system for pronunciation. At the time, teaching traditional Chinese characters and Pinying phonetic together was an innovation. We ignored the political implications by using Pinying. Time tells us we made the right decision, and the teaching method obviously was an advantage for our children. We were also fortunate to have the famous linguistics professor, C. C. Cheng of the University of Illinois, to be their first teacher.

Looking back, we felt the reason that Iris later had no identity problems as a minority in the U.S. may be due to the fact that she had been exposed to Chinese culture in her very early years. She was aware of her roots and was proud to be a Chinese-American.

⁕

The house on Broadmoor Drive was really too small for a family of four, although it had that nice big yard. Iris and Michael were big enough now to need their own bedrooms. After we returned from Europe, I spent time trying to find a bigger house for the family. In 1974, Shau-Jin was promoted to full professor in the Department of Physics. It seemed that we were going to stay in Champaign-Urbana for a while, so finding a better place to live was vital.

We bought a new house under construction in southeast Urbana, in a district with an excellent elementary school. After the house was finished, we moved into our new home in April 1974, and Iris attended Yankee Ridge Elementary School in Urbana, near our new house.

While I was busy decorating the new house that summer, Shau-Jin was starting a new vegetable garden in the back yard. Again, we erected a new gym set beside the garden. Because the house was new, we had done all the landscaping ourselves. After we laid the sod down, Shau-Jin and I planted trees and brushes in the front and back yards. Both of us did the digging and planting in the intense, hot summer sun. Doing this gave me some idea of what the lives of the American West settlers had been like, but minus the cattle! It was a period during which we worked very hard to provide a good home for our children and to fulfill our own American dream.

Our house was next to the last lot on the block. The last lot was empty, and beyond the lot was a vast cornfield. Iris was starting to ride her bicycle with training wheels on the sidewalk, exploring her surroundings. Michael stayed busy catching butterflies and other insects with his baseball hat in the empty lot next to our house. The empty lot was full of weeds, including clovers, which attracted many butterflies. For a period of Michael's childhood, he was obsessed with catching the most beautiful butterflies and moths in that region. He shared his interest with Iris, and we often saw the two of them go on insect hunts: Michael carried a glass jar, and Iris held an insect-catching net. Once they caught a most beautiful and delicate moth, the size of a baby's palm.

In the summer before the new school year started, we settled into the new house. We bought a new upright Baldwin piano for Iris to learn to play. When I was young, I'd never had a chance to learn any musical instruments. Playing the piano was one of my childhood obsessions. As I mentioned, I was born in Chungking, the war capital of China, in the intensive Sino-Japanese War during the ruthless Japanese invasion. After the war ended in 1945, China fell immediately into a civil war. My parents brought us thousands of miles to escape the war. My memory of my childhood is full of fears, worries, pains, and frights. My parents were constantly planning how to survive, with no time to think about anything more than our basic education. Of course, there was no such luxury as piano lessons. When Shau-Jin and I were finally able to buy a piano in 1974, my childhood dream was transferred onto my own children. I love classical music, and I wished to cultivate my children's love for it too.

Gradually, we met many Chinese families in our area, and their children were all young and attending Yankee Ridge School. One time I did a count: there were about ten Chinese families living close to our house, and we all became very good friends. All of these families were associated with the University, and they had a similar family background to ours.

During the summer of 1974, on August 29, Shau-Jin and I celebrated our tenth wedding anniversary. We were indeed very content with our new house and our family of four. We had a new community and a new school district. Our lives were starting a new chapter, dynamic and filled with excitement. It was an American dream come true!

⚬◦⚬

In September 1974, Iris started first grade at Yankee Ridge School in Urbana. It is a very emotional moment for a mother to watch her child go off to school on the first day.

Most of the children in our area came from families of the University faculty; thus it seemed that every family emphasized its children's education. There were high expectations from the parents, and there was competitiveness among the children in the school.

When Iris got home, she always had something to tell me about her day in school. She would often tell me that someone had been teasing or picking on her. Iris was easily hurt, and it took us time to comfort her and to persuade her to think differently. These daily talks helped us establish a very close mother-daughter relationship when she was very young. She surprised me sometimes with how sensitive she was; such sensitivity was absent in other children I encountered. I reminded myself that she was unique and I needed to approach her with extreme patience.

When Thanksgiving arrived in 1974, I was planning to celebrate it as a typical American family would. We had a brand-new house with new furniture, and I wanted the family to feel that it was a home—a home full of love, joy, and thanks. At past Thanksgivings, we had usually been invited by our American friends to go their homes to celebrate; if not, we did not do anything special. But the real reason for our celebration of that year's Thanksgiving was a report from Iris, our proud first-grader. She said that her classmates in school had asked her whether our family celebrated Thanksgiving.

They said, "Does your mother cook a big turkey or a pumpkin pie?"
She was so ashamed that our family did not.
So I told her: "Oh, yes, we are going to have a big Thanksgiving dinner this year!"

A week before the day, I pulled out our cookbooks and tried to figure out how to cook a turkey. Alas, the bird was really too big even for a family of four; and besides, a whole baked turkey was not my favorite. I convinced Iris that the meat of baked big birds was tough and tasteless, like wooden sawdust. And I told her that there was a recipe I had found in the *American Better Homes Cookbook* that was easy to cook and was similar to the Chinese style of cooking. The turkey breast was cut into small bite-size pieces, first dipped in melted butter, then rolled in bread crumbs and baked until tender. She seemed to agree with me. I also "baked" a pumpkin pie, a pecan pie, and bread rolls, but of course they were all from frozen sections of grocery stores. Pumpkin pie was Iris's favorite.

I remember that day being unusually cold. The wind was so strong that we could hear it whistling over the cornfield; but we were all inside, in our warm house, breathing in the butter and cinnamon aroma. Iris and Michael were following me around in the kitchen and waiting for the turkey and the pies. Iris told me incessantly about the stories of Thanksgiving her teacher had just told them in class, such as the stories of American Indians and English pilgrim settlers. She said Thanksgiving dinner should have cranberry sauce, too. But oh, sorry, we forgot cranberries, I said. She said it should have yams too. Oh, I was so sorry, I did not know that either, I said. How could I forget that lovely scene?! I can still remember the anticipating sparkling eyes of Iris and Michael waiting for their first *real* American Thanksgiving dinner—complete in spirit even without the cranberry sauce and yams!

When Christmas came, Iris and Michael helped me put up a Christmas tree. We are not Christian, but we were just like anyone else in the country that celebrated the holiday and the New Year with enthusiastic spirit. We bought an artificial plastic Christmas tree, since I had always had an environmental conscience and hated to waste trees for any occasion. Before the Internet era, we always mailed Christmas cards to relatives and friends. I did not forget to remind Iris to mail one to both grandparents. It was a tradition that I helped Iris make a homemade Christmas card to send to Po-Po (my mother) and Gong-Gong (my father) in New York. Iris wanted to write her name in Chinese to show off her skills. She wrote her Chinese name so big, it occupied half the card. My parents were very happy to receive the card, and the result was a big package of Chinese candies and cookies from them. It was a tranquil and blessed family life, indeed!

4

A Passion Emerges

Beginning in January 1975, Shau-Jin was on leave from the University of Illinois for one semester. He visited the Fermi National Laboratory near Chicago and lived in the onsite housing during the week, and came home on weekends. My parents were waiting to move into a new apartment building under construction called Confucius Plaza, in New York City's Chinatown. Rather than renewing their lease on their temporary living quarters where they had lived since they arrived from Taiwan, I persuaded them to come live with us while they were waiting for their new apartment. The plan seemed to make sense, so my parents came to stay with us for three months.

From February to May 1975, my parents lived with us, so Iris and Michael gained a strong picture of their grandparents, their lives, and their history. My father was very happy that I had established a children's Chinese class in the community and that I had taught Iris to read and write Chinese. My father's pride in being Chinese and his love of Chinese culture and civilization were apparent in every word he spoke to them.

The three months passed very quickly, and when the time came for my parents to return to New York, we had taken many family photos together. The pictures became treasures to me, and I hung them on the wall of our family room for all the years that Iris and Michael were growing up. This visit from my parents in 1975 was the last time they were ever able to travel and to live with us.

Iris grew into a very beautiful girl who always caught people's eyes when they saw her. Many in the street would tell me how beautiful she was; she was used to hearing that kind of praise. One day, when one of our good-hearted Chinese friends told me again in front of Iris how pretty she was, I secretly pulled my friend aside and told her that she shouldn't praise Iris to her face so much about her looks. I was worried that too many compliments would make her vain.

In this period, Iris loved to listen to the fairy tales we read to her. In the summer of 1975, when Iris's first-grade year ended, the whole family drove to Florida's Disney World. There, Iris was thrilled to see the fairytale princes and princesses in the Magic Kingdom. She looked just like the little Alice in Wonderland when she was sitting in a big carved wooden Dutch shoe, the size of a canoe, wearing a red Swiss folk costume that I had bought for her in Vienna in 1973. She loved the story of *Alice's Adventures in Wonderland*; when she grew older, she read Lewis Carroll's original edition, and loved it like she was a little girl all over again.

In the fall of 1975, Iris started second grade and Michael became a kindergartener. I thought they were old enough for me to go back to work, after three years as a stay-at-home mom. The only problem was that the kindergarten class was only a half day, and I needed to find a sitter to take care of Michael until I got home at 3:00 P.M. I went back to work as a Research Associate in the Department of Biochemistry of the University of Illinois, and worked part-time. Dr. Hager, the professor I had previously worked with, had a new grant for cancer research on the Simian Virus SV40, so I was re-hired by him. My past research experience was on bacterial membranes and I knew nothing about human viruses, but I accepted the job because I was eager to go back to work.

Working and raising young children at the same time was not easy, but I tried to manage it. Needless to say, my life was very hectic. During the week, I was focused on my own research; but on the weekends, my time was totally devoted to the children's activities such as Iris's Chinese class, Iris's group piano lesson, Michael's group violin lesson, going to the public library, going to the skating rink in the winter, going to the swimming pool in the summer, and so forth, not to mention grocery shopping and driving to and from all the other activities. I was very systematic about scheduling all my time in my Weekly Planner.

On April 5, 1975, President Chiang Kai-shek died in Taiwan. In the 1970s, Taiwan faced a series of setbacks on the international stage. In 1971, the Communist People's Republic of China was admitted into the United Nations, including "inheriting" China's seat on the Security Council, and the Republic of China in Taiwan was kicked out of the United Nations, since the UN recognized only one China. In March 1973, the U.S. withdrew its troops from South Vietnam. In April 1975, Saigon fell quickly to the Viet Cong. After President Chiang died, people in Taiwan were uncertain about the future of Taiwan. Shau-Jin's parents were also thinking of emigrating to the U.S. since all their children were now here.

In June 1976, Shau-Jin's parents came to the U.S. for a visit. It had been several years since they last visited us, not since Iris was only one year old. Now Iris was eight. Iris and Michael were very excited to see their paternal grandpa and grandma, Ye-Ye and Nai-Nai, respectively, as they were called in Chinese. Although Nai-Nai did not understand English and spoke a Jiangsu dialect, which was hard for both children to understand, you could see that both grandpa and grandma loved their grandchildren dearly, without any reservations.

In the several weeks Ye-Ye and Nai-Nai were with us, we took the opportunity to bring them and the children to visit Lincoln's tomb near Springfield. We were eager to use the trip as an educational tool for our second-grader, who was enthusiastic about learning more about the American presidents, especially President Lincoln. Shau-Jin and I had applied for U. S. citizenship almost six years previously; finally, in the summer of 1975, it was granted to us. We were sworn in as naturalized U. S. citizens in Danville, Illinois on October 15. We told Iris and Michael that we now had the right to vote, but, as naturalized U.S. citizens, we could not be elected president of the U. S.; but *they* could become president, because they had been born in the U. S. and were therefore American citizens by birth.

Nineteen seventy-six was the two hundredth anniversary of American independence. When July 4 arrived, Iris was thrilled when the whole family, plus Ye-Ye and Nai-Nai, went to downtown Urbana to watch the July 4 parade. She was always the one in the family who was most excited about these things. Iris's eyes were sparkling with tremendous excitement when the parade procession passed in front of us! That evening, the whole family went to the University of Illinois football stadium to watch the spectacular firework display.

When we brought Shau-Jin's parents to visit his older brother Shau-Yen in New York, I took the opportunity to bring our children to visit my parents in New York's Chinatown. At this time, my parents had moved to the newly built high-rise apartment building there, at Confucius Plaza. It was a new experience for Iris and Michael. The streets of Chinatown were lined with interesting shops: Chinese grocery stores, Chinese restaurants, Chinese herb and tea shops, antique stores, and much more. Iris and Michael were impressed by the Chinese words displayed on the windows and storefront. The street was very crowded, filled with all sorts of races coming from different parts of the world. The crowd and the high noise levels were in high contrast to the quiet of Urbana.

When Shau-Jin went to Taiwan in 1976, he brought a number of Chinese children's books back with him. There were books on Chinese literature for children, and some on famous ancient Chinese legends. Because Iris was fond of the Western fairy tales, we wanted to show her that there were Chinese folktales too. We had told her many ancient Chinese folktales at the dinner table, such as the stories from *The Adventure of Supermonkey*, the story of *Mu Lan*, and the stories from *The Three Kingdoms*.

When the Chinese Mid-Autumn Festival came in September, we bought moon cakes for the celebration. The Mid-Autumn Festival is one of the three most important Chinese holidays in the year, and it is on the fifteenth day of the eighth lunar month, according to the lunar calendar. When I was little, my parents and our whole family usually sat outside the house on the patio and ate moon cakes while we enjoyed the beautiful bright full moon. It's a festival that originated in ancient China, to celebrate the abundance of food after the harvest, when the moon is at its fullest. We did the same thing that night. We sat on the patio and looked at the moon, and we told Iris and Michael the story of the beautiful lady Chang'e Wo who ascended to the moon after she drank the elixir of life, according to the legend. And we also told them the legend about how on the anniversary of Chang'e Wo's ascension, there was an uprising of Han Chinese against the Mongol rulers of the Yuan Dynasty in the fourteenth century. Although the legend might not be entirely historically accurate, we told them the tale nevertheless. Iris was fascinated by all the Chinese stories we told her. To her, China was far away, mysterious, and enchanted. She was quite aware that her ancestors had come from that mystical ancient country.

The Chinese New Year fell on February 18 in 1977. It could occur either in January or February in different years according to the lunar calendar. Po-Po and Gong-Gong in New York, as well as Ye-Ye and Nai-Nai in Los Angeles, mailed a big parcel of goodies to Iris and Michael. In addition, they also asked us to give each of their grandchildren a red envelope on behalf of them—an old tradition on Chinese New Year's Eve. In the envelope we put money, and we gave it to the children on

New Year's Eve as a gift, a welcome symbol for starting a prosperous New Year. Needless to say, Iris and Michael welcomed all the gifts; they were the beneficiaries of both cultures. They were glad to celebrate both Chinese and Western holidays!

Iris's school teacher wanted her class to learn different cultures in the world. Iris had the chance, and was proud to "show and tell" the Chinese New Year traditions to her class. Once she brought her Chinese notebook, so she could show her classmates the Chinese characters she wrote neatly, column after column, from top to bottom and from right to left.

Shau-Jin not only brought back Chinese children's books from Taiwan; he also brought back a sheet covered with hundreds of silk-worm eggs, each egg the size of a sesame seed. Raising silkworms was a common hobby for almost all Chinese kids in China when we were young. Shau-Jin especially cherished this practice and had fond memories of raising silkworms as a boy. He was very happy he had gotten the eggs from a friend in Taiwan, so he could show Iris and Michael how to raise them.

When the spring finally came in 1977, Shau-Jin saw that the mulberry trees along the Boneyard Creek near the U of I Physics Department were covered with tender leaves. He carefully took the eggs from the refrigerator, where they were stored and hibernating, and put them in the warm kitchen air. Over the course of a couple of weeks, the tiny eggs hatched and the black larvae came out of the shells, and the whole family was busy raising the baby silkworms. Every evening when Shau-Jin came home from work, he would bring a branch of mulberry leaves for the baby worms to eat. Iris and Michael would hover over the box and watch the baby silkworms chew on the leaves. They ate day and night. The old dried-up mulberry leaves from the previous day were replaced by fresh mulberry leaves each evening. We had to clean up the tiny black excrement left behind in the box. The baby silkworms grew very fast and gradually became white caterpillars, with a horn at the end of their backs.

Iris and Michael were very excited each day to check the worms after school. They also shared their excitement with their friends by inviting them to come to our house to see the silkworms. The worms molted four times and finally reached about two or three inches long, and they consumed more and more mulberry leaves each day. A week after the last molt, the worms became semi-transparent, their bodies full of silk fibers, and started looking for a place to make a cocoon.

Both Iris and Michael were fascinated watching the worms make their cocoons; the worm's mouth spit out the thread of silk fibers while its head moved back and forth and left and right. Day and night, it spun the silk thread around itself until its body was enclosed inside and out of our sight. The cocoon was made of a single continuous thread of silk at least a thousand feet long, according to the silkworm experts.

The first year we got close to fifty cocoons, mostly white. We also got some yellow, gold, and even pink cocoons. Raising silkworms in our family became a tradition that lasted several years.

One night, Shau-Jin excitedly called us from the family room and asked us to come quickly. Iris, Michael, and I went immediately, and Shau-Jin showed us that several moths were squeezing out of a small opening in a cocoon. Some of the male moths were mating with the females. After mating, the eggs were released from the female moth. Iris and Michael witnessed and learned the complete life cycle of the silkworms. Because of this experience, Iris mentioned silkworms in the poems she would write a few years later. It's interesting—and perhaps not a complete coincidence—that Iris's first book's title, many years later, was *Thread of the Silkworm*. The Silkworm in this instance was the name of a Chinese missile developed by rocket scientist Dr. Tsien Hsue-shen, the father of the Chinese missile program and the primary subject of the book.

One day in the spring of 1977, Iris's third-grade teacher, Mrs. Hemp, sent the parents of her class a note asking the parents to come to the class for a class unit called "American Hero." Iris was a diligent student, so, a couple of weeks before, she went to the public library to find a book for the unit. Finally, she chose Clara Barton's *The Angel of the Battlefield* for her book report. I learned alongside Iris that Clara Barton was a dedicated woman caring for wounded soldiers in the American Civil War and later became the founder of American Red Cross. On the day the parents were invited to the class, I saw that Iris was wearing a white early American colonial hat, apparently provided by her teacher to portray a nurse. The long medieval-looking dress I bought for her to wear with that hat made her really look like a woman from the nineteenth-century Civil War era. Iris told me she had chosen Barton because of "her courage" and because "she cares."

—◦◦◦◦◦—

In the summer of 1977, Shau-Jin visited Aspen, Colorado for a summer physics conference. We brought Iris and Michael along to hike on the many beautiful trails nearby. At the end of the conference, we drove to Arches National Park in Utah, and to the Grand Canyon and then the Petrified Forest National Park in Arizona on our way home. This part of America had the most beautiful landscapes we had ever seen. The magnificent sandstone arches were so grand and impressive that they took our breath away. The color of the red sandstone under the sun was more bright and beautiful than any photos we had ever seen. I felt that Iris, in particular, was the one who was really inspired by these wonders of nature, as she was always curious about the world around her, and here were landscapes beyond people's wildest dreams.

It was when Iris was almost ten years old, in the fourth grade, that she began to derive a real joy from writing. Iris not only read books like a bookworm, but she enjoyed writing so much that she compiled her own stories and poems into a self-made "book" and proclaimed that she was the author. Her fourth-grade teacher taught the class to make a so-called "Poetry Book." Iris showed me with passion what she wrote in her book. On the front of the book, bound by brownish wooden-patterned wallpaper, the title "Poetry Book, by Iris Chang" was displayed. On the first page, there was a Foreword wherein she introduced herself as a fourth-grade student and said she liked to write poems. On every page, she wrote with a pencil in the best neat cursive she could muster. Each poem or story had a title and date.

On March 21, 1978, titled "I used to . . . A poem," she wrote:

> I used to have tadpoles,
> But now I have baby frogs, . . .
> I used to write stories,
> But now I write poems. . . .

The next was her prose on "The Wonderful World of Cat." Then "A Haiku Poem" and a "Limerick," which I believe her teacher taught the class how to write.

There was also a description of "Loneliness," which she wrote in several short sentences:

> Loneliness is a silent chirp of a cricket across a lake
> Where the leaves on the trees rustle at sunset.
> It smells like a violet patch.
> It sounds like wind blowing through the tall prairie grass.
>
> . . . .

Reading her words, I could imagine that she was reflecting on what she saw in her surroundings and in her mind. In the summer of 1978, we had just moved to the big brand-new house at 309 Sherwin Drive in the Yankee Ridge Subdivision, which was more secluded; it was surrounded by woods, prairie grass, and cornfields. From the wide front windows of her second-floor bedroom, Iris could see the beautiful oak and maple trees lining the stream and the acres of cornfield. Indeed, the landscape could inspire feelings of loneliness, especially when we were separated from her accustomed surroundings. At the time, her loneliness was also compounded because a girl in her Chinese class had tried to ostracize her, and despite the fact that she had many other friends, this petty cruelty still hurt her. Fortunately, I completely understood how she felt, and she could pour her misery on me. We had endless talks, which I believed soothed her lonely sensitive feelings and gave her strength.

It's interesting to note that all the little things that happened during that time, Iris wrote into her stories and poems. For example, there was a little pond in the Yankee Ridge Subdivision that was not far from our house, hidden in the woods. During the spring it contained swarms of tadpoles. Iris and Michael were fascinated by the tadpoles. We helped them catch a bottle of tadpoles and brought them home. We put them in our fish tank, and the tadpoles eventually became tiny frogs—so small, like the size of a lima bean. The transformation of tadpoles to frogs amazed them.

Iris loved cats, starting from when she was very little. When we moved into the new house in the Yankee Ridge, there was a tabby that always came to play with Iris and Michael. At first, we did not know why this cat was so friendly to them. We learned later that both of them saved the meat from the dishes I cooked to give to the cat. No wonder the cat just sat outside of our back sliding door and waited patiently in the evening. Iris begged us to adopt the cat and finally I gave in, but with the condition that the cat should live outside, not in the house. She named the cat Cat, short for Catherine, but she later renamed her Tash, although the cat always remained Cat to me.

In many of the stories and poems that Iris wrote, she mentioned cats. It was Cat who was her best companion after school. She took many pictures of Cat. When she did her homework or read a book, Cat was always beside her, even though I told her that Cat should not be in the house. She managed to smuggle Cat into her room behind my back. She was no longer allergic to cats at age ten; at least not *this* Cat. One day, when I opened Iris's bedroom door, I found Cat sleeping on her bed! This cat became one of our family members and lived until 1999, twenty-two or twenty-three years.

Our interest in reading Iris's writings had given her a sense of achievement and encouraged her even more onto the path of literary writing. The impact of parents' attitudes on their children is unbelievably significant, which we sometimes did not realize.

Iris's love of writing was even more apparent in a note she wrote in class in 1979: "Writing is one of my favorite pastimes. It improves my English. It makes me think, and I understand more about things. I never think of it as work. I always think of writing as something enjoyable, because it is something that I really like to do."

From 1978 to 1979, she wrote many poems and recorded them in several booklets that she made. When Iris was in fifth grade, Yankee Ridge School held their first Young Author writing competition. Since I had read many of Iris's poems and other writings, I encouraged her to enter the competition. I also volunteered to type her work for her. Iris submitted a collection of her poems and a short story titled "The Mouse Family." The poems were selected from her writings and titled "Where the Lilies Bloom" (which was the title of one of the poems in the collection).

Both submissions won the Yankee Ridge School competition. Then her two pieces represented Yankee Ridge School to compete in the Urbana School District. Again, her collection of poems and the short story won and were chosen to participate in the Central Illinois Regional Young Author Conference in Bloomington.

"The Mouse Family" described a mouse family of seven; Father Mouse, Mother Mouse, and five children mice. The most elaborate part of the story was a newspaper published in Mouseville called *The Mouseville Gazette*, in which Iris was able, on one page of the "newspaper," to give readers the news that "Mr. Mouse wins a house-building contest," "Mouseville Bank robbed," and, of course, Letters to the Editor and the Dear Anne Gerbil Column.

In the fall of 1978, when we had just moved to our new house in the Yankee Ridge Subdivision, Iris had developed a strong interest in newspapers. She not only read the local newspaper of Champaign-Urbana, *The News-Gazette*, but also "published" her own homemade newspaper.

She and her good friend Elaine, who shared her fascination, often spent hours after school working on their newspaper. They used the back of Shau-Jin's discarded physics computer printouts to make a sophisticated "newspaper" layout. The newspaper "The Mouseville Gazette" in Iris's story "The Mouse Family" must have derived from these homemade newspapers. It's particularly interesting to see that Iris had such passion for solving others' problems, which were shown in the Dear Anne Gerbil Column's question-and-answer section. These must have been inspired by the "Dear Abby" column of *The News-Gazette* of Champaign-Urbana.

In the spring of 1979, a man came to Iris's school and talked about his idea to publish a newspaper for children called *That Newspaper,* and tried to collect writings from the students. Iris immediately submitted her writings to the newspaper. Her two poems and one advertisement, as well as Elaine's, were accepted and published in the first sample issue of *That Newspaper.* She got excited, and she and Elaine went so far as to peddle that issue of the newspaper on the University of Illinois campus. Iris and Elaine asked students to buy the issue and support the continuous publication of *That Newspaper.* Their presence on the campus caught the eye of the reporter Karen Brandon of *The Daily Illini,* the UI student newspaper. Brandon wrote an article in *The Daily Illini* on April 19, 1979. She described that "Iris Chang, a fifth-grader at Yankee Ridge Elementary School, 'hoped' that the paper will continue to be printed and had further suggestions for it to include comics, more poems, and horoscopes. Chang not only writes for *That Newspaper,* but also co-writes with a friend a 'very private newspaper' she refused to comment on." In the article, Brandon continued, "Who knows? *That Newspaper* may be fostering future Erma Bombecks, budding Art Buchwalds, or even prospective publishers of underground newspapers at the grade school level." Indeed, who could have predicted that eight or nine years later, Iris herself would become a major contributor to *The Daily Illini* and later a best-selling author? Perhaps it all really did begin with Mr. Mouse!

On Sunday, April 26, 1980, we drove Iris to Bloomington to participate in the Central Illinois Regional Young Authors Conference. It was a very big and exciting event for Iris. When we arrived, there were many young authors about Iris's age. The conference gave every representative from each school district a certificate. Iris was one of the representatives from the Urbana School District and went to the stage to accept the certificate congratulating her for her achievement. The conference also invited a best-selling author to give a speech and later to have a book signing. Iris's eyes were sparkling throughout the conference. From that moment, I think the fact that being an author was glamorous was planted in Iris's mind.

When Iris's poems and story were selected by the Yankee Ridge School for the Young Author competition, one of Iris's friends told her that her mother did not believe that Iris had written the poems. "Iris's mom wrote them," the girl told Iris her mother had said. Iris was upset and told me the story. I laughed and told Iris that she should not be bothered by those comments, but should consider it a compliment. "Alas!" I said, "I wish I *could* have written them!"

From 1978 till 1983, Iris made all greeting cards by herself for Christmas, my birthday, Shau-Jin's birthday, Mother's Day, and Father's Day. She wrote the words and added hand-drawn pictures. I was always moved to tears when I read the words she wrote on her self-made cards, such as these lines in the card she gave me on my birthday in June 1980:

> *I hope that this card will make you happy and glad,*
> *For I mean to tell you that you are the best mommy I ever had! . . .*

Iris was very interested in making greeting cards for any occasion and wished to make a career out of it. She wrote to Hallmark to ask whether they needed a freelance greeting-card writer. To her dismay, the company replied that they had too many already.

Nineteen seventy-nine was a time of transition for both Iris and me. Iris found her interest in writing, and she was like a flower in bloom.

As for me, I was surer of what I wanted in life: to be not only a mother to my children and a wife to my husband, but also a useful researcher in the science I loved.

On February 27, 1979, I got an unexpected call from my mother in New York. She informed me that she had just discovered a lump in her left breast. I flew to New York immediately. On March 26, my sisters and brothers and I were gathered and accompanied our mother to the Memorial Sloan-Kettering Hospital for the biopsy procedure. After several hours, the doctor finally came out and informed us that the biopsy showed that the lump was cancerous, so he had immediately performed the necessary surgery and removed the lump. My mother was sixty-five years old.

My mother's illness put my life in perspective. Upon returning home, I continued to ponder the question: what should I do with the short life a person had? I was not happy with my research on SV40 in the Department of Biochemistry. After almost four years in Dr. Hager's lab, it seemed like I hadn't gotten anywhere. I became determined to go back to the biochemical research on bacterial membrane lipids, on which my earlier thesis research had been based. At that time, I found a professor, Dr. John Cronan, who came to the Department of Microbiology at UI from Yale University, whose research was on bacterial membrane lipids. In April, I went to see him. To my surprise, he told me that he knew my PhD thesis work with Dr. Eugene P. Kennedy at the Harvard Medical School, whom he admired. He said he had a grant with which to hire me. In September 1979, I joined his lab and started a long research journey with him. Happily, we published a number of very good research papers together, and my time collaborating with him lasted twenty-one years, until I retired in 2000.

Although we encouraged Iris's love of books, she almost loved them too much: her eyes became nearsighted and she started wearing glasses when she was in the fifth grade. Her reading speed was very fast, and she was reading all kinds of books. When we drove both our children to the public library every weekend, she would borrow at least ten books at a time. She was a real "bookworm." This made me think of the silkworms, which consumed mulberry leaves day and night during their growing period. Their only goal at that period was eating. Like silkworms, the books Iris read or consumed over the years were transformed internally and later became her own words in her own writing.

Iris never missed a chance for a reading or a writing activity, even at this tender age. I remember that she was very serious about her school-sponsored "Battle of the Books" activity. The school tried to encourage students to read, so it sponsored a reading competition among the children. At first, their parents were asked by the children to donate reward money for each book the children read. The money collected would be used for a school project, such as purchasing video equipment for the class. We had to pay 25 cents for each book they read. Iris would inform me which books she had read. The speed with which she read those books, and their sheer number, made us jokingly say to her that we were going to be bankrupted.

Iris and Michael made a good pair of playmates; they played well together, but also competed and fought with each other as all siblings do. Iris was always Michael's big sister. At this time, Iris was very interested in magic. She was fascinated by it, and she wondered how the magicians did their tricks. She borrowed many magicians' trick books to read and secretly practiced by herself in her room. She liked to carry a soft flowing silk handkerchief in her left hand and a wand in her right hand. She was often twirling her wand and pretending she was a magician on stage with the words "Abracadabra!" and "See!," pointing the wand at me. Michael was busy trying to find a way to ruin his sister's magic tricks. Iris did perform several magic tricks in front of us and fooled us. Once Iris was interested in something and was driven by her curiosity, she would devote her time and energy passionately to work on it; that was the hallmark of Iris's character.

Iris also loved to play the piano and really enjoyed her lessons. By this time, she could play many classical pieces by Mozart, Bach, and

Beethoven. It was an absolute pleasure to listen to her practice on our piano in the living room. I usually stopped my work and listened when she was playing Beethoven's "Für Elise" or "Moonlight" Sonata. The images of her profile in front of the piano—her long black hair on her shoulder and the reflections of the wavering birches in our tranquil back yard on the living-room window—had been eternally sealed in my memory.

Iris was open and very talkative at home, but she was shy and more reserved in public. I don't know if she was conscious about her minority status, or if she just felt more comfortable within her family. Iris was a child who was very frank about expressing what she liked or disliked; she would not hide her feelings. She was sometimes very naïve and believed everyone was just as outspoken and open as she.

She liked to ask a lot of questions and made many thought-provoking comments. When we could not answer her questions, we encouraged her to look things up in the encyclopedia and reference books. We were very open and democratic in our family discussions. Everyone could have a voice to express his or her opinions over the dinner table. Iris had by far the most opinions, about anything and everything. She was very talkative and often dominated the entire conversation. We sometimes needed to stop her to give Michael a chance to talk. Because Iris spent most of her time talking at the dinner table, she ate very little or ate slowly. Sometimes everyone else had finished the meal, but she had not even started her main course, so concerned was she with finishing her train of thought. However, everyone enjoyed listening to her because of her eloquence and dramatic expression.

I think it was around this time, in the 1979–1980 school year, when Iris was in the fifth grade, that she developed a great interest in her own roots. She was extremely curious about our family history and background. When my parents lived with us for three months in 1975, she had been too young to understand the historical significance. But by this time she would ask Shau-Jin and me many questions, such as where we came from, respectively, and why we'd had to come to the

U.S. What had it been like when we were her age in China? We usually told her over the dinner table about our parents' stories*: How my father was orphaned at the age of nine, and, in spite of his poor family background, he was able to beat the odds, challenge his fate, and struggle through and make a name of his own by working hard. I told her about my father's hard working ethics and his emphasis on education. I told her the words my parents said repeatedly, "Money can be lost or stolen but the knowledge inside our brains can never be taken away by others."

We also told her of the sufferings of both our parents' lives during the Sino-Japanese War and the subsequent civil war between the KMT (the Kuomintang: the Nationalists) and the Communists. Among the many stories we told her, the one about how my parents were almost separated from each other during the 1937 Japanese invasion of Nanking was particularly prominent in her mind. The story was described by my parents numerous times when we were growing up, so we repeated the story to our children. In brief:

On July 7, 1937, Japan attacked the Marco Polo Bridge near Beijing and started a full-scale war with China. On August 13, Japanese warplanes bombed Shanghai and Hangzhou. My parents still lived in Nanking, the capital, at the time. All branches of the government of Nanking were planning to retreat inland. My father was informed that he and his family could take a ship provided by the government to travel upstream on the Yangtze River with the working unit to the Hunan province. On November 14, a month before Nanking fell to

---

* My father Tien-chun Chang, Iris's Gong-Gong (grandfather) (1899–1994) was a legendary figure. He was a follower of Confucius's thoughts and had passionately advocated Dr. Sun Yat-sen's "Three Peoples Principle" as the basis for building a democratic new China. He was also a loyal member of the Kuomintang party. He authored many books, including a two-volume autobiography. He was also a political commentator and writer for newspapers and magazines in China and Taiwan. He was never a military general, as some Chinese news media wrongfully reported.

the Japanese Army, my mother took my sister Ling-Ling back to her home village near Yixing, to retrieve her mother and her younger brother, so they could escape together with her family, since my mother's father had just died. Ling-Ling was one year old, and my mother was seven months pregnant with my brother Cheng-Cheng. After my father learned that his working unit was going to retreat to Wuhu, he immediately sent a person with a message to inform my mother that when she came back, she should take the intricate waterways to Wuhu, a city southwest of Nanking, upstream on the Yangtze River, instead of coming back to Nanking, because public transportation—buses or trains—was often interrupted by the Japanese bombings.

On the day my father was boarding the ship at Wuhu, my mother and her family still had not arrived. They had been supposed to get to Wuhu four days before. My father waited and waited on the waterfront every day. He walked up and down the piers and checked every little boat loaded with refugees approaching the dock, but my mother was not in sight. When the government ship was about to depart on the last day, my father almost went crazy. In desperation, he started screaming my mother's name "Yi-pei, Yi-pei" at every arriving boat. Then, a miracle happened. Along came a little boat and my mother's head popped out and answered "Yes, I'm here." My father repeated this story many times in family gatherings when we were growing up, and told us that he thanked God for the miracle: otherwise, my mother and all the family members with her would not have survived the Sino-Japanese War.

We also described the subsequent Nanking Massacre and told Iris that every Chinese person should remember the brutal war crimes that Imperial Japan committed during the war. We never anticipated then that those stories at the dinner table would later become the impetus for her to write the book *The Rape of Nanking: The Forgotten Holocaust of World War II*, which would become an international best seller and change the world's view of World War II forever.

5

The High–School Days

In the fall of 1980, Iris entered University Laboratory High School, or Uni High, in Urbana, after she passed the entrance exam. Uni High is an experimental high school of the University of Illinois under the Department of Education. It combines middle school and high school into five years, namely, Sub-freshman (Subbies, as they are called), Freshman, Sophomore, Junior, and Senior. The school is small, with each class having fewer than fifty students a year. The school is quite famous—alumni include Nobel laureates (Philip W. Anderson for physics in 1977, Hamilton O. Smith for medicine in 1978, and James Tobin for economics in 1981), and Pulitzer Prize winners, including the columnist George Will.

When Iris first went to Uni High, she was happy and full of expectations. But the following couple of years were difficult for her. Whenever we later mentioned the years in Uni High, her mood turned dismal. Indeed, the first couple of years comprised one of the unhappiest periods of her life. I believe this was not due to Uni High itself, but to her passage of life, as high school can be an emotionally trying time for many people, and it was for her.

Iris and a group of her girlfriends from grade school went to Uni High together. They had known each other for a long time, and eventually there were some conflicts among them. One day, Iris told me that one of her best friends was not talking to her anymore. She said that the friend criticized almost every aspect of her. Iris was devastated. I tried to comfort her and serve as a sounding board. I also gave her my advice. I told Iris that she should analyze her own behavior and ask herself whether her actions could have offended the others. I told her she could improve herself during the reflection, in the meantime forget the unhappiness and move on. When Iris got older, she had told me that she learned that many other girls, just like her, were unhappy at this age. Eventually, they all had overcome the growing pain of life.

The breakup between Iris and her best friend from grade school was very unfortunate. Iris became quieter and sank into her own world. She read even more. She often told us that she found freedom in books. Books were her best place to forget her troubles and her misery. In books and in the imaginary world she found comfort and felt liberated. Books set her free.

Iris spoke of the freedom she enjoyed so much at Uni. There were several bookstores on Green Street next to the main campus of the University of Illinois and Uni High. The one Iris loved the most was Acres of Books, which was a popular used bookstore on campus. For a quarter or forty cents, you could buy an old secondhand copy of a world classic in literature.

After Iris graduated from grade school, there was a short period of time when she said she could not find a good book to read. That did not last very long. Very quickly she jumped into the world of literature classics when she went to Uni High. She read one book after another, just like a bookworm again. The bookshelves in her room were soon filled with secondhand books she had bought from Acres of Books or from book sales at the Urbana Public Library or the U of I Library. The public libraries and the U of I library usually had annual book sales in which they eliminated duplicate or damaged copies of books and books from donations. If she found a book she liked costing her only a dime, she was as jubilant as if she had found a gold coin in the trash.

At this time, Iris would sacrifice her sleeping time to read. We had a house rule that everyone should go to bed before midnight. We found that Iris had a difficult time getting up in the morning for school. Later we realized that she was still reading when she was supposed to be asleep. We caught her once—she secretly cracked her bedroom door open after the lights were out and used the dim light of the hallway to read her novel after midnight. To wake her up in the morning for school became a perpetual problem during her high-school years.

Iris's excessive book reading resulted in even more advanced nearsightedness. Her glasses became thicker and thicker. Fortunately, at this time in 1981, contact lenses were available on the market. Both Iris and Michael started to wear contacts. Our visits to optician Dr. Sorkin's office became so frequent and routine over the years that he became a good friend of Iris's. Dr. Sorkin loved to read too, and often they talked about books and other issues besides fitting contact lenses during their appointments.

In this period at Uni High, Iris thought herself ugly, especially when she wore thick glasses and orthodontic gear or braces on her teeth. She felt unhappy and lonely. During this period, I comforted her as much as possible and gave her my support. It was at this time that we, a mother and a daughter, formed a strong bond that would last a lifetime. She confided her sadness and worries to me. I understood her, and she trusted me. I feel this was reflected in the poem she wrote in June 1981 for me on my birthday:

My Mother
by Iris Chang
Who gave me so much love and care?
Who for me always had time to spare?

My mother.
Who, through love and laughter, time and tears,
Finally raised me after so many years?
My mother.
Who is it that I owe my entire life to?
Who is it that even a million treasures
To replace her would never do?
My mother.
Dear Mother, one day when your limbs are stiff and old and weak too . . .
It will be my turn to take care of you.

Since she has gone, I have read it on every Mother's Day and my birthday, and I cannot stop my tears.

Uni High had very heavy coursework, and all the students were very strong academically. Most students at Uni had parents that were on the faculty of the University of Illinois who prioritized education, and there was definitely competition among the students. Iris, however, studied according to her interests. When she loved a subject, she would study hard and get a good grade. When she disliked the subject, or the teacher of that subject, she would not spend as much time on it.

Iris loved math and English. She represented her class and took part in math contests for her entire high-school career. She won several awards, singly and as part of her team. The traditional view in the U.S. that girls were not good in math was a total myth for Iris. In our family, we never thought there was any gender difference as far as achievement in math was concerned. Shau-Jin was of course very good in math, and Iris always asked her dad if she confronted a problem. Whenever a math competition was over, she would bring the test home to show Shau-Jin. Iris would check each question on the exam with her father and determine how many she had gotten right. She was very happy whenever she got a problem right. She loved to be challenged and was very competitive.

In later years, Iris had told us that she was grateful for our attitude about the competition and winning. She said the mom of one of her friends told the friend "If you can't win a competition, don't bother to enter," while we simply told her to do her best. In the end, her friend stopped entering competitions altogether.

On the other hand, Iris had a tendency to obsess over the things she was interested in or working on. When she was pondering ideas or indulging in her own thoughts and imagination, she was in another world. If that happened, she would not hear what her teachers said or how her classmates responded in the class. For that, her classmates would laugh at her and label her a "spaceout" or say she was day-dreaming in class. She was quite sensitive to people labeling her as a "spaceout." Because of that, she withdrew even more into herself and put a distance between herself and the rest of the class.

Iris was weak at sports. In PE class, she was often among the last ones chosen for a team. This hurt her pride and made her hate sports even more. Besides this, in general she was working hard and loved her classwork. She was enjoying English, math, science, and Mr. But-ler's ancient history class. Iris also loved music. She liked to sing and joined the mixed chorus.

When the school year ended and summer arrived, we took the chil-dren on trips to visit their two sets of grandparents on the east or west coast, alternatively. In the summer of 1980, we visited my parents in New York, so in the summer of 1981, we visited Shau-Jin's parents on the west coast. This coincided with Shau-Jin's summer plans too. He was scheduled to visit the Department of Physics at the University of California at Santa Barbara (UCSB).

In Santa Barbara, we visited Ye-Ye and Nai-Nai, and together we went to the Mission of Santa Barbara and learned the early history of California. Iris and Michael were very impressed by the Santa Bar-bara Fiesta. We were lucky to be there at the right time. They saw the dazzling California horsemanship and the gorgeous ladies dressed in Spanish or Mexican costumes in the parade, and they saw what a difference in culture there was between the Midwestern and Pacific states.

In January 1982, Shau-Jin took the spring semester off for his sabbatical. He visited the Institute for Advanced Study at Princeton for one month and then was scheduled to visit the Department of Physics at National Tsing-Hua University in Taiwan. Iris, Michael, and I stayed behind because both children were in school and I had to work. When the spring semester ended, we joined Shau-Jin in Taiwan for six weeks, in the summer of 1982.

In Taiwan, a big industrial revolution was also in progress: Taiwan could build computers cheaply. We bought a Taiwanese-made computer similar to the Apple II, for which we only needed to pay a fraction of the price we'd have paid in the U.S. It was a very exciting period when all of us were hearing what wonders a computer could accomplish.

While we were in Taiwan, I enrolled both Iris and Michael in a local Taiwanese middle school and elementary school, respectively. The semester of Taiwanese schools was longer than that of the U.S. Iris and Michael had one month in Taiwanese school, which was a big experience for them.

In Taiwanese schools, the students had to wear school uniforms and cut their hair short. We got the principal's permission to keep Iris's long because Iris loved her long hair and did not want to cut it short just for one month in a Taiwanese school. She looked so conspicuous among the hundreds of students with their hair cut short above their ears, even though she wore the same school uniform as the others.

The change from Uni High to a Taiwanese middle school was a shock to Iris. The new environment helped her come out of her shell. She was welcomed by her fellow classmates and was bombarded with interesting questions. She had a good time practicing her Chinese and teaching her classmates English. They were very curious about her life in the U.S. But gradually she learned of the weakness of the Taiwanese education system. She would tell me that a class of fifty or sixty students sitting in fixed seats and listening to the teacher quietly, without expressing opinions of their own, was too passive for her. She also did not like the school rules, such as forcing students to cut their hair so short and making them wear uniforms every day. She told me that she was grateful that she was able to attend school in the U.S. and that she valued the freedom she enjoyed at Uni High even more after her brief stay in a Taiwanese school.

I also brought Iris and Michael to see the house where I had lived in the suburbs of Taipei when I was a little girl their age in 1951. I told them the story of how my parents moved to the place (after they escaped from the Communists and arrived in Taiwan in 1949) with almost no neighbors around, and now it had become a populated town. Also, I told them how my mother raised fifty chickens at one time so we could have eggs. She also planted vegetables and flowers in our yard, which was very beautiful in the spring when the flowers were in blossom. But now when they looked at the yard, it was a polluted home factory. Both Iris and Michael accompanied me to the elementary and middle school I used to attend nearby, but they never could feel the same nostalgia I felt when I walked on that path in 1982.

When Iris was in her third year at Uni High, as a sophomore, the report cards for the first quarter of the year came, and she had done poorly in French. It was not surprising, because I had never heard her listen to the language tapes. Right at this time, Uni added a new language course, Chinese, in addition to the French, German, and Latin that were on the original curriculum. Iris immediately dropped French and took Chinese. We knew this was an easy way out because she had been studying Chinese for six years, but we had no reason to prevent her switch. We knew one day she would realize that she had to face the problem and overcome it.

The first semester of her sophomore year, all I can remember about Iris is her obsession over her IQ score. She had learned there was a Mensa organization and subscribed to its monthly publications. Iris read these carefully and wanted to take an IQ test to see what her score would be. Finally, one Saturday morning in December 1982, she asked me to drive her to the place to take a supervised IQ test. Actually, I had never worried about her IQ, so I didn't care what her score was. At the time, I was irritated by her obsession with this. I told Iris that I did not think that the fact one had a high IQ score could prove anything. My feeling was that working hard was the most important condition for someone to achieve his or her goal in life. As my mother used to say to me, the success in one's life was dependent on seventy percent hard work and only thirty percent talent or genetic makeup. That's what I stressed to Iris at the time.

When Iris first entered Uni High, she had found out there was a school newspaper called *Gargoyle*, and she immediately wanted to join the editorial board. She did not know, though, that there was a hierarchy among the editors. Seniors or juniors would be the editors and Iris, a subbie, would have to wait for her turn. Iris was disappointed, but she said, after all, the school newspaper was not a literary magazine, more or less just a newsletter for the school. About this time in 1982, she found a magazine called *Unique*, which was a school literary magazine, started in 1961, which had been discontinued recently because no one at Uni was interested in continuing its publication. Iris was overjoyed and immediately told us that she wanted to revive the magazine.

The discovery of *Unique* and her determination to revive it occupied Iris for much of her free time after school. She had finally found an outlet. I remember she talked about the magazine all the time, from finding a teacher to sponsor it to finding a team of literary lovers as contributors. She put out a working plan and tried to recruit school-mates to join her in this endeavor.

She found Ms. Adele Suslick, her English teacher, to serve as the magazine's adviser. Iris talked to Ms. Suslick many times after school about the revival of the magazine. Because of the work relating to *Unique*, Ms. Suslick became a good friend and remained so even after Iris graduated from Uni. The magazine *Unique* was revived and was finally published in 1983, her junior year.

At that time, there was a girl in Iris's class who was labeled by her classmates as "weird," cruelly singled out as a target for fun or name-calling in the class. Iris told me she felt very sorry for the girl. Iris felt injustice. She also told me that she did not like one other aspect of Uni High—the size of the school was too small. Everyone knew everybody else, and they were all under scrutiny from others, and it was hard to meet new people when you already knew everyone. She told me that she would never be the kind of person who would follow the crowd. She had her own opinions, she said, as opposed to most people who followed the trends or the fashion or "political correctness." For example, she never thought that she had to buy a name-brand sweater or signature jeans to wear to promote her status. Very early on, she gave me the impression that she was unique. I had the feeling that most of her fellow classmates did not know her potential.

Besides working on *Unique*, Iris spent a lot of her after-school and weekend hours on computers. Iris had loved computers since she was in grade school. Every Sunday morning Shau-Jin brought both Iris and Michael to the physics building. He dropped them in the computer room near his office. While he was preparing his lecture notes for the week, they were happily playing PLATO, a computer-based educational system developed at the U of I, which was a pioneer in computer-based teaching tools.

At this time, Iris found out that there was a computer club called "Summit," which consisted of computer wizards on the UI campus. Iris found the group challenging and wanted to pass the tests and become a member. She studied hard and passed all the tests, then found out that the club had changed the rules and she had to pass more tests in order to get in. Later, she found out that the Summit group was all-male. After hearing of a girl wanting to join in, they had held an emergency meeting. They did not want to have a female in their group, so they changed the rules. Iris felt that this was totally unacceptable. She said that they could not change the rules after she had taken and passed all the tests. In a second, she told us that she did not care about it anymore and told them to "forget it."

In spite of this incident, she continued attend CERL (Computer Engineering Research Laboratory) on the UI campus for her junior and senior years as a Junior Programmer and did research for PLATO. She met and made friends with a number of computer engineering students there. Her love for the computer only increased, and she felt the computer was part of her future.

In the summer of 1983, the end of her sophomore year, I saw another change in Iris. She opened up gradually and tried out everything that was offered to her. For example, she found a week-long computer workshop taking place at Bradley University, a small college in Peoria, Illinois. This was a typical trait of Iris's. She always initiated things by herself. She told us she wanted to go so she could learn a new computer language, Pascal, which the camp would teach.

One day in June 1983, Iris told me she had found out about a teenage volunteer service called the Candy Stripers. She told me that the Candy Stripers was a national volunteer organization, and the local chapter was doing volunteer work in Carle Hospital in Urbana. I had never heard about Candy Stripers, and so I called several department stores in town, asking whether they carried the uniform that Iris needed. Later, I realized that the name Candy Striper came from the fact that the uniform was a striped red and white pinafore. Iris applied to the program and was accepted. She went through several weeks of training in order to become a volunteer and was then allowed to work in the hospital. She was well liked there, and some of the patients told her she was a very pretty young lady, which no doubt was refreshing to hear during these years of high school insecurity. I no longer worried as much about her vanity as I had when she was a child.

Looking back, as parents, we feel very lucky to have had a daughter such as Iris who initiated so many activities that we did not know about. Without her introduction, we would never have known about Mensa, *Unique*, Summit, Bradley's summer computer camp, or the Candy Stripers. Our lives were enriched tremendously by her presence.

In later years, Iris often told me that she had begun writing down her goals when she was fifteen years old, and it had proved to be a turning point in her life. To her astonishment, she said, by the end of the year, she had achieved everything she had set out to accomplish on her list—the grades, the extracurricular activities, the awards. She said it was as if the words themselves were possessed by magic. It was then that she realized that she had control over her own destiny.

In the fall of 1983, Iris became a junior at Uni High. One day she proudly showed us the issue of *Unique* she had been working on for so long. The revival issue had finally been published. Although the issue was thin, it was the product of more than a year of planning and working, along with her and her team's busy school life. In the issue, there were two of Iris's poems:

A Soap Bubble
by Iris Chang
A sheen of iridescence
Lustres on a sphere
Glossing a slippery surface
So translucent and crystal clear. . . .
Nature's paragon of fragility
Hovers in delicate ascent
Glistening in the sunlight
With a shine so scintillant. . . .
Enchanted, I gaze with wonder
At the miracle so near
But perfection is ephemeral
And too soon will disappear. . . .

Sunrise
by Iris Chang
Rosy luminance appears
Over the edge of the earth
Banishing all the darkness
To reveal a new day's birth. . . .
Streaks of flaming gold

Etch the glowing pink heavens
When a crimson disk emerges
Casting embers as it ascends. . . .
The sun, growing more vivid,
And taking a golden hue
Transforms a magenta sky
Into a deep azure blue. . . .

When I re-read her poems today, it seems like her life was described in her poems: her life was as magnificent as the sunrise, and yet the miracle of her life was ephemeral like a soap bubble, soon gone.

In that issue of *Unique* was a story written by Iris (but labeled as anonymous), about a little dandelion that had a conversation with a big tree next to it. The dandelion was asking the big tree what the big tree could see over the horizon. The dandelion was impatient and wanted to know more about the universe. The dandelion was searching for a purpose to its existence. The article portrayed exactly, I think, what was in Iris's mind and her thinking at that period of her life.

Iris grew to love science fiction in those years and read many books in this genre. Shau-Jin and I have fond memories of her talking about the books she read, such as H. G. Wells' *The Time Machine* and *The War of the Worlds*. She also loved the book *2001: A Space Odyssey*, written by Arthur C. Clarke (with whom she later had corresponded in the 2000's). Iris also loved to watch the *Twilight Zone* TV series. Shau-Jin had introduced her to *One, Two, Three . . . Infinity* by George Gamow and *What is Life?* by Erwin Schrödinger. These two books, I believed, had great influence on her.

She was also very interested in nature and science. I remember she talked a great deal about the book *The Immense Journey* by Loren Eiseley and *The Lives of a Cell* by Lewis Thomas. Shau-Jin and Iris also loved the book *Surely You're Joking, Mr. Feynman!* by the famous physicist Richard P. Feynman. When they discussed the stories of Feynman, both had a particularly good time. Even now, Iris's crisp laughter was still floating in my ears.

The second semester of Iris's junior year was college SAT and ACT test time. I knew the ACT and SAT scores were important for admittance to a good college, but I was not very involved in that process. She seemed to know what she should do. She handled everything by herself. Iris wished to get into Harvard or Stanford, but she also knew her grades at Uni and her SAT scores were not good enough. Students at Uni were pre-selected, and they were all exceedingly good academically. Therefore, to make it to the top of the class was not easy.

After the SAT test, it was application time. In May 1984, parents of Uni High students were invited to see the school counselor, who would advise and recommend universities to which each student should apply. We went with Iris to see the school counselor. The counselor looked at Iris's grades and she immediately told us that there was no need for Iris to apply to any Ivy League universities. In her opinion, there was no chance for her to get in. We were somewhat surprised by her blunt attitude and the way she understated Iris's potential. At least, she should give a little room for Iris to try, I thought. Needless to say, Iris felt somewhat insulted.

Iris knew her dad and I had gotten our PhD's from Harvard, but we never tried to convince her that she should go to an Ivy League university. Both Shau-Jin and I always stressed to her that a person's success in life eventually depended on himself, not on what kind of school he attended. There were plenty of examples, as we told her, of famous and successful people in history who never even had a college degree—and of people who went to prestigious schools and ended up floundering. Nevertheless, in spite of her counselor's discouragement, she applied to a number of universities including Ivy League schools. She got admitted to Cornell University, the University of Michigan, the University of Chicago, and UC Berkeley, in addition to the University of Illinois.

Iris wished to go to Cornell or the University of Chicago, but we told her the University of Illinois was just as good as Cornell or Chicago, reminding her that she was a year younger than average students entering colleges; to be near home might be better for her. In the end, she chose to attend the U of I. Indeed, she had a good education at the U of I and was a loyal Illini alumna ever after.

In the summer of 1984, we drove to Los Angeles via Yellowstone National Park in our new blue Dodge Aries. Although Iris was only sixteen years old and Michael was a little short of fourteen, both were taller than I was. Michael was as tall as his sister. I felt that I was sandwiched between two giants when I talked to them. When they sat in the back seat of our car, they looked just like a pair of adults.

When Shau-Jin was driving from Illinois to Yellowstone, we not only enjoyed the moving scenery we saw through the window, we also listened to Iris's comments and opinions along the way. She talked about the books she'd read, the news she'd heard, or her stories in school. She was very talkative and a good storyteller. It seemed that talking never tired her. I really enjoyed listening to her. When she talked, her face was full of expression. She also liked to tell jokes. When she heard a joke, she laughed louder than anyone else. She was reserved in public or in school, but she had no reservations in private when she was talking to us. We asked her to stop talking only when we got lost on the highway or when I needed to take a nap.

After Yellowstone, we drove straight south to Salt Lake City. We took a tour at the big Mormon Church of Jesus Christ of Latter-day Saints and listened to their version of history and the religion of Mormonism. When the church video said that American Indian art and culture could be attributed to the Jews who left Israel to discover the New World, I could see that Iris was frowning with disbelief. We were not Christians, but we were not against any religion or anybody's belief. As a scientist, I'm always in pursuit of truth. Our views might have influenced Iris. When her friends asked her whether she was Christian or whether she believed in any religion, she would say she was "agnostic" but not an "atheist."

That summer, the Olympic Games were taking place in Los Angeles. The People's Republic of China, for the first time, was going to participate in the Games. Before that, only The Republic of China on Taiwan was in the Games. Watching that year's Olympics in L.A. on TV was very popular among Chinese-Americans, and Iris and Michael were excited about it too. Very naturally, we talked about the two Chinese political systems and the historical background involved. At this time, there was a game between the PRC and the U.S. In front of the TV set, Shau-Jin and I were in favor of the Chinese team, whereas Michael supported the American team. Iris seemed undecided and she said she did not know which side she would prefer. This reminded me an incident Iris told me about when she was in grade school. One of her classmates asked her, if America and China were at war, which side she would be on. Iris told her friend that she hoped there would be never a war between America and China. When she came home, she told me that she was confused and did not know how to answer. She said she loved both countries. In 1984, she still loved both countries. She was not too concerned about which country would win the medal count in the Olympics.

On our way back home from L.A., we passed through Utah again, but this time we accidentally visited Cedar Breaks National Monument near Cedar City. It was raining. When we reached the Monument, the sun suddenly broke through the clouds. The sunshine made the rain-washed sandstones brilliant red. The scene was stunningly beautiful and unforgettable. Could all those scenes Iris saw from the trips we took over the years to the West and to the East Coast have made her more appreciative of nature? The family trip we took together in 1984 spanned more than half of the country; we saw from the vast flat plains of the Midwest to the majestic Teton peaks of Wyoming, from the white sand desert of the Salt Lake to the bright red sandstone of Cedar Breaks, from the glittering neon signs of Reno to the blue seashore of Santa Monica. . . .

In the fall of 1984, Iris began her last year of Uni High. She became the senior editor of the magazine *Unique*. With the SAT and ACT examinations behind her, the last year of high school was really a free time for all the seniors. Iris collected many articles from her schoolmates for *Unique* to be published, and she herself also contributed many. When the 1984–1985 issue of *Unique* came out, it was thicker than before, and she had four poems in it.

During her senior year, Iris's English class had a senior debate. Iris prepared for the debate very carefully. The topic was social reform in the U.S. Iris went to the U of I main library to gather materials and prepared for the debate. I remember that she carried a gray metal index-card box to school with her every day. She wrote down her arguments on each notecard. She often mentioned to me that the debate at Uni was good training: it prepared her for public speaking and debating later in her career.

In February 1985, she was almost seventeen years old and got her driver's license. She was like a bird, ready to have her solo. As a senior, she now had many literary friends and enjoyed her life and was very busy with her social activities. When it was time for the Prom, we went together to look for a prom dress and the necessary accessories. Indeed, she had grown up as a beautiful young lady, but she somehow did not realize it yet.

In June, Iris graduated from Uni High. It was an important time for all the seniors. Iris was no exception. All the seniors received the Uni High Yearbook with their senior class pictures. Each graduate had been asked to write a few words of their own or use a quotation from their most admired personalities. Iris chose Matthew Arnold and Albert Einstein, a literary figure and a scientist. The quote from Matthew Arnold read:

> *"Poetry is simply the most beautiful, impressive, wildly effective mode of saying things, hence its importance."*

And from Einstein:

> *"Imagination is more important than knowledge."*

On graduation day, all the students were busy writing in each other's yearbooks. The seniors were especially excited since they were embarking on a brand-new stage in their lives. Iris's friends from the editorial board of *Unique* wrote words of appreciation and admiration for her literary talent and hard work. But there were others who did not know Iris very well, and they expressed regret that they had not made the effort to know her better.

It was a paradox. On the one hand, Iris tried her best to be accepted by her peers; on the other hand, she was very independent. She held her own views and opinions, and resisted following the crowd. Some of her classmates considered her to be a loner lost in her own world. In reality, she was constantly reflecting and striving to become the best in whatever she was doing. She was extremely competitive and motivated.

On graduation day, as Iris watched some of her classmates being voted to be one of the most likely to succeed, she felt left out and depressed. She knew that it was just a popularity contest, but it was disturbing to her. She was restless. She talked to me for a long time that evening after graduation. I did sense her ambition, her strong determination to succeed, and her confidence in proving herself. I told her that I believed in her and that one day she *would* succeed. I told her that all she had to do was work hard and have patience. It went without saying that she had my full support. It was a mutual commitment we had.

Iris's English teacher, Adele Suslick, knew Iris well, as she was the faculty sponsor for *Unique* and the two spent a lot of time together. Ms. Suslick spoke about Iris at the memorial service held on the University of Illinois campus on December 2, 2004, which gave us an accurate glimpse into her days at Uni High. She said on that occasion that "'Colorful' pales as a descriptor for her. She was one of the most passionate individuals I have ever known: very intense, very focused, totally committed to the cause at hand. . . .

"Iris's first published work may have been this haiku (which appeared in the 1980–1981 issue of *Unique*):

"Time
Moving steadily
Destroys, mystifies, conquers
Absolutely impossible to stop
Eternity."

Ms. Suslick continued: "Iris may not have considered knowledge paramount back then, but she knew a lot about a great many topics, as demonstrated by her outstanding performance in Senior English. What's more, she had an innate talent for public speaking and could nail an argument with compelling evidence. She made meticulous notecards, I recall. Grades did not seem to motivate her as much as her desire to understand something thoroughly, and she always looked you directly in the eye when she spoke. There was no doubt that she believed in what she had to say and that she wanted you to believe it too." These words were a good characterization of Iris as we knew her.

In August 1985, after her high-school graduation, we headed east for a family vacation to see Po-Po and Gong-Gong in New York. We drove to New York via Ann Arbor, then from Toronto to Boston. When we reached Cambridge, we showed Iris the Harvard campus along the Charles River. We showed her the Memorial Church on the campus quad, where Shau-Jin and I had married, and the Holden Green, the married student housing, where we had lived. We also took her to see Harvard Medical School, where I had spent five years as a medical science student. We also showed her the famous century-old Filene's bargain basement store where I'd found the few fancy clothes that I could afford to buy. It was a trip to recount Shau-Jin's and my graduate student days. Now, twenty years later, Iris was going to move to a dormitory and get her own taste of college life.

6

Standing Out in Crowds

I ris was admitted into the University of Illinois in 1985, double-majoring in mathematics and computer science. Before she started her freshman year that fall, she had already registered with the U of I for a summer math course in calculus. She studied hard every day, since the summer course was short and intense. She got an A for her hard work. At the end of the summer, after we returned from our vacation to the East Coast, Iris moved to Hendricks House, a privately owned high-rise building in Urbana very close to the campus. It was on the same block as the Physics building and one block from my laboratory in Morrill Hall.

The day she moved in, we all were there, including Michael, to help her. The campus was full of students and helping parents. The town was awakened by the noises, which were a huge contrast to the summer silence. Finally, Iris was out of our house—an independent person. In reality, it only took ten minutes for her to drive home and five minutes to walk to her dad's office or to my lab during the day. Nevertheless, she was living on her own.

The first weekend, Iris came home. She was very happy and excited. She brought all her dirty laundry with her. While she was doing her laundry, she described to us the things that had happened in Hendricks House and her coursework. The girls she shared her suite with were nice, but they did not study as hard as she, she said. Most of the students in the house came from the Chicago area or nearby towns, and they all got along just fine. Looking at her beautiful and happy smile, she was just like a flower in full blossom. I was as happy as she was when I saw her smile.

Iris told me that she loved the fact that UI was so big, so that she was able to meet many different kinds of people. She enjoyed the freedom on the campus too. She said that no one really knew anyone else in such a big university, so no one would be judged as closely by peers, as would be the case in a small school. She was happy like a fish that had found water.

During registration and course selection, Iris had consulted Shau-Jin as to what courses she should take for her first semester. After all, Shau-Jin had been the course advisor for students in the Physics Department for many years. Shau-Jin told Iris that if she wanted to major in math and computer science, even if she was only required to take Physics 101 and 102, he advised her to take the Physics 106 and 107 series instead. Math and computer science were part of the College of Liberal Arts and Sciences. Only engineering students needed to take the harder Physics 106 and 107 rather than the easier Physics 101 and 102. But Shau-Jin told her that physics was a basic science for students who really wanted to major in math and computer science. Iris listened to her dad and signed up for Physics 106.

Iris studied hard, and the only time she came to see me or her dad in our offices was when she needed money to pay tuition or rent, or to buy meals and books. In addition, we gave her an allowance for clothes. At this time, she was quite aware of her appearance, and she started to enjoy shopping for clothes. She found an Indian shop on Green Street carrying many exotically colored clothes imported from

India that were comparatively inexpensive. Because she was tall and slim, any clothes looked elegant on her. She showed me a multicolored skirt made of soft cotton fabric imported from India and a black long-sleeve top. Wearing those clothes, with her long curling black hair (she had her hair styled in a beauty salon in her senior year at Uni High), she looked like a gorgeous young lady from an ancient Middle Eastern country.

Iris did not usually spend too much time shopping, except for necessities. She wore T-shirts and jeans to go to class. The only times she really needed fancy clothes were when she went to a party. Whenever she was shopping, she looked at the price tag first. I think we had influenced her in this regard. Both Shau-Jin and I had come to this country on scholarships with limited resources. We were very careful in spending, quite frugal. It became a habit, even when our income later improved. We had always told her that we should not waste time and money on something we did not really need.

Iris told us that she was often noticed and admired by male students she met on campus. She seemed to enjoy the attention. I knew she was going to parties and watching movies in addition to studying. She was really enjoying college life. She not only met many students in her computer science courses, but also met students from other departments, such as engineering or English majors.

Every weekend Iris came home to do her laundry and see the cat, as she missed Cat very much. In the meantime, she would ask Shau-Jin about the math or physics that she did not understand in her courses. Her first semester ended happily, with a grade point average that qualified her for the Dean's List.

The year of 1986 was an extremely exciting year for me professionally as well. In January 1986, I found that the protein sequence of a bacterial enzyme with which I had worked for several years had a strong homology (similarity, affinity) with the protein sequence of another enzyme. The discovery of the homology of these two proteins explained several things about their unique properties. I attended two national meetings to report my results. In March, I went to Washington, D.C. for the annual American Society of Microbiology meeting; and in June, I went again to D.C. for the annual Biochemistry meeting. I was busy wrapped up in my own research. I had been working full-time in the lab since 1984, when Michael was in his sophomore year at Uni High. I was sure the children did not need me when they came home from school. I now had a number of papers published in scientific journals, almost one paper a year.

The second semester of Iris's freshman year, the spring of 1986, Iris had some difficulty with her Physics 107 course. She often came home to ask Shau-Jin for help, but I could see that her heart was not in the physics. At the time, she told me she was going to start a student literary organization called the Illini Literary Society. She found out that she could apply to the University for financial support if she submitted a budget for the organization. Eventually she did get some funds that way. She later used the funds to start a magazine called *Open Wide*. She was talking about recruiting literature-loving students to submit poems, fiction, or original musical compositions and artwork for publication in the magazine. Again, she was enthusiastic about the new magazine and talked about it with passion, just like her high-school days with the magazine *Unique*.

In the final few weeks of the second semester Iris was struggling with Physics 107 and eventually got a C for that course, which made her unhappy. Maybe she secretly blamed her dad, who had advised her to take the more difficult physics course for engineering students. When her freshman year ended, that summer she wanted to take a summer-credit math course: differential equations. We thought it was a good idea. In our family, taking classes was always encouraged, and this was no different.

In that summer of 1986, our house needed some repairs and maintenance work, such as painting the outside wooden trim and replacing the rotten wooden deck above the garage. I was too busy to use my one-month vacation in the summer to carry out the house repairs.

We told Iris, a college student, and Michael, a rising senior in high school, that they should share some responsibilities while they lived under our roof.

Both Iris and Michael, just like average teenagers, were reluctant to do any household chores without enforcement and reward. Iris in particular was constantly reminding me while we were working outside, such as painting the siding of our house or mowing the lawn, that humans should invent more machines to substitute for manual labor. It was clear that Iris believed she would do better with her brain than she would laboring with her hands. That summer was the last one Iris spent at home. She looked for jobs that required her brain, not her hands, ever after.

In the fall of 1986, when the first semester of her sophomore year started, Iris moved to the university dormitory, Illinois Street Residence Hall (ISR), which was so close to the campus that Iris essentially needed only a few minutes to walk to her classes.

This second of Iris's college years was the year she tried to figure out what her real passion was. In the fall semester, she took a required math course, Abstract Algebra, which she had been struggling with from day one. After a few classes, one day she came to see her dad and complained that she had spent a whole afternoon trying to understand the first page of the textbook, and she could not grasp the meaning of it. She was frustrated, to say the least. Shau-Jin took the textbook and read it and agreed with her. He said that he did not understand why the mathematician had made the statement so hard for students to understand. Shau-Jin started to explain the content of the mathematic theory to Iris in his way. Iris seemed to understand this time, for page one; but there were many new theories as the class went on. On the first exam, she did badly, so she dropped the course immediately. This discouraged her and made her reconsider whether she really wanted to be a theoretical mathematician. She told us that she had previously found math fun, but now she no longer felt that way.

One of the reasons that she failed her math course, in my opinion, was due to the fact that she was doing so many other things at the same time—she had many, many interests! She joined music chorus, recruited students to join her literary society, read books she was interested in—plus she liked to go to parties, as any college girl would. She told me that she wanted to taste all kinds of college life. On Halloween night, for example, she showed me a number of the pictures she had taken at a party. She had dressed as a Hawaiian girl and posed as she was dancing Hawaiian dances. She said that in the ISR, there was a party going on every night if one wanted to go.

When Iris dropped the Abstract Algebra course, it shook her. She started to ask herself whether she should continue to major in math and computer science. She came home to talk to us seriously one day. She said that she loved math and computer science, but she loved writing and psychology even more. She was thinking about transferring either to English literature or psychology. We had a long talk that night. We told her that we had no objection if she wanted to change majors. We told her that we understood that only when one loved a subject would one spend time on it and consequently succeed in that field. Iris was quite relieved—she had thought we would be against the change. Shau-Jin and I loved science and no doubt we encouraged our children to study it, but we stressed to her that we believed that she would succeed only in the subjects she was interested in and wanted to spend time studying. In later years, Iris had expressed her gratitude to us for allowing her to follow her own interest in choosing her career path. In contrast, some Chinese parents, Iris said, forced their children to study subjects, such as medicine or law, instead of their children's true love.

Then she started pondering whether she should major in literature, journalism, or psychology. I encouraged her to find out by gathering information on each field and talking to the students and professors in each of the departments. Finally, she decided she would like to transfer to journalism after speaking with several friends in both the English and Journalism departments. In journalism, she said that she not only could write, but she could also get in contact with many interesting people who would enrich her experiences.

After she decided to transfer to the Journalism Department, she went to see the Dean of the College of Communications. Iris reported to us that when she saw the dean, he asked her to think twice before transferring. He told her that the students in the Journalism Department had difficulties getting jobs after graduation, but that, on the other hand, computer science students had no problems getting jobs. He asked Iris to think further and come back again if she still insisted on transferring. It took Iris another semester to decide whether she should transfer to journalism or not. Actually, Iris did very well her sophomore year; she was on the Dean's list for both semesters. She was taking not only math and computer science courses, but also rhetoric, psychology, philosophy, and music courses. She took far more courses than were required for graduation.

In January 1987, Professor John Cronan's recommendation to promote me to Visiting Assistant Professor was passed in the departmental meeting. The whole family thought it was great. Iris, in particular, felt very happy for me. She thought that I should have been promoted long before this date. Very early on, Iris and I had discussed the role of women in society. We agreed that although women in this country had gained equality with men in many aspects, there were still places unfair treatment existed—such as the pay in the workforce. Women's salaries and promotions still lagged behind men's, not to mention the fact that it was still quite difficult for women to have both a family and a career, whereas men usually did not have to make such sacrifices and were not expected to "choose" one or the other.

Iris had read many feminist books; she was influenced greatly by Betty Friedan. She told me she shared the same view as Friedan. She felt that there had been a lot of injustice for women in the society of the past. We had a number of discussions whenever we touched on women's issues, and I shared her views. From very early on, she had been aware of all this, and she did not want to fall into the trap that most women fell into. She had a strong desire to have her own identity. She was ambitious and determined to have a career of her own.

Iris's second year in college ended in May 1987. As early as January, she had already started to look for a summer job. She told us that she had met a classmate, James, in her computer science class. James had worked in a computer company in suburban Chicago the summer before, and he was going to work in the same company the coming summer. James was nice to Iris and said he could introduce her to the same company. The company, called Microsystems, was located in Hoffman Estates in suburban Chicago. So, on one Saturday in January 1987, Iris asked us to take her to Chicago. She was introduced by James to the head of Microsystems for an interview. Several weeks later, Microsystems accepted her application for a summer job as an intern. She was very excited and immediately started looking into summer housing near the company. She posted an advertisement on the bulletin board of her dormitory. Very soon she got a call from a student in her dorm whose family lived in Palatine, Illinois, which was close to Hoffman Estates. Her family had an extra room for rent. Iris never thought she would have such good luck and was amazed that she could resolve everything in such a short time.

This was the first time that Iris left home to live independently for a paid job. She was very excited about it. She was paid $300 a week for forty hours. For overtime, she was paid more. After working at Microsystems for ten weeks, she was able to save a net of around $1,400. She deposited her paycheck each month and showed me the bankbook proudly.

This summer job for Iris at Microsystems was supposed to involve writing software for the company, but very soon they discovered that Iris was also a good writer—of words. Iris found that the manual for teaching employees how to use the software in the company was badly written and not easily understood. Because of Iris's complaint, the company asked her to improve the manual. She made sure that she understood the whole system first, and then she rewrote the manual as if she had never used a computer before. She worked hard and wrote fast. She finished the first assignment on schedule. The president of the company was very impressed and asked her to do another manual. She was able to finish the second manual before the summer internship ended. Iris showed us the thick manuals she had helped to write when she got home. The company loved her, and the president wrote a superb recommendation for her and told Iris that they would welcome her back any time and would guarantee her a job after her graduation.

During her ten weeks at Microsystems, she also enjoyed her life with her co-workers. She showed me the pictures she had taken at a party at the president's home where she was swimming in the pool and laughing wildly. She was no longer the same shy girl as before; she was very happy and got along with everyone.

On August 7, Iris finished her job at Microsystems. Two weeks later, she moved back into her ISR dormitory and started her junior year at UI. She had made up her mind that she wanted to transfer to the Journalism Department. She had found that her love was writing, and the job in Microsystems had given her the confidence that she could do it.

One more thing that firmed up her decision was the magazine *Open Wide*, which she was able to publish in August 1987. Throughout her sophomore year at UI, alongside her coursework, she was publicizing the Illini Literary Society, which she had founded, and asking for contributions of original works for her magazine. She met a number of literary friends from different departments at UI and finally the first issue of *Open Wide* was published—financed by the UI office for student activities.

In this first issue of *Open Wide*, Iris wrote one poem titled "End of the Mirror Tunnel." The poem reflected her impatience and restlessness:

. . . .

I was searching for the world
Where anything=possible
Where infinite ends as

parallel lines kiss
and time is a rolling wheel
Where
Life is a hologram
shifty, swirly rainbow of
infinite possibilities
infinite dimensions
infinite way for intuition to see it

. . . .

She still had so much to learn, to know, and to experience. It seemed as if she was always racing against the clock to learn something new or experience something different.

When the new semester started in the fall of 1987, since Iris had decided that she was sure that she wanted to transfer into journalism, she went to the dean's office and talked to him again. This time, he agreed with Iris when he saw she was so determined. Iris told him that she loved writing and that she had been able to write two technical manuals for a computer company in ten weeks over the summer. She told him that she wanted to combine science and writing, and felt that journalism training would help her in her future science-writing career. The dean was convinced. For the formal transfer to the Department of Journalism, Iris had to wait until the spring semester of 1988, the second semester of her junior year.

Once Iris had determined that she was going to be a student of journalism, she did not wait. She threw herself full force into the field. She immediately went to the office of the *Daily Illini*, or *DI* for short, the official student newspaper on campus. She talked to the editor and introduced herself to the staff there. Most students working in the *DI* were journalism majors. Iris told them she would like to write for the *DI* and told them that she would be a formal student of the Department of Journalism the next semester. She also showed them that she was the founder of the Illini Literary Society and published the magazine *Open Wide*. People seemed to respect her once they learned that she came from a double major in math and computer science. Iris joined the *DI* as an important contributor.

The first article Iris wrote for the *DI* was on October 12, 1987. The title was "Pop Rocks, are they fun or fatal?" It was a well-researched Features article about a candy called Pop Rocks, which would sizzle and had a popping sound when put it in your mouth. Iris called me in excitement when I was in the lab. She informed me that her article had been published and asked me to read the article in that day's *DI*. Our lab had a free copy of the *DI*, so I read it immediately. I shared in Iris's excitement at seeing her first article published. The article was accompanied with a huge cartoon of a man with his mouth wide open and a blast of Pop Rocks!

Pretty soon, Iris was writing concert reviews. On Friday, November 6, she told me that she was going to the Assembly Hall to listen to Whitney Houston's performance. Frankly, we never took our children to any American popular music concerts. We usually listened to either Chinese folksongs or Western classical music at home. Iris loved classical music as well as popular movie songs, but I never would have thought she could write concert reviews. On Monday when I read the article "Whitney Houston Rouses Audience to New Heights" in the *DI*, I was surprised that she had written it so well.

Iris had always loved opera, and she had been taking singing lessons in the UI Music Department. She had a very good voice. When I listened to her practice singing the aria "O mio babbino caro" from the Puccini opera *Gianni Schicchi,* it moved me to tears. She had asked the voice teacher to teach her this aria because she was inspired by the movie *A Room With A View.* We went to see the movie together, and both of us were quite moved by the music adapted from the Puccini opera in the film.

Because Iris wrote concert and theater reviews and because she was doing volunteer work as an usher, one day she called me and said that she had a ticket for that night. She wanted to invite me to see the production of Mozart's opera *The Marriage of Figaro* by the UI Department of Music. She knew I liked to watch opera too. It was a memorable evening. At the end of the opera, I thought we were just going home, but instead Iris invited me to go to the Performance Center's famous coffee shop to have a piece of her beloved chocolate cake. While she ate the chocolate cake, she talked about the opera. Not just the opera itself, but the disgusting feudal system described in the opera—the ancient European feudal privilege of a noble having a night with his servant-bride before giving her away to the groom. This was Iris: she always felt strongly about injustice whenever she saw it, even in a 200-year-old opera.

One day Iris told us she had found out that there was a summer internship program sponsored by the American Society of Magazine Editors (ASME). The internship was a ten-week summer training program for junior journalism majors for thirty or forty American domestic business magazines such as *Newsweek, Time,* and *Reader's Digest.* Usually one intern was selected from each university's Journalism Department, one who was recommended by the dean or the department head. Then, if accepted, the student would be assigned to a participating magazine. Iris said this internship would be the best training for her, and she wanted to apply. The deadline was in December, for the following summer.

In December, Iris had not yet been formally transferred to the Department of Journalism; that would not happen until the beginning of the next semester. Not only that, but the department head could only recommend one student from the department. Iris was worried that she would not be qualified; therefore, she called the ASME and asked if there was any alternative. Out of desperation, she went and talked to the head of the English Department. Iris had taken a number of courses in the English Department and knew several of the professors there. She had done very well in the English literature and rhetoric courses. Somehow, she was able to persuade the head of the English Department to write a recommendation letter on her behalf to the ASME. She sent off her application, together with her essay on why she wanted to apply for this internship and why it was so important for her.

During this period, Iris was uncertain about her future. She was very ambitious, but also very impatient. During the winter break of her junior year, in January 1988, she asked us to give her a ride to Chicago to visit the *Chicago Tribune*. When we walked in the chilly air of downtown, she was continuously complaining. She lamented why we had to stay in Urbana rather than in a big city such as Chicago where there were more opportunities. She asked why were we so satisfied with our placid lives, staying risk-averse, and so on. This was the first time Shau-Jin and I had ever been upset with her, as we were surprised that she would say these things. She had never criticized us before, and even now I still don't know what made her so unhappy at that time. Later, she did apologize to us, and now I think she had just been bursting at the seams to take the next step in her life and her impatience was getting the better of her.

After her visit to the newspaper, Iris was able to persuade the *Chicago Tribune* editor to appoint her as their campus stringer for UI. In the second semester of her junior year, Iris not only wrote news and reviews for the *DI*, she also wrote campus news for the *Chicago Tribune*.

On February 1, 1988, when I reached my lab, the students came up and told me that Iris had written a big fiction story titled "The Secret Admirer," published in the *DI* Features section that day. The story was long and its title was in big type, with a drawing of a huge heart next to the article. It was a love story of college students living on campus. Now Iris was a frequent writer for the *DI*. She not only wrote news, theater reviews, and short stories; she reviewed books, too, which I know she enjoyed tremendously. At this time, all the students and colleagues in my lab knew that I had a beautiful daughter on campus who wrote for the *DI*. Some of the students told me that they enjoyed reading Iris's articles and were eager to meet her in person.

From February to May 1988, Iris, as a campus news stringer, sent numerous campus news articles about UI to the *Chicago Tribune*. The news ranged from a story about the new collections in the UI Library to the supercomputer UI would purchase for the school. But the most sensational news was that a female first-year UI veterinary student, Maria Caleel, was murdered on March 6, 1988. That day, Iris called us early in the morning, which was unusual because she was usually a night owl and seldom got up early. She said in a shaking voice that she had just received a call from the *Chicago Tribune*, and they had asked her to gather information on the slain student. We were also shocked, since Champaign-Urbana was a relatively safe town. Iris told us that she was going immediately to work on the case and she wanted to borrow our car. Her devotion and passion as a journalist had already been demonstrated. The article on the murder was published on March 8 in the *Tribune* with her name as one of the contributors at the end of the article. Many years later, the killer of Maria Caleel still had not been found. Maria's father was a prominent Chicago cosmetic surgeon, and her family had offered a huge reward for any leads to find the killer, but so far the case had not been solved. Years later, Iris still sometimes mentioned the case of Maria Caleel.

On April 19, Iris called us in excitement because she had received a letter from ASME telling her she had been awarded the summer internship. More significantly, she was assigned to *Newsweek!* She was so happy that she almost screamed. She later told us that two students from UI were accepted by the ASME internship, one from the Department of Journalism and the other, Iris, from the English Department. Iris told us later that it might break a record, since it was very rare for two students from the same university to be accepted by the ASME in a single year. It was a very pleasant surprise to me that she had been assigned to *Newsweek,* one of the two hottest and most desirable magazines, a dream internship for anyone. When Shau-Jin told one of our Chinese friends that Iris had been awarded a summer internship at *Newsweek,* our friend repeated twice *"Newsweek?"* with the suspicion that he was hearing it wrong.

Iris was able to get the summer internship with the ASME not by chance, but through hard work. During the application process, Iris was demonstrating her ability in writing and her passion in journalism. By this time, she had published many articles in the campus newspaper, plus she was a campus stringer for the *Chicago Tribune*. The Department of English recommended her because of her excellent classwork, her dedication, and her eagerness to learn. She had a goal, and she worked hard to reach it. She was very persistent; this was her strong trait. And, most important, she was not afraid to try to beat the odds.

On June 5, Iris flew to New York City for her ten-week internship. All the interns lived in dorms at New York University. She shared a room with another intern and had the opportunity to talk to many other interns assigned to other magazines. She said that she and the intern who was assigned to *Time* magazine got the most attention from their peers. Iris was assigned to the Business section of *Newsweek* and got to know the writers and editors of the magazine and gained firsthand experience on how the magazine was published.

On June 14, she sent us a postcard of a picture of the famous New York waterfront skyline with the words "I Love New York." In her message, she wrote:

> Hi, Everyone!
>
> I want to say Happy Father's Day to Dad! I'm doing very well in New York and I have met other ASME interns as well as the ones at Newsweek and Time Inc. Everyone gets along amazingly well because everyone has very similar interests. I'm going to be reporting and fact-checking at Newsweek, and I might get a byline. The New York Times gave me a personal tour to see the paper yesterday, and they were very friendly and want me to write for them. I miss you all and I'll write back. Love, Iris

Iris called us regularly and told us about her life at *Newsweek*. She told us that writing for a magazine as opposed to a newspaper was very different. *Newsweek* only published once a week. The staff did not write simply to fill space; they picked and chose stories out of a pool of ideas. Very few ideas were chosen and published. And a few of the reporters were also writers. It was difficult to get a byline at *Newsweek* unless you were one of the few writers. Iris told us that she did her best to suggest many ideas to the editors, but only one of her ideas was accepted. Unfortunately, the idea was killed even before it started when they found out that the story had been reported in a newspaper a year before.

In spite of all this, Iris told us that she learned a lot and that the experience was one she could not have gotten in journalism courses. She was delighted to be treated as nicely as one of the staff members working there. There were fringe benefits at *Newsweek* too, she said. Every Friday, the business department went to dinner on the expense account because they worked so late. She was treated to lunches and dinners at the Waldorf-Astoria Hotel and many Fifth Avenue and Park Avenue restaurants.

In the last few weeks of her internship, Iris tried to speak with several *Newsweek* editors to seek their advice on her career. On July 4, Iris called to tell us how wonderful it was to see the splendid fireworks explode in the sky, illuminating the images of the New York skyscrapers. How exciting to live in a big city, she said. She told us she wished to live in a big city like New York after she graduated—and besides, she said, New York was the center of the publishing world!

In New York, Iris also visited Gong-Gong and Po-Po at Confucius Plaza. Not long after Iris got to New York, Michael and I flew there for my father's ninetieth birthday. Iris came to join us for the big occasion.

While Iris was doing her internship in New York, she also visited the *New York Times* and talked to the editor about the possibility of becoming a campus stringer for them. They were convinced and gave her the opportunity. When she retuned home, during her senior year at UI, she had submitted campus news to both the *Chicago Tribune* and the *New York Times*. This was another common trait of Iris: she never missed any chance or opportunity she thought might help her reach her goal. Iris submitted UI campus news to the *Times* very frequently. The editor of the Campus Life section of the *Times* used her news pieces one after another; but finally he told Iris that he could not use her pieces anymore, otherwise the readers would think the Campus Life section of the *New York Times* was specifically for the University of Illinois!

In 1988, Iris continued working hard for the magazine *Open Wide*. She had a number of literary friends on campus who contributed poems and stories. Her second issue of *Open Wide* was published in her last year of college. In this issue, Iris wrote a story, "The Halloween Prince," in which she described debating whether a captured toad should be set free or put in a glass tank. At the end, the girl and the boy decide that to set the toad free in the creek, which "might be a dangerous, short life threatened by a million things. . ." was still better than to life in a glass tank, where life would be "a secure and long one, year after year, the same rocks, same food, same water, able to see the world on the other side but never able to reach it. . . ." Very clearly, this was Iris's philosophy of life. She preferred to lead a colorful risky life rather than a secure long one.

Iris read novels and nonfiction when she could find time in her busy coursework. Sometimes she would tell me what books she was reading and the names of the authors. I remember her mentioning a number of famous American writers, poets, and playwrights such as Henry Wadsworth Longfellow, Edgar Allan Poe, Washington Irving, O. Henry, Mark Twain, Walt Whitman, William Faulkner, Carl Sandburg, Ernest Hemingway, and Tennessee Williams.

When Iris fell in love with the work of one particular poet or writer at the time, she would be very passionate and would enthusiastically describe the life and work of the author to me. One time she was quite taken by Carl Sandburg's poem "Fog." She told me she loved the line "The fog comes on little cat's feet." When she recited the poem, her hands would mimic cat's paws and her back arched like a cat approaching me. Iris was a cat lover, and I could see that she loved this line of the Sandburg poem. Sandburg's birthplace was Galesburg, Illinois, and she badly wanted to visit the place. One summer, she and one of her friends did visit Galesburg. I wish I could have appreciated all those literary works as much as she did, but at the time I was very busy with my own research and did not discuss them further with her. Now that I look back, I realize I had lost the best chance to learn from her.

When the first semester of her senior year started in the fall of 1988, Iris moved to the Phi Beta Chi sorority house on Lincoln Avenue in Urbana. She had always been fascinated with the Greek system on campus. She said that since this was her last year in college, she wanted to find out what life in a sorority was like. Phi Beta Chi was a low-key sorority, and members were more academically oriented than in most sororities. She applied to join and was accepted. Although she was a senior, as a newcomer she had to live in the basement of the house. Shau-Jin helped her to move her stuff in, including the Apple IIc computer that she used all the time. She was using it to send news to the *Chicago Tribune* and *New York Times*; she was ahead of many of her journalism professors in using the computer as a daily tool at this very early stage. After all, she had been a computer science major.

Life in a sorority was different from living in a dormitory. In a sorority, like in a big family, each girl was assigned a number of responsibilities, such as cleaning the house. Iris never liked to clean, but she had to do it. She came home, took our portable vacuum cleaner, and persuaded me to donate it to the sorority. I gave it to her and hoped she would keep her room clean.

In general, Iris was enjoying living in the sorority house. Living there gave her an opportunity to know several students who came from a family background drastically different from her own. For example, she said she talked to a sorority sister who came from a blue-collar family and a small town. Her main goal was to find a good husband after graduation and settle down. To Iris, this was unthinkable. On the other hand, Iris was considered by others to be too idealistic.

Iris continued writing for the *DI*, but her articles now became long and in-depth, more like investigative reporting and commentary. On

October 12, 1988, she had an article published in the *DI*, "How to take the sting out of criticism," which was a review of a book titled *When Words Hurt: How to Keep Criticism from Undermining Your Self-Esteem* by Mary Lynne Heldmann. Iris wrote in the article that, according to Heldmann, we must brainwash ourselves to believe we can succeed. Heldmann emphasized "positive self talk," which was her technique to combat criticism hurled toward *When Words Hurt*. Heldmann also emphasized the importance of daydreaming and picturing yourself achieving your goals in situations where you were in control. She also discussed ways to let those hurtful words bounce right off. Heldmann described four skills for dealing with criticism: silent observation, defusing, genuine inquiry, and stating your position.

Heldmann's book influenced Iris tremendously. Iris had taught me these techniques to deal with hurtful words when my colleagues or even my relatives threw criticism at me. In high school, Iris had been laughed at by her peers and criticized for her constant day-dreaming. And now, she had found that nothing was wrong with daydreaming. Now she knew how to deal with the criticism. In Iris's writing career, especially with her second book *The Rape of Nanking*, she received a huge amount of criticism from Japanese right-wing groups, but she took the criticism in stride and no doubt applied these four techniques to help her cope. Years later, I saw that Iris wrote, on notecard after notecard, lists of "positive self talk" to confirm her beliefs and "brainwash" herself that she could succeed and not let the harsh words of others lead her to doubt herself.

In October 1988, Iris told me that she was going to compete for Homecoming Queen. This was another unexpected thing to many of her peers. To me, it was not entirely surprising. She had told me repeatedly that she wanted to experience college life as much as possible, plus she was also very competitive. I always supported whatever she wanted to do, as long as it was a sound activity. I never paid attention to the sports events on campus, even though I knew that students and many people living in Champaign-Urbana were crazy for the football games played in the stadium, especially at Homecoming weekend. Our experience of the stadium was limited to the July 4 firework display years ago.

When Iris informed me that she was one of the ten female students selected into the Homecoming Court, I was very excited for her. The selection process was based on a good GPA and involvement in campus activities. In addition, an essay to describe the applicant's life goal was one of the criteria; a face-to-face interview was also involved. Each of ten female students was paired with one of ten male students elected to form a pair representing one of the Big Ten schools. Among these ten couples, a Homecoming King and Queen were chosen. In the final, Iris was not chosen as Queen, but she and her partner, who represented Purdue University in the Homecoming Court, would still participate in the parade.

When the news came that she was going to participate in the Homecoming Parade, and then when we were invited to the next day's football game in the stadium to watch her appearance in the halftime show, I was very excited but also nervous. I felt ashamed that I did not know anything about football or Homecoming. I quickly dug out the navy sweatshirt for Shau-Jin with the big white words "Illini Dad" on the front—a Christmas gift from Iris that Shau-Jin had never worn. For myself, I thought the orange sweater I'd bought for Halloween night would do. At least I remembered that the color scheme for the "Fighting Illini" was orange and navy blue!

Iris did not have any formal dark suits to wear for the parade, and there was not enough time to go shopping. It put me at ease that one of her sorority sisters was nice enough to lend her a suit for the occasion. But the parade was in the late afternoon and the weather was quite chilly. Iris needed a nice overcoat; she caught cold easily. I told her that I had just bought a beautiful green overcoat and I could lend it to her. Iris and I had shared clothes frequently since the time she had been a senior in high school.

On Friday, October 21, 1988, I quickly finished my work in the lab and went to Wright Street, where most of the fraternity and sorority houses were located. I learned from the *DI* that the parade would start on Wright Street and turn onto Green Street. I carried my camera and waited on the side of the street. At this moment, huge crowds of students gathered on the side of the street. The noise of music from loudspeakers was blasting, and the colorful flags with the Fighting Illini logo were swinging in the sky. I saw there were several convertibles carrying the Homecoming Court approaching and waving to the crowds. From the songs and slogans I heard, I realized that the next day's football game was Illini versus Michigan State. I also learned that the team color of Michigan State was green. I was immediately regretting that I had lent my green overcoat to Iris; she should be wearing navy or any other color, but not green.

When I saw Iris riding in the convertible in the procession of the parade approaching me, she also spotted me in the crowd and I took several pictures of her. She was smiling and waving to me, and I was sure that she was not aware that she was dressed in the "wrong" color.

When the parade was over, I couldn't find her. It turned out she and the entire Homecoming Court were at the Quad in front of the Auditorium. They had a pep rally late into that night. It was so exciting for her that she forgot to tell me where she was. I tried to call her about the overcoat and advise her that she should not wear the green coat again at halftime the next day. The next day, early in the morning, I finally reached her. She and I immediately went to Market Place Mall. I bought a new black overcoat for her.

That afternoon, Shau-Jin dressed in his "Illini Dad" navy sweatshirt and I dressed in the bright orange sweater, and we proudly accompanied Iris to the stadium. Michael also came to join in. Michael was now a sophomore in the UI Electrical Engineering Department. We, as parents of a Homecoming Princess, were invited to sit in the front row of the back section of the stadium. This was our first time, after nineteen years of being in Champaign-Urbana, to attend a football game. We were quite close to the players, only a few feet from them.

Although I did not understand the rules of the game, the cheering, the noises, and the enthusiastic crowds excited me all the same.

Finally, at halftime, they announced the names of the Homecoming King and Queen. The entire Homecoming Court appeared in the center of the stadium with the Illini marching band and music. With thousands of students and people watching and cheering and waving, I was terribly moved, and proud. For Iris, I believe this experience enhanced her confidence and her longing for visibility and fame.

After Homecoming, Iris told me that she had received a lot of attention from male students who were eager to date her. One night, several weeks after Homecoming, Iris called us to say that she had met a UI electrical engineering student named Brett Douglas at a campus fraternity party. From what she described to us, she seemed quite taken by this tall, handsome young man. So we told Iris to invite Brett over for dinner.

In December, Iris did just that. I had prepared several good Chinese dishes for this special guest. We learned that Brett was a graduate student in electrical engineering and was two years older than Iris. He was indeed, as Iris had described to us, tall, handsome, and courteous. His family lived in Mason City, a small Illinois town about sixty miles west of Urbana. His father was a farmer, and his mother was an elementary-school teacher. He had grown up in Mason City and had graduated first in his class from his high school. He planned to get a doctoral degree in electrical engineering. I could see that Iris received full admiration and attention from Brett throughout the evening.

Later, Iris showed me many pictures of her campus activities. Among those were ones of her and Brett, taken together at many of the fraternity and sorority parties. One was Brett giving a big heart-shaped box of chocolates and a bunch of red roses to Iris on Valentine's Day, 1989. Another one was Brett embracing Iris so closely that my face turned red when I saw it. Iris showed me and told me everything about her inner thoughts, and sometimes I wished she would keep some of that to herself. No doubt, Iris was falling in love with Brett, even though she had told me in the past that she wanted to concentrate on her career first.

When the fall semester of her senior year ended, Iris was actively looking for a summer job for the next year. She thought she would need an extra year to graduate because of having changed majors. She told us she was applying to many newspapers for internships, but the job situation in newspapers was always grim. Sometimes she got discouraged, but she was working hard at her job search. She borrowed our car to drive to Chicago a couple of times to talk to people at the *Chicago Sun-Times* and *Chicago Tribune*.

On our side, for the second semester of the 1988–1989 academic year, Shau-Jin was on sabbatical leave to the La Jolla Theoretical Institute, near San Diego, for half a year. Because of that, I was applying to the Department of Biology at UC-San Diego. Professor Milton Saier replied and invited me to work in his lab as a visiting scientist. Therefore, we were busy preparing to move to La Jolla for half a year. We rented our house to a visiting professor who was hired by UI, who also promised to take care of Iris's cat. Because there was a month of winter break between the semesters, Iris and Michael went with us to California for the holiday.

Due to the rush in our preparation for moving to La Jolla, we all bought instant gifts for each other for Christmas, 1988. Among the gifts we gave Iris were a yearlong subscription to the *New Yorker* and *Atlantic Monthly*. She gave us a collection of classical music on CD. While we were in La Jolla, both Shau-Jin and I worked hard. I helped Saier's lab characterize the gene expressions of several bacterial genes of their interest by the genetic fusion technique in a few week. Both children called us regularly.

Iris wrote us on January 25, 1989. This was her last semester at the University of Illinois:

> *Dear Mom and Dad,*
> *I hope both of you are enjoying the sunny California weather. . . . It's not very cold in Urbana, but it rains a lot.*

Today is the third day of class, and I spend most of my time writing, sending off applications, studying or attending meetings. Brett and I decided to study together yesterday and both of us got an incredible amount of studying done because we made a date to sit down and study. We're going to do this once or twice a week; both of us will probably become more disciplined. There were no interruptions because we studied in Brett's EE office.

The moment I got home everyone has been throwing paper at me, . . . Someone called me "Miss P. R." I'm not going to have time to do all this, so I won't. . . .

At least I'm not lonely here at the U of I, even though you are away. There are now seven people living in the basement. Two of them caught colds and gave it to everyone else. . . .

The entire house is gloomy these days. It seems that half the girls in the sorority broke up with their boyfriends during break; the other half got engaged. Everyone in Phi Beta Chi is worried about their future. Every day I see girls sobbing into the phone or screaming at each other. I'm rather happy these days, though. I'm lucky. . . .

Love you, Iris

Then Iris told us that the Department of Journalism had informed her that she had enough course credits to graduate in four years. This was a surprise to her; she had thought she would need to take more required courses in order to graduate. But the Department of Journalism acknowledged the courses she took in math, computer science, and English as the equivalent credits. This threw her into distress, since it meant that she needed to look for a job immediately. On February 7, her letter was depressing. She wrote: ". . . Every day I get rejection letters from newspapers. I'm very upset." She added: "I'm doing my best to juggle my courses with writing, dating and job searching. I miss both of you very much right this minute, but to tell you the truth I've been too busy to miss you most of the time. This semester will be even busier than the last."

On February 12, 1989, Iris called and talked to us on the phone for two hours. She was unhappy because of the fact that so far she had not gotten any job offers. And she was going to graduate in May!

Iris also told us that she and Brett were thinking of visiting us in March, during their spring break. Brett and Iris had been in a steady friendship since they'd met in October the year before. We told her we would welcome their visit during the spring vacation. On March 16, 1989, they arrived, and very soon Michael came to visit too. We toured the famous San Diego Zoo, and we even went together to the Mexican border town Tijuana, where we bought many Mexican native handmade art products. We also went to Los Angeles to see Ye-Ye and Nai-Nai, who met Brett for the first time. The good weather of California refreshed all of them, and they returned to Urbana happily.

Near Mother's Day, 1989, I received a card, dated May 12, from Iris to show her thanks. She chose a funny card. On the front, it read: "Mom, the <u>brighte</u>r the child, the more <u>difficult</u> they are to raise." The drawing showed a scared mom next to a naughty, smiley boy holding a snake from a pile of books. Inside, the card was signed "Love, Einstein (alias <u>Iris</u>)." In the card, she also wrote:

Dear Mom:

Have a wonderful Mother's Day. . . . This is probably the first Mother's Day I've had with you so far away.

Today I handed in a 30-page paper and now I'm studying for four finals. Some of the classes I have are really boring. . . .

I hope you feel better soon. . . . I was upset and worried when you told me you are now restricted to a bland diet of rice, vegetables, etc.

Take care of yourself, please. Sometimes I think we worry too much about things we forget about a couple of years later! Maybe we should take up some mindless hobby to soothe the stress away. . . .

Love, Iris

At the time, Iris knew that my stomach was flaring up and, as a matter of fact, that I had been quite ill at the end of our stay in La Jolla. I was diagnosed later as having a gastroesophageal acid reflux (GEAR) problem.

Iris continued writing for the *DI*. From November 1988 to April 1989, she wrote articles on leading and top-notch scientific research on the UI campus. She combined her writing skill with her science background. She wrote a number of excellent articles such as "Talking Minds. Computer: A new hope for those who can't move or speak." She interviewed graduate students and professors from the Psychology Department and described the technology available for people who were unable to communicate physically to speak through a computer. She also wrote an article on "The Fifth Force" by interviewing Shau-Jin's physics colleague, Professor Steven Errede. She was able to transform difficult physics laws into common, everyday language.

Iris also wrote a three-part series on AIDS. She went to libraries to do research to understand the disease, and she interviewed researchers and doctors in the field. She also went to a local hospital to interview an AIDS patient about his struggles and suffering and the current discrimination against AIDS patients. She told me she interviewed the AIDS patient without a mask or gloves. I was somewhat uneasy about that, but she told me that as long as she did not come into close contact with the patient, she would not contract the disease. She said the AIDS virus was transmitted through blood only. "You will not get AIDS even through shaking hands," she assured me.

When I read the three-part series on AIDS, I was really moved by her dedication in understanding the disease and promoting awareness.

But to me, among the articles she wrote for *DI*, the most impressive one was an article on the "Third Kingdom," the archaebacteria. She interviewed Professor Carl Woese of the Department of Microbiology, who classified archaebacteria as the third kingdom of life; she also interviewed other professors in the field. She thoroughly understood the research they were working on and the method they were employing to decipher the mysterious life forms. No wonder, after the article was published, she received a letter from Chancellor Morton W. Weir, who wrote:

> *Dear Ms. Chang:*
>
> *I have just finished reading your Features article in* The Daily Illini *of March 1, 1989.*
>
> *Congratulations on an excellent job. You have made the work of Carl Woese and his colleagues intelligible to a layman. I have read many articles about Professor Woese's work, and have talked with him often about it. Yours is the most succinct and understandable account of his research that I have run across.*

Iris was very happy to give me a copy of Weir's letter. Anything she was proud of, she would not forget to let us know.

Even with all the above-mentioned well-written articles published in the *DI, Chicago Tribune,* and *New York Times,* Iris had difficulty landing a job at this time. Fortunately, her professors in the Department of Journalism, particularly Professor Robert Reid, who recognized her talent in writing as early as 1987, wrote very strong recommendations on her behalf.

The best gift that Professor Reid gave to Iris—and to his other students too—was his willingness to listen. Besides us, I guess at this time Professor Reid was the person who listened to Iris the most. Whenever she needed journalism advice, she would go to Professor Reid. The recommendation letter he wrote for Iris, dated April 15, 1989, stated: "Iris Chang is one of the very brightest, most energetic and most talented students I have seen in my 10 years of teaching at the University of Illinois. She has a keen analytical mind, writes extraordinarily well, does exceptional independent work and is a tenacious worker. . . ."

With such strong recommendations and her numerous newspaper clippings, Iris finally got a job as an intern for the Chicago bureau of the Associated Press. The job started on June 1, 1989.

Iris's graduation ceremony was May 21, 1989. We were determined to return home for the ceremony, even though I did not feel well at the time. I had had a stomach problem since the summer of 1988, when I hurt my esophagus eating hot peppers. Since then, I'd had an acid-reflux problem that was getting worse in La Jolla. On May 14, I went to New Orleans for the American Society of Microbiology meeting. The food I ate there made me sick again, but I still flew to Urbana. Iris was delighted to see Shau-Jin and me come for her graduation, but the photo I took with her in front of the Assembly Hall showed that I was sick.

Shau-Jin and I flew back to San Diego after the graduation ceremony to conclude our half-year sabbatical, and we started to drive back home on June 4—when Iris had already reported to work in Chicago for the AP. In the summer of 1989, Iris happily told us that she'd been awarded a $1,000 national scholarship from the Asian American Journalists Association. Again, her unfailing hard-working spirit had paid off.

In 1990, Iris returned to the University of Illinois campus after a brief stint working at the Associate Press and the *Chicago Tribune*. She was approached by an editor of a college guidebook called *Barron's Top 50, An Inside Look at America's Best Colleges* (Barron's Educational Series, Inc., 1991 edition). The editor was looking for a person who had graduated from a university to write about his or her personal experience about the particular university in question. Iris was delighted to accept the invitation and wrote a superb chapter in the book for the University of Illinois. Many people may not know that she wrote that article for the U of I. I felt that her description of the U of I was accurate, vivid, and inspiring. She described not only the student lives at the U of I in general, but she also injected her own personal life into those four years (1985 to 1989).

Iris's own words are:

> *Choices, choices, choices! I was stunned by all of them at the University of Illinois. During my four years as an undergraduate, I took courses*

in news reporting, differential equations, Shakespeare, computer science, sociology, and voice. The professors had won the Nobel Prize and Pulitzer Prize, and I remember one semester I tried to decide whether to study under a former New York Times correspondent, a Broadway and Hollywood star, or a world-renowned expert in artificial intelligence. I started my own magazine, joined the Oriental Cultural Organization, and listened to speakers invited by the British history club. Never again will I have the supermarket of choices that were available to me at the U of I.

I started out as a math and computer science major; and later switched into journalism. This confused people in both fields. In the dorm cafeteria, my C. S. buddies urged me to come to my senses: "At least get a science degree as a backup." In my creative writing classes, my teacher and classmates would tease me for being too rational. "Where's your sense of romance?" There's no way to get only one perspective at a school as large as the U of I. That's what I like about it—hearing these different opinions all the time.

Iris described her journalism class at the UI:

I heard all the horror stories about journalism professor Robert Reid, before I took his in-depth reporting class. A man of inflexible deadlines, he was known to flunk people who stumbled in class a few minutes late when handing in their 40 page papers.

I was pleasantly surprised when I sat with 14 other people on the first day of class. Reid wanted us to be more than reporters. He wanted us to be writers. Creative nonfiction writers who, like novelists, would capture details and make a story so real a reader could see it and smell it and taste it. Reid hated reporters who insisted on punching facts into a cold news formula. "If I had any such robots in my newsroom, I'd fire them," he liked to say, cracking a piece of chalk onto the ground for emphasis.

Later in the year, Reid became my mentor. I would spend hours with him after class to discuss writing techniques, journalistic ethics, and the works of literary journalists like Tom Wolfe, Lillian Ross and John McPhee. And since he was convinced that each student in his class would do something important one day, he told us to quit worrying about our grades and start trying to do our best.

Under the Social Life section, Iris wrote:

At least once a week, I would get together with some of my buddies and—over Chinese food and pizza boxes in our dorm room—we might talk until three in the morning. The subjects of conversation ranged from boys to comic books to thermodynamics, depending on the group I was with.

I especially liked being with journalism friends—we would read each other's writings, suggest changes and toss around story ideas. We swapped books and discussed John Steinbeck and Guy de Maupassant and Franz Kafka; we slammed on bad articles in the local newspapers, sometimes highlighting key paragraphs. These nightly chats were some of the best times I had at the U of I and what I learned from them was as valuable as anything taught in the classroom.

Iris described the extracurricular activities:

"I remember the first article I wrote for the Daily Illini, I was assigned to do a feature about Pop Rocks, the candy that allegedly killed Mikey, star of the Life cereal commercials. After experimenting with ten packs of Pop Rocks—sprinkling them on my tongue, feeling them sizzle and explode in my mouth—I tried the candy out on my friends, carefully researched the history of the candy, and typed the story in the DI computer system.

A few days later, I snatched up the DI that was thrust under my door. There it was, a full-page article next to this cartoon of a man with his mouth shattered open from a volcano of Pop Rocks! I did it! I had broken into print! My stomach felt as if all ten packs were bursting out at once.

An hour later, my phone was ringing off the hook from excited friends who had seen the article. Although I was later writing for bigger newspapers like the New York Times, *nothing could match the thrill of seeing my first byline in the* Daily Illini.

Then Iris described another personal experience at the U of I:

I was a junior when I first wandered into Professor Stegeman's office. He was the placement officer for the journalism department and I asked him for some advice about breaking into the newspaper business. Stegeman smiled, stroked his white beard, and told me about his first job as a reporter in a coal mining town in southern Illinois, his adventures in Africa and even his investigative reporting crew in East St. Louis.

Stegeman was the one who suggested that I apply to 50 newspaper and magazine internships; he gave me a big batch of application forms and even proofread my resume and cover letters to make sure they were free of typos. He gave names of U of I alumni to contact and frequently stopped me in the hall to tell me about new job opportunities. Unlike the machine-like career placement center I expected of a Big Ten university, the journalism placement office was very personal.

From all the descriptions Iris wrote about her experience at the U of I, we could get a better glimpse of part of her college life, which was full of excitement and fun. She was so eager to learn everything and full of hope for a bright future.

She was genuinely in love with the U of I. In the Summary Overview of the U of I, Iris concluded:

Few schools can rival the University of Illinois in academics, size and price. Its world-class status and excellent faculty attract the brightest students everywhere, many who cross oceans to get an education at Illinois. The school boasts of such things as having the third largest academic library in the country, the biggest alumni network, the biggest Greek

system, the best centers for science and technology and all for low, low,
state university tuition.

Iris received a check for $200 from the book's editor as a reward for writing about the U of I. Iris was quite happy about it. A couple years later, Iris told us that a paragraph of her article on the U of I in *Barron's Top 50* had been used in one year's reading test on the SAT exam. She felt honored.

7

Fresh Out of College

In the spring of 1989, Chinese students in mainland China launched a pro-democracy movement that grabbed the attention of the world. For Shau-Jin and myself, both born in China, the events really hit home. We were riveted to the television for weeks.

When the student protests began, I was still at UC San Diego, working in Professor Milton Saier's lab with a couple of students from mainland China. The students and I talked constantly about the news from China and couldn't contain our excitement. We all thought that our homeland was inexorably heading down a democratic path.

In addition to students, we saw older workers and intellectuals demonstrating in the streets of Beijing and in Tiananmen Square. Hundreds of students went on hunger strikes to demand that the Chinese government reform, guarantee freedom of speech, and crack down on corruption. The students also erected a Goddess of Democracy statue, which looked remarkably similar to our own Lady Liberty in New York Harbor. Tears of joy welled up in my eyes.

In late May, Iris called to tell us she had reached Chicago and was living in a dorm room of Mundelein College. She shared our excitement about the events in China.

After we finished our sabbaticals at UC-San Diego on June 4, Shau-Jin and I started driving back to Illinois. On the way, we heard on the radio that Chinese tanks had rolled into Tiananmen Square in a violent, bloody crackdown. We couldn't believe it. As soon as we reached St. George, Utah, where we'd planned on spending the night, we called Iris. She said that the AP had told her to head to Chicago's Chinatown to gather reactions to the massacre.

The next time we called her from the road, Iris told us that she had interviewed Chinatown shop owners and people on the street. Her story, the first one she wrote for the AP, was used by hundreds of newspapers around the country. Her new colleagues enviously told her how lucky she was to be allowed to work on such a hot news story her first week on the job. And Iris was excited to have an AP photographer assigned to her story.

After we returned home, she mailed us a copy of a letter written by her boss, James Reindi, the AP's news editor in Chicago. The June 7 letter read:

> *Dear Iris:*
>
> *Congratulations on your first A-wire (story) for the AP. I trust it is the first of many.*
>
> *Your story on Chicago's Chinatown reaction to the situation in Beijing is in the newsroom of every afternoon newspaper in the country today. It deserved to be. The story is loaded with excellent detail and good quotes. A first-rate job!*
>
> *Sincerely, Jim*

We also got a copy of her story as it appeared in the *Champaign-Urbana News-Gazette*. It was headlined: "Chicago's Chinese hunt for news on homeland." The byline was "by Iris Chang, Associated Press Writer." The story began:

> The old man raised his cleaver and slammed it into the neck of a duck at a Chinatown grocery store. "Killers," he spat out as he repeatedly chopped the duck and spoke with two other men listening to a Chinese-language radio broadcast Tuesday morning.

The day after we arrived home, Chinese faculty members and the Chinese Student Association organized a huge protest on the University of Illinois campus. The demonstrators condemned the military crackdown, as did the American people as a whole. To show their anger and disgust, the U.S. scientific community boycotted conferences held in China. Shau-Jin and I signed numerous petitions. We couldn't comprehend how the Chinese government would slaughter defenseless students who we thought were genuine patriots.

Iris often came home from Chicago on weekends to see us and to see Brett, who was still at the University of Illinois working on his doctorate in electrical engineering. Iris told us her job at the AP was demanding; she had to pump out story after story. Because she was a fast writer, she was always able to make her deadlines, but the flow of news was unrelenting. She could barely find the time to eat. So she mostly grabbed fast food on the run. That alarmed me, and I told her to make the time to eat more healthful food. I don't know how much she listened to me. She also told us she didn't know whether she should marry Brett or wait for a few years. I was reluctant to steer her in either direction, knowing that that was a decision she could only make for herself.

Once Iris became an adult, I never made a major life decision for her. But at the same time, I did emphasize that women, just like men, needed to become financially independent by developing skills to support themselves, whether or not they were going to marry. Iris agreed, telling me: "To gain equality with men, women need to educate themselves first."

About two months after Iris went to work for the AP, she called to tell us that the *Chicago Tribune* had offered her a four-month internship. About the same time, she said, the AP offered her a full-time reporting job. She told us she had decided to work at the *Tribune* so she could write in-depth feature articles. At the AP, she said, the job was mostly writing hard news.

August 29 was the twenty-fifth wedding anniversary for Shau-Jin and myself. That Saturday, Iris came home from Chicago to help us celebrate the occasion. Brett and Michael joined us for dinner at a Chinese restaurant. After dinner, we took a family portrait. Iris was twenty-one years old. She looked so happy and carefree in the picture. She had lost some weight because of her frenetic pace at the AP, but she looked beautiful and happy.

Iris began her internship at the *Tribune* on September 1. As an intern, she worked for all the departments in the newspaper: the national desk, metropolitan desk, features, and sports. She particularly loved writing feature articles and generally disliked writing local news. She said she hated to go to City Hall for press conferences because she found most municipal issues boring.

She wrote articles headlined "Fire Forces Museum to Close" and "Young Muralists Put City in Perspective." She wrote about the University of Illinois being urged to scrap its Indian mascot, and she whipped up an article for the food section before Christmas titled "Adding Memories to Sugar and Flour." Her long articles in the Tempo section, such as the one headlined "Do Bugs Give You the Creeps? Get to Know Them," showed her strong science-writing ability.

One of the best and most widely read articles she wrote for the *Tribune* had the headline: "To Scientists He's an Einstein. To the Public He's— John Who?" The story was about Professor John Bardeen, the two-time Nobel Prize winner who had been on the University of Illinois faculty in the engineering and physics departments since 1951 (emeritus since 1975). In the early eighties, the young Iris had met him at our house because he and Shau-Jin were in the same department, so she knew how famous he was in the scientific community. In that early-eighties meeting, Iris asked if Bardeen would do her the honor of autographing a copy of the *News-Gazette of Champaign-Urbana* in which an article had just described Bardeen's world-famous discovery. Iris was very impressed by Bardeen's achievement, and was proud that she had met him personally. Whenever someone asked her about the U of I, she would always say that Bardeen was on the faculty there and he was a two-time Nobel laureate, whereas the questioner might have only been interested in the Fighting Illini football team!

Iris was fascinated by Bardeen's research on the transistor and the theory of superconductivity, so we suggested that she interview him for a story. We also reminded her that Bardeen was eighty-one years old, and if she wanted to interview him, she should do it soon.

She immediately contacted Bardeen and interviewed him over the phone many times and at length in his office. Her story was published in January 1990, a year before he died. The article was reprinted by several University of Illinois publications to memorialize his life.

Because of Iris's science background and her tenacious research, she was able to write an accurate, passionate article about him. Bardeen was well known for being quiet and modest and not showing much emotion in public. But Iris told us she found him warm and kind. Perhaps Iris reminded him of his own granddaughter.

Iris had interviewed many of Bardeen's former students and post-doctoral researchers in the physics and engineering departments on campus, including Nick Holonyak, a physics and electrical engineering professor. Iris told us that she had gained insight into physics—which still intrigued her even though she had not taken a physics class in many years—from Holonyak, who in turn appreciated Iris's passion for learning and her talent in science writing.

Holonyak, Bardeen's first graduate student, later invented the light-emitting diode used in digital watches and pocket calculators. After Iris's article was published, we ran into Holonyak a couple of times on campus, and he told us how much he enjoyed talking to Iris. Later, he told us that he had followed Iris's career and read her books. Iris always felt lucky that she had grown up in an academically rich community such as Champaign-Urbana.

In late September, my brother Bing called us from his Manhattan office to tell us about a two-hour special called "China in Revolution, 1911–1949" that would soon be shown by PBS. My father, a witness and survivor of that period of Chinese history, was interviewed for the special. When we got a tape of the program and gave Iris a copy, she showed a lot of interest and told us that some day she would like to interview her dad and me about our family history.

Three weeks after the PBS special ran, my mother called me from New York. She said she had coughed out two pea-sized blood clots from her throat that day. My brothers and sisters were all alarmed and urged her to see a doctor immediately. The doctor told her she had a tumor in her lung that could be cancerous.

The diagnosis shocked our whole family. I took time off from work and flew to New York to help out my mother. On November 27, my sister Ling-Ling and I accompanied her to Memorial Sloan-Kettering Hospital for a biopsy. The doctor found that the tumor was indeed cancerous, but that the cells originated from her breast, not from her lungs. That was actually good news, because there were drugs to stop the growth of breast-cancer tumors, whereas lung cancer was much harder to treat. After the biopsy, the doctor decided against removing the tumor and prescribed cancer-fighting drugs instead. For a while, we were relieved there was a cure for the tumor, but we knew that my mother's breast cancer had metastasized to other organs—a bad omen for her overall health. I came home from New York exhausted.

Then Iris called us from a public phone booth down the stairs from her office with more bad news. The *Tribune*, she said, was not going to hire her after her internship was over at the end of December. This was a big setback. She had been hoping to land a job at a major newspaper to establish her journalism career. Her dream was dashed. We asked her whether the *Tribune* had hired any of her fellow interns.

"Yes, they did," she replied weakly. I could hear the humiliation in her shaky voice.

Shau-Jin and I talked to her for a long time, and she began a self-examination of her work and her life. She told us that in the newspaper industry, she would be limited in what she could write. She also realized that she was not the kind of person who liked taking orders or being at the whim of whatever was deemed newsworthy at the time.

Shau-Jin told her that in any profession, you had to work your way up from the bottom. "You cannot be a general the first day you enter the army," he told her. "You have to work first as a foot soldier." But Iris was exceedingly ambitious and impatient. During this phone conversation, Iris told me: "You know, Mom, I'm not the kind of person who is willing to conform in a corporate setting." She admitted that she was too independent, too individualistic, and didn't really enjoy being part of a team.

She told me about some of her confrontations with her editors. One time, she said, her boss had asked her to call members of a family whose loved one had just died tragically. She told the editor she had tried several times, but the family refused to be interviewed. Not showing much sympathy, the editor asked her to try again. So Iris picked up the phone and dialed the phone number, in front of other colleagues. She handed her boss the phone and said "*You* talk to them." He, of course, was not happy. But Iris told us that she felt the family had a right to grieve in private. That, she said, was more important than getting a quote for a story.

There were also issues in her social circle and within standard "office politics." Iris, for example, didn't like to gossip behind other people's backs. She said she found it meaningless and a waste of time.

Still, Iris was heartbroken about not being offered a job at the *Tribune*, as there were other parts of her work there that she truly enjoyed. I comforted her and said "We learn lessons from our mistakes. There will always other opportunities."

Iris was quite blue for days. But she got over it and was soon back to her old self. She urged us to come to Chicago to visit her while she was still living there. She said she would move back home soon and regroup and figure out what she wanted to do.

Two days later, she phoned and said the *Tribune* had called her in the middle of night after a jet had skidded off the runway at Midway Airport because of freezing temperatures. She immediately drove to the scene so she could interview people to get the full story.

My maternal instincts took over. I remember thinking that the life of a reporter must be hard. I imagined her driving in the darkness in the early-morning hours all by herself in subzero temperatures with a strong wind blowing and ice and snow all around. Iris had lived a sheltered life with us in Urbana all her life. Shau-Jin and I immediately made up our minds to visit her as soon as possible.

Eleven days before Christmas, we drove to Chicago to see her, despite the frigid temperatures. Her small apartment, in a high-rise in the fashionable downtown district, was minimally furnished since she had been living there only a short time. It seemed as if she only went there to sleep. Nothing in the kitchen showed that she did any cooking. The rice cooker I had bought her was still brand-new without any sign of use. I was disappointed. I could not imagine someone being so busy that he or she couldn't find the time to cook and eat properly. But Iris told us that she didn't have time to even think about eating. She was totally dedicated to her professional life.

A few days later, Brett also went to see Iris. Unfortunately, while he was Christmas shopping, something caught in his contact lens and he developed an eye inflammation and had to go to an emergency room. Iris later took care of him in her apartment. He decided it would be best to go home to rest, so on December 21 he took Amtrak but was stranded for hours when the train broke down because of the extreme cold. Iris, meanwhile, could not come home for Christmas; she was assigned by the *Tribune* to work over the holidays. Besides, she told us she needed to be alone anyway to figure out what she wanted to do after she left the *Tribune*.

Late on Christmas Eve, when I called her, she told me she was lonely. I tried my best to cheer her up. But it was difficult to find the right words. It made me sad, thinking about my daughter spending Christmas alone in a big city, and I thought about our family's joyful Christmas celebrations of the past.

Iris told me she had just walked down Michigan Avenue to get a good look at the night scene. She knew it might be a while before she could walk down the avenue again in the cold of winter.

She was freezing, but she still enjoyed standing next to a building, tilting her head back, and watching the skyscrapers shoot into the sky. She enjoyed the trees along Michigan Avenue that sparkled with tiny bright-yellow lights. The streets, she said, were jammed with people with big shopping bags filled with gifts. She told us she would miss Chicago. As she walked the city streets, assaulted by the wind and cold, she imagined I was roasting a duck in the kitchen, Dad was making steamed Chinese bread, and Michael was poking at the logs in the fireplace. She said she missed all of that.

I told her we would see her on New Year's Day when she moved back to Urbana. Yes, Iris said, she wanted to come home and start over.

8

Starting Over at Twenty-Two

On January 2, 1990, Brett went to Chicago to help Iris move her stuff back home. By this time, Iris had decided to go back to school instead of looking for a new job. We agreed with her, saying that a higher degree would increase her chances for job opportunities.

Iris was a person of action. She immediately went to the U of I campus to look into the possibility of academic enrollment. It was too late to enroll as a degree student, but she could enroll as a non-degree student for the semester. She decided to enroll in the Department of History. She was also actively looking for an apartment on campus. She insisted that she wanted to live on campus rather than at home, which would be more convenient for her. She wanted to be more independent. We promised to support her one semester financially and gave her time to ponder what she should do next.

Within several days, she found an apartment on Stoughton Street; it was within walking distance of the campus. She was lucky, because the apartment was a sublet and she got a discount on the rent. On January 9, she moved in and started to be a student again.

Iris was happy to return to the familiar campus. Many of her friends were still there—and besides, she and Brett could now see each other every day.

After Iris had met Brett in 1988, she'd never dated anyone else, although many men were always pursuing her. When Iris was working at the *Chicago Tribune*, she told us there were always some professionals or businessmen on trains or buses who tried to initiate a conversation with her and gave her their cards and telephone numbers. Iris said she had a stack of cards an inch thick!

Iris and Brett had been talking about marriage for some time. Brett asked Iris to marry him on the day after Thanksgiving, 1989, at the same spot where they first met in October 1988. On January 13, 1990, Brett and Iris went to a gift shop and Brett bought a diamond engagement ring for her. So, Iris was engaged to be married. We were not surprised at all and took it as a natural turn of events.

Several years later, Iris told us that one of her friends, who was Jewish, asked her whether her parents would be against her marrying a non-Asian. Iris told her friend that there was no barrier whatsoever from the parents on both sides. Her friend commented, "You are lucky. My parents want me to marry a Jew!" Indeed, we had no objection to who Iris would marry as long as the person was sincere and honest and really loved her.

Before Iris met Brett, during discussions about dating and marriage, we had told Iris that usually a successful marriage involved two persons with similar cultural backgrounds. Shau-Jin and I were hoping that Iris would marry a Chinese-American or an Asian-American if only so he could relate to her experience as a child of immigrant parents, but Iris told us that she had not had many chances to meet Chinese-Americans—and besides, in her dreams her boyfriends were always white Caucasians. She added that this probably was influenced by the books she read and the movies she saw. We were convinced that it was up to her to decide.

When the university semester started, Iris told us she was taking a number of courses in history and philosophy. She was serious and studying hard. The termination of her intern position at the *Tribune* had not deterred her enthusiastic spirit and passion in pursuit of her dream. Actually, the setback further enhanced her determination. She was quite confident. I never doubted that she had potential. I believed in her. I knew that she would achieve something one day.

Iris was not only taking non-degree courses; she was also in the process of applying to graduate school. She felt her true love was writing and publishing. She wanted to be a writer even more than a news reporter. After the *Tribune* episode, she realized that she wanted to be her own boss. I never asked her how many universities she applied to, but I knew she had applied to many. Later she was awarded an assistantship from the Johns Hopkins University writing program, a one-year master's program. At the time, I was focused on my own research, and I had obtained good results, so I had my own research grant proposal to worry about, too. It was a nerve-racking time for us both. Professor Cronan told me that my title of "visiting assistant professor" would be changed to "senior research scientist" because I could not be "visiting" too long; three years was the maximum, according to department regulations.

Iris told us that she had talked to Professor Lillian Hoddeson of the Department of History, who was originally a physicist and a colleague of Shau-Jin's in the Physics Department. Hoddeson later joined the History Department because her area of study was the history of science. Iris told Professor Hoddeson that she was interested in writing a biography of John Bardeen. Iris's article on Bardeen was published in the *Chicago Tribune* in January of that year. Iris proposed to Hoddeson that she had a lot more material on Bardeen and was interested in continuing the project by interviewing and conducting research on him. Iris said she could expand the materials into a book. Hoddeson thought it was a good idea, but in order to support the project she suggested that both of them needed to write a proposal and apply for a grant. This was just one of Iris's ideas at the time.

Professor Hoddeson indeed wrote the grant proposal on a biography of John Bardeen; but when she received the grant, Iris had been already awarded an assistantship from Johns Hopkins University and gone to Baltimore. Nevertheless, several years later, in 2002, Hoddeson and Vicki Daitch published the book, titled *True Genius: The Life and Science of John Bardeen.* When the book was out, we met Hoddeson one day when we still lived in Urbana. She told us that she felt that the book should have been written by Iris. She praised Iris and said she was truly a good science writer! It was very humble of her to say that; her book on Bardeen was excellent, according to Shau-Jin, who read the book.

The time Iris spent at the U of I campus in the spring of 1990 not only gave her a chance to take the courses she wanted to explore, but also enabled her to talk to a number of professors in various departments. Many of our professor friends from the departments of Physics, Microbiology, and Electrical Engineering, who knew Iris, told us that they found Iris pleasantly curious and her questions intriguing. But among all of them, Professor Robert Reid of the Journalism Department had given her the most encouragement. Iris shared Professor Reid's belief that a good reporter should be a good writer—and Iris was determined to become a good writer, and her acceptance into the MFA at Johns Hopkins was the first step.

With the spring break approaching, Iris wanted to visit her grandparents in New York. She always loved seeing them, but this time she wanted to introduce them to Brett, as she and Brett were now engaged. The year before, when they'd visited La Jolla, Brett had met Ye-Ye and Nai-Nai when we drove them to Los Angeles. Iris loved big cities and New York was one of her favorites. Therefore, we decided that the whole family would visit New York over spring break. Po-Po and Gong-Gong were very happy to see them. My mom smiled all the time and could not close her mouth. It was one of the happiest days for her, both because she got to see the grandchildren and because now she knew that Iris, her favorite granddaughter, was engaged. Iris, Brett, and Michael also took the chance to tour the Statue of Liberty and to see a Broadway show—a must for Iris, who loved the entire spectacle of a Broadway performance. They had a wonderful time in New York.

Once Iris learned that she had been awarded a place in the Johns Hopkins University writing program, which would start in the fall of 1990, she was busy fulfilling the necessary requirements for the fall term and for her teaching assistantship. The program also had a foreign-language requirement, either German or French, and Iris chose French. Because she had been awarded an assistantship, her tuition was waived, and she intended to obtain the degree within a year, meaning she had to pass the foreign-language requirement at the beginning of the program. When the semester at the U of I ended in the middle of May, she moved to French House on campus, where only French was spoken; English was not allowed. I still remembered that when Iris was at Uni High and did not pass the French exam, she'd dropped French and taken Chinese as an easy way out. Now because she was determined to get a degree in writing from JHU in a year, she devoted three months to intensively studying French and living in the French House. She passed the French proficiency test when she arrived at JHU and thus fulfilled the foreign-language requirement for the degree, showing that once Iris was motivated and determined to do something, she would work hard to reach that goal.

June 16, 1990 was my fiftieth birthday, which happened to be on a Saturday that year. Michael came home from his summer job in Chicago specifically for the occasion. Shau-Jin sent twenty red roses to me. Professor John Cronan threw a big birthday party at his house in the evening. All the people working in the lab were there, and Brett and Iris came too. Betsy, Professor Cronan's loving wife, baked a big birthday cake for me. That morning a family portrait was taken in a professional studio, and that portrait has hung on the wall of our family room for all the years since. It is the formal family portrait we took before Iris got married. In the portrait, both Iris and Michael look innocent and full of joy, and Shau-Jin and I could not be happier.

Everyone gave me a present, but the words in the card Iris gave me touched me the most. Apparently, she had taken time to choose a card carefully to express her feelings:

"The worlds we've grown up in are very different, calling for different choices in each of our lives. I know that you may not agree with every choice I make, but I think it's great how you've taught me to choose for myself. It's been a precious gift to me, and I just want to say thanks, Mom, for loving me enough to let me be me." And in addition, she added, "Thanks for being not only my mother but the best girlfriend I've got."

At the end of May, Brett's thesis adviser, Professor Hua Lee, decided to leave UI for a position at the University of California at Santa Barbara. Brett had two more years to go for his PhD, so he was going to Santa Barbara with his thesis adviser. And Iris was going to Baltimore to attend JHU. There was no other way but for them to separate for a year. Before they parted in August, they decided to get married the following year. This was an important date to set, since the reservation of a church and a reception location usually needs to be made a year in advance, so they were right on schedule. Iris and Brett had discussed their wedding plans before they left for the East and West Coast. They decided to get married in the United Methodist Church right on the U of I campus. And the reception would be in the Illini Union next to the church on Green Street. The wedding date was set for August 17, 1991.

Once the date of the wedding was set, I started to plan. After all, I had been told that, according to the Western cultural tradition, the bride's family was supposed to spearhead the wedding plans. On July 29, Brett's parents, Ken and Luann Douglas, came to visit us, and that was the first time we met them. Ken was tall and sturdy and was a farmer in Mason City. Luann had red hair, the same color as Brett's. She was teaching in a grade school and was more talkative than Ken was. We happily discussed the plan for Iris and Brett's wedding in the coming year.

Iris was scheduled to move to Baltimore in the middle of August, and I knew once she left, we would not have time to go shopping together for the wedding gown and the accessories. So in July, Iris and I went to a wedding shop to choose her wedding gown and all the other necessities including the bridesmaid's dress, the shoes, the veil, and so forth. We were quite efficient; in one afternoon we got most of the things done.

While we were shopping for her wedding gown, Iris seemed somewhat absent-minded. It seemed she wanted to get the things done as soon as possible. Iris had never liked shopping; but, I thought, this was for her own wedding, after all. It turned out that I was more interested in the wedding than she was. I had the feeling at the time that she was very single-minded about her career, and it seemed her mind was only on the forthcoming trip to Baltimore. The excitement of studying in a prestigious university on the East Coast excited her. To her, the wedding was something she wanted to get over with and out of her way as soon as possible, so she could embark on the path of her dream of becoming a writer. Perhaps the wedding ceremony was a mere formality in her mind. What was really important to Iris was their mutual commitment for their future hopes and dreams together.

Iris told me that she did not want to waste time on the dating game as most girls in college did. She had met Brett in 1988, when she was twenty years old. They had been together ever since. Iris had many male friends, but all for academic or business purposes. Since she met Brett, she had never dated anyone else as far as I knew. One of my friends said to me that Iris was a person who gave people a strong impression at the first meeting. Iris was quite aware that she was beautiful, judging by how she said that many male admirers gave her compliments all the time; but she seemed to really not be too concerned about how she looked. Rather, she was quite wary about whether she could achieve something in her life. She valued human existence very differently from the rest of pop culture.

On August 11, Iris moved her stuff back home from French House. On August 13, Shau-Jin and I helped her load her suitcases, the sturdy

Apple IIc computer, books, and other necessities in the car and drove her to Baltimore. My younger sister Ging-Ging lived in Potomac, Maryland, not far from Baltimore. We visited Ging-Ging's home first and then, on August 15, we moved her stuff into her dormitory, Homewood Apartment. As soon as we settled her in her dorm, Brett called from Santa Barbara. He had recently moved to Santa Barbara and said he'd found an apartment and would be sharing it with three girls. Three girls? I was a little surprised, but Iris told me that I worried too much. Indeed, I was too old-fashioned and had not been able to adapt to the current pop culture of young people at this stage in their life. When I was a graduate student in 1962, there were no co-ed dorms that I knew of, let alone any male students sharing apartments with female students.

After we bought some necessary furniture for Iris and met her roommate, who was a nice Chinese-American girl, we toured the campus. Iris led us to see the Baltimore harbor district. She had been to Baltimore for an interview given by the University program in May, so she knew the area better than we did. She even introduced us to a special local seafood dish in a famous restaurant near the harbor. We enjoyed the harbor scene while we dined. We gave Iris our best wishes, and the next day we left Baltimore. Iris was left on her own to pursue her dream!

Not long after we left Baltimore, Iris called and said she was lonely and missed home. After all, this was the first time she had lived that far from home. On August 27, 1990, about ten days after we left her, she wrote us a long letter describing her life at Johns Hopkins and her observations of her surroundings:

Dear Mom and Dad:

I'm sorry I cried and made such a big emotional scene over the phone last night, but I was lonely.

Actually, I'm often quite happy being alone. It gives me the freedom to devote myself entirely to my books. Within the past few days I've read almost 30 short stories from an anthology of 81, a few plays by Eugene

O'Neill, several nonfiction pieces by John McPhee (renowned staff writer for the New Yorker), *an autobiography of a black comedian and civil rights worker,* The Year of Silence *by Madison Smart Bell,* Woman Writer *by Joyce Carol Oates,* Lost in the Funhouse *by John Barth, stories by Franz Kafka, Pearl Buck, John Updike, Truman Capote, John Steinbeck,* White Fang *by Jack London, four plays by Tina Howe (she'll be teaching at Hopkins next spring),* Beowulf *(the oldest English epic) plus* Dubliners *by James Joyce. From the moment of I woke up I would read, run errands and study French. I think my roommate was worried about my spending so much time in my room. Occasionally she'd knock on my door to see if I was still alive.*

It was, I admit, a thrill for me to borrow books from the Hopkins library (and be allowed to keep them for the next four months!) I also visited the local used bookshop and bought a heap of classics for less than $10. Do you ever get so excited in a bookstore that you feel a spattering of ice drops running down your legs and a cold fist squeeze your bowels and a crawling of the skin—thousands of tiny ants!—until you almost fall to the knees? Other people must feel this way. . . (I can't be the only one!) Other people, like the couple who ran the bookstore. I love talking to owners of used bookstores! Unlike many people I know (who confine their reading material to Cosmopolitan *and Harlequin romances), these commercial librarians are as well read as any English professor. They are likely to have read every book by any author you can mention and they'll recommend at least ten more books before you're out of the store. They tend to be curious, liberal, politically active and very opinionated. I asked the young man behind the counter if he had a copy of the* Best Short Stories of 1989, *edited by Margaret Atwood, and he got all excited and asked me if I had read Atwood's* The Handmaid's Tale. *I said yes and suddenly he was running all over the store and yelling that he loved Atwood's* Cat's Eye *and that it was a must-read; then the other owner, a Jewish woman in her 40's, asked me if I liked women's literature—I said yes and soon she was running down the aisles and came back with a copy of Mao Tse-tung's writings in her hand. She said she* *was a feminist in the 1960's and that some big women's center in San Francisco grew out of the teaching of Mao! "Every feminist I knew was reading Mao at the time—it was the thing to do!"*

Then Iris continued about the people and the street scenes in Baltimore:

By the way, I have to admit that the people in Baltimore are nicer than the ones in Chicago. Sometimes I feel as if I'm in Champaign-Urbana again when I walk down a street of rowhouses, it seems no different from a neighborhood in a suburb except that all the mansions are fused together. And each block is flanked with trees, lawns and bushes. Often the street is so peaceful it's almost eerie. There are times when Sandra and I are walking down through a neighborhood, and I don't see a single person, car or cat. It's as if everyone died during the night and all that's left are the houses.

One thing that intrigues me about Baltimore is the class structure. The people one block west of where I live talk differently from the people one block east. As you know, one block west brings me across N. Charles St. and onto JHU turf where people discuss Max Weber and existentialism and the Hubble Space Telescope. One block east takes me into the drugstores or delis where the cashers chew gum and use "ain't" in every sentence.

And there's one point where three roads intersect and form a star-shaped crosswalk. If you stand right in the middle, you'll find that one road slides into an upper class white neighborhood with stained glass windows and mansions, another road winds into a predominately black professional neighborhood where you can see black men wearing ties and suits and well-dressed black women pushing babies in strollers, and still another road that leads to a block of rowhouses with broken windows and littered with garbage and black panhandlers sitting on sidewalks. Three different worlds, side by side. It was the strangest thing I had ever seen.

Iris was keen in her observations and sensitivity. We always enjoyed reading her letters. No doubt, Iris read so much classical and contemporary English literature voraciously in the year she was at JHU. She was like a sponge, absorbing as much as she could.

Iris's coursework in the writing program was heavy, and besides that she had to help grade students' papers as a teaching assistant. Even with such a huge workload, Iris told us that she continued to look for career opportunities by submitting writing proposals to major magazines and building up her published portfolio of "clips."

When Thanksgiving was approaching, Iris decided to visit Brett in California and said she would come home for Christmas. Her assistantship was really not enough to support her. When she complained that the meals in the dorm were poor, we immediately sent money and asked her to buy healthful food to supplement the deficiency. When she returned to the JHU campus after Thanksgiving, she wrote humorously, "People have come back to Hopkins with colds so I hope I don't get sick AGAIN. Really, I consider myself a careful person, but Johns Hopkins seems to be loaded with sick people all year round (maybe that's why they have such a good med school!)"

In November, I too had a cold and took the antibiotic ampicillin. A month later, on December 3, I found blood in my stool. I was very scared and thought I had colon cancer. I immediately saw a doctor and did tests. To my relief, it was only inflammation of the colon, not colon cancer. However, I was tired and had constant abdominal pain and diarrhea. When Iris came back home from Baltimore during the Christmas break, my health had not improved. Brett also came back from Santa Barbara to his home in Mason City for Christmas. For Christmas, 1990 and New Year's Day, 1991, because of my illness, I was not able to do any cooking or house chores. Even with this condition, I forced myself to be with Iris and Brett when they were shopping for a bridal registry for their forthcoming wedding.

After Christmas and during the winter break, Brett brought Iris to Mason City, to visit his hometown, see his parents' home, and meet his grandparents, whom Iris hadn't met yet. Iris also visited Luann's classroom, and the children in the class enthusiastically welcomed her and commented on how beautiful she was. Iris sensed that Luann's mother was worried when she learned that Iris was not a Christian. However, Brett assured her that even though Iris was not a Christian, she had very high morals, and that was comforting to his grandmother.

Over the winter break, Iris was working on a proposal called "Chinatown" for *National Geographic*. She also constantly toyed with ideas for a possible future book. This became her habit. She was always thinking about a book idea at any place and any time. When the winter break ended on January 15, 1991, she returned to JHU, and Brett to UCSB.

My gastrointestinal discomfort, in spite of my seeing a number of doctors, continued on and off for several months without being completely cured. Finally, another test on a stool specimen and a colonoscopy revealed that I had "pseudomembranous colitis," which was caused by an intestinal pathogenic bacterium, *Clostridium difficile*. The toxins released by the bacteria had destroyed the protective lining of my colon and caused the inflammation of the colon and the bloody diarrhea. My case of colitis was considered to be a severe one and was finally cured by the last line of antibiotic, vancomycin. It took me almost another half year to recover fully.

Because of my illness in the first half of 1991, I was physically weak and tired all the time. The failure to find the real cause of my illness for the first several months compounded my anxiety and distress. Worse yet, Iris's wedding was coming up and there was still a lot to do, stressing me out even more during those months.

In February 1991, President Bush ordered the bombing of Baghdad and the war in Iraq was dominating the headlines. Iris immediately called us, saying that all her classmates in JHU were watching the news in the TV lounge and were very concerned. We were also watching the news attentively. But the most important thing I was concerned with at the time was Iris's wedding. Because my gastrointestinal illness had not improved over time, I was very worried that I would not be able to prepare a good wedding party for Iris. However, Iris seemed not to be worried about her wedding at all, and urged me to relax and take care of my health.

On Valentine's Day, Iris mailed us a card. On the front was a kitten licking the mama cat's cheek and the mother cat was closing her eyes and enjoying the moment. Inside, Iris wrote:

> *I miss both of you very much and I can't wait to see you again in May! Brett sent me half a dozen roses today and told me he might have a chance to be in a submarine—his research on sonar imaging will be used by the Navy.*
>
> *I'm pretty busy writing fiction, nonfiction, teaching and reading novels and poetry. (Baltimore has a rich literary heritage. . . did you know that Edgar Allen Poe, H. L. Mencken, F. Scott Fitzgerald, Francis Scott, they all came from this city!) In all honesty, I think my stay at Johns Hopkins has been quite exciting and well worth the year-long separation from Brett. He's going to love it out here when he visits me in March. He has the most incredible memory for historical facts, and yet he's never been to Washington!*

Very soon after this letter, she called us in excitement with good news. Her adviser, Professor Barbara Culliton, told her that her friend, Susan Rabiner, a book editor at HarperCollins, was trying to find a writer for a book on a Chinese rocket scientist named Tsien Hsue-shen. Culliton seemed to like Iris's writing style and thought she was a good candidate to be this writer. Professor Culliton was a renowned science writer and editor for many prestigious science magazines such as *Science* and *Nature*. According to Culliton, Susan Rabiner heard the story of Tsien at a scientific conference in 1990 and felt his life was worth a book.

Iris said that Culliton had recommended her to Susan Rabiner because of Iris's Chinese background and her scientific writing skills. Iris did not know anything at all about Dr. Tsien, however. Over the telephone, Iris asked us, "Do you know this Chinese scientist, Tsien Hsue-shen?" Shau-Jin told her, "Of course I know him. He is quite famous in China." In fact, Shau-Jin had met him in person in 1980 in Beijing, when Shau-Jin had been invited as one of the overseas Chinese physicists for a physics conference. Shau-Jin told her what he knew about Tsien and, in addition, told her that on our bookshelf we had a Chinese book on him. Iris got very excited and said she would tell Susan Rabiner about it. Several days later, Iris told us that Susan had really responded to the fact that Shau-Jin and so many other contemporary Chinese scientists knew about Tsien and asked Iris to gather as much information on Tsien as she could. This was the beginning of a huge transition point in Iris's life.

Dr. Tsien Hsue-sen was a brilliant Chinese-born scientist who was educated at MIT and Caltech. He had made enormous contributions in rocketry and had helped America enter the space age. At the peak of his career, he was caught up in the witch hunt of McCarthyism and was accused, falsely, of being a Communist. After being deported back to China, he became the father of the Chinese missile and space program.

Iris ended up writing three books in her short life that were all related to China. Many people thought that it was her own idea to write something related to her ethnic background and cultural heritage, but actually the first book on Dr. Tsien was completely due to Susan Rabiner's suggestion. I remember Iris told me that she had talked to Susan about her book idea about John Bardeen, the American two-time Nobel laureate in physics, but Susan thought Dr. Tsien's life was more interesting and would make for a better book.

In March, Brett flew to Baltimore to visit Iris during her spring break. They went to Washington, D.C., not only to visit the museums, but because Iris wanted to go to the National Archives to see whether there were any files there on Tsien. On March 19, 1991, Iris wrote us a postcard :

Dear Mom and Dad:

   Brett and I went to the FBI museum today! . . .

   By the way, Susan Rabiner at HarperCollins talked to me today and she wants me to write up a proposal on Chien Xue-xin (more than one of its spellings) . . . She was really excited about the project, esp. after I told her about the info Dad told me. More later . . . Love, Iris

Then, on March 24, she mailed us another postcard that said:

Dear Mom and Dad:

   . . . Brett and I went to Washington on Friday, so I could do some research on Tsien Hsue-shen. NASA had a file on him that was more than an inch thick! I spent an hour xeroxing all the articles on him, then went to the National Archives. There was no information on him there because Tsien is still alive. I will have to file a Freedom of Information Act form to get the FBI files on him, and that can take 2 to 5 years!!! Anyway, Susan Rabiner had called me early Friday morning and told me Barbara Culliton (my advisor) is really excited about this and that Nature may print an excerpt or article about the book if it works out. More later. . . . Love, Iris

She was working hard and using her spring break to collect information on Tsien. Several weeks later, she gave Susan Rabiner a written report. Susan was really impressed.

I had been continuously working in my lab, in spite of my abdominal discomfort, until May. I was so sick in May that I could not work further. I finally took some sick leave. At the time, I had lost almost fifteen pounds. In the latter part of May, the doctor finally confirmed that it was pseudomembranous colitis again and prescribed vancomycin, and I was back on the healing track.

For Iris's wedding, Luann visited us several times and brought a book to tell us how to prepare a good wedding. We had discussed the reception in detail. With Iris and Brett on the East and West

Coast, respectively, the planning was on the shoulders of both sets of parents.

On Mother's Day, Iris mailed me a card and wrote:

I wish I could spend Mother's Day with you. . .especially now that you're resting at home most of the time. You must be exhausted from planning the wedding reception and I feel pretty guilty about staying on the East Coast for a few extra weeks instead of coming back to Urbana as soon as possible. But at the same time, I'm glad to be spending so much time with Grandma! She told me an interesting story tonight (a Chinese version of Romeo and Juliet) of a woman scholar who dresses as a man and falls in love with a poor student, ending with the woman crawling into his grave, from which two butterflies sail into the sky—perhaps you know the name of this fairy tale? I hope to find you relaxed and well when I see you again. I love you very much. . . . Iris.

Because of my illness, I missed Michael's college graduation ceremony on May 12. Only Shau-Jin attended. Michael graduated from the Electric Engineering Department of the U of I and received an assistantship from the Department of Electric Engineering of UCSB. He was going to study in Santa Barbara, the same place Brett was. I was happy that Iris, Brett, and Michael would be in the same place starting in May.

On May 24, finally, Iris came home from Baltimore, having completed her one-year writing seminar program and having obtained a master's degree in writing. She did not stay home long. Two weeks later, on June 9, she went to Santa Barbara to be with Brett. She was eager to go to California to collect information on Tsien in preparation for her book proposal, as Dr. Tsien had graduated from Caltech and spent a number of years in Los Angeles, and Iris wanted to interview his friends and colleagues while she was out west. Another reason, of course, was that she wanted to be reunited with Brett. She and Brett missed each other terribly during their separation.

Iris came home on August 7, just ten days before the wedding. By then, arrangements for the ceremony and the reception had already been made.

On the morning of Saturday, August 17, 1991, the weather forecast was cloudy with possible rain. The wedding ceremony was at 5:00 P.M. In the early afternoon, a summer storm brought a brief shower. I went with Iris to the church a couple of hours prior to the storm. Iris and all the bridesmaids were busy changing clothes and setting their hair in the back lounge of the church. Iris did not want to put too much makeup on her face and insisted that she look natural. I was the one who was nervous, whereas Iris was quite relaxed.

When the time was near, I was ushered to the front seat of the church, whereas Shau-Jin was waiting near the entrance door with Iris since he would be giving her away. When the guests settled, we heard Schubert's "Ave Maria," which was sung from the balcony above by a music-major student of the U of I whom Iris had invited. The song was beautiful and touched everyone's heart. Just at this time, the sun suddenly broke through the clouds and its rays penetrated through the rainbow-colored stained glass of the church. United Methodist Church was huge, with a three-story-high cathedral ceiling and gigantic windows. The whole church was quiet but bright, and the melody was resonating in the spacious open air. The atmosphere was solemn and holy. I could barely breathe as I listened to the beautiful music and soaked up the moment.

The bridesmaids, Amy Orfield, Kathy Szoke, and Carolyn Wu, and the maid of honor, Janice Karlovich, paraded down one after the other toward the altar. All were Iris's best friends; they wore elegant bright fuchsia-colored dresses. When the wedding procession music was played on the old church organ, we saw Shau-Jin accompanying Iris walking slowly down the red-carpeted aisle to the altar. Iris smiled along the way and finally joined Brett, who was standing in front of the minister. Minister Palmer officiated the ceremony and Andrew Lloyd Webber's "All I Ask of You" was sung midway through the ceremony.

When the ceremony ended, everyone told us it was the most beautiful wedding they had ever seen!

I was quite happy—and a bit relieved—that the wedding was over. It had taken me almost a year of preparation, and it went flawlessly. Iris and Brett left for Santa Barbara immediately after the wedding. They had decided to take their honeymoon after resting for a while first.

It was a fairytale to many of our friends as well as to Iris and Brett's friends: a beautiful princess married to a handsome prince.

9

Struggles of a Young Writer

After the wedding, Iris lived with Brett in Goleta, a small town next to Santa Barbara where the University of California at Santa Barbara (UCSB) is located. Brett was working on his PhD in electrical engineering.

Over the Labor Day weekend of 1991, Iris and Brett went to Las Vegas for their honeymoon and stayed at Caesar's Palace. Later she mailed us a big photo portrait of them taken during the Vegas show *Splash* at the Riviera Hotel. In the photo, both look so young and beautiful; this is one of the best photos of them. Her smile is quite cheerful and her eyes glitter with intelligence and drive. The portrait was on the wall of our family room in Urbana for many years. It was also displayed in every house Iris and Brett ever lived in together.

On October 6, Iris wrote us a three-and-a-half-page single-spaced typed letter that touched on several topics. She said that she had talked to Susan Rabiner, and Susan thought her book should have "enormous reviews," but "how well it sells depends on a number of factors: the details I am able to gather, the quality of the narration, the subject matter, the timing of the book and the promotion." Iris also mentioned that "There should be three markets for this book: the scientific community, the Chinese-American community, and the political community—particularly those interested in the McCarthy era of the 1950's." She was very focused and wanted her first book to be successful even before she got the contract. She was learning every possible bit of information on the book-publishing business while she also gathered information on Tsien.

In the letter, she also told us:

If you are looking for any good books to read, then you should check out American Steel *by Richard Preston. It's an excellent example of literary journalism, and I highly recommend it. . . . I'm also reading* Cross Creek *by Marjorie Kinnan Rawlings and* The Rise of Theodore Roosevelt *by Edmund Morris in my spare time. Just the other day I read that a woman won the Nobel Prize in literature—Nadine Gordimer of South Africa. I plan to read some of her novels when I get the chance. The caliber of writing in Nobel Prize literature is several cuts higher than even the best of most contemporary American writing, yet so few people put the works of Nobel Prize authors on their reading list. Had it not been for the Nobel Prize committee, I probably would not have discovered the Icelandic epic novels of Halldór Laxness, or the Yiddish short stories of Isaac Bashevis Singer or the poetry of Czeslaw Milosz, from Poland.*

I really admired her passion for reading and learning, even when she had so much work to do.

In the same letter, she also wrote:

I really miss both of you very much, I've been thinking about my family quite a bit these days, especially after my visit to Grandma and Grandpa's home (in L.A.). . . . It depresses me to see how young, muscular and handsome Brett is now and then to imagine him sixty years later, stooped, coughing and old. One fourth of my life is over already and for Brett, it's almost one third. People sometimes don't understand why I'm so impatient, but how can I NOT be when time passes so quickly? It doesn't seem to bother most people, however.

Then she was talking about a new book idea:

Every day, I think of a new idea for a book. For instance, the history of commuting in the United States. How did it begin? From the highway grew the suburb, the "bedroom community," the community college, the commuter college, the shopping mall, the chain store, the mobile home and smog. To find the heart of our national soul, as many writers seek, we must start with the web of arteries that we call our highways. What has commuting done to the American community? Has it contributed to the decay of our inner cities? Has it brought people closer, or has it forced people to live and work farther away from each other, placing not just physical but emotional distance between the American people? What kind of psychological toll does a daily one or two-hour commute impose upon us? What does the rampant machine gun shootings on the highways of Los Angeles or the cross-fire of the streets of East St. Louis tell us about our society?

Apparently, she was not only writing her book proposal, she was also reading other books, thinking about ideas for a new book, and reflecting on her life.

On October 10, 1991, she finished her book proposal and mailed it to Susan Rabiner. On that day she wrote to us:

Dear Mom and Dad:

I just sent off the final version of my proposal to HarperCollins, and before long I will enter negotiations and a contractual agreement! Before I sign anything, however, I plan to read a couple of books on the subject in the library. Can you believe the proposal was 102 pages long, with an

additional 6 pages of sources? The best investment I have made so far is
my laser printer.

Brett and I have both been very busy, but when he comes home at
night we take long walks together. This weekend will be a wonderful
break for both of us. Sometimes Brett doesn't come home from lab until 9
or 10 pm, and sometimes I'm typing away at the computer until 2, 3 or 4
am, occasionally waking him up, but he doesn't get mad at all. Anyway, I
miss both of you very much. Love, Iris

However, the break she had after she sent off her book proposal
was filled with loneliness. She called us and complained that
she was extremely lonely in Santa Barbara. One major factor, of
course, was waiting for the answer to her proposal from Harper-
Collins. Iris told us that Susan Rabiner liked her proposal very
much. Susan said she did not expect Iris to do so well on the book
proposal; "It's marvelous," Susan said. And Susan assured her
that she would be stunned if proposal did not get approved. Susan
asked her to be patient, though, as the process would take time. In the
meantime, Iris was worried that even if the proposal got approved,
she still had to find other resources to support herself in addition
to the book advance. She was actively looking for and applying for
grants to support her research. She said she went to the UCSB library
to find the names of grant agencies and had started applying. Then
she said she was still lonely even after she had met a number of
people in town. She even found two people from Urbana and had
lunch with them. She missed the big cities like Chicago or New York
and hated smaller towns such as Santa Barbara, populated mostly
with "the newly wed and the nearly dead." She said she felt trapped.
She would love to live in Los Angeles, but Brett hated the traffic and
the smog. She missed Chicago, Michigan Avenue, Water Tower Place. . . .
I comforted her and told her to be patient. At the end of the phone
conversation, she told me that this was just one of her down days,
and she admitted that she should feel lucky for what she had.

On the phone, she also mentioned that she hated cooking and cleaning the apartment. Not the cooking and the cleaning itself, but the everyday routine. She said that she felt a sense of accomplishment when she finished the cleaning, but the fact that it always got dirty again, and the routine of constant cleaning, seemed hopeless. She vowed that she would delegate the cleaning to someone else when she had enough money.

At this time, Iris was desperate for money to support herself, but we did not really realize this until we visited her during the Christmas–New Year's holiday at the end of 1991.

In November 1991, she had been happy again when she was about to go with Brett to a conference in San Francisco, where Brett was presenting a paper. On November 3, she wrote us a postcard from San Francisco in such small scribbles that I had to use a magnifying glass to read it:

> *Dear Mom and Dad:*
>
> *Brett and I are staying at Peter Kim's apartment in San Francisco and I LOVE IT!!! Never have I been in such a romantic city on the West Coast—(Forget Santa Barbara and Los Angeles! If I ever get the chance I want to live here!). . . . Today we rode down the hills on a cable car and ate crab sandwiches and squid and shrimp along Fisherman's Wharf. The crowded booth of sea food, cheap jewelry and T shirts reminded me of the street markets of Taiwan. Brett and I enjoyed "Bread Bowls" of clam chowder: hollowed out rolls of bread filled with creamy white soup, with flaps of crust for lids! We crawled through the quarters of a World War II submarine and peered through telescopes at Alcatraz (the penitentiary that housed such felons as Al Capone) and Angel Island, where many immigrants from China had been detained. Then we walked up and down the streets, every corner a surprise: a gallery of original Disney animation sketches, a shop of romance and massage, a wax museum, a street magic show. In some ways, this city is Chicago, Baltimore and New York rolled into one—and warmer and cleaner as well.*
>
> *Tomorrow we go to Monterey . . . I'll write you then! Love, Iris*

Shau-Jin went to Taiwan for a conference at the beginning of November for two weeks. Both Iris and Michael were in Santa Barbara, so I was alone at home if I was not working in the lab. Iris called and wrote often to check up on me. After San Francisco, she and Brett went to Monterey for an electrical engineering conference. Iris wrote me a postcard on November 8, 1991 and said that "During the 3-day Asilomar Conference, I did nothing but read, buy books, walk along the beach and eat bowls of clam chowder. By the end of our 'second honeymoon' I was itching to get back to work. I can hardly wait to see you again at Christmas!"

I told Iris we had decided to visit them after Christmas and then go to Hawaii for a much-needed vacation. I had just recovered from my illness, and Iris's wedding was over; Shau-Jin and I thought we needed some time for ourselves. Michael came home for Christmas, which was lovely, as we had not seen him since Iris's wedding. So, after Christmas, on December 30, we flew to Santa Barbara and drove to Goleta to visit Iris. Iris and Brett lived in a small apartment at 312 Ellwood Beach Drive. They lived like typical graduate students. Iris took us to see the UCSB campus and the beaches. The beaches and the architecture of the build-ings were beautiful, and the student culture in Santa Barbara was very liberal. The five of us then drove down to Los Angeles to visit Shau-Jin's parents, where we stayed with Shau-Jin's brother Frank in L.A.

On the last day before we flew to Hawaii, in the early morning of January 3, 1992, Brett told us that Iris was spending money without proper planning and she had spent most of their savings. Brett sug-gested that Iris should find a regular job. Because we were in a hurry to catch the plane to Hawaii, we did not have the chance to find out exactly what had happened.

Iris never thought much about money. She usually spent it on books and all the things related to writing or publishing. She wanted to buy computers, laser printers, and file cabinets, for example. She never wasted money on clothes or cosmetics, so I could not say she was wasting it, although she did buy a large number of books.

We later learned that Brett wanted Iris to look for a nine-to-five regular job, such as a teacher in a high school or a college. She did apply to the UCSB Department of English and several small colleges near Santa Barbara. She complained that in Santa Barbara, not like Baltimore or Chicago, there was a very limited job market.

In December 1991, Iris found a book agent, Laura Blake of Curtis Brown, Ltd., one of the most prestigious literary agencies in the country. Laura represented Iris after HarperCollins approved the book proposal. As far as I remember, Iris got a $30,000 advance from HarperCollins— not enough to cover her living expenses, considering the book was going to take two to three years to write, let alone the money needed for her research. That was why Iris was under tremendous pressure to seek an additional source of income. She applied for a number of grants from foundations, big or small, such as the National Science Foundation, the National Endowment of Humanities, the MacArthur Foundation, the Woodrow Wilson Center, and the United States Institute of Peace. She also contacted her former professors at the U of I to ask them to write recommendation letters, particularly to Professor Bob Reid, who wrote numerous letters on her behalf.

During the first half of 1992, Iris was not only continuing the research on the biography, but also applying for all those grants or fellowships, on top of looking for teaching jobs. During the waiting period, she tried all the ways she could think of to find a freelancing job at business magazines or newspapers. One time, she called us and said she'd met a person working in the local Kaplan, Inc. who said that if she wanted, she could teach the Kaplan classes to students for test prep and college admission; there were openings. Another time, she said she could work as a telemarketer for a product company. But when she heard nothing from the grant agencies or received rejection letters one after another, she was desperate. When we heard she was delivering pizzas, my heart sank! We couldn't believe she would do this; we immediately expressed our concern. Fortunately, it didn't last long. Shau-Jin and I, as well as Brett, immediately asked her to stop. We were not against the job itself, but we worried about her safety, since we had all heard horrible things about how people who delivered pizza got kidnapped or killed, especially if they were women. Even under these circumstances, however, Iris still remained optimistic and very focused on collecting materials for the biography.

Due to my illness the year before, I had not seen my parents for more than a year, and their poor health had prevented them from attending Iris's wedding in 1991, so I decided to visit them in May 1992 around Mother's Day. I arrived at my parents' apartment in New York on May 18. Iris was already there. Iris's trip to the East Coast was multi-purpose. She had a business meeting with Susan Rabiner at HarperCollins in New York, and she wanted to do some research at the National Archives in Washington, D.C. She also wanted to go to Boston to visit MIT, where Dr. Tsien had taught from 1947 to 1949, and to interview his colleagues as well as the librarians and archivists there. Iris also wanted to go to Providence, Rhode Island for Kathy Szoke's graduation from Brown University, as Kathy had been one of the bridesmaids in Iris's wedding and the two were very close. Iris had planned the trip carefully and tried to accomplish many things in one trip.

I was very happy to see Iris, even though we had just seen each other at New Year's and she called us almost every week. Still, she seemed to have endless things to tell me. She now was not only my daughter, but also my best friend. We could talk about anything and everything. I clearly remember the night of May 19, 1992; we spent it together in my parents' New York apartment. We slept together and talked and talked till past midnight. She was very happy and in a good mood and told me that she and Susan Rabiner had discussed how the book would come together. It seemed like Susan had high hopes for the book, and her enthusiasm rubbed off on Iris. She also updated me about what she had found in the Archives about Tsien's life, and about the interviews she'd conducted with his friends and colleagues (and had recorded on numerous tapes). She was a good investigative journalist, digging deep and following leads wherever she found them.

Then our topic turned to her next book project. At the time, she had just started working on her first book and was far from finishing it, but she had already begun to think about what would come next. She even showed me a list of possible topics. Her list of book ideas varied widely, from deep-sea industrial diving to the rise of the city of Las Vegas. I told her that, quite frankly, the topics she showed me were not personally interesting to me, and I feared it might be the same for others. Then we talked about fiction. Iris told me she wished one day she could write a book such as Margaret Mitchell's *Gone with the Wind*—a novel of a love story mixed with a historical war in the background.

I told her that many heroic and love stories had happened in China during the wars of the twentieth century. I said that since she had a bilingual and bicultural background, she should write about China, which would be something new and fresh to English-language readers. There was too much competition if she wrote the same kind of stories about the West. I told her it was a pity that there were not many epic novels in English describing China in the era of the Sino-Japanese War. Then she remembered my parents' war experience during the Japanese invasion in the 1930s. We talked about the Nanking Massacre. I repeated the story of how my mother had almost been separated from my father forever in Nanking, just a month before Nanking's fall at the hand of the Japanese Army in 1937. She said she remembered that, and would like to do some research on that war once she had some free time. That was the beginning of *The Rape of Nanking* book project, although we did not know it yet. I will never forget that night—we talked so much that we almost lost our voices.

After the trip, Iris returned to Santa Barbara. Brett and Iris immediately moved to a new apartment at 50 South Patterson Avenue in Santa Barbara. According to her description, the apartment was newer and located in a much quieter area. In front of their second-floor apartment was a swimming pool that belonged to the apartment complex and was used exclusively by the residents. She said the apartment was bigger and brighter than the previous one, and she loved it.

On June 17, 1992, Iris wrote us a long letter updating us on her life:

Dear Mom and Dad:

I've been sending out some resources in response to some advertisements that were published in the Santa Barbara News-Press *and the* LA Times. *Perhaps, if I am lucky, I can get a job working as a part-time "freelance editor" for a national bimonthly business magazine. I wrote to them and explained that I have a home computer system, which includes a laser printer and modem, and that I can receive and transmit manuscripts electronically, making it possible for me to work out of my own home. There are other positions about which I have made inquiries: educational video, scriptwriter, grant proposal writer, catalog writer, technical writer.*

Starting tomorrow, I will work four hours a night as a telemarketer, from 5 pm to 9 pm. The company that just hired me, Tri-County Productions, is only a block away from where I live, so I can easily walk there and back.

In the meantime, I've been busy answering correspondence related to the book and pulling ahead on my research. Susan Rabiner and I write to each other through E-mail, now that she finally got a sign-on from the MIT media lab. I've informed a number of sources that I will be calling them between July 7 and August 7 (my month of free phone calls) and before long I will receive from Sprint a confirmation letter that the calls made on my Sprint card will be free as well (this will permit me to let Dr. Hua Di use my Sprint card number to call China to inform certain missile scientists that I will be in touch with them). In the next few days I will also be meeting with local Chinese graduate students who will give me a verbal translation of those articles about Tsien that appeared in the People's Daily *and the* Chiao Tung *alumni year book. And I've arranged for one retired scientist in Santa Barbara, Bob Meghreblian, to help me sort through the voluminous scientific papers of Tsien and to pinpoint the ones that have made the biggest impact on the field of aeronautical engineering.*

*My goal for the next few months is to try to transcribe at least one
tape a day. For the past few days, I have been able to accomplish that,
but who knows what will happen in the next few months. By the end
of June, I hope to finish most of my research for a NSF grant proposal
and preliminary research for the July 7-August 7 interviews. It may also
interest you to know that the Center for Investigative Reporting may fund
a documentary about Tsien or the Chinese missile program, of which
I would be a consultant or collaborator. I certainly have enough background material and photographs in my files.*

*I've been cooking a lot more these days, making dishes such as
cuttlefish ball soup, Chinese marinated chicken, chicken drumlets and
sliced carrots, almond Jello, avocado-ham-alfalfa sprout sandwiches. . .
Love, Iris*

Certainly she was pulling together all her energy to do research on
her book, but in the meantime she was desperately applying for a job,
although she maintained her calm in the letter. Finally, around this
time, one piece of happy news arrived. She'd been awarded a grant of
$15,000 from the John D. and Catherine T. MacArthur Foundation.
The money was given just in time to support her to go to a conference
she wanted to go to very much, the World Space Congress in Washington, D.C., at the end of August.

On August 28, Iris attended the first World Space Congress. Iris said
it was the largest space conference in history. It drew a huge number
of space research scientists from all over the world. She met many
Chinese space scientists from China there and took the opportunity
to tell them that she was writing a biography of Tsien. There was a lot
of interest in her project, and many people were eager to help her. Iris
was able to interview a number of prominent Chinese missile scientists
in the convention center and nearby hotel. They also gave Iris many
names for contacts in China if she was going to go there. Indeed, her
next planned trip was to China, and the MacArthur grant helped her
finally make concrete arrangements.

One notable episode during this time showed how mesmerized she was by her research: One night, Iris called us from the National Archives in Washington, D.C., and said that she was locked in the archives and could not get out. I asked how on earth that could have happened! She said she'd been reading files and documents about Dr. Tsien, and she was so focused that she hadn't realized it was past the closing time of the Archives. Apparently, the archivist didn't realize that she was still there and had locked the entrance door when he went home. She called us from the public phone in the hallway. We told her we were in Urbana; there was no way we could rescue her, and urged her to call the local emergency phone number. Just while she was calling us, Iris heard some footsteps and said it might be a night guard passing by. She quickly called out to him and was finally let out. Another time she was riding the train from D.C. to Baltimore, and she was so focused on what she was reading that she didn't manage to get off until she was in Delaware. These episodes were quickly spread among her friends and she became a laughing-stock at the dinner table. But, joking aside, everyone agreed that Iris was working too hard.

On October 5, 1992, Iris wrote us a detailed letter about her life and her research:

> Dear Mom and Dad:
>
> Enclosed please find a copy of a biographical essay about Dr. Tsien that appeared in a book about China's leading scientists. The book was mailed to me by S. I. Pai, the fellow you had breakfast with in Taiwan. Is it possible for you to take a look at the essay and see if there is anything new? If there is, the next time we talk you can mention the page numbers to me over the phone and I'll have a Chinese UCSB student do a little oral translation for me.
>
> I think it's important for me to write more letters to you to keep a record of events. I do this regularly with my friends but not with you, because of the convenience of the telephone. After spending a year of

research on this book I have learned that the best way to control how history is written is to

(1) be a compulsive letter writer, or

(2) outlive your enemies.

Because as I piece together the event of Tsien's life I have two resources: the written record and the oral record. One of Tsien's best friends, Frank Malina, was a prodigious correspondent who, at the time of his death, left behind 40,000 documents to the Library of Congress. Although his papers have been consolidated into the Frank Malina Collection, no one to my knowledge has ever spent a great deal of time looking through it. During the 1930s, when he and Tsien were experimenting with rockets made from junkyard parts, Frank Malina wrote to his parents two and three times a week. Years later, when he was retired in Paris with plenty of time on his hands, he compiled a collection of excerpts from those letters that pertained to his days as leader of "The Suicide Squad" which have never been published. Frank Malina desperately wanted to be famous; even as a young graduate student at Caltech he was actively sending out press releases about his rocket experiments, holding press conferences with LA Times reporters or lunching with AP science writers at the Caltech Athenaeum. (Luckily for me, this has generated a lot of good newspaper photographs of Malina, Tsien, Parsons and Forman launching rockets in the desert.) In later years he wrote historical articles about the Caltech days and carefully kept records for the historian "100 years from now." It is unfortunate he died 10 years ago . . . I think he would have liked to talk with me.

Every night, I transcribe two or three of my tapes, and it is a thrill to see the stories come to life on the page. It's a lot of work, but I can type very quickly now. When I stare at the words moving across the screen, in rhythm with my hands on the keys and my feet on the transcription pedal, I am strongly reminded of the piano lessons I had as a child! It is piano playing in reverse—instead of following the notes and trying to create music, I am listening to the flowing sound and putting it in symbol form back on the page!

Brett and I estimate that we work anywhere between 50 to 100 hours a week. Brett gets up at 8 every morning, rides his bike into UCSB, rides back for dinner around 6 or 7, and then takes the car back in to the lab and works until midnight. Like Brett, I work from the moment I wake up until I fall asleep at night. Recently Brett spent a few days sleeping late because he was so tired. . . . Then I was afraid I was pregnant. That put more stress on us until it was confirmed today that I was not.

I don't want to have any children until I've spent a few years estab-lishing my reputation as an author. Brett, too, needs the freedom to move about and take the risks required to advance his career. . . .

I will write back as soon as I can. Love, Iris

I was very glad that Iris wrote us in detail about her life at the time; so, as she said in the letter, her letter became a historical record. Because many materials about Dr. Tsien were in Chinese, Iris automatically sent these documents to us for our comments all the time. She had transcribed many interview tapes herself, one by one. She did not have the budget to hire others to do the transcribing for her; the practice she gained doing it herself was another reason she could type so fast. Sometimes you didn't know that the disadvan-tages you had at the time would prepare you for something useful in the future.

In January 1993, Brett finished his PhD thesis and returned to the U of I with his thesis adviser for the final oral examination. On January 11, he came to Urbana to stay with us. We were very happy that he finally had received his PhD. We invited him, his parents, and his brother Jeff for dinner after he passed the exam. Iris did not come home with him; she said she was busy with her research and the travel back home cost too much; but the main reason, she revealed to us, was that she was struggling to get money to support herself as well as the money for research for her book. Her book advance and the small amount of grant money were not enough to support her living plus her research, and both of them were living on Brett's graduate-student salaries. This forced Iris to take extra jobs. It made her life very difficult. We did not truly know her financial situation until then.

When Iris had first met Brett, she thought highly of herself and told Brett with confidence that her chance of becoming a bestselling book author was ninety percent! Iris might have said that she could even support Brett after their marriage. But the fact was that now, Iris couldn't even support herself. The consequence was that Iris, always very proud and independent, was working harder to prove herself.

However, the biggest event of 1993 was when Shau-Jin underwent heart surgery in February. Early that month, he had experienced chest pains after shoveling snow, and I drove him to the ER immediately for tests. The test results showed that he had a blockage in a heart blood vessel. The next day he underwent an angioplasty procedure (balloon) to open up the blockage, but unfortunately the procedure failed and he needed immediate open-heart surgery. I almost fainted when I learned the news—such a big, critical operation on such short notice.

During the long waiting hours in the hospital lounge while Shau-Jin was in the operating room, I called Iris and Michael to tell them about the situation. Of course, they were shocked. It seemed like everything around me was a blur at the time. Thankfully, Shau-Jin survived, but it was a harrowing experience. Despite a severe winter storm and the huge amounts of snow in the area, both Iris and Michael immediately flew in to help.

On March 7, 1993, Iris wrote a letter after returning home to Santa Barbara:

> Dear Mom and Dad:
>
> I'm ecstatic to learn that Dad is feeling much better now. It was certainly a shock when he had to have the operation.
>
> Brett and I are determined to eat healthier now. I have sworn off all soft drinks and fast foods from this day on. I am also determined to exercise at least once a day. Yesterday, Felice Chu invited me to her step

*aerobics class and it was a lot of fun. Today, Brett and I took a long walk
down the beach.*

*The sea had the lowest tide of the century, and tonight we had the
largest full moon of the century. There were many people on the beach
this afternoon. We watched some of them slice through the water with
their "jet skis"—a contraption that works like a miniature motor boat and
looks like a motorcycle. They leapt over waves and swerved around each
other in circles, leaving behind wide arcs of foam.*

*It was pleasant just to walk down the beach. When the waves washed
over the shore, it made a delicious seething sound, hissing as it sucked
greedily at our toes, then pulling back and smoothing the surface of the
sand until it was shiny and flat as a mirror. The sand was warm under
our feet and with each step the sand seemed to dissolve under our heels,
like sugar. The walk was timeless to me, transfixed as I was by all the
patterns of sand—the tight ripples and slender braids and intricate
convolutions.*

*Many things came to my mind but all of them disappeared, like words
etched in silt before a wave, and I thought: what are words anyway,
but an attempt to hold still—if only for a moment—that elusive, liquid
quality that is life? Love, Iris*

It seemed that Shau-Jin's heart attack and the emergency surgery
put Iris's view of life in perspective: life is short and elusive and could
disappear very quickly.

For the next several months, I was obsessed with Shau-Jin's physical
condition, which occupied all my time and thoughts, so I did not pay
much attention to Iris's life or her progress in writing her book. All I knew
was that she was busy preparing for her trip to China, using the MacArthur
foundation grant. In spite of the shock and trauma of the surgery, Shau-Jin
was still able to give her advice. He gave her all the names of his physics
and engineering friends or colleagues in China in case she needed help.
I gave her a list of things she should take with her. After all, this was
the first trip she had ever taken alone out of the country. My biggest

concern was drinking water, and I told her that she should not drink the tap water (even to brush her teeth) in China. She appreciated all of our love and concern. Before she got on the plane, she mailed us a joking upside-down card that read: "Don't worry, Dad—I've got everything under control. Happy Father's Day!"

Actually, the trip to China was carefully planned. Iris mailed us her itinerary and a long list of names of people she was going to meet in three cities in China: Hangzhou, Shanghai, and Beijing. The itinerary included dates, and the places she could be reached on those dates.

On May 31, Iris flew to Hangzhou, the city where Tsien had spent his earliest childhood years. On June 6, she took a train from Hangzhou to Shanghai. At that time, the National Science Foundation grant agent tried to contact her about her grant proposal; he managed to reach us instead. Her proposal was passed, under the condition that she would modify her proposed budget. We passed this good news to her when she reached the prearranged hotel in Shanghai. She was quite happy and surprised. She immediately revised her budget accordingly. Her carefully written grant proposal had paid off, although it had taken a long time.

In the same phone call, Iris told us that upon arrival in Shanghai, she found that the rate of the guest house at Chiao Tung University in Shanghai had doubled, more than she had anticipated, and she was worried about having enough money to cover the whole trip. Finally, she told us that one of the professors in Beijing had offered her a place to stay in his house once she reached there. That solved her problem.

On June 10, 1993, Iris wrote us a postcard from Shanghai:

Dear Mom and Dad:

Thank you so much for letting me know about the news from NSF! After talking with you on the phone, I called Brett and he faxed me the information. I went to the Sheraton Hotel and faxed back a revised budget and explanation of the figures. I reduced the budget from $70,000 to $60,000.

As I mentioned to Brett, local historians in Hangzhou helped me find Tsien's childhood home, his ancestral temple, his father's old home and even his father's alma mater and workplace. On the 6th I took a train to Shanghai. As I watched the scenery from my window, I was struck by how many people lived in China. Even in the countryside you are never out of sight of other people. On Brett's farm, corn and soybean stretch unbroken to the edge of the horizon without another barn or house in sight. In China, the farmer's houses look like dormitories or condominiums, and the land is a patch of rice paddies and maize.

Today, I walked about Chiao Tung University and took photos . . . Tsien's old dorm, library and classrooms. Tomorrow, a history major will help me search for material in the Chiao Tung archives. I'll write back soon. Love, Iris

Iris went to Shanghai, where Tsien had spent his college years at Jiaotong (Chiao Tung) University. There, Iris visited the school archives and found old yearbooks and photographs of Tsien, even his class rank and scholastic records. Iris hired a junior editor at a Shanghai publishing company to help her in searching secondary source material about the school and Shanghai in the 1930s. The editor also accompanied Iris on important interviews with Tsien's former college classmates still living in the city.

Aside from researching Tsien's college years, Iris attended the International Space Conference of Pacific Basin Societies, held in Shanghai. She had learned of the Shanghai conference when she was at the 1992 World Space Congress in Washington, and had gotten an invitation from the Chinese missile scientists there. At the Shanghai conference, she met and interviewed more missile scientists and colleagues of Tsien's and obtained more contact names in Beijing. As a Conference delegate, Iris was also given a tour of models of certain Chinese launch vehicles and satellites.

On June 15, Iris took a train to Beijing. We had not heard from her for several days, so we called her at the hotel she was scheduled to be in. She was fine and happy and told us that she was able to meet people in Beijing who helped her a great deal. We got a postcard from her, dated June 20, 1993, which she wrote in small scribbles:

> *Dear Mom and Dad:*
>
> *Thanks for calling me yesterday . . . I'm amazed you actually got through to me. Today I moved to Room 3202 of the Tsinghua Hotel. Dr. Tsien's secretary's son and daughter-in-law took me to see the Great Wall and the Ming Tombs today (Wang Shouyun, who is away on a conference, arranged for a special car and chauffeur) seems incredible to me that such a wall could have been erected hundreds of years ago, with raw manpower and stone. Spent a lot of time wondering how many lives were lost building the wall, and how it must have felt to be a laborer, walking up and down those mountains carrying those rocks. I also wondered if the wall symbolized a deep suspicion and paranoia of foreign ideas during the time of the wall's construction, as well as tremendous bureaucratic and organizational skills. Felt kind of embarrassed when Wang's son asked me to name American's natural landmarks . . . Grand Canyon, Yellowstone, Sears Tower, Walt Disney Land. . . . How uncultured we must appear to China! Love, Iris*

Iris spent two and a half weeks in Beijing, where Tsien had spent most of his life—first as a student in the late 1910s and 1920s, and later as the founder and administrator of the Chinese missile program from the 1950s until his recent death (in 2009, at the age of ninety-six). During Iris's stay in Beijing, she visited Tsien's grade school and high school (where she obtained priceless class photographs from the 1920s), and the Qinghua University archives, and the compounds where Tsien had worked and lived after he returned to China in 1955.

Iris conducted a series of taped oral-history interviews with Tsien's former scientific colleagues as well as people who had been very close to him such as secretaries, family friends, and high-school and college classmates. Iris said she had gathered unpublished documents and memoirs about Tsien, as well as more than fifty hours of interviews. However, she was never able to get an interview from Tsien himself or his wife, who were still living in Beijing at the time. According to Iris, Tsien was an exceedingly private person. His refusal to grant an interview did not come as a surprise: Tsien, since his return to China, had never granted an interview to any American writer, perhaps still hurt about being falsely accused by the American government during the McCarthy years. Iris told us, according to Tsien's secretary, that he also forbade anyone in China to write a biography on him (except the person he appointed to do so) while he was still alive.

The fact that Iris was able to talk to Tsien's secretary and a number of powerful officials and military generals in Beijing was based on their presumptive hope that Iris would write a biography according to *their* wishes. However, Iris had clearly expressed to them that she had to gather all the materials, sort them out, and write a fair account. She told us that her frank and non-appeased attitude put them on uneasy terms.

In the summer of 1991, a few months after Susan Rabiner had given Iris the book idea on Dr. Tsien, Iris was able to locate Tsien's son, Yucon, in Fremont, California, who (against his family's wishes) granted Iris an interview in his car. That Iris was able to track down Tsien's son and secure an interview with him in the U.S. impressed Susan Rabiner, who fully appreciated Iris's journalistic ability and dedication.

The trip to China completed the research on Tsien and gave Iris a full picture of his life and a deep understanding of the impact of his work on China's missile program. On her return on July 4, 1993, Iris had far more materials on Tsien than she could write about in one book. The NSF grant, which finally arrived in September 1993, helped Iris tremendously.

On January 14, 1994, we flew to California to attend the wedding of Shau-Jin's nephew, Bernie, in Los Angeles. While we were in Los Angeles, we experienced the violent earthquake on early morning of

January 17, 1994. It was 6.7 magnitude, and the epicenter was near Northridge, a mere twenty miles north of Santa Monica where we were staying. Fortunately, we escaped the disaster and were able to get back home safely.

Sadly, there were more tragedies to come in 1994. On Monday, March 14, I got a call from my brother in New York telling me that my father had passed away in the early morning. He had been very sick for the past year, and we knew he would not live long, but still, the feeling of sadness and loss is hard to describe. He lived to be ninety-five years old, but this was the first death I had experienced in our family. Up to that day, I had not really felt the sting of death. My paternal grandparents had died when my father was very young, and my maternal grandpa died when my mother was in her twenties, so they were never a part of our lives. My mom's mother died in old age, but she was trapped in mainland China under Communist rule and we could not visit her or be present at the funeral because of political reasons. Therefore, there was never a death in our close family until my father died in 1994. I immediately flew to New York. On the plane, my tears would not stop. The flight attendant looked at me with curious eyes.

All of the children and their spouses and grandchildren of my father flew to New York for the funeral, including Iris and Michael. The funeral was on Friday, March 18, at a funeral home in lower Manhattan's Chinatown. Besides family members, some Chinese community leaders and Chinese newspaper reporters were there too because my father had a reputation as a writer and author in the New York Chinese circle. In the ceremony, my two brothers and my younger sister and I each gave a short speech on how our father had influenced us when we were growing up. My older sister Ling-Ling, who had taken care of my father in his last years, was so devastated that she could not speak. While the members of my family spoke, I saw that Iris was quickly writing something down on a small piece of paper; and then, at the end, she stood up and said she would like to speak a few words. What she said at the funeral was recorded in a memorial pamphlet that my brother Cheng-Cheng compiled. Iris said:

My grandfather had an incredible life. He was born in 1899, the year when the Boxer Rebellion swept through China. He was twelve when the Qing Dynasty collapsed, ending more than two centuries of rule. He was a teenager when the Republic of China was established and World War I broke out. He was thirty-eight when the Japanese invaded China. He was forty-six when World War II ended. He was fifty when China fell to the Communists. He was seventy-three when he first stepped foot on American soil, the very same year Nixon made his historic visit to the People's Republic of China. He was ninety when Chinese tanks massacred students in Tiananmen Square.

I caught only glimpses of that life. They came to me first through stories my mother would tell over the dinner table when I was a little girl—stories of grandpa being captured by bandits, writing stories that got him arrested, inciting riots in prison and even suffering torture. They created in my mind a portrait of my grandfather as an intensely headstrong, vociferous and individualistic man—a man who was determined to air his opinions even during politically dangerous times.

. . .

My grandfather may have passed on, but I'll never forget his courage, his dedication to education and most of all, his passion and enthusiasm of life. He died a fighter.

I was really impressed by this speech. First, she told me later, her desire to talk had been driven by a last-minute impulse. She quickly wrote down an outline on the back of a small piece of a sales receipt. She could write down the historical events chronologically in her grandpa's life in such a short time—which must be due to her latest research on the book she was writing, as well as her previous career as a news reporter. It was impressive, not just that she could relate to her grandpa's life with history, but the fact that she could speak so eloquently despite being so emotional at the same time. I remember that she was wearing a long-sleeve black brocade dress that showed her elegant figure. She stood very gracefully with her long dark hair while she spoke, standing out in the crowd.

After the ceremony, several cars carrying family members escorted the casket to the New Jersey Rosehill Cemetery burial ground. When we reached the cemetery, it was late afternoon and it had started raining. The rain soon changed to a wet snow. All of the family members opened umbrellas to shield themselves from the snow, and we surrounded the freshly dug hole in the earth. The huge snowflakes dropped down like small cotton balls being dumped on the tops of a sea of black umbrellas. We huddled together in the cold, wet wind and witnessed the coffin of my father being lowered into the grave. My eyes blurred with the warm tears and the icy snowflakes falling on my face.

That night after the funeral, the four of us stayed in the warm room of a hotel in Manhattan. Shau-Jin and I started to tell Iris and Michael about our childhood, telling stories from when we were growing up in China and Taiwan. We also told them about our early days when we came to the U.S. to study.

We stressed to them that we, not like them, had had nothing when we came to this country. All we had were our scholarships. We alone had to support ourselves. Our parents could not support us once we reached this country. To secure a job and to survive in this country after graduation was our prime goal at the time. We were not like them; they could take a risky route or try out a new path based on their interests. After all, they always had us to fall back on in case they failed. We explained this part of our lives to them because sometimes they said that Shau-Jin and I were too timid, that we did not take enough risks. We still remembered the day on Michigan Avenue in Chicago, when Iris had criticized us, saying that our lives were too conventional and that we were too apprehensive to try something new. The discussion was candid and the emotion was high; maybe the death of my father had made me very sentimental. The conclusion was that my father's generation was a generation that strived to survive poverty and the wars, whereas our generation was better than my parents', but the next generation, the generation of Iris and Michael, was even luckier than ours. "Here is the opportunity," we told them, "if you work hard enough, you will achieve something in this country!"

We flew back home right after my father's funeral, but Iris stayed in New York for several more days. She went to see Susan Rabiner, and Susan gave her a timetable and urged her to give her a completed section of the book, which she would then edit and help Iris polish and revise. Iris also showed Susan the incredible photographs she had collected for the book, and they discussed the title and subtitle of the book. Iris was also wondering what name she would use as the book's author: Iris Chang, or Iris Douglas, or Iris Chang Douglas. She had thought about that for a while. She said she had been using Iris Chang as the name on all her previous publications and she might just keep her name as it was.

The most important thing, though, was that Susan wanted Iris to give her the first draft of the entire manuscript by August 1994, just four and a half or five months away. Iris said Susan praised her writing lavishly and said that, so far, she had found her writing "marvelous! Impressive!" This gave Iris tremendous confidence and the stamina for the final push in her research and writing.

The next day, Iris went to see her book agent Laura Blake at Curtis Brown. Laura Blake was very satisfied with the progress of the book and praised Iris highly for her writing skill. Laura said her next book advance should be much higher than this one; maybe as high as $50,000. It turned out that her next advance, for *The Rape of Nanking*, was $60,000, which was double the advance of her first book and would give Iris a little more of the financial security she needed to keep researching and writing at a high level with minimal distraction.

At this time, Iris disclosed to me her worry about the fact that she had become more materialistic. Perhaps the financial strain she had been under for the past few years had helped bring this on. She told me that she did not care about money, only the experiences and adventures money could bring. She said she just couldn't stand the idea of someone sneering at her, simply for her lack of money. I asked Iris if California could be the wrong place for them to live, because when she'd been in Urbana, money had never been in her thoughts. Indeed, I suspected that Brett and Iris were influenced by the more materialistic culture in California.

Iris told me that she had recently joined a local writer's group and met many interesting people. Some were retired entrepreneurs, professors, or novelists, and some were even movie stars. Talking to them, she said, broadened her horizons. She told me she'd been invited to a local Celebrity Author's Luncheon in March, and she said people there had been impressed by her youth and surprised to learn that she had already landed a book contract. The people she met were also impressed by her book ideas and her opinions. She also met a number of famous contemporary authors around Santa Barbara, and she sought their advice on book publishing and other aspects of the writing "life."

Iris told me that she also continued reading many books, such as Jonathan Spence's *Search for Modern China*, David Brinkley's *Washington Goes to War*, and Walter A. McDougall's *The Heavens and the Earth*.

For my own life, in the next few months after my father died, I was in a sad mood. On April 22, former president Nixon died, and on May 22, Jackie Kennedy died. I was super-sensitive to the word "death"; it seemed that I could not expel my father's death, or death in general, from myself.

To move past my grief, I decided to go with Shau-Jin to Taiwan in the middle of May. Shau-Jin had been invited to the Academia Sinica in Taiwan to give lectures at a physics workshop. We stayed in Taiwan for a month. This was my second trip to Taiwan since I'd first left home in 1962. The first trip had been in 1982, when Iris was in high school and the whole family was visiting there for two months. Twelve years had passed since our last trip to Taiwan, and it had changed completely. When I visited my old house where we used to live, in the suburbs of Taipei, the house was gone and the surroundings were barely recognizable. I did not take a photo of this new landscape, because I wanted the memory of my childhood to live forever.

On May 27, 1994, while we were in Taiwan, Iris wrote us a long e-mail:

> Dear Mom and Dad:
>
> It was great to receive your E-mail letters. . . .
>
> Carolyn came to visit the very weekend you left for Taiwan. We went to the Channel Island on May 14. . . . The trip was an all day affair. . . .
>
> During the past week, I've been writing additional chapters of my book and looking at the chapters Susan Rabiner has edited. She thinks my writing is "fabulous" "terrific" "charming." She couldn't edit it at first—she was too absorbed by the story. Lately, she's had nothing but good things to say about my book, which, of course, may be her way of keeping me confident and motivated as I finish the rest of the material.
>
> Over Memorial Day weekend, I plan to attend the American Booksellers Association convention in Los Angeles. From what I've heard, some 30,000 to 50,000 people will be there: authors, agents, editors, publishers, bookstore owners, and representatives from the biggest book chains—how exciting! I'm sure I will learn much about the business of books there. All my other writer friends from Santa Barbara will be present.
>
> Keep in touch—I'll write back to you sometime next week. Hope to hear from you soon. Love, Iris

In Taiwan, we met Professor C. N. Yang, the Nobel laureate in physics, at a banquet after a conference. He asked Shau-Jin about Iris's book progress. We were impressed that he still remembered that Iris was writing a book on Dr. Tsien. Iris had written to Professor Yang in 1991, more than three years earlier, at the beginning of her book project, to inquire about Dr. Tsien. We told Iris about our meeting of Professor Yang in Taiwan, and we encouraged her to finish the book as soon as possible since "the world was waiting to read the book, including a Nobel laureate!" we joked in our e-mail.

At the end of our stay in Taiwan, we went to Tianjin in northern China for a physics conference, and then to Beijing. This was the first time I had returned to mainland China since 1949, when my parents had brought the whole family to Taiwan to escape the Communists—that was forty-five years ago. I left China as a little nine-year-old girl and returned as a woman of fifty-four!

My family's journey, after the retreat from Nanking to Chungking (the war capital) during the Japanese invasion in the 1930s, and then to the escape from the Communists in the 1940s, had been all through the southern part of China, so I had never been to Beijing before, although Shau-Jin had been there many times, all at the invitation of physics-related Chinese academic organizations. Yet this was the first time we had been together in Beijing. Of course, in the week we were there, we went to the Great Wall, the Forbidden City, and other historical landmarks to pay our respects and show our admiration to the great heritage of our ancestors. It was very emotional for me, since Beijing was the capital of so many legendary dynasties. My father had talked about Beijing a lot, about his love of Beijing from tea house to opera, yet he was no longer alive to see it—nor could I relay my impressions of modern Beijing to him—making my visit bittersweet.

Iris called us after we got back from China and updated us on her progress in writing the book. She said she worked very hard; usually she slept during the day and worked at night. Brett had been working at Sonatech, a company in Santa Barbara, ever since he'd obtained his PhD. They had completely different working hours. When Iris was about to go to bed, Brett was waking up. She got up in the afternoon in time to have dinner with Brett, and they took a walk together afterwards.

Sometimes Iris got frustrated. One day, she called me up to say that she was very tired and could not write as fast as she wished. I had to comfort her and ask her to take a nap; I told her that the next day might be better. Writing was not an easy profession, I thought. She also told me that her car had been broken into when she was in Los Angeles at the book convention. Her pair of eyeglasses and contact lens solution, together with other things in a bag in the car, were gone. Her newly ordered glasses had not arrived yet; it was a bad week on top of an already stressful time.

On September 28, Iris called and exclaimed that she had finally finished her book. It was a milestone, I told her, and I was thrilled for her. But Iris was very tired, and she said she was going to relax for a while. Her recovery plan was to watch lots of movies and eat well and read some good books.

On October 18, 1994, Iris wrote me an e-mail:

Dear Mom:

Yesterday, I printed out a double-spaced copy of my book on the laser printer, which came to 574 pages, and stored the file on two disks. Then I federal-expressed the entire bundle to Susan Rabiner. By the end of the year, I will deliver a final draft with Susan's revisions, along with footnotes and permission forms to use quotes and photographs. From January to the end of February, I will be working closely with a line editor to perfect the manuscript, and then it is printed in galley form, ready to be reviewed by other authors and the media. At the same time, I am working on applications for teaching positions and ideas for other books. So there is a great deal of work to be done in the next few months. Originally, I had hoped to plan a pool party, but now I don't think there will be enough time. Brett and I decided to restrict our socializing to going out with couples for dinner or lunch, which is more intimate and less time-consuming, maybe I can throw a party when the book actually comes out in print.

Your E-mail of homecoming brought back warm memories. Can you believe it was five years ago! I supposed much HAS happened during

those five years: my job at the Tribune *and AP, Johns Hopkins, my marriage to Brett and now this book. But it really doesn't feel like much time has elapsed at all. . . .*
Love, Iris

She asked us to visit them at the end of the year, but not during Thanksgiving because she and Brett were going to go to Maui for a vacation, a much-needed break for her, one that I was happy to learn about.

Only a couple of weeks later, she wrote to tell us that she had just submitted a sixteen-page single-spaced letter to her agent describing some of her ideas about a number of possible books she could write in the future. She had told us, not once but many times, about her many book ideas; for example, the Sino-Japanese War, women's biological clock, Chinese immigrant stories (including everything from smuggling and prostitution rings to the highest achievements, such as Nobel laureates). I was amazed that she could submit her future book ideas immediately after she finished her first book, without any rest in between.

In the meantime, Iris said, she had been interviewed by a professor at California State University at Northridge, for a possible teaching job at their Ventura campus. They needed a teacher in ancient and modern Chinese history, the history of women, the history of California, and possibly the history of Asian-American immigrants. Santa Barbara City College had also expressed interest in hiring her for a part-time teaching job alongside UCSB, which was interested in her as an instructor for their writing program. But all these plans were put on hold once Iris went to a conference in Cupertino in December 1994 and saw a photo exhibition on the Nanking Massacre!

10

The Photos that Changed Her Life

Although Iris talked to us about her many book ideas for her next book while she was writing her first book, her decision to write *The Rape of Nanking* came all of a sudden, in December 1994. As Iris told us, and as described in the book, she made up her mind to write about this most atrocious chapter of history when she was attending a conference in Cupertino, California on December 13, 1994. In November that year, Iris had heard that a documentary film describing the Sino-Japanese War and the war crimes committed by the Japanese military in the 1930s had had problems getting funding. She was curious, and then she connected with a number of people involved in the project. She was informed that there was a conference to be held in Cupertino on the subject. They told her that if she was interested in the subject, she could come up to the Bay area and attend the conference. She was not only looking for a new book topic, she was also extremely interested in this period of history. She had been hearing a lot about the Sino-Japanese War from both Shau-Jin and me since she was little. It was perfect timing, too: she had just finished her biography of Dr. Tsien.

At the conference, there was a photo exhibition of the Japanese war crimes committed in China in the 1930s, taken when the Japanese Army invaded Chinese territory. Iris wrote in her book: "Though I had heard so much about the Nanking massacre as a child, nothing prepared me for these pictures—stark black-and-white images of decapitated heads, bellies ripped open, and nude women forced by their rapists into various pornographic poses, their faces contorted into unforgettable expressions of agony and shame." And she continued: "In a single blinding moment I recognized the fragility of not just life but the human experience itself." Later she told us, in a telephone update, that she simply must write about the rape of Nanking for her next book. It was a moral obligation, and it would be justice for the victims as well.

In 1998, after *The Rape of Nanking* had been published, one Japanese reporter, Kinue Tokudome, interviewed Iris and asked her, "Why did you decide to write this book?"

Iris replied: "When I was a little girl, my parents shocked me with the story of the Rape of Nanking. They told me that the Imperial Japanese Army massacred thousands of civilians in the capital of China—and butchered even small children. This left a powerful impression on me, and I went to the local libraries to learn more details. But I couldn't find a shred of information on the subject. There was nothing in my local school libraries, or public city libraries, or in my world history textbooks. Still worse, my teachers were completely ignorant of this event.

"The event remained a question mark in my mind for years, until I saw an exhibit of photographs on the subject in 1994. The horror of those photographs inspired me to write the book." Indeed, prior to that, Iris thought we might have exaggerated what had happened in Nanking in 1937–1938 when we told her those stories all those years ago.

At the Cupertino conference, Iris learned that, so far, there was no English-language book to deal with this subject exclusively. She had learned that many American missionaries, journalists, and military officers had recorded their views of the event in diaries, films, and photographs, which were stored in archives and libraries. Immediately, with the help of the Bay area activists and the organization Global Alliance for Preserving the History of World War II in Asia, she was introduced to several activists on the East Coast. She wanted to go to the National Archives in D.C. and the Yale University Divinity School Library to do research on the materials.

On January 4, 1995, we flew to Los Angeles to see Shau-Jin's parents and then drove to Santa Barbara to see Iris and Michael. This was a kind of annual ritual after Christmas, since now both children were not coming home for the Christmas and New Year's holidays. Besides, California weather was so nice in the winter, and this was another way to escape the cold in Urbana. However, January 1995 was bad for Los Angeles. As soon as we arrived, it had the worst rainy season on record. Throughout the trip, it rained almost every day.

Iris told us she was planning to go to the East Coast in a few days. Everything had been arranged, with the help of activists in the Bay area. She left for Washington on January 8 while we were still in Los Angeles. When we returned home, I had written Iris an e-mail asking whether she'd reached D.C. safely. On January 24, Iris replied from the Yale Divinity Library computer that she was fine and just too busy to answer my e-mail in more detail. After she returned home on February 12, five weeks later, Iris said there was a stack at least three feet tall of mail waiting for her, including boxes of photocopied documents that she had sent from the East Coast to herself. The visit to Yale was extremely successful: she found a lot of source material for the book. Iris said she owed us a long letter about the trip, and she was going to write to us once she found the time.

On March 12, Iris mailed us a twenty-five-page, single-spaced typed letter about the trip—which, by itself, could have been expanded into a major article. She described the trip in such detail as to the house where she lived and the people she met and each person's characteristics. She said she had written us such a detailed letter so it would also serve as her diary, to remind herself of the details later. Indeed, as she said before, such a letter gave us a full understanding of her thoughts and her life at the time. It was a historical record of her research on the book *The Rape of Nanking*.

In the letter, Iris said that she flew to Washington on January 8 and reached Dr. S. Y. Lee's home at 11:30 pm. Iris did not know Dr. Lee at all and had been introduced by Bay area friends. Dr. Lee and his wife graciously allowed Iris to live in their house while she was doing her research in the National Archives. She wrote:

> Dr. Lee and his wife were an elderly Chinese-American couple who had lived in the Washington, D.C., area for decades. He talked past midnight about their early years in China and how when he was a sophomore in college his university literally packed up and moved inland during the Sino-Japanese War. Typical of many Chinese-American professionals, Dr. Lee and his wife fled to Taiwan before the 1949 revolution and later migrated to the United States. After getting his PhD in chemistry, Lee worked as a chemist in a number of government research institutes, such as NASA.
>
> Now retired, the Lees devote their time to publishing the Chinese American Forum, a journal they founded for the purpose of airing the opinions and stories of Chinese-Americans from all professions and ages. Dr. Lee eagerly hoped that I might contribute to the journal in the future. Lee told me how gratified he was to see someone working on this book and said there was no such book like it in the English language. Even the ones in Chinese are distorted, he said.

Then Iris described her daily life in D.C.:

> I stayed at Lee's home for one week, sleeping in a guest room on the second floor of his house. There was a wooden desk in the room, on which the Lees had placed several books on the Sino-Japanese War for me to read along with articles about the Nanjing massacre. The Lees rarely saw me except in the evenings, for I spent almost every waking moment at the National Archives.

On a typical day, I would rise between 7 and 8 am and take the bus to the Silver Spring metro station. Fortunately, there was a bus stop directly across the street from Lee's house. The trip to the National Archives took about 45 minutes on public transportation, and the building was open by 8:45 a.m. I spent my mornings in the military reference branch of the archives on the 13th floor, looking through finding aids and filling out cards to request archival boxes from different collections of papers. Dozens of boxes would be pulled from the shelves, placed on carts and made available to me in the second floor reading room, which stayed open until 9 pm on Tuesdays, Thursdays and Fridays. I was usually there in the afternoons and evenings, scanning the documents, tagging the ones that pertained to the Nanjing massacre and xeroxing them as quickly as possible.

At the end of the day, Lee would pick me up at the Silver Spring train station. If I worked late, I had to rely on him to give me a ride because the buses stopped running after a certain hour. In the beginning, I felt bad to trouble him in this way, but he insisted that it was all right because he had nothing much to do anyway. Besides, Lee was curious about my daily findings at the Archives and relished our long discussions about the Sino-Japanese War in the car on the way back to his house. For instance, he was fascinated by the question of how the Japanese soldiers could have been so polite at home and so brutal abroad. The answer, he believes, lies in the history of the Japanese samurai culture, which he thinks is nothing less than a cult like religion.

Iris also wrote details about the National Archives and the archivist, John Taylor:

The records on the Nanjing massacre were voluminous and scattered throughout many holdings in the National Archives. The person who guided me through them was the same man who helped me on the Tsien book: John Taylor, a white-bearded elderly archivist with sagging jowls, baggy clothes and an encyclopedic memory. After fifty years of service in the archives, he had worked his way up to the highest rungs of the military reference branch and proved indefatigable in his efforts to help me and all the other scholars in his office. He introduced me to the recently declassified American intercepts of messages from the Japanese Foreign Office, the complete collection of transcripts from the International Military Tribunal of the Far East (also known as the Tokyo War Crimes Trial), the investigative files for the prosecution of the IMTFE, the Shanghai Municipal Police Records, and the microfilmed records from the Department of State and military intelligence for 1937–1938.

Taylor is one of the hardest working employees of the federal government, even though he is past retirement age. He is the first one in the office and the very last to leave. He even eats his lunch at his desk so that he will never miss a phone call. One of my most vivid memories is watching him play the phone like an operator with one hand while holding a sandwich with the other. Once, when I was staying at Marian Smith's home and got sick for a day, John Taylor actually called me at her home to see if I was all right. On the day of my illness, I was supposed to have taken the shuttle bus to the Suitland branch of the National Archives from the main building at 8:15 am. Mr. Taylor noticed that I wasn't at the bus stop at the side of the building and grew concerned. His phone call to Marian's home signified to me two things: one, that Taylor was concerned enough about my general welfare to make the call, and two, he was actually in the vicinity of the National Archives as early as 8 a.m. to notice my absence! (In a city where many federal employees work ten to three with two hours off for lunch and who are reported by their secretaries as either "not in yet," "busy at a meeting," or "gone for the day," whenever you call, it seems inconceivable that someone like John Taylor actually exists.)

I was so busy I missed the opportunity to take the general tour at the National Archives, which exhibits the nation's most precious documents: the Declaration of Independence and the Constitution of the United States. However, I did have the chance to meet an interesting man with whom I corresponded: namely, Arnold Kramish, a nuclear physicist turned author.

Then Iris talked about Arnold Kramish, who later wrote the first blurb praising her book on Dr. Tsien:

> *Years ago, Kramish started writing to me after a notice of my book appeared in a newsletter for intelligence officers. I didn't know much about him except that he was a scientist who was also a respected author, and that he had recently written the book* The Griffin, *which was the story of Paul Rosbaud, a science editor for the German firm Springer Verlag, a good friend of the top nuclear physicists in Germany and a pillar of Nazi society. Rosbaud was also Winston Churchill's most valuable spy during World War II. In many of his letters to me, Kramish offered to take me out to lunch if I visited DC. On January 11, I met Kramish at Luigi's, a famous Italian restaurant in the city. He was a plump, white-haired gentleman—so exuberant, talkative, and good natured that he reminded me of a beardless Santa Claus.*
>
> *Like Dad, Kramish once studied under Julian S. Schwinger at Harvard. He later worked for the Manhattan Project during World War II and the RAND Corporation, the US Atomic Energy Commission and other government agencies. At some point in his life he also served as adjunct professor at UCLA and the London School of Economics. He has written at least six books and won a number of prestigious awards in his lifetime. . . . Throughout his lifetime, he has accumulated a number of inside stories about scientific espionage and knows a number of spies personally.*
>
> *A prolific letter writer, Kramish has a wide range of personal contacts . . . Kramish is the only surviving participant of the Manhattan Project who conducts meticulous historical research about the Manhattan Project in the National Archives. In many ways, he is a real threat to historians who specialize in this aspect of World War II history because (1) he was an eye-witness observer to these events (2) he truly understands the science and (3) is comfortable with the techniques of historical research as well. It makes historians of science nervous.*

Next, Iris wrote about her meeting with the independent film producer Nancy Tong in New York City:

After a week in Washington DC, I took a train to New York. On January 15, Martin Luther King Day, I spent the morning looking for photographs of the Nanjing massacre at the Bettmann Archives, one of the biggest photo repositories in the world. Then I met with Nancy, a Chinese-American independent filmmaker who had produced an hour-long documentary on the Nanjing massacre called In the Name of the Emperor. *We had lunch at a Chinese noodle restaurant to exchange information and contacts.*

Nancy worked briefly as a reporter for a Hong Kong television station, but grew so disgusted with the petty politics there that she decided to strike out on her own in New York City as an independent filmmaker. I found Nancy to be talkative, warm and affable, and took a liking to her at once.

Over steaming bowls of soup, Nancy warned me about the problems she had encountered with the PRC bureaucrats. In August 1993, Nancy went to Nanjing by herself to interview the survivors of the 1937 massacre . . . a historian gave her a list of people to contact and recommended a student to accompany Nancy to help translate Nanjing dialect into Mandarin. They took a taxi and talked with four survivors in their homes, most of whom were reluctant to be interviewed.

The first survivor whispered to her in the dark stairway of her compound: "Young lady, if you want to talk to me, go through the proper channels. If you don't, I will be in big trouble."

Nancy decided not to interview any of them. She already had the testimony of one woman on film, and didn't want to risk putting their lives in jeopardy.

"They lived in tin shacks!" Nancy said. "They didn't even have money for medicine! They had absolutely no furniture! You should see how the former Japanese soldiers live in contrast to their victims in China. They have beautiful homes with beautiful art and gorgeous furnishings and gardens. They received large financial compensation for

their services to the Japanese Army. These people are the criminals and
here are the victims, who are still suffering from what they did. I could
not believe how the victims were treated by the police after talking to
foreign journalists. . . ."

After I read Iris's description of Nancy Tong's encounter in Nanjing, I told Iris maybe it was not a good idea to go to Nanjing to interview the survivors.

In the same letter, Iris continued to brief us on her meeting with her book agent and book editor in New York:

The next day, I met with my agent and editor: Laura Blake in the
morning, Susan Rabiner in the afternoon. At the Curtis Brown Ltd office
at 10 Astor Place, Laura and I discussed all the possible places for serial-
ization of the Tsien biography: Popular Science, *the* New York Times
magazine, the Wall Street Journal, US News and World Report,
etc. She seemed very excited about the Rape of Nanjing *book and told*
me that a scholarly, literary publisher like Basic Books, Alfred Knopf or
Farrar Strauss Giroux would be perfect for it.

After our meeting, I went to HarperCollins. . . . Before my arrival in
New York, Basic Books had already held a large marketing meeting about
the Tsien book to serve as a pep rally for the sales representatives.

I gave Susan the thick author questionnaire that she had requested,
which contained information about me and the book and lists of poten-
tial publications that could review the book in the future: journals and
magazines and newspapers about aerospace, Chinese, history, espionage
and numerous other topics. The topic of our meeting was marketing and
serialization. I was told that the challenge to Basic would be to get orders
from bookstores, so it was important for me to as much publicity as pos-
sible before the book is released. We discussed three tactics of getting pub-
licity: . . .

Susan and her team also decided to put me on a six-city tour: San
Francisco, LA, San Diego, New York, Boston, Washington, DC. . . .

Did I tell you that Susan and I have finally agreed on a title for the book? It is THREAD OF THE SILKWORM. After the meeting, Susan brought me to the art department and showed me the cover of the book, which displays a picture of a Chinese rocket over a backdrop of red silk embroidered with a dragon. It was a lovely cover, and I was very pleased with it. Then we went to Susan's office and spent some time discussing the revisions on the manuscript. The conversation later turned to more personal matters and we talked about my future plans of combining motherhood with authorship. Susan said when she was my age, she had already had her two children. She told me that children grow up fast and by the time they are in school, mothers can return to a more normal work schedule. When I have children, she said, my career will be put on hold for not for the next 20 years but only for about four years.

Before I left the office, I asked her about the kinds of authors who get the 6-figure advances you read about in the newspapers. Do they have to be famous? I asked. Susan said not necessarily: if the topic is big, and if you can write well and quickly, you can get the money. That's why many of these advances come with strings attached. If the author can't make the deadline (which is sometimes only nine months after the contract is signed) then they have to return the money. Certain topics are so timely that if the author can't produce a book within a short time frame then it won't sell. Typically, Susan said, these advances go to men because "women have too much sense to commit themselves like that." Women, she said, prefer to take their time when writing a book, while men are more willing to take risks.

The next stop was the Yale University Divinity School Library. Iris was introduced to Mr. Shao Tzeping, who lived in Rye, Connecticut. Iris had pre-arranged to meet him in New York's Grand Central Station. It's such a small world. I realized later that I knew Mr. Shao Tzeping. Shao's family had lived close to my parents' house in Taiwan. My parents knew his parents. I didn't know him personally, but according to Iris, Shao became an activist in the East Coast in the movement to preserve the history of the Sino-Japanese War. Iris wrote about her meeting with Shao and his family:

> Shao had promised to house me for the next two weeks so that I could do my research at Yale University. I arrived at the booth shortly before he did, and together we boarded the commuter train to the suburb of Rye. Shao sat across from me, wearing a Russian-style brown hat and holding a black briefcase. . . .
>
> Rye is a wealthy suburb, and the passengers on the train looked like Wall Street types.
>
> The train ride took only half an hour, and then Shao and I took a bus down Purchase Street, Rye's tiny "downtown" section of expensive boutiques, cafes and restaurants. The town seemed quaint and peaceful.
>
> Shao's home on Grace Church Street was a few paces away from the church where George and Barbara Bush married. Built in the 1800s, his house was a white, three-story wood and stone structure that was very attractive on the outside. . . .
>
> For almost two weeks, I spent my evenings in the guest room in their attic. During the day, I pored through missionary diaries and letters at the Yale Divinity School library. Shao lent me his car, an old grey Buick, so that I could drive from Rye to New Haven every day. The commute took me about 50 minutes each way. When I arrived on campus, I would park the car along Canner Street, go up the stairs of the school, pass through the library, curve around a rotunda and emerge in the archives. I spent most of my time in the John Mott room, sitting at a table between walls lined with grey archival boxes. A Xerox machine stood next to a window with a view of the courtyard. The archivists, Martha Smalley and Joan Duffy, were everything the Caltech archivists were not: calm, friendly, trusting of researchers. There I worked—opening boxes and xeroxing documents—until five or six pm. Then I would drive back to Rye, eat dinner with the Shaos and go to bed.
>
> These records I examined at Yale included the papers of John Magee, a minister who took motion pictures of the atrocities with a camera; Robert

Wilson, a doctor at a Nanjing hospital; Lewis Smythe, former Univer-
sity of Chicago sociology professor who was teaching at the University of
Nanjing; Minnie Vautrin, who taught at Ginling College and set up a
refugee camp for Chinese women. Those were only a few of the foreigners
in Nanjing whose diaries and letters ended up at Yale—foreigners who
were compulsive writers, meticulously documenting the Japanese atroci-
ties and their own emotions. These missionaries took enormous risks by
remaining in Nanjing to help the Chinese. All of them, at some point
of their stay in the city, had been slapped or beaten up by the Japanese.
One was even thrown down a flight of stairs. Of course, this was nothing
compared to what had happened to the Chinese civilians in the city. As
I placed one brittle, yellowing letter after another on the Xerox machine,
I caught glimpses of sentences about men being machine-gunned by the
thousands, women and small girls raped by bayonets, broken bottles or
golf clubs.

If just reading about the violence made me feel physically ill, try to
imagine the effect it had on the missionaries, who witnessed it first-hand.
David Magee, the surviving son of John Magee, told me it contributed
to the early death of his father. One missionary woman went insane.
Another woman, Minnie Vautrin, killed herself shortly afterwards. (As
I mentioned to you on the phone, Vautrin left behind a 500-page diary
that is as compelling as The Diary of Anne Frank. *I would like to edit*
and publish the diary in the future.)

When I wasn't at Yale, I worked at Mailbox Etc. or Staples at Rye,
xeroxing copies of documents for Shao (he would reimburse me after-
wards) or xeroxing papers lent to me by Shao, or mailing big boxes of
material back to myself. I must have xeroxed literally thousands of pages
of documents.

In my free time, usually on weekends, I drove around Rye, looking at
the big houses and the palatial country club. Rye was the home of CEOs,
Wall Street executives, investment bankers, a real bastion of the East
Coast establishment. Everywhere about me, I saw WASPY old men in
plaid caps, tweeds, and beige trench coats, or elderly women in expensive

wool coats lined with fur. The town looked even more monied and exclusive than Santa Barbara.

During my stay, I tried not to be a burden on the Shao family. I washed the dishes without being asked, babysat the kids whenever the elder Shaos went out, later gave the girls a $30 gift certificate for Barnes and Noble before I left for DC. At the end of two weeks, I felt as if I knew the family pretty well.

On January 28, Shao and the children accompanied me to the train station in Rye for a final farewell. I traveled to Grand Central Station, and from there took Amtrak to Union Station in DC, where my friend Marian Smith picked me up. I would stay at her home for the next two weeks.

Iris dug up many documents and records from the Yale Divinity School library. Of course, I would never forget the call Iris made to us while she was there. After she read Minnie Vautrin's diary, she was so moved that she broke down and cried and right there she called us and told us Minnie' story. Iris said Minnie Vautrin was born in Secor, Illinois, and, like Iris, had graduated from the University of Illinois at Urbana. Her diary vividly and sadly recorded the rapes and the killings and the other acts of brutality she witnessed when she was the acting head of Ginling Women's College in Nanking. Because of her admirable courage, humanity, and tenacity, she saved thousands of Chinese women and children from rape and other crimes by Japanese soldiers in the Safety Zone. However, after Minnie Vautrin returned to the U.S. in 1940, she took her own life out of sheer physical exhaustion and mental suffering. Minnie's diary and her suicide had affected Iris greatly, perhaps because Minnie was a woman with such courage, or perhaps because Minnie had also graduated from the U of I as Iris had. In any case, Iris described Minnie's story whenever the Nanking Massacre and Safety Zone were mentioned in the years to come. Right there on the phone at the Yale Divinity School library, Iris told us that she wanted to publish Minnie's diary once her Nanking book was done. Minnie's suffering and suicide was so tragic and her life was continuously haunting Iris. Minnie too was one of the victims of the Rape of Nanking.

For the next two weeks, Iris stayed with her friend Marian Smith, a historian working in the U.S. Immigration and Naturalization Service. Iris had met Marian several years before while doing research for the Tsien book. Iris wrote in the letter:

From January 28 to February 12, I stayed with Marian and continued my research at the National Archives. This time, I spent most of my time looking at microfilm records on the fourth floor. On weekends the room was crowded with people conducting genealogical research. You heard them chatting about their ancestor's participation in the civil war or discussing the complexity of trying to find their land property records. Occasionally, I went to the Library of Congress to xerox giant city maps for Nanjing from the year 1937 or to look at microfilm of old newspapers or to examine indexes of microfilmed Japanese records. I spent a day at the Holocaust Museum, working with archivists and scholars to get citations on books about the Jewish holocaust, genocide, and the psychological portrait of wartime killers. I even dropped by to see Frank Winter, a curator of the National Air and Space Museum, because he wanted to give me an unpublished article about Tsien's leadership in the Chinese satellite program, which had been written by one of Tsien's former students.

The most important meeting I had in Washington was with Barbara Culliton, my former professor at Hopkins. On February 8th, I met her at the offices of Nature *magazine in the National Press Building and had coffee with her in a cafe on the bottom floor.*

Barbara seemed very happy to see me and we spent the next couple of hours catching up on all the news. She still teaches at Hopkins and she started a new magazine called Medicine *for the company that owns* Nature *and officially resigned from* Nature *to work on this magazine.*

Barbara was eager to hear more about the Nanjing Massacre book, because she said she has always been more interested in the Asian side of World War II than the European side.

She urged me to continue writing books, saying that no other student
of hers has been as ambitious and successful in this line of work as I have
been. She wondered how some of her other students were doing and wist-
fully talked about organizing a reunion one day.

Iris spent five weeks on the East Coast, and indeed it was a fruitful trip. She said she obtained so many source materials for her book that it would take her the next few years to digest all of it.

The most important thing that happened at this time is that when Iris was in New York visiting Susan Rabiner at Basic Books, she mentioned to Susan her determination to write the book on the Rape of Nanking. Iris told Susan that she wanted to write this book so badly that she would publish it out of her own pocket if necessary. Susan asked her what was the Rape of Nanking and why did she want to write about it? Even Susan did not know the full story of Nanking, making Iris's need to write this book and tell the world all the more real. Iris described to her the photos she'd seen at the exhibitions and the materials she'd collected in the National Archives and the Yale library. Susan was fascinated with the story and asked Iris to write a book proposal for her immediately.

Iris told an interviewer later about her passion for writing this book: "I wrote *The Rape of Nanking* out of a sense of rage. I didn't really care if I made a cent from it. It was important to me that the world know what happened in Nanking back in 1937."

On March 13, 1995, the first anniversary of my father's death, my mother fell and broke her hip in her New York apartment while my older sister Ling-Ling was busy getting ready to visit my father's grave in New Jersey. My mother was admitted into the hospital immediately.

My mother's breast cancer, discovered in 1979, had spread to her lung in 1989. Now, in 1995, the cancer had spread to her bones.

Due to my mother's illness, I visited her in New York four times that year. As soon as I heard about my mom falling and breaking her hip, I flew over on March 23 and stayed there for a week to help Ling-Ling take care of her. By then she had already been released from the hospital. But when I returned home, her condition worsened and she was readmitted to the hospital. Two weeks later, I flew to New York again and this time I stayed for two weeks. At that time, all my siblings were working and I had research obligations; the travel and the uncertainty of Mom's condition took a toll on everyone in the family. In May, my mother was transferred to another hospital called Calvary Hospital in the Bronx, which specialized in terminal cancer.

Iris called us often and tried to find out more about her grandma's condition. She wanted to call her in the hospital, but I advised her to make the calls short since Grandma needed rest. She also continued to update her work on Tsien's book:

> May 14, 1995
>
> Dear Mom,
>
> I just finished all the footnotes—what a long, tedious process it was! In the future I plan to write more books based on my personal experience so I never have to deal with footnotes again. . . .
>
> You might want to mention to Dad that the relatives of Minnie Vautrin have given their consent for me to edit her diary. It's the kind of project that might take only a few months of my time. If I'm lucky a commercial publisher will be interested in putting out the diary, but I think this is a university press-type book. My agent wants me to work on this only after I have written my third book because she doesn't want it to compete with the Rape of Nanking book for sales.
>
> Next Wednesday, I will interview the former KMT general who disguised himself as a monk and witnessed the massacres in Nanjing. He is in his 90s and living in Monterey Park, LA.
>
> Have a wonderful Mother's Day—I may call you tomorrow.
>
> Love, Iris

Then, miraculously, my mom's condition was stabilized. After she stayed in the Calvary Hospital for three weeks, where she was supposed to die, she became well enough to go home. I feel it was largely due to Ling-Ling's hard work taking care of our mother all those many long months.

On May 20, I had to present a research paper in a national microbiology meeting in Washington, D.C. After the meeting, I traveled to New York and arrived at Calvary Hospital on May 25 to help Ling-Ling bring my mother home. Mom was so happy to see me. Indeed, she looked better than the last time, when she was in Memorial Hospital. That night I stayed in the hospital too, with Ling-Ling beside our mom. In the wee hours and in the dim light of the hospital room, I heard the most horrible and painful sounds of all kinds from the patients' ward. It was terrifying. No wonder my sister and mom insisted that they go home no matter what, now that she was stable. Mom said she preferred to die in her own home.

Iris wrote to me that she and Brett would come home over the Memorial Day weekend for her 10th Uni High School reunion in Urbana, and also Brett could pay a visit to his parents. On May 28, when I got home from New York, they were already in Urbana. At the high-school reunion, Iris told us she had met many of her former classmates. Many of them had changed, not only in their looks but also their attitudes. She said they seemed very impressed by the fact that Iris was now a book author and surprised that her book would be published soon. I was very pleased to hear that Iris was now confident in front of her classmates.

On June 4, 1995, Iris wrote to us about several pieces of good news, the most important that she'd gotten a formal contract from Harper-Collins to write the book *The Rape of Nanking:*

> Dear Mom and Dad,
>
> Wonderful news awaited me when I got home! The Pacific Cultural Foundation offered me a grant for the Rape of Nanking project, albeit smaller than my original request for $12,000 (the maximum one can ask for) due to "limited funds"; the grant was $2000, enough for a plane

ticket to Taiwan. In addition, there were several urgent messages from representatives of HarperCollins concerning the interest of a Chinese publisher to translate and publish the Tsien biography. . . .

Over the phone I gave my approval for Commonwealth to publish my book in Chinese. . . .

The contract for the second book has already arrived in the mail, so Laura Blake and Susan Rabiner have moved faster on this project than I had predicted. I am seriously thinking about turning your home into "a writer's retreat" during your trip to Copenhagen and India and working quietly in Urbana for a few months. You have no idea how relaxing and therapeutic I found last week to be. . . .

Love, Iris

Shau-Jin was qualified for his sabbatical for the fall of 1995, and he wished to go to the University of Copenhagen Niels Bohr Institute of Physics and to India. In both places he had physics friends who had collaborated with him before. I tried to look up whether there was any opportunity for me to work in the Department of Molecular Biology at Copenhagen University. As both of us were busy making arrangement for visiting Copenhagen and India, Iris was making arrangements for her forthcoming research trip to China and Taiwan for the book *The Rape of Nanking;* she wanted to interview the survivors of the Nanking Massacre in Nanjing. Michael was planning a trip to China, too! He was taking a Chinese class at UC Santa Barbara and would join a Chinese language and culture tour to China.

It turned out that we eventually abandoned the plan to visit India; instead, we decided to visit Mexico. One of Shau-Jin's students now was a professor of physics in Mérida, Mexico, and he invited Shau-Jin to give a series of physics lectures there. The final plan for Shau-Jin's sabbatical was to first visit Copenhagen from August 21 to October 30, and then come home for Thanksgiving. After Thanksgiving, we would visit Mexico for three weeks. I was also very lucky that Professor Bjarne Hove-Jesen in the Department of Molecular Biology,

Copenhagen University, accepted me into his lab to continue my research at the same time Shau-Jin would be visiting the Niels Bohr Institute.

In the meantime, Iris told me that she was working hard till the early dawn hours on revisions of the source notes section of her Tsien book. She wanted to get the book done in the final stage before her trip to China and Taiwan, and all that time she was also getting things ready for the trip. She wrote me that she got her immunization shots, and she also got a home video camcorder, laptop computer and recorder, many tapes, and so forth. It seemed that she was well prepared.

On July 18, Iris flew to Hong Kong, her first stop. She called us from there, the night she arrived, from her hotel room, where she complained that the noise in the street was so loud that she could not fall asleep. She said she was going to Shenzhen the next day, the city at the border of China and Hong Kong, and would take a train from there to Canton (Guangzhou).

Before the trip, I had been against the way Iris said she would reach Nanjing. I thought to fly there would be the most direct and safe way; however, she wanted to fly to Hong Kong and take a train from Shenzhen to Canton and then to Nanjing. She said that on her first trip to China in 1993, she'd flown directly to Shanghai. She'd always regretted that she did not take a train, as Dr. Tsien had when he was returning to China from the U.S. This time, since she had finished her book on Tsien, she wanted to have the same experience that he had and see the countryside.

When Iris called me from Hong Kong, I asked her to be careful and let us know as soon as she reached Guangzhou. However, we waited and waited and did not hear from her. I started to get worried and called Brett a couple days later. Brett told us that she had taken a train at Guangzhou and had already reached Nanjing, but that she was sick. After we learned that she had already arrived at Nanjing, we called directly to the room where she was staying. Before the trip, Iris had reserved a guest room on the Nanjing University campus for foreign visitors (formerly Ginling Women's College, where Minnie Vautrin had protected thousands women from rape by Japanese soldiers).

We finally reached Iris in her room in Nanjing and asked her what had happened. She told us the story: As soon as she reached Guangzhou, the biggest city in Guangdong Province, she could not believe that thousands of people, most of them looking homeless, had crowded around the train station. She could not even find the place to buy a train ticket without bumping into someone sitting or lying on the ground. She could speak Mandarin, the official Chinese language, but it was useless in Guangzhou, for most of the people speak the local Cantonese dialect. She asked many people where the ticket window was, but got different answers. It turned out the lines leading to the ticket windows were quite long and no one was sure where to stand. Finally, in confusion and frustration, she saw a policeman who was there to maintain order and she asked him for help. She thought, after all, a policeman must be able to help her. After a struggle to explain it to him, Iris asked whether he could help her to buy a first-class slumber train ticket to Nanjing and she would give him double the money for the ticket. The policeman said he would try and went to the ticket window for some time and came back with a ticket. Iris was so happy and thanked him with the promised amount of money. She finally boarded the train with her big and small luggage, going through the huge crowd on the train platform.

On the train, she started looking for her seat. She started in the first class section, but the people there told her that she should go to the other sections. After passing through several sections, she arrived at another section of the train and realized that her ticket was not first class, but second class. There was no bed; but on the side of the train, there were two hard wooden boards staggered on top each other. One of those hard wooden boards was her bed.

She was angry and shouted out in Chinese, "He cheated me! I should have a first class ticket!" Many people there were starting to surround her and asked what happened. At this time, a train conductor came, a female, and the first thing she said was "Show your identification papers!" After Iris gave her her passport, the conductor said "Oh, you are an American!" Iris felt that her identity had been disclosed and regretted that she had shouted out and made a scene. Iris explained to the conductor what had happened: she'd given the money to someone to buy a first class ticket, but what she got was a second class. The conductor said that although she was sorry, she couldn't do anything about it and asked her to settle down.

Iris complied. Now she had to climb up to her hard board for a rest. She surveyed her surroundings and found there was no privacy in the car. Over a dozen people were crowded into the space. Some were old men, some women with children, and some were young men and women. Now some were staring at her. Iris thought: "Now they all know I came from the U.S., and I have to be very careful of my belongings. . . ." Poor Iris, she could not close her eyes while sleeping; she was holding tight to her purse and ID while lying on that hard board for two nights.

There was no air conditioning in second class. The window of the train was wide open to allow wind to come in, but so too came the dust, the train soot, and the aroma of buffalo shit and sewage. The weather was hot and humid and the noise from the wide-open window pierced her ears. Each time she needed to go to the toilet, she had to climb up and down from the "bed." She had not brought any food with her, so she bought food from the vendors on the train. No wonder she was sick by the time she reached Nanjing.

Over the phone, I told her that I was concerned about her illness and asked her to see a doctor immediately. We also called Shau-Jin's cousin in Nanjing, who was a nurse, and asked her to buy some antibiotics for Iris. We called Iris almost every day for the rest of her stay in Nanjing. Our telephone bill for that month was over $600!

Before we left for Copenhagen, in fear that my mother would die during our trip, I decided to pay her a visit once more. On July 27, while I was visiting my mom in New York, Shau-Jin called and said Iris had called him from Nanjing to say that her diarrhea had stopped, but that she had a stomachache. In addition, she had a sore throat and cough. She did not know whether it was the flu or just allergies to the dust and pollution in Nanjing.

I sat beside my mother's bed in New York. At my side was my mother lying there in pain from cancer-destroyed bones. Across the continent and the Pacific Ocean, I imagined that Iris must be coughing along with pain in her stomach. My part in all this was to feel such pain in my heart.

As soon as I returned from New York, I called Iris and was relieved to hear that she felt better. She said she had already interviewed several survivors of the Nanking Massacre, and now she was busy transcribing the video interviews from tapes to a Word file on her computer. She had a translator in Nanjing helping her translate the Chinese interviews of the survivors into English orally. Although Iris could understand some of what the survivors said, the Nanjing dialect prevented her from understanding fully. She said she was working very hard and unfortunately had no time to call us if there was nothing major happening.

Iris told us the following about her interviews with the survivors: "Every single survivor I met was desperately anxious to tell his or her story. I spent several hours with each one, getting the details of their experience on videotape. Some became overwrought with emotion during the interviews and broke down in tears. But all of them wanted the opportunity to talk about the massacre before their deaths."

Iris was heartbroken when she found out that all of the survivors lived in poor conditions. She felt the injustice for the victims and said that writing this book was important and urgent. She also told us that she wished to be a lawyer someday, so she could help those poor victims seek justice in the international court. She said the testimony and eyewitness accounts of the survivors confirmed the accuracy of the records and documents she had read in the archives.

In the meantime, I learned that Iris had been bitten by a swarm of mosquitoes when she and her guides went to inspect massacre sites in the outskirts of Nanjing. She said the execution sites now were covered by weeds and abandoned, even though some of them had had memorial markers built to help preserve the sites. When she returned to her room, she found her legs were covered with red mosquito bites. They were so itchy that she was not able to fall asleep at night. I was also worried about whether she would get malaria. I quickly went online to the Center for Disease Control and Prevention to check whether China was in the malaria region. Fortunately, Nanjing was not in the malaria-warning region, but Iris was regretting not bringing mosquito repellent (as I had suggested to her before the trip).

I visualized what Iris told me on the phone: Under the intense summer sunshine of Nanjing, with her guides she was walking through the weeds in the suburbs of Nanjing to look for the marked and unmarked graves and massacre sites of 1937–1938. The sweat wet her hair and her T-shirt. It was an incredibly hot afternoon. Enormous sorrow engulfed her while she read the numbers and the dates engraved on the headstones, where innocent Chinese people were massacred and then forgotten in the field. After she and the guides visited many such sites scattered around the outskirts of Nanjing, it was approaching evening. Standing near a stone marked for anonymous victims, she looked at the beautiful sunset in the west. She fell silent. The evening wind blew through her hair, and sadness swallowed her heart. . . .

Another problem Iris encountered, as she told us over the phone, was finding a machine with which she could duplicate the videotapes of her interviews. She was worried that the videotapes of survivors she interviewed, the most precious from the trip, could be confiscated at the airport checkpoint. We were very glad when we heard later that she'd been able to find a machine to duplicate her tapes in Nanjing. She asked to store the copies of the duplicated tapes in the house of the translator (who we later learned was Professor Yang Xiaming) and told him that if her copies were lost, at least he had copies as backups. Happily, her copies of the tapes passed through the checkpoint of the airport without any problem.

There were a couple of things that made us nervous while Iris was in Nanjing. One was that HarperCollins sent the galley proof of the Tsien book to her in Nanjing. Because the book had criticized Communist China's Cultural Revolution and various policies at that period, the Chinese government was bound not to be happy with it. We were very worried that the Chinese government would find out about the book while Iris was still in Nanjing. Fortunately, the proofs of the book arrived in Nanjing without incident and Iris was able to hide them in her suitcase and bring them out of China.

Another troubling event was the arrest of Harry Wu. Harry Wu was a Chinese human-rights activist who severely criticized Chinese Communist's labor camps. While he was sneaking back to China from the U.S., he was arrested at the Chinese border. We were afraid that the Chinese government would tighten up all regulations concerning American journalists in China after Wu's arrest. Over the phone, we told Iris the news and asked her to keep her profile low.

We left for Copenhagen on August 21, two days after Michael had arrived in Nanjing on August 19, which was the same day that Iris left Nanjing for Taipei, Taiwan.

After we had lived in Copenhagen for a week, we received an e-mail from Iris in Taiwan on August 29:

Dear Dad and Mom:

I'm sorry I was not able to email you earlier. . . . Today I visited the National History archives near Xingdian; tomorrow I will interview a couple of Taiwanese helpers in the Japanese army at Nanking, if all goes well. . . . I hear there is a typhoon headed this way.

I'm so relieved to hear that Harry Wu has been released from China. Everyone in Taiwan seems to be talking about Wu and the upcoming women's conference in Beijing—I'm sorry I'm going to miss it. In female infanticide, the woman shortage, the comfort-woman issues should be the hot topics of debate, but I don't know how the PRC will handle such topics . . . according to an email Associated Press report, PRC officials confiscated videotapes and film and notes from reporters after a seminar given by a Korean comfort woman—they even turned off the lights to interrupt her speech.

Otherwise, I'm still a little weak though I seem to be suffering from allergies rather than a cold . . . every foreigner I meet and virtually every Chinese I talk to has the same problem—we suspect it's the air pollution and pollen and dust and bad air conditioning. Will be in touch soon . . . all is going well.

Love, Iris

Then on September 2, four days before she returned home, she wrote us again:

Dear Dad and Mom:

I have some good news and bad news—the good being that there was no major typhoon after all, only a slight drizzle, the bad being that all the former Taiwanese soldiers in the Japanese army at Nanking in 1937–1938 are dead. My contacts at the local military association here made a series of frantic phone calls trying to find one surviving soldier; no luck. Turns out the two Taiwanese soldiers I planned to interview weren't at Nanking at all but in nearby Shanghai or were at Nanking years after the Massacre.

Coincidentally, the Center of Academic Activities is hosting a conference on the history of World War II (Sept. 1–3) and I've met some very interesting people so far . . . two are Chinese experts on the Rape of Nanking (one is Wu Tienwei, the SIU professor who gave me a good letter of recommendation for the Pacific Cultural Foundation grant). My health seems to have recovered and I look forward to going home . . . will put details of my trip in a long letter to you later.

The former soldiers are still looking for people who might have served in the Japanese army in Nanjing in 1937 but I'm not holding my breath . . . if they locate one person, I will try to correspond with him. So far, I've interviewed more than 10 survivors of the massacre.

Love, Iris

After returning home on September 15, Iris was apparently fully recovered and wrote us a long letter to update us about her Tsien book and her concerns over her safety in writing her next book on the Nanking Massacre:

> Dear Mom,
>
> . . . Susan Rabiner and I talked yesterday and she told me that Walter McDougall, the Pulitzer Prize winning author of the book The Heavens and The Earth *wrote me a blurb for the book jacket in time for publication—I now have three great blurbs (the other two are from Arnold Kramish, the author of World War II books and books on espionage and a former physicist for the Manhattan Project, and John Bluth, the official historian for the Jet Propulsion Laboratory.) Also, she alerted me to the fact that* Publishers Weekly *ran a picture of the cover of the book with my name on it (p. 40, September 4th issue)—it's a beautiful cover, with a silhouette of a rocket over a dragon embroidered piece of red silk.*
>
> . . .
>
> *Now for the bad news. I'm somewhat concerned about the future of Basic Books/HarperCollins as a scholarly book publishing firm. When I was in China, there was a major shakeup at Basic and a lot of editors got fired. Susan, fortunately, was not only kept on but promoted, so she's busier than ever. The new Basic Books is a much more commercial imprint, although it still claims to put out serious books. Apparently, any editor or author at Basic who isn't bringing money into the company will be on his or her way out. Susan said that I should survive because I tend to pick subjects that are not only literary but commercial—and it is hard to find an author who is both literary and commercial, she said. . . .*
>
> *I think Dad and Robert Reid were right when they urged me to write as many books as possible before going to grad school (if I ever go), because the printing presses might not be open to me forever. More so than ever before, publishing is turning into a "winner takes all" market.*

The September 18th Newsweek *declares that the "$1 million-advance syndrome is the latest example of an industry gone slightly bananas trying to satisfy the chain super-stores that want blockbusters and the entertainment conglomerates that dream of synergy between books, movies and television. There's no longer time to groom an author through three or four novels, hoping that eventually he'll find an audience. Today's publishers are scrambling to strike it rich by signing up the next* Bridges of Madison County. *The article describes how Nicholas Evans, a 45-year-old unknown British screenwriter, sold his first novel,* The Horse Whisperer *for $6.15 million ($3.15 million for the book, $3 million for the film rights)—before his novel was even finished!*

The only thing preventing me from completely self-destructing when I hear such news is a flicker of hope that the Nicholas Evans of the next millennium will be ME!

Love, Iris

The second e-mail came right after the one above:

Dear Mom,

I forgot to mention that Brett and I will be moving to a two-bedroom apartment when we find the time. We're moving because we need the space and also because I want our new home to be untraceable by some Japanese fanatic. Several people in the US expressed concern for my physical safety. (Most of my friends feel that I will be in far less danger when the book is published, because then the "secret" of the Nanking Massacre will be out.) I don't know if they are paranoid, but I do know that the PRC government will not permit their scholars to write on the Nanjing massacre, for fear of jeopardizing their lives should some right-wing extremists find them.

Today I talked with some private detectives on the phone to find out how one might hide from the public eye. These detectives have helped local celebrities and battered girl friends "disappear." It's amazing what people can find out about you if they have only your name and phone

number. . . . One detective used my name and phone number to find
out my social security number and all my addresses for the past five
years. . . . They gave me a lot of advice over the phone. . . .

The basic principle of maintaining a low profile is this: fill in a PO
Box address on all forms and correspondence; avoid giving out my actual
address whenever possible. HarperCollins and my new literary agent
should have only my PO Box and phone number unless they decide to
come and visit me. . . .

Brett is annoyed by all this because he doesn't think anyone is
going to come after me. . . . Brett's mom, who had earlier urged me
to cancel my trip to China, now wonders whether I should write the
Nanjing book at all.

Meanwhile, I remain intrigued by what the detectives and FBI told
me over the phone: did you know that individual sheets of paper can
sometimes be traced back to the state or company from which they
came, and that the saliva on a postage stamp can be traced with DNA
analysis?

Love, Iris

In respond to Iris's long e-mails, I reminded her in my reply that she, as
a responsible writer, should represent truth, beauty, and humanity. As
for potential dangers posted by Japanese fanatics, I said that she should
follow detectives' suggestions and to protect herself properly. However,
I did not feel that there was any need for her to panic or be paranoid.

While we were in Copenhagen we could get American news by
watching the CNN English-language news channel. Around the end of
September, the hottest news was the trial of O. J. Simpson. On October 2,
the day before the verdict, I received an e-mail from Iris, who wrote that
she was sure that the jury would find him guilty. Then, on October 3, the
court announced that O. J. was not guilty. Iris wrote us immediately:

Dear Dad,
I'm devastated . . . the jury found OJ not guilty. How could they?

Mom probably told you about my euphoric email yesterday when I was absolutely convinced that the jury [had] found Simpson guilty. . . .

News reports say that Simpson made more money in prison this year than he did as a free man the year before . . . defense analysts were stunned: one said people had been convicted and executed on far less evidence than in this case. . . .

How could they? How could they?

Iris

And another e-mail, written right after the one above:

Dear Dad,

. . . Perhaps I was naive when I assumed that OJ would be convicted. Apparently the politics of race have become so polarized in this country that the central issue of murder can be ignored.

I felt physically ill when the verdict was announced. How much more evidence did the jury need? . . .

One can always say that evidence has been fabricated but after a point it becomes ridiculous. The defense team's tactics remind me of those of the hard-core Japanese who still deny that the Rape of Nanking ever happened. Even after being presented with a mountain of photographs and documents and witness testimony some Japanese still believe the massacre is a pack of lies made up by the Chinese. Photos can be altered, they say, documents forged. Witnesses can be bribed. What about Western newsreel footage and their newspaper articles? Nothing but propaganda and sensationalism. Even primary source material like burial records in the Chinese archives and US intercepts of the Japanese Foreign Office communication can be dismissed if one believes there is some grand conspiracy between the US and China to frame Japan. Some Japanese historians then try to confuse everyone with semantics and metaphysical arguments: what IS truth, anyway? Isn't it all relative, depending on your viewpoint? Maybe there is no such thing as truth anyway. And how can you really trust what you see as reality, etc, etc, ad nauseam. Some even hint that one can never write about the Rape of Nanjing because it was such a brutal large-scale event and no one can ascertain the exact number of casualties. Does it mean that no historian can ever write about the US civil war or World War II or any war, because of the impossibility of an exact body count? What nonsense!!

    Love, Iris

We returned home from Copenhagen in time for Thanksgiving. Both Iris and Michael came home for Thanksgiving too. Iris and Brett came home also to attend Brett's brother's wedding in Indiana. For Iris, there was another important event to attend, her book signing for her newly published book *Thread of the Silkworm* at the Champaign Pages for All Ages bookstore. The morning of November 22, 1995, Iris was interviewed by Jack Brighton of WILL-AM Radio. At 7 P.M., when Shau-Jin and I went with Iris to the bookstore to attend the signing, we met many of our old friends, Iris's high-school classmates, college friends, her teachers, professors, and so forth. Indeed, it was a big homecoming party!

For Iris, her first book was her first "child." To me, it felt like my first "grandchild" when I held that copy on November 22, 1995! It took Iris, as well as us, numerous hours, days, and months in discussions about the book, from application grants to support her research to making a trip to China, from translating Chinese articles about Dr. Tsien to rescuing her from being trapped inside the National Archives. Shau-Jin and I were always her cheerleaders. It was a journey for her, and also quite an incredible journey for us!

11

The Biological Clock

After the book signing and Thanksgiving were over, Iris and Brett went back to Santa Barbara on November 26, 1995. As for us, we departed for Mexico for the rest of Shau-Jin's sabbatical. One of Shau-Jin's students, now a professor at the Institute of Physics in Merida, picked us up at the airport and drove us to a nice apartment where we would stay for three weeks. During our stay, Shau-Jin gave a series of physics lectures to the students at the Institute there, while I was earnestly reading Iris's book. Although Iris had told us about Dr. Tsien's life all along with her progress of the writing of the book and even though we had translated some of the Chinese articles and letters for her, we did not actually see her manuscript of the book before its publication. While I read the book, I also tried to keep a sheet recording any errors I spotted, so Iris could ask the publisher to correct them in the next printing.

By the time we returned home on December 17, I had finished reading Iris's book and was ready to give her my comments. No question, I was very impressed by the book, but not just because my daughter was the author. It was fair to say *Thread of the Silkworm* was a well-written and thoroughly researched book. We had received many compliments about the book from other people, including our professor friends in aeronautic engineering and physics who were not afraid to "tell it like it was" and would not easily praise a book. They were really impressed by Iris who, though not trained as an engineer, could understand and write so accurately about aeronautical and rocket sciences. The book had taken Iris a total of more than three years to research and write. Iris said Susan Rabiner praised her for it, as well as a number of her friends. We had always known Iris was a talented writer, but the publication of this book proved it to the outside world.

On Sunday morning, January 21, 1996, Iris called us from Santa Barbara and exclaimed that John Taylor in Washington had just called her to say that there was a review of her book on the front page of the *Washington Post* Book World! She was so excited, it seemed like she could hardly breathe. She asked us to buy several copies of that Sunday's *Washington Post* and save the copies for her, because she had called around her town and found that the *Post* would not arrive in stores there until Wednesday! Shau-Jin and I immediately drove to the Barnes and Noble and bought as many copies of the newspaper as they had. Right there, we read the review, which was straightforward and positive and contained no criticism of her. It was a big relief, and we were very happy and impressed. We imagined that it was not easy to get a book reviewed in a big newspaper, let alone to be reviewed by a major national newspaper such as the *Washington Post.*

Pretty soon after that, many other major newspapers and magazines reviewed Iris's book. On March 5, the *Chicago Tribune* ran a review, and on March 14, *Nature* reviewed it favorably as well. Not long after that, *Science* magazine also reviewed *Thread of the Silkworm*. In the *Science* book review, there was a photo of Dr. Tsien in front of a chalkboard, which was displayed conspicuously. *Nature* and *Science* are considered two of the most important scientific magazines in the world, with wide circulations in the U.S., and Iris told us she felt honored that her book could be reviewed in such prestigious magazines.

One of the reasons her book generated such wide interest and media coverage at the time was also due to the tension between the People's Republic of China on the mainland and the Republic of China on Taiwan. A general democratic presidential election was going to take place on March 23 in Taiwan. The PRC was worried that presidential candidate Li Teng-hui would advocate an independent Taiwan. The PRC carried out a cross-strait military exercise and missile test on March 8 to show their military power by launching M-9 missiles into the water of the Taiwan Strait. The PRC considered Taiwan to be part of China and had warned Taiwan for a long time that they would use military power to stop any possible action leading to Taiwanese independence.

We read both Chinese and English news reports, so we were well aware of the tension between mainland China and Taiwan. I called Iris and reminded her that she should point out in media interviews for her book that the missiles used in the cross-strait military maneuver had been developed and advanced by Dr. Tsien, the father of the Chinese missile program. Very soon, Iris was interviewed by a number of radio stations on the East Coast about her book, and on March 14 she was invited by NPR's *All Things Considered* program to their station studio in Thousand Oaks for a personal interview. All these activities were related to the tension on the Taiwan Strait. On March 23, the *South China Morning Post*, the largest English newspaper in southern China, had an article on Iris's book, with a huge photo of Dr. Tsien wearing a military uniform and the missiles he helped develop prominently displayed at the top of the article. Certainly, this was incredible publicity for her book and helped establish Iris even further in the literary community.

In February, Iris told us that she had book signings in local bookstores in Santa Barbara; and in March, she was interviewed at Santa Barbara's Celebrity Author's luncheon. And the local newspaper profiled her and her book. People found that she was a good public speaker and could handle interviews very well. Indeed, she became a local celebrity.

Iris was somewhat disappointed, however, when Basic Books told her that the sale of her book was not so great, about average, although the book got great reviews in important newspapers and magazines. On March 11, 1996, Iris wrote to her dad:

> *Dear Dad:*
>
> *Today I was interviewed by a major New York radio station (WOR) on a syndicated talk show program with only three hours advance notice. . . . The WOR station received a fax I had sent them last night and made a snap decision to book me on the show. It's easier for me to get on the air now that tensions are rising in the Taiwan Straits.*
>
> *Susan said that while my book is attracting more review attention (and favorable review attention) than the average book at Basic, it is generating average (or below average) sales. In other words, the book is noticed and well-respected by the reviewer but people who read the reviews aren't buying SILKWORM in droves. In contrast, Basic has some books that sell tens of thousands of copies within months while getting virtually no reviews. But Susan said good reviews are important in establishing an author's reputation. . . .*
>
> *Love, Iris*

She also complained to us that Basic Books had broken the promise that they would put her on a six-city book tour to promote the book. Iris said she would remember this when she was shopping for her next book contract.

With all this publicity, Iris had great confidence in herself as an "author": she had had a book published, and there was another one on the way. In the conversations we had over numerous telephone calls to each other during that period of time, she disclosed her ambition that she wanted to be a famous author; a world-class, best-selling book author. She had been reading many famous well-written books and studied their writing styles carefully, the way priests scrutinized the Bible. She said "I do not go to church; I go to the library. I worship books." "Books are the ultimate way for writers to reach immortality," she would say. She wanted to be remembered after her death.

She also recalled the years when she was in grade school and high school. "I was a loner in grade school and in high school. I do not mind. I found eternal happiness when I was reading a book." She remembered how happy she was when she found a book she wanted in a library's card catalog. She said, "I would scrawl down the call number of the book from the card catalog and run through the aisles. My heart was pounding, and I was so excited that I hardly could breathe and it seemed like I might faint."

Besides reading and writing books, Iris also watched many movies in her leisure time. She was a true movie buff. She told me she was interested in scriptwriting, too. She realized very early on that the greater the power of a movie, the greater the impact the movie could have on viewers. She watched Oscar-winning movies systematically. She had been studying movie scenes segment by segment. "The movies I like are tightly structured, beautiful cinema graphic films with survival themes," she would say. She mentioned the movies she liked such as *Terminator, Apollo 13, The River Wild*, and *Witness*. "My favorite movies are ones in which the central character wants something badly, takes her fate into her own hands, overcomes obstacles, fights against odds, and succeeds at the end!"

She also mentioned movies about class struggle or class envy or war in epic films such as *Gone with the Wind, A Place in the Sun, Giant*, and *Shane* that she enjoyed. She said that a book she would like to write in the future would be also along the lines of a survival theme. She would always tell me a number of ideas for her next book. It seemed that her well of inspiration and curiosity were limitless.

On February 12, 1996, Iris called us in panic after she saw a *Newsweek* cover story on baby's brains. She had a book idea on "how to raise baby's IQ" or "how to raise a genius," which now seemed to be overtaken by the *Newsweek* cover story. We told her, "You have hundreds of ideas, but you can only work on a few. You can't write two books at the same time." "The man who runs after two hares will get none," Shau-Jin added. We advised her that the book she was currently writing was an important, serious book, and she needed to finish it with her full attention. "You should not be distracted," we said to her.

At this point in Iris's life, she felt she had reached a goal she'd set for herself, or at least she had become what she wanted to be, a book author. She now tried to help Brett excel in his career. Iris said Brett was very smart and should go to a business school to obtain an MBA. He could be a CEO, she said. The next thing I knew, Iris had persuaded Brett to apply to the country's best business school—Harvard Business School, and she was quite energetic in helping Brett with the application. On May 19, Brett was informed by Harvard Business School that he had been admitted to the school for the fall of 1996. Iris was overjoyed, but Brett also had several good job offers from high-tech companies, and he wanted to work in Silicon Valley. Iris was insistent that Brett should go to HBS, so Brett finally agreed to enroll at HBS by delaying a year and also under the condition that Iris secure a big book advance for her next book, and thus their finances would remain secure while he was at school.

To secure a big advance for her next book became Iris's major concern in 1996. She toyed with ideas for her next book proposal almost all the time, besides working on her book *The Rape of Nanking*. Iris had expressed to me repeatedly over the phone that she felt life was unfair for a woman such as she, who had a dream and ambitions but was limited by her biological clock—the time to have children coincided exactly with the time she could write most productively in her life. She felt trapped because she was a woman. "By the time I reach the point when I'm commanding six-figure advances, I'll have to slow down to have babies!" she shouted. Thus, the next book idea on women's biological clocks was born. The book she was going to propose, she said, would find a solution so career women and female intellectuals could have both family and career. Iris believed that if there was no biological clock barrier for women, they could compete with men equally. And there was modern technology available for women who wanted to delay or prolong their biological clocks. She began active research on the topic and tried to perfect the book proposal.

To her dismay, when Iris mentioned the idea to Susan Rabiner, Susan disliked the idea right on the spot. At that time, Iris told us she had found a new agent—Mel Berger, of William Morris Agency (now William Morris Endeavor), to be her next book agent. According to Iris, Mel was a powerful book agent with a number of famous clients. Iris said he had represented the author of *Apollo 13* and had helped make the book into a successful movie. She believed Mel would help her to get a big advance for her next book. Iris was thrilled that when she contacted Mel, he agreed to represent her. Mel told Iris that she could submit any book ideas to him; apparently he was impressed by *Thread of the Silkworm*. Iris mentioned her idea on the biological clock, and Mel asked Iris to write it up and send him the proposal.

On Mother's Day, a cheerful call to me ended up with her admission in tears. She confessed that she felt caught between two arenas—to excel by her own merit and to excel as a woman married to a successful man. She felt she was caught in her own biological clock.

On May 18, 1996, I went to New Orleans for a national microbiology meeting and planned to visit my mother in New York right afterward. My mother's condition had worsened with time. From my frequent phone calls to her, I found her voice weak and her backache severe due to the cancer. She was crippled and bedridden. I had told Iris and Michael about the condition of their grandma. When Iris heard I was going to New York, she arranged her trip to the East Coast to coincide with my visit, so we could meet in New York. She said she needed to go to the National Archives again to see some documents. She also needed to go to New York to talk to Susan. On May 23, when I arrived in my mother's apartment at Confucius Plaza, Iris was already there.

In the little garden in front of the high-rise building that was Confucius Plaza, Iris told me all her worries and concerns. She had apparently lost some weight. Writing *The Rape of Nanking* definitely had taken a physical toll on her. She said she had lost a lot of hair and she could not sleep well at night. Besides the fact that the story of the Rape of Nanking depressed her, Iris was also unhappy about a number of other things. For one, she was not certain that she could get a big advance for her third book. She was under tremendous pressure. I told her I was amazed that she would drive herself so hard. Why should she torture herself? I advised her that she should concentrate on finishing the Nanking book. I cheered her up by asking her to think about how much she had accomplished so far. Her dad and I were very proud of her, I said. I could see my words lifted her spirit somewhat.

In June, Brett accepted a job offer from a company called Applied Signal Technology. They were scheduled to move north to Sunnyvale from Santa Barbara in July.

Before the move, Iris had many boxes of files that she had accumulated in the past few years when she had done the research for *Thread of the Silkworm*. Iris treasured any written records. Her research files were always neatly organized in folders and in file cabinets and meticulously labeled. She would never throw away even a piece of her research papers, but since the book had been published, there was no point in moving those papers with her. The archivists at UCSB had been eager to acquire Iris's papers and told her they would start a collection in her name. Finally, Iris decided to donate her collection of research on Dr. Tsien to the Multicultural Center of the UCSB library; her materials would be stored in a room specifically designated in her name. But she admitted that to be separated from the files she had been with for the past three or four years would be emotionally difficult.

On July 15, 1996, Iris informed us that they had moved into an apartment located at 655 South Fair Oaks Avenue in Sunnyvale, about thirty miles south of San Francisco in the heart of Silicon Valley. Iris described to us how their apartment was in a huge apartment building complex in a courtyard setting, and the residents were young, professional, and culturally and ethnically diverse. She said she couldn't wait for us to come to visit her.

Iris also mentioned that she had finished the book proposal on the biological clock just before moving and would mail us a copy for our comments. She was also sending the book proposal to a number of her friends for suggestions. Soon afterward, we received Iris's book proposal outline, titled *Turning Back the Biological Clock: The Fertility Revolution of the Next Millennium*. She asked us to give her our honest comments before she sent it to Mel.

The proposal of twenty-four pages, single-spaced, was divided into three parts. In the Overview, Iris pointed out that "The woman's fertility clock is probably the final barrier to true female emancipation. It hurts women during years of crucial career development, forcing some of the best, brightest and most ambitious to make the unpleasant choice of stepping out of the fast track or forgoing motherhood altogether. Also, the very fact that women face an earlier deadline for procreation than men casts them in a weaker position in the dating game." But she added that "Scientists have reached the point, on the eve of a new millennium, of shattering this ancient barrier." In part one, she said she would "examine the history of the woman's biological clock—the role it has played in the subjugation of women in the agricultural and industrial age. Part two will investigate the present manifestations of the clock's influence on our global society—how it continues to oppress women in both work and sexual relationships with men. Part three will forecast the future implications of technological forces that are, at present, eliminating the biological clock and hurtling our society into a new age."

Shau-Jin read her proposal more carefully than I because I was so busy with my own research at the time. Nevertheless, I read it as thoroughly as I could and gave Iris my comments. I told her that the book would be for general readers, so she should not go too much into scientific detail, such as the technical details how eggs can be preserved in liquid nitrogen. I also asked her to not stress waiting to have children too long, perhaps only at most to the mid-forties. I told her that if a mother was in her sixties, it would be hard to raise children even if she could have a normal and healthy baby, as, based on my own experience, young children have so much energy that it could be difficult for an older person to keep up.

A couple of months later, Iris said that Mel told her the proposal had been rejected by most of the publishers he sent to. It was a big blow for Iris. She told Mel that she wanted to revise the proposal and try again. Mel told her he would resubmit the revised proposal for her again, so Iris worked hard trying to make the necessary changes. At that time, we did not realize how much this book proposal meant to her on a personal level. Each time when she called us and talked about it, we asked her about *The Rape of Nanking* instead. We advised her to concentrate in finishing the Nanking book first before considering anything else. But something outside of books and publishing was bothering her.

The competitive urge was always deeply rooted in Iris. One day, she complained, "If only I had more time! If only I wasn't hindered by my own biological clock!" Another day, she told me that Brett and she had written down their goals for the next twenty years. She said it was painful to see how few "productive" years were left for her, and that could have meant either professionally or biologically. I told her she should not drive herself so hard and should not approach life on such a tight schedule. She should relax, I told her. Those things always have a way of coming together, and many women were able to reconcile professional fulfillment with a family.

On September 12, 1996, Iris mailed us her revised biological clock proposal. Again, both Shau-Jin and I read it over and gave her some suggestions. After that, I did not hear about it very much because an important thing happened at that time in all of our lives—the discovery of John Rabe's diary in Germany became international news. Iris and the forthcoming book *The Rape of Nanking* were now in the center of a media maelstrom.

12

The Breakthrough

Nineteen ninety-six was a very complex year for Iris. She had to put the finishing touches on *The Rape of Nanking*, which was scheduled to be published in 1997. She was also busy promoting *Thread of the Silkworm*, which had just been published in November 1995. In the meantime, she was also actively revising her proposal for what she hoped would be her next book, on the "biological clock." But the most exciting thing was the discovery of John Rabe's diary in the spring—a big breakthrough in Iris's career and a huge asset to her efforts to tell the full story of the Rape of Nanking, something that was almost in danger of being sidelined by her work on her biological clock proposal.

Iris first learned of John Rabe when she was doing the research on the Nanking Massacre at Yale in January 1995. His name was repeatedly mentioned in a number of diaries and letters of the missionaries who had stayed in Nanking at the time of the massacre.

When the Japanese military invaded the Chinese capital, Nanjing (then called Nanking), on December 12, 1937, within just six to eight weeks the Japanese had slaughtered some 260,000 to 350,000 Chinese civilians, and had raped between 20,000 and 80,000 Chinese women and girls in the most heinous and barbaric ways. During the carnage, a group of Westerners—European and American missionaries, scholars, and doctors, who had chosen to stay behind—had established a Safety Zone to protect some 250,000 refugees in a neutral area of two square miles in Nanking. The head of the Safety Zone was a German businessman, John Rabe, who was also the head of the local Nazi Party in Nanking.

Iris told us that she had always been curious about John Rabe. She had been told by activists in the U.S. and historians in China that Rabe had virtually vanished after he returned to Germany in February 1938. Where was John Rabe now? Was he still alive? If not, did he have descendants? What happened when he returned to Germany? Her curiosity drove her to find out more about him.

When Iris came back from Taiwan in the summer of 1995, she brought back some documents related to the Nanking Massacre from the National History Archives in Taiwan. The document was a stack of German diplomatic reports about the Nanking Massacre. Since the reports were in German, she needed someone who knew both German and English to translate them for her. A friend of Iris's introduced her to Barbara Masin, who also lived in Santa Barbara, because Barbara Masin could speak five languages and was fluent in German.

In December of 1995, Barbara dictated the translated text orally into a tape recorder while Iris took notes. Iris later told us: "As she spoke, the living room of her house reverberated with the stories of hundreds of atrocities." Iris learned from the reports that John Rabe had permitted some two to three hundred women to live in tiny huts on his property in Nanking. There were numerous stories in the reports that John Rabe had protected those refugees from rape and murder by Japanese soldiers. Rabe toured the city of Nanking and the countryside to record the extent of the massacre. The reports also recorded his departure, in February 1938, back to Germany. Rabe had promised his Chinese friends that he would let his government know what had happened in Nanking. He planned to deliver a report and a film of the Nanking atrocities to the highest power in Berlin: Hermann Göring and Adolf Hitler himself. (The film was shot by Minister John Magee, and one copy of the film had been smuggled to the U.S. and later provided the famous images of the Nanking Massacre for *Life* magazine.) People in Nanking prayed that Rabe's presentation would compel Nazi leaders to exert pressure on the Japanese government to stop the carnage. Iris was very curious: had the film and the report reached Hitler? And what had happened to Rabe after his presentation of the film and the report?

From the diaries and letters of the American missionaries in the Safety Zone, Rabe emerged as a man who worked tirelessly to protect Chinese women from rape and Chinese men from execution. He wrote to Japanese officials repeatedly, demanding that they end the violence. Because of his Nazi status, Japanese soldiers were hesitant to commit atrocities in his presence. Rabe was revered among the Chinese refugee community as a savior—the "Schindler" of Nanking, if you will.

Iris told us that the more research she did on the Massacre, the more she wished to know the fate of John Rabe after he left China. After all, unlike his Safety Zone colleagues, he had not come forward to testify against the Japanese during the International Military Tribunal of the Far East (IMTFE), and no one ever heard from him again after his return to Europe. Iris had contacted a number of scholars and political activists and descendants of the Nanking Safety Zone committee members, but none of them knew what had happened to him. Iris then determined to embark on a journey to track him down, while simultaneously working on her book.

First, Iris told us she had written to the Siemens Company headquarters in Germany, where Rabe had once been an employee. The archivist of the company wrote back and said indeed they had a file on him, but alas, the last information on him was that he had been transferred to the Siemens office in Nanking in 1931. The archivist

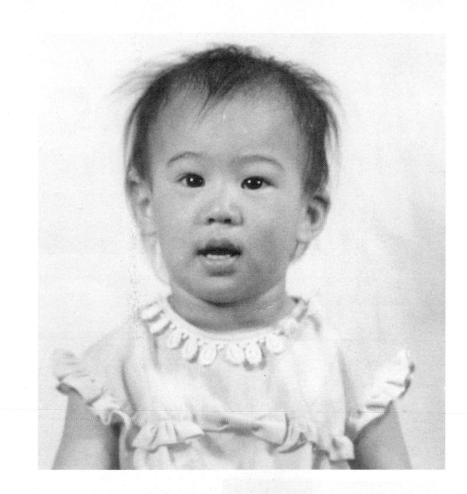

ABOVE: Iris as a one-year-old in Princeton, N. J. RIGHT: Iris at 15 months with Ying-Ying and Shau-Jin during a trip to Vienna, Austria.

TOP LEFT: As a three-year-old in Urbana, Illinois. TOP RIGHT: Iris was celebrating her 5th birthday in Princeton, N. J. with her brother, Michael (far right) and her friends, over the much-beloved gingerbread house. CENTER: A family portrait with Iris (aged 7) and her maternal grandparents. BOTTOM: Mother's Day, 1978.

TOP: A family portrait with Iris (age 10) and paternal grandparents. BOTTOM: The family trip to Yellowstone National Park in the summer of 1984 when Iris was 16 years old that she referred to throughout her whole life.

TOP: Iris's high school graduation photo. BOTTOM: Iris, Ying-Ying, and Shau-Jin in the football stadium at the 1988 University of Illinois Homecoming game. Iris was selected as one of the princesses for the Homecoming Court.

TOP: Iris as a college student at the University of Illinois. BOTTOM: Iris's graduation from the Journalism Department of the University of Illinois in 1989. On the right is Professor Robert Reid, her mentor.

TOP: A family portrait taken on Ying-Ying's 50th birthday when Iris was 22 years old working at the Associate Press in Chicago. BOTTOM: Iris and Brett on their honeymoon in 1991 in Las Vegas.

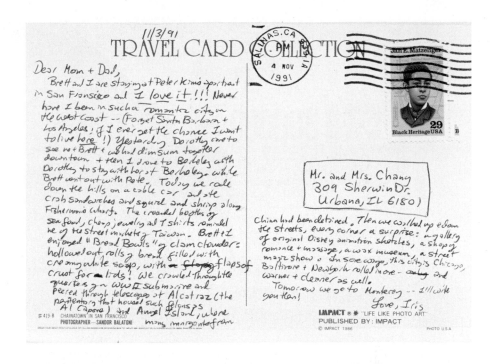

TOP: One of the postcard letters Iris sent home, Nov. 3, 1991. BOTTOM: Iris at the Great Wall of China in Beijing in 1993 conducting research for her biography on Dr. Tsien.

TOP: Iris in Nanjing, China in the summer of 1995 interviewing the survivors of the Nanjing Massacre. Photo was taken in front of the Nanjing Memorial Hall for the Victims of the Nanking Massacre. BOTTOM: With Nanjing survivor Xia Shu-qin (second from left), who witnessed the killing and raping of her family members when she was nine years old.

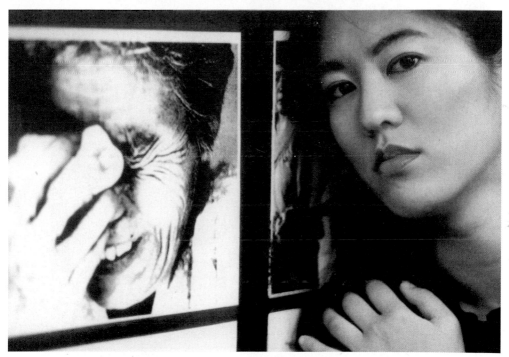

TOP: Iris and Ying-Ying at a signing of her first book, *Thread of the Silkworm*, in Champaign, Illinois in 1995. BOTTOM: Iris at a photo exhibition of the Nanking Massacre. The photos in this exhibit would change her life. (Photo courtesy of *San Jose Mercury News*.)

TOP LEFT: Iris in 1997, the same year *The Rape of Nanking* was published. (Photo by Jimmy Estimada.) TOP RIGHT: The cover of the November, 1997 issue of *Johns Hopkins* magazine. This article was the first intensive coverage of Iris's *The Rape of Nanking* book. BOTTOM: Signing copies of *The Rape of Nanking*.

TOP: Copies of *The Rape of Nanking* displayed in a bookstore. BOTTOM: Iris and her parents with Uni High School Principal Shelley Roberts (right) and her former English teachers, Adele Suslick (left) and Charlene Tibbitts (seated) at the 1998 Max Berberman Award ceremony.

TOP: The cover of the September, 1998 issue of *Reader's Digest* magazine. BOTTOM: Iris and *Washington Post* columnist George Will.

TOP: Iris and President Bill Clinton at the Renaissance Weekend New Year's Eve Party, December 31, 1998. BOTTOM: Iris and Diana Zuckerman (left) with First Lady Hillary Clinton at the White House, 1999.

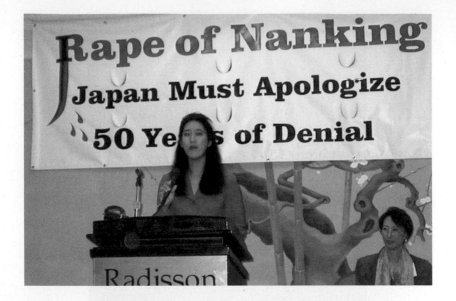

TOP: Delivering the keynote speech in San Francisco in September, 2001, at a conference counteracting the official commemoration of the 50th anniversary of the San Francisco Peace Treaty. BOTTOM: Iris in 2003. (Photo by Jimmy Estimada.)

TOP: In an interview with Orville Schell. BOTTOM: Iris was one of the keynote speakers at the 50th anniversary of the United Nations Universal Declaration of Human Rights on December 9th, 1998, in the San Francisco Masonic Center. With her, other speakers were Martin Luther King III, the son of civil rights leader Martin Luther King, Jr., and Arun Gandhi, grandson of the legendary Indian leader Mohandas K. Gandhi (second and fourth from left, respectively). At left is Ignatius Ding, VP of Global Alliance for Preserving the History of WWII in Asia.

TOP: Her new book, *Chinese in America* in 2003. CENTER: At a press conference at Toronto in 1998 with David Magee (right), son of John Magee, who showed the camera his father had used to record many Nanking atrocities. John Magee was a minister who served as chairman of the International Red Cross Committee of Nanking during the massacre. BOTTOM LEFT: In an interview with Charlie Rose. BOTTOM RIGHT: Delivering a speech at the Committee 100 conference in 2003.

TOP: Iris with her one-year-old son, Christopher, at home in 2003. BOTTOM: Iris met the descendants of Nanking Safety Zone Committee members in Michigan in 1998. Harriet Mills and Angie Mills (left and second from left, respectively) are daughters of Wilson Plumer Mills, who was the Presbyterian missionary in Nanking in 1937, and Neal Brady (right) is the son of Richard Brady (a surgeon who worked for the safety zone committee after the worst of the massacre was over). Brady gave the original Safety Zone Red Cross flag to Iris, who later donated it to the Hoover Institution.

TOP: Iris at a book signing in 2003 for *The Rape of Nanking* and *The Chinese in America*, one of her last before her suicide. BOTTOM: Friends light candles outside the funeral home during the visitation on November 18, 2004.

TOP: Iris's grave at Gate of Heaven Cemetery in Los Altos, California. BOTTOM: A statue of Iris stands near the front of the Memorial Hall for the Victims of Japanese Invaders in Nanjing, China.

Iris and Ying-Ying attending the memorial service for the victims of the Nanking Massacre and photo exhibition on December 13, 2001 in San Francisco.

TOP: Iris and Ying-Ying in Champaign-Urbana, 1998. BOTTOM: Ying-Ying's Chinese article published on May 15, 1998 in the Chinese newspaper *World Journal* Sunday magazine. The article described the mother's journey with Iris behind the *Rape of Nanking* book.

Oct. 5, 1992

Dear Mom + Dad,

Enclosed please find a copy of a biographical essay about Dr. Tsien that appeared in a book about China's leading scientists. The book was mailed to me by S. I. Pai, the fellow you had breakfast with in Taiwan. Is it possible for you to take a quick look at the essay + see if there is anything new? If there is the next time we talk you can mention the page numbers to me over the phone and I'll have a Chinese UCSB student do a little oral translation for me.

I think it's important for me to write more letters to you to keep a record of events. I do this regularly with my friends but not with you, because of the convenience of the telephone. After spending a year of research on this book I have learned that the best way to control how history is written is to
(a) be a compulsive letter writer or
(b) outlive your enemies. Because as I piece together the events of Tsien's life there are only two resources:

© Hallmark Cards, Inc.

TOP AND OPPOSITE TOP: A hand-written letter, October 5, 1992. OPPOSITE BOTTOM: Iris's postcard from June 10, 1993.

the written records + the oral record. One of Tsien's best friends, Frank Malina, was a prodigious correspondent who, at the time of his death, left behind 40,000 documents to the Library of Congress. Although this papers have been consolidated into the Frank Malina Collection, no one to my knowledge has ever spent a great deal of time looking through it. During the 1930s, when he + Tsien were experimenting with rockets made from junkyard parts, Frank Malina wrote to his parents two or three times a week. Years later, when he was retired in Paris with plenty of time on his hands, he compiled a collection of excerpts from those letters that pertained to his days as leader of "the Suicide Squad," which have never been published. Frank Malina desperately wanted to be famous; even as a young grad student at CalTech he was actively sending out press releases about his rocket experiments, holding press conferences with LA Times reporters or lunching with AP science writers at the CalTech Athenaeum. (Luckily for me, this has generated a lot of good newspaper photographs of Malina, Tsien, Parsons + Forman launching rockets in the desert.) In later years he wrote historical articles about the CalTech days + carefully kept records for the historian "100 years from now." It's unfortunate he died 10 years ago -- I think he would have liked to talk with me.

Every night, I transcribe two or three of my tapes, and it's a thrill to see the stories come to life on the page. It's a lot of work, but I can type very quickly now. Alan I

THE NEW YORK TIMES **INTERNATIONAL** TH

to save people who would later become his country's enemies. Indeed, Mr. Rabe's outspoken support for the Chinese upon his return to Germany appears to have ruined his career.

Some who have followed his case say that he, like Oskar Schindler, the German industrialist who protected Jews under very different circumstances, offers another example of the durability of humanitarian impulses in the cruelest of times.

Scholars say Mr. Rabe's diary, which includes reports from other foreign observers, photos and other memorabilia, is valuable not so much for revealing new historical facts, but because it provides an unusually detailed and personal account from a German witness to an incident considered among the most brutal in modern warfare. They believe the diary to be authentic, because American missionaries in China who were Mr. Rabe's contemporaries knew of his actions and supplied similar accounts of atrocities.

The diary also offers a counterweight to claims by some Japanese officials who have long denied either the existence or the scale of the massacre in Nanking, which is now known as Nanjing.

"It's an incredibly gripping and depressing narrative, done very carefully with an enormous amount of detail and drama," said William C. Kirby, a professor of modern Chinese history at Harvard University, who has read parts of the diary in German. "It will reopen this case in a very important way in that people can go through the day-by-day account and add 100 to 200 stories to what is popularly known."

The diary has only now come to light because of the efforts of Iris Chang, a Sunnyvale, Calif., author. While researching a book on the Nanjing massacre a few years ago, she stumbled upon a few references to Mr. Rabe's humanitarian efforts. She tracked down Mr. Rabe's granddaughter, Ursula Reinhardt, in Berlin, and upon discovering that Mr. Rabe had kept a diary, persuaded the family to make it public.

That will formally happen today at a news conference at the Hotel Inter-attend. The public announcement is being organized by the Alliance in Memory of Victims of the Nanjing Massacre, a Chinese-American group, said Tzuping Shao, a past president. Eventually, copies of the diary are to be donated to Yale Divinity School Library and Nanjing Massacre Memorial Hall, in China.

Martha L. Smalley, research services librarian at Yale Divinity School, said Mr. Rabe's accounts are corroborated by documents on display at a current Yale exhibition called "American Missionary Eyewitnesses to the Nanjing Massacre."

One such missionary, Robert O. Wilson, a Harvard-trained doctor who worked in China in the 1930's, wrote of Mr. Rabe:

The 1937 diary of an unlikely hero bears witness to Japanese atrocities.

"He is well up in Nazi circles and after coming into such close contact with him as we have for the past few weeks and discover(ing) what a splendid man he is and what a tremendous heart he has, it is hard to reconcile his personality with his adulation of 'Der Führer.' "

It is not clear whether Mr. Rabe embraced the oppression of Jews and other groups in Nazi Germany. He lived outside Germany during the time of Hitler's rise to power, and there is no record of the extent of his activities in the Nazi Party after he returned to Germany in 1938, according to Ms. Chang. Because scholars, who received the diary only a few days ago, have not finished reading it, they cannot say if it contains expressions of anti-Semitism.

But Mr. Rabe was outspoken in his support for Nazism. In a lecture he delivered after his return to Germany in February 1938, he said, "Although I feel tremendous sympathy not only in the correctness of our political system but, as an organizer of the party, I am behind the system 100 percent."

Born in Hamburg in 1882, Mr. Rabe spent much of his life in China working for the Siemens Company, rising to become its top representative there, selling telephones, turbines and electrical equipment. His children and grandchildren were born in China, and he had many Chinese friends. He spoke the language fluently.

But by 1937, Hitler's Germany was shifting its loyalties away from China and toward Japan. So when Japanese forces converged on Nanjing, many Germans who were working in China felt torn, Professor Kirby said.

Mr. Rabe was ordered by Siemens to leave for the safer grounds of Wuhan, a few hundred miles west on the Yangtze River. But he refused. Instead, he became chairman of a group of about two dozen German and American missionaries, doctors and professors who established a neutral zone in Nanjing as a haven for Chinese refugees.

It was a daunting task. Mr. Rabe witnessed people who were shot, doused with gasoline and burned alive. He saw bodies of women lanced with beer bottles and bamboo sticks.

In his diary entry for Jan. 1, 1938, Mr. Rabe wrote: "The mother of a young attractive girl called out to me, and throwing herself on her knees, crying, said I should help her. Upon entering (the house), I saw a Japanese soldier lying completely naked on a young girl, who was crying hysterically. I yelled at this swine, in any language it would be understood, 'Happy New Year,' and he fled from there, naked and with his pants in his hand."

In another entry, referring to the Chinese he had hidden, Mr. Rabe wrote that it was hard to sleep with 650 people snoring in his backyard. On Dec. 10, with water and power failing and the city ringed by fire, he noticed that his canary, Peter, sang in rhythm to the sound of gunfire.

Upon his return to Germany in February 1938, Mr. Rabe wrote a But he was arrested by the Gestapo, interrogated for three days and ordered to keep silent on the subject.

From there Mr. Rabe's life headed into a downward spiral. Between 1938 and 1945, Mr. Rabe worked on and off for the Siemens Company, including a brief stint in Afghanistan.

As World War II intensified, Mr. Rabe wrote increasingly in his diary about hunger and the ravages of war; he and his family in Berlin had to eat nettles and acorn soup.

Because Mr. Rabe was one of the about 9 percent of Germans who were members of the Nazi party, he had to petition to be de-Nazified by the Allies after the war in order to hold a job. His first petition was denied, and Mr. Rabe had to appeal.

Ultimately, in June 1946, Mr. Rabe was granted de-Nazification status because of his humanitarian acts in China, according to Ms. Chang. But the investigation proved draining, and he died of a stroke in 1950.

"He was humiliated because he had to go through de-Nazification," Mrs. Reinhardt said in a telephone interview from her home in Berlin.

Mr. Rabe's diary may bolster the efforts of Chinese organizations like Mr. Shao's alliance, who contend that as many as 300,000 Chinese were killed in Nanjing massacres, to extract an apology, or possibly war reparations, from the Japanese Government. Unlike Germany, Japan has been perceived as resisting responsibility for wartime atrocities. Some high-ranking Japanese officials, including a former Minister of Justice, Shigeto Nagano, maintain the incident never happened.

Ms. Chang, whose book, "The Rape of Nanking: The Forgotten Holocaust of World War II ," is to be published next year by Basic Books, said of Mr. Rabe: "I think he felt that he could make a difference, that if Germany knew what Japan was doing, then maybe Germany could have influenced Japan to stop it. It may have been naïveté. But to me, John Rabe is the Oskar Schindler of China, another example of good in the face of evil."

:Week in Review, Sec. 4, P.7

THE NEW YORK TIMES, SUNDAY, DECEMBER 15, 1996

Word For Word / *The Rape of Nanking*

A Nazi in China Who Used His Swastika to Save Lives

RECENT works like "Schindler's List" and "Hitler's Willing Executioners" have stimulated public debate about what German civilians did and did not do during the Third Reich to lessen some of this century's signal horrors. Add to that discussion now the case of John Rabe, a German businessman and Nazi organizer in China who worked to protect Chinese civilians caught in the two-month rampage by invading Japanese soldiers known as the Rape of Nanking.

Last week in New York, Mr. Rabe's diary and other writings were made public by his family and a group commemorating victims of the Nanking atrocities. The writings chronicle the Japanese Army's frenzy of killing, rape and looting in the Nationalist Chinese capital (now transliterated as Nanjing) in the winter of 1937-38, and offer details of Mr. Rabe's humanitarian role, which in general terms has been corroborated independently.

His writings are a counterweight to Japanese efforts to whitewash the Nanking episode. Above all, his story embodies a rich paradox: an unarmed Nazi — a standard-bearer for notions of racial superiority — was defending Asians against the brutal army of a country edging closer to Germany as world war approached. Here are excerpts.

DAVID W. CHEN

• • •

As the Japanese advanced on the city, Mr. Rabe (pronounced RAH-bay), the top representative in China for the Siemans manufacturing concern, joined with other foreign businessmen and American missionaries to designate a square-mile area of the city a "safety zone" for Chinese refugees. They counted on the Japanese to respect the neutrality of foreigners. But it became clear early that this neutrality would be often honored in the breach. Mr. Rabe writes vant's closet and the rest, about 100 people, are either in the foxholes or out in the open. ...

In an entry soon after the Japanese have overrun the city, he encounters their atrocities:

I drove with some Americans to the southern part of the city ... where I found out how much damage the fighting had inflicted. ... We found many corpses of Chinese civilians. I examined them and determined that they had probably come from nearby and had been shot in the back while trying to flee. ...

He mistakenly assumes that retreating Chi-

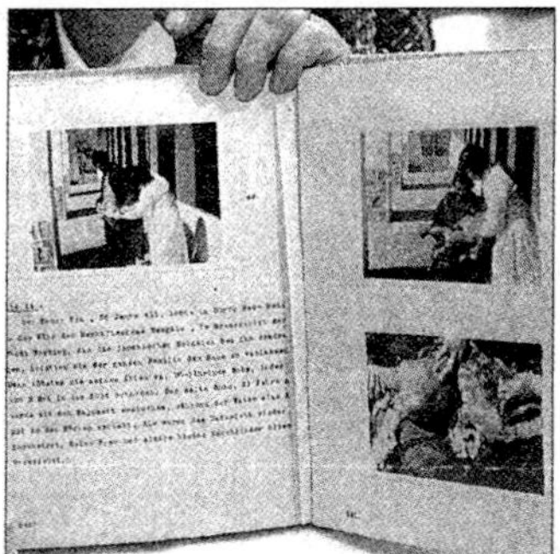

Associated Press

Ursula Reinhardt with her grandfather's diary last week.

these atrocities. One was powerless against these monsters. ... They had respect only for us foreigners, but nearly every one of us came close to being killed dozens of times. We asked each other, "How much longer can we maintain this bluff?"

•

Still, he wrote, he couldn't refuse people's pleas to intervene on their behalf:

On the way to the zone's command center, my car would regularly be stopped by someone in the way who begged me desperately to protect either their wife, sister or daughter from being raped by Japanese soldiers. I then had to go, accompanied by a group of Chinese, to the place where the rape was occurring and chase away the Japanese, many of whom were caught in the act. I don't need to tell you that these incidents were quite dangerous. The Japanese had pistols and bayonets and I ... had only party symbols and my swastika armband. One had to overcome the lack of weapons with a domineering presence and energy, which normally helped.

On New Year's Day, 1938, he recounted this incident:

The mother of an attractive young girl called out to me and, throwing herself on her knees, crying, said I should help her. Upon entering the house, I saw a Japanese soldier lying completely naked on a young girl, who was crying hysterically. I yelled at this swine, in any language it would be understood, "Happy New Year!" and he fled from there, naked and with his pants in his hand.

Soon Mr. Rabe and the other foreigners who formed the committee overseeing the safety zone devoted themselves to documenting the atrocities with photographs and accompanying descriptions, like this one written by Mr. Rabe:

A Japanese soldier demanded cigarettes from [this] employee of an enameled-goods shop. Because he didn't have

New York Times articles on the discovery of John Rabe's diary, December 12, 1996.

said they had no information concerning his whereabouts after 1938. However, the file revealed that between 1900 and 1903, Rabe had worked as an apprentice to a merchant in Hamburg, and Iris tried to pick up his trail there. Because of this information, Iris thought he might have had some ties to the city of Hamburg.

Iris told us she planned to put an advertisement looking for him in the Hamburg newspapers. In the meantime, Iris turned to John Taylor, the archivist in the National Archives in Washington who had helped Iris a great deal when she was doing research there on Dr. Tsien and *The Rape of Nanking*. He was well connected and seemed to know every historian in the world. Taylor suggested that Iris contact a German history expert in California; from there she was directed to a German lady who knew the history of Hamburg in great depth. On April 26, 1996, this kind lady wrote to Iris that she was able to locate John Rabe's granddaughter, Ursula Reinhardt. All of these details on how Iris tracked down Rabe's descendants were recorded in chapter 9, "The Fate of the Survivors," in Iris's Nanking book.

Iris shared every move and every discovery in her research with us. Each time there was big news to share, she would call us immediately, even in the middle of the night. After Iris found Ursula Reinhardt, she corresponded with her constantly. Iris and Ursula exchanged letters that ran for tens of pages. One day in May, Iris called us in excitement and said that Ursula had told her that Rabe had kept a diary about his time during the Nanking Massacre! According to Iris, Ursula was Rabe's favorite granddaughter. Her mother, Rabe's daughter, had given Rabe's diary and other documents to Ursula after Rabe died. Ursula had carefully saved her grandfather's papers, diaries, and photographs, including invaluable documentation about the Rape of Nanking. Ursula was very generous; in her letters to Iris, she translated several of the last entries in the diary into English. Ursula could speak English, and Iris had talked to her and interviewed her on the phone, sometimes as late as three in the morning (California time). Iris even mailed us a copy of Ursula's letters to share her excitement!

We recognized how important and valuable the diary of John Rabe was, as well as the reports and documentations about him. Rabe's diary was one of the most powerful testimonies that could refute the Japanese rightwing politicians' denial of the Rape of Nanking. Iris and I had many discussions on how and what to do with the diary. Iris's book would be out in November 1997, but that was still a year and half away. We all agreed that the announcement of the discovery of Rabe's diary and his story should coincide with the publication of her book as closely as possible. However, my instinct told me that we might not be able to hold the news that long. It was always a worry that the discovery would be leaked out. I was very much on the cautious side, and worried for Iris.

Iris brought back from libraries and archives a tremendous amount of material on the Rape of Nanking. One time Iris commented to us that when she was writing *Thread of the Silkworm*, she wished she had more information on Dr. Tsien; whereas for *The Rape of Nanking*, she felt like she was overwhelmed by the amount of material. Too much information was just as problematic as too little, she said. She had American missionaries' letters and diaries, American intelligence reports during the war, IMTFE records, Chinese eyewitness testimonials, Japanese soldiers' confessions, and so forth. In addition, she had documentation and books on the subject in Chinese, Japanese, and German. She also had personal recordings of her own interviews with survivors in Nanjing.

During this period, Iris worked at night so she could concentrate on writing without interruption. Brett was working during the day, from nine to five, whereas Iris would get up around noon and run errands in the afternoon before sitting down to work until Brett came home. After dinner, she would take a long walk with Brett, and then she would go write when Brett went to bed. It was a lonely schedule. Sometimes she would write until four or five in the morning and call us before she went to bed. Because Illinois time was two hours ahead of California time, when she called at 5 A.M. her time, we were already up. Sometimes she called us when we were about to go to bed at mid-night, while she was at the peak of her writing.

We always welcomed her calls and listened to her, no matter what the hour. That was also why she would pour upon us many of the inner emotions that she couldn't find time to tell Brett. Besides, Brett was very busy with his own work, and Iris said that he was also getting worn out by all the gruesome stories of atrocities she described to him, one after another. There was a cultural difference, too; Iris found that we could understand her emotional anguish more because we had common Chinese roots and the tragedy hit closer to home.

Iris told us that the most difficult thing was to read one case after another of the atrocities Japanese soldiers had committed in Nanking in 1937–1938. The Japanese soldiers carried out the rapes, tortures, and executions of innocent women and men with unspeakable cruelty. She read hundreds of such cases. She felt numb after a while. She told me she sometimes had to get up and away from the documents to take a deep breath. She felt suffocated and in pain.

One day in March 1996, she read a document that described a nine-year-old weeping girl being dragged screaming into bedrooms to be raped by Japanese soldiers. She felt a cold rage sweep through her. She could hardly contain her anger.

One night in April, she called and told me that she could not fall asleep lately. She had nightmares and had lost weight. Her hair fell out in clumps in the shower. I was alarmed and very worried when I heard that. As her mother, Iris's health was my prime concern. I asked her whether she really wanted to continue to write this book. She said "Yes, Mom. What I'm suffering right now is nothing compared to those victims who perished in the massacre." She added "As a writer, I want to rescue those victims from oblivion, to give a voice to the voiceless."

I was really moved by her determination and tenacity, but on the other hand I was worried about her physical and mental health being affected by the content of the massacre. I reminded her that she should take more breaks from her writing to refresh herself. I also advised her that she should try to finish the book as quickly as possible so she could move on to other things. The deadline for handing in her first draft was in January 1997, but she said she would hand it in earlier than that.

On May 25, 1996, when Iris and I met in New York at my mother's apartment, Iris conducted a thorough interview with Po-Po, her grandma. Iris asked her grandma about the details of the story about how she and Iris's grandpa were almost separated during the war in November 1937. Although we had told Iris the story many times, this time she took down all the details in her notebook. She also interviewed my sister Ling-Ling about the horror of the Japanese bombing and her memories of the war. My mother was surprised and commented that she had not met a single young Chinese-American who was so interested in the history of the Sino-Japanese War. She was very impressed indeed.

Iris had corresponded with Ursula Reinhardt continuously and learned the whole story of Ursula's grandfather John Rabe. The diary of John Rabe was extremely valuable, and we worried about its safety. We discussed this with Iris for a long time and decided that the best and safest way, before anything could happen, was to ask Reinhardt to donate a copy of the diary to the Yale University Divinity School library as quickly as possible and let the world know about it. Maybe we were being overcautious, but we wanted to rule out any chance that the diary could be stolen or destroyed. On September 23, Reinhardt finally agreed to donate it. We also reminded Iris that she should ask Reinhardt to donate a copy to the Memorial Hall for the Victims of Japanese Invaders in Nanjing, China.

Iris and Ursula had corresponded with each other through numerous letters and also through telephone conversations, but Iris had never had a chance to go to Germany to meet her. Later, in the summer of 1999, Iris was invited to Switzerland for a conference, but she did not have the time to make a side trip to Germany to visit Ursula. She told me later that was one of her biggest regrets.

Iris spend the last week of September 1996 writing a 3,000-word article about how she had tracked down John Rabe and found his granddaughter Ursula Reinhardt, who possessed his diary recording the Nanking Massacre. She also wrote a short press release about the discovery. She mailed a copy of the article and the press release to us for our comments. When Shau-Jin and I read the article, we were greatly impressed by Rabe's life story. Besides Iris and the family of John Rabe, we were the first in the world to learn of his story. In the article, Iris included the last few entries of Rabe's diary, about his hardship in postwar Berlin in 1946 (translated by Reinhardt). Rabe had written:

April 18, 1946 . . . We suffer hunger and hunger again—I had nothing to tell, so I didn't write down anything. In addition to our meager meal we ate acorn flour soup. Mummy (his wife) collected the acorns secretly in autumn. Now as the provisions come to an end, day after day we ate stinging nettle; the young leaves taste like spinach.

Shau-Jin wrote to Iris that he had cried when he read the article. In reply, Iris wrote on September 27, 1996:

Dear Dad,

Thanks for scrutinizing the story so carefully. . . . I still need to read it over a few times before sending it anywhere.

Your reaction to Rabe's diary touched me deeply. I have to admit tears came to my eyes, too, when I read the excerpts that Ursula Reinhardt sent me. For a moment, I wanted to put in my article the fact that while poor Rabe was starving to death in his tiny apartment, bewildered and afraid, many of the perpetrators of the Nanking massacre lived on, rich and comfortable, to the end of their days. For instance, Prince Asaka, Hirohito's uncle whose headquarters was responsible for sending out the order KILL ALL CAPTIVES before the Nanking massacre, retired in glory and spent the rest of his life playing golf. And some of the Japanese war criminals who were executed after the IMFTE have been enshrined in Tokyo.

Love, Iris

As soon as Iris finished the final draft of the Rabe article, she mailed a copy to all major newspapers such as the *New York Times, Washington Post, Chicago Tribune,* and *LA Times.* On September 26, Ignatius Ding, of the Global Alliance for Preserving the History of World War II in Asia, posted Iris's article on the Internet with the title "Rabe's Records of 'The Rape of Nanking' Discovered." We were holding our breath and waiting to see the reaction of the world.

The first person who picked up the news of John Rabe was Shao Tzeping, the activist in the Chinese-American community who had generously allowed Iris to stay in his house in Rye when Iris was doing research at Yale in early 1995. He called Iris on October 9 and talked to her excitedly for three hours. He later told Iris he had been very worried about the possibility that the Japanese right-wingers might destroy the diary, and he was on a mission to bring the diary to U.S. as soon as possible.

On October 14, the U.S. bureau of *Asahi Shimbun,* one of the biggest newspapers in Japan, contacted Iris and interviewed her about the discovery of John Rabe's diary. In a letter to me, Iris described the interview:

> *Dear Mom,*
>
> *Don't worry, I already had my meeting with the reporters at 1 pm, which went well. One was Japanese; the German interpreter was American. They are going to send me a copy of the English-language translation of the report when it is finished.*
>
> *We talked in the City Hall building. . . . The Japanese reporter took numerous pictures of me both inside City Hall and in the Rape of Nanking photo display room. The reporter asked me a lot of questions about Rabe and my book. He was keenly interested in knowing more about the total number of deaths in Nanking. He claimed that the topic is very controversial in Japan and the right-wingers claim only 30,000 people died and that the PRC has been accused of spreading all kinds of anti-Japanese propaganda on this issue. I cited plenty of studies that show that*

the death count exceeded 260,000—possibly 300,000 or even 370,000.
I also asserted my opinion that, if anything, the PRC has been too lax in
publicizing this event for fear of injuring diplomatic relations with Japan.
They gave up their right to seek national reparations from Japan for the
incident (even though international law stipulates that individual vic-
tims still have the right to demand reparations).

He said he had to be careful about getting the facts right because after
this article comes out, the right-wing people will do everything they can
to criticize and discredit him.

Love, Iris

Iris told us later that *Asahi Shimbun* held on to the news for a long time,
two months, as it hesitated over whether it should be published or not.
Finally, it was published on December 8, a few days before the *New York
Times* article. The *Asahi*'s German translator, Jeff Heynen, translated the
German report into English and gave Iris a copy, which was later used
by the *New York Times* in their article on December 12.

On October 15, Iris was interviewed by a reporter from the *San Jose
Mercury News*, the biggest English newspaper in the South Bay area. On
November 3, a big article on Iris and her discovery of Rabe's diary was
featured in the *Mercury News*. Iris mailed us a copy of the article, which
was accompanied by three photos: one was a side view of Iris standing
and looking at the photos hanging on the wall of the photo exhibition,
one was a photo of John Rabe, and lastly there was a photo of Iris next
to a photo of a woman with an expression of unspeakable agony. With
the publication of this article, Iris was instantly known in the Bay area
and became famous in the Chinese-American community.

On November 10, 1996, Iris wrote to me:

Dear Mom,

Here is the latest exciting news. . . .

I shall be the master of ceremonies for what I believe will be the
biggest Rape of Nanking conference ever. The event will take place at

Stanford University during the first weekend of December. Hundreds of people from more than 50 activist organizations all over the globe will be there—as well as representatives from all the major news organizations of California, China and Japan. The goal of the three-day affair is to discuss legal strategy. How can we seek reparations for victims through international law and UN resolutions? How can we gather evidence of atrocities for lawsuits? What methods should we use to force the Japanese to accept responsibility for its [sic] past misdeeds?

The turnout for this conference will be twice as large as the one I attended in December 1994. So many scholars and international lawyers and survivors plan to attend that Ignatius Ding had to turn down requests from prominent academics to present papers on subjects unrelated to the main theme of the event.

Therefore, I was truly surprised, but honored, when Ignatius called me last week and asked me to kick off the opening ceremony as the keynote speaker and MC.

This evening I talked about my book and John Rabe before a packed audience in the Mountain View City Council Chambers (Ignatius Ding had invited me and another person to speak on the subject). Virtually every seat was taken, and some people stood near the door or against the wall. Afterwards, I was literally BESIEGED. A crowd of reporters, activists, World War II veteran types, and interested readers, both Asian and Caucasian, swarmed about me, offering congratulations and asking a million questions (while rifling through my lecture notes). I think I got the lion's share of the attention because my English was better than that of the other speakers. Everyone wanted me to lecture at his particular organization/school/college. Parents insisted on taking photographs of me with their children (one introduced me as "a famous author" to a daughter who aspired to be a writer because she had won the local "Young Authors" competition at her school). Some people wanted me to autograph the article that appeared in the San Jose Mercury News.

And . . . here's more good news:

A big TV network is interviewing members of the Chinese activist community next weekend, and I've been invited (once again by Ignatius Ding) to speak on the Rape of Nanking.

Basic Books told me that Thread of the Silkworm *was one of the bestselling books on their list. Also, it was one of the few books they published that received frequent and consistently good reviews.*

More later. . . . Love, Iris

In the meantime, the activist group, Global Alliance for Preserving the History of World War II in Asia, was going to put an ad in the *New York Times* and asked Iris to write up a short summary about her book on the Rape of Nanking and on Rabe's diary. This summary would be included in the ad.

On November 17, 1996, Iris wrote me in an e-mail: "A 600-word article of mine about the Rape of Nanking, complete with byline and description of my book, will be published in a giant *New York Times* advertisement sponsored by Chinese activists nationwide. It may appear anytime next week, but probably next Sunday. Susan Rabiner is thrilled about all this publicity and said that Basic Books hopes my book will become a blockbuster (by their standards, of course), selling 25,000 to 75,000 or even 100,000 copies."

On the first weekend of December 1996, Iris attended the conference on the Rape of Nanking as the MC, sponsored by Chinese-American activist groups on the Stanford University campus. She said it was a great experience for her, since she had never had the chance to speak in front of several hundred people before. She said in her e-mail, written at midnight on Saturday, December 7, 1996:

. . . the conference is going well, and everyone is impressed by my duties as MC—more details later. I'm exhausted by the entire event, as well as by giving interviews to the media. The New York Times *is going to run a long story about my discovery of the Rabe diaries on 12-12-96, the* Asahi Shimbun's *story should appear on 12-8-96, and the* Metro *is*

almost certain to print a cover story on me. I've been mentioned in the World Journal already, and the Christian Science Monitor *is probably going to quote me in their story on the conference. Tomorrow I will be interviewed by a Japanese TV station at Stanford.*

Indeed, as Iris said, a big article on her was published in *Metro*, a free Santa Clara Valley weekly newspaper, on December 12. We were delighted to see that Iris's face was on the front cover of the newspaper. The article must have made a big impact on the readers in Silicon Valley, as the buzz about *Nanking* continued to grow.

A press conference was held in New York on December 12, organized by Shao Tzeping, because December 12, 1996 was the day before the fifty-ninth anniversary of the fall of Nanking and, subsequently, the beginning of the massacre. After Shao talked to Iris, he contacted Ursula Reinhardt in Germany and invited her to New York to formally announce and introduce her grandfather's diary to the world.

When we saw the big article published on December 12 in the *New York Times*, I wondered why Iris was not going to New York for such an important press conference. I immediately called her, but she said that long before the event she had already reserved a plane ticket and paid the fee for a scriptwriting class in Los Angeles and was scheduled to fly there that weekend. She did not want to change her plans at the last minute.

Fortunately, before December 12, the reporter from the *New York Times*, David Chen, got hold of Iris and interviewed her extensively on the phone. The article on Rabe's diary and his life story occupied half of the International page, with a headline that read "At the Rape of Nanking, A Nazi Who Saved Lives." The subtitle was "The 1937 diary of an unlikely hero bears witness to Japanese atrocities." With the article, there was a photo of John Rabe and a number of Safety Zone members standing in front their office in the Safety Zone in 1937. The article mentioned Iris: "The diary has only now come to light because of the efforts of Iris Chang, a Sunnyvale, Calif., author. While researching a book on the Nanjing massacre a few years ago, she stumbled upon a few references to Mr. Rabe's humanitarian efforts." At the end, the article quoted Iris: ". . . to me, John Rabe is the Oskar Schindler of China, another example of good in the face of evil."

During the press conference on December 12, Reinhardt donated a copy of John Rabe's diary to the Yale University library. The event was reported not only by the *New York Times*, but by almost all major newspapers and TV and radio stations throughout the world. It was major international news. Shau-Jin was in Taiwan for a meeting, and he brought home all the Chinese newspapers in which the news of discovery of Rabe's diary was prominently reported.

Iris did not realize that the news would be so hot internationally, and now she had some regrets that she had missed the New York press conference. On the other hand, she was very interested in learning scriptwriting at the time, and it was difficult for her to give up the opportunity—especially because she had already paid for the class. Iris said the publicity department of Basic Books wished the announcement of the discovery of Rabe's diary could have been held off until October of the next year, just before her book hit bookstores—that would have been ideal. But we knew the discovery could not wait that long. Iris said both Susan Rabiner and the publicist were thrilled by the *New York Times* article and said that the publicity would still help her forthcoming book tremendously.

After the copy of John Rabe's diary was donated to Yale, Iris had asked Yale to make a copy of the diary for her; in turn, she made two more copies. On March 11, 1997, we received a box of several thousand pages of a Xerox copy of John Rabe's diary from Iris. She was worried the diary would be destroyed by some unforeseen cause in the future. An extra copy stored in a different place would be safer, she said. The copy of Rabe's diary was stored in our basement for more than five years, until 2002, when we moved to California. We donated that copy to the University of Illinois Archives in the summer of 2002, with Iris's permission.

Another copy of the diary was donated to the Memorial Hall for the Victims in Nanjing. As early as October 1995, after Iris returned home from her research trip to China and Taiwan, she made a huge effort to make copies of many important materials she had found in the U.S. National Archives and the Yale University library and donated them to the Memorial Hall for the Victims in Nanjing. Those materials included John Rabe's report to Hitler, the diaries and letters of Minnie Vautrin and other missionaries in the Safety Zone, and the records of the International Military Tribunal of the Far East (IMTFE). Iris did this voluntarily when she found out that the Memorial Hall in Nanjing lacked Western source materials. She spent many hours of her time and a good amount of money copying those materials, consisting of thousands of pages, for them. Iris felt that it would be a shame if the museum in Nanjing, where the massacre had occurred, did not have those documents. I thought it was a very generous act. I was impressed that she was willing to share her findings and make the information available to other scholars and researchers, when her book had not yet even been published. She was more concerned with sharing knowledge.

The world now knew that Iris was writing a book on the Rape of Nanking and that it would be published in November 1997, and the pressure was beginning to mount.

13

Overcoming Obstacles

The publication of *The Rape of Nanking* ran over several bumps in the road along the way. On October 25, 1996, Iris told us that she had finished the first rough draft of the book and would mail a copy to us for our comments. She added that there were still two chapters to go on the topic of "cover-up" (later called "The Second Rape") and the "Fate of the Survivors." In her e-mail of November 13, 1996, Iris wrote:

> *Dear Mom,*
>
> *Thanks for the email! Susan Rabiner is overwhelmed with work right now, but she said she will read my manuscript soon. Let me know what you think of my writing—please don't hesitate to write in the margins and take notes and to relay your honest opinions to me. I respect your judgment.*
>
> *Sometimes, when I reread my book, I wondered if I should have inserted more scenes (stories of individuals) into the text. There is still*

time to include those stories, because I have a surplus of information. I'll
wait until Susan gets back to me.

   Love, Iris

I was very busy at the time because the whole Department of Microbiology was in the process of moving into a brand-new building. It took about two weeks in November to set up my workplace in the new lab before Thanksgiving.

It took us a few weeks to read her 140-page, single-spaced first draft. Both Shau-Jin and I gave up our nights and weekends to read her manuscript. Our first reaction to the manuscript was disappointment. We told Iris that some parts of the writing gave too many details, whereas some other parts were oversimplified. Also, we told her that quite frankly, the story was told with a lack of emotion. Iris listened and said she would wait to see what Susan Rabiner said.

Susan did not have the time to read the draft until a month later. Finally, Iris called us and said that Susan was disappointed with the first draft too, and her comments were similar to ours. Iris asked us if she could have somehow lost the ability to write. We tried to lift her spirits by assuring her that she could revise it—that was what drafts were for. Shau-Jin and I also pointed out that there were some parts of the draft that were excellent; it wasn't *all* bad, by any means. We gave her all the assurances we could and reminded her to look at the specific questions and remarks we had written on each page. Susan also gave Iris many suggestions in the next few months to improve the manuscript. Iris felt that the root of her problem was that she had so much source material that the actual narrative was getting lost. She read every instance of atrocities and felt numb in the end, and it came through stylistically. When an author loses his or her mental sensitivity, it is not possible to write with the proper emotion.

In retrospect, unlike the time when she was writing her first book, *Thread of the Silkworm*, she was doing more than one thing in 1996. That year, Iris was writing not only *The Rape of Nanking*, but she was also writing a proposal for her next book and trying to help the *Thread of the Silkworm* backlist. She was under stress to accomplish many things, and part of the pressure was from herself. Another reason was that *The Rape of Nanking* had a deadline: it had to be finished in two years. Iris and the publisher wanted the book to be published on the eve of the sixtieth anniversary of the Nanking Massacre to attract world attention, which was the best marketing strategy.

At any rate, I knew few scholars who could digest so much information in such a short time; besides, the story was so sad and depressing that it took an emotional toll on her as well. I could see why the first draft of the book was somewhat disappointing.

Neither Iris or Michael were coming home for Christmas 1996 and New Year's Day 1997, and we planned to visit them after the New Year. During the holidays, I translated a number of Chinese articles into English for Iris because she wanted to know what the Chinese media reports said about John Rabe. It took me the entire day before Christmas to translate all of them. I mailed the translations to her that evening with the note, "My God! It took my whole day, Iris, you sure are right; it's expensive to hire someone to translate. You get it free!"

She replied to me:

> Dear Mom,
>
> You were a saint to translate the articles for me. Yes, I know, translation is time-consuming and expensive—this is why Jeff Heynen's and Barbara Masin's free translations are so invaluable! I'm really touched that you spent the day helping in this manner. . . . Love, Iris

Shau-Jin and I flew to California on January 3, 1997 to see Iris, Brett, and Michael. January 7 was Shau-Jin's sixtieth birthday. It was considered an important milestone for a person to reach sixty, and deserved a special celebration in Chinese culture. Iris had urged us to come to California to celebrate—and, at the same time, she said that we could visit her and Brett's new apartment in Sunnyvale and Michael's in San Francisco. We had not had a chance to visit them since they moved from Santa Barbara to the Bay area in the middle of 1996. And there was another important reason for the visit—to help Iris translate some more Chinese materials for the second draft of the book.

Iris and Brett's apartment was one of the units of an apartment complex centrally located in Silicon Valley. As they had described, the apartment complex had a swimming pool and other sports and physical fitness facilities on-site. Their unit was a two-bedroom. My first impression of their rooms was that there were very many book-cases lined along almost all the walls of their small apartment. The bookcases were essentially filled with Iris's book collections. I was not surprised, because I was totally familiar with Iris's beloved hobby of reading and buying books. In addition to a bedroom, a living room, and a kitchen, they had a small room that served as her office, which had a big desk that was equipped with a computer, a printer, a fax machine, and more books and notebooks. Wasting little time, she showed us the Chinese documents she wanted us to translate. She said she was working on revising the Nanking book according to Susan's and our suggestions and had no time to waste, as she was currently working on the section that told the Chinese side of the story during the Massacre. She wanted to find out why the Chinese capital, Nanking, had fallen to the enemy so quickly on December 13, 1937. The materials she had collected from the Chinese Archives included the telegram exchanges between Chiang Kai-shek and Commander-in-Chief Tang Sheng-chih, who had defended Nanking in the last hours of the battle. She wanted to know the content of the telegrams and needed to find some clues. To translate Chinese docu-ments into English usually was not too difficult for us, but telegrams were a different story.

In China in the 1930s, the telegram industry usually used only minimal necessary words to save time and money encoding and decoding each Chinese character during the transmittal process. For this reason, at that period of time in the telegraphy field, there was a group of Chinese characters, each of which was used to represent a certain defined meaning, such as the hour and the date at which the telegram was sent. If people did not know this convention, then it would be almost impossible to understand a telegram. This convention was abandoned after the war with the new developments in telegraphy technology.

When I first read the telegram exchanges between Chiang and Tang, I had difficulty understanding them fully. Fortunately, Shau-Jin had learned this convention in grade school, so he and I together were able to translate the desperate telegrams that Tang had sent to Chiang Kai-shek on December 9 and 11, describing the severe damage to the gate of the wall surrounding Nanking by the brutal attacks of the Japanese military. We read how Chiang Kai-shek ordered Tang to retreat at the last minute, even though Chiang had asked Tang to defend the city to the end in the beginning of November. The telegrams are brief but hold tremendous historical meaning.

Shau-Jin and I sat on the futon in Iris's small apartment in Sunnyvale and dictated our translations to Iris, who was writing them down on her notepad. She also showed us the collection of photos she intended to include in the book. I had difficulty looking at the gruesome photos of the massacre that she laid down on her bed to show us. I also remember that I had reminded her that she should check the source of each of the photos carefully. She said that all the photos were from archives and that most of them had previously been published in the news media.

Our visit to Iris and Michael in California was short but was memorable, with the sixtieth birthday party for Shau-Jin proving to be a fun and festive occasion. Iris, Brett, and Michael surprised Shau-Jin with a big ice-cream birthday cake at the end of the dinner, and it was great for all of us to be together.

Iris was continuously revising her manuscript, and on January 22 she wrote to me:

Dear Mom:

Thank you for your inspirational email. I've been working on my book all week and feel more confident about my material. . . .

The sections [of the book] are so short that I organized each chapter as I would a speech. . . . Thinking of the chapters as speeches forces me to distill each idea into a tiny, hard gem.

Lately, I've been reading many of the world's classic speeches for inspiration. They are breathtaking in their power—and so much more pungent than prose! In the evenings, when I read the speeches of Napoleon or Clarence Darrow or Winston Churchill, I feel engaged in actual conversation with them. Words are the only way to preserve the essence of a soul. What excites me about speeches is that even after the speakers are dead and buried, their spirit lives on. This, to me, is true religion—the best form of life after death. (And, for now, probably the ONLY form of life after death.) This is the first time I have ever devoted much attention to speeches. My previous reading had consisted mainly of essays, plays, novels and poetry.

. . .

Love, Iris

On February 20, Iris wrote to me that she had finished the revision of the main section of the book and was going to spend the rest of the month working on the introduction and the section about the cover-up. We received the revised manuscript that Iris sent us for our comments. She had improved it tremendously, and we told her so.

In March, Iris finished the Introduction. It took another month for her to finish the chapter about the cover-up. In every revision, she would send us a copy via e-mail or U.S. Mail for our comments. In the end, we received no fewer than four or five different versions of the manuscript before she and Susan settled on the final version. The manuscript printouts were bad because of her old over-used printer: the letters "a" and "o" were totally black. Also, at the margins of the manuscript, the ink was so dark that sometimes we couldn't read words discernibly. She needed a new printer, but she didn't have the time, and maybe the money, to buy a new one—it was a hard life for an independent writer under the pressure of time and financial strain.

Finally, in May, Iris mailed the whole revised manuscript to us. After I read her Introduction, I was moved by her passion, something that had been missing from the original draft. She genuinely wanted to be the voice for the victims, and now it was coming through in print. As Iris had told us, we found that Susan had edited her Introduction and other sections of the book brilliantly. In reading the "Second Rape" chapter, I clearly saw the Japanese right-wing groups' ongoing attempts to hide the truth of the massacre from the Japanese people and the world. Although I was applauding Iris's efforts and courage to disclose the cover-up, I was also very worried about her safety. This worry was not without basis. We had long learned from Chinese history that the Japanese imperial government had used intimidation and violent methods such as assassination during the war to eliminate many Chinese leaders in the Japanese struggle to conquer China. I told Iris those stories and asked her to be careful. She assured me that she would be all right and that there was no way she could omit the chapter on the cover-up from her book. But I knew that after publication of the book, she would be a thorn in the side of the Japanese right-wing groups.

In April, my mother's health had further deteriorated. Shau-Jin and I planned to visit her around Mother's Day. When Iris heard about her grandma's poor health and our plan to go to New York, she immediately made a plane reservation to join us there.

Iris was very considerate and mailed me a beautiful Mother's Day card before she left for New York. The card was purple with a beautiful iris flower, a thoughtful tribute to her namesake. Inside, she wrote:

> *Mom—I'm really touched by all the work you have put into* The Rape
> of Nanking—*the proofreading, the translation, the countless hours of*
> *invaluable discussions. You're the kind of mother most authors can only*

*dream of having—wise, passionate, endlessly supportive, inspirational. I
love you more than I can say. Iris.*

My eyes started to well up with tears. Those words really touched my
heart!

On May 9 we arrived in New York, and the next day we all went to
see grandma. We were appalled to see that Po-Po, always so feisty and
full of life, had shrunk to a skeleton. It was hard for me to see her in
such a condition. On Mother's Day, we gathered around her hospital
bed with flowers decorating the room. That was the last Mother's Day
I was with her.

Iris stayed in New York several more days to see Susan Rabiner and
other people at Basic Books. After we retuned home, Iris told us what
had happened at Basic. Apparently, big changes were in progress. Basic
would be taken over by Perseus Books Group, and the whole house
was being restructured. Most of the people who currently worked there
would be let go, including Susan. Iris was very surprised—and scared.
She wondered whether her book might be cancelled. Susan assured her
that her book would be published, but told her that she should finish
it as soon as possible. Iris said the entire Basic Books office looked
like a funeral home. People looked grave and were whispering in low
voices. Susan told Iris she was leaving at the end of June; after that,
Iris would have a new editor.

As I heard this bad news, I was worried for Iris. Besides the fact that
she and Susan had such a wonderful working relationship, if Perseus
Books decided that they did not want to publish the book after all,
then Iris would have wasted at least two years of her precious time and
the story of Nanking would still remain untold.

Twelve days after we came home from New York, on May 23,
Shau-Jin and I flew to Los Angeles to attend Shau-Jin's nephew Eric's
wedding. At the end of the wedding ceremony on May 24, when we
returned to our hotel room, we received very bad news from my brother
in the form of a telephone message saying that my mother had passed

away that evening at 7:40 P.M., New York time. At that moment, Iris and Michael were in the room. The four of us immediately discussed what to do. Shau-Jin and I decided to go back to Urbana immediately, regroup, and then go to New York for the funeral. I spent a lot of time on the phone canceling the old itinerary and making a new one, but perhaps keeping so busy helped distract me from my grief. On May 30, all my sisters and brothers, their spouses and their children, and Shau-Jin, Iris, and Michael were at the funeral home in New York to say good-bye to Po-Po. She was eighty-three years old.

Although I knew my mother was going to die one day, especially since she had been sick for so long, I was still devastated when her death eventually came. She had fought breast cancer for eighteen years, going through various types of treatments and suffering. Her spirit, the way she never gave up hope and never stopped her fight to live, was an inspiration to me.

When I returned to the lab to work after my mother's funeral, I could not overcome my sadness over her death. I kept thinking about how many things I could have done for my mother while she was alive. A sense of guilt and regret overwhelmed me. I blamed myself—why had I never quit my job for a while to be with her in her final days? How selfish I was! My mother had sacrificed so much for me and our family, but I could not give up a few months of my job to be with her. I couldn't sleep at night thinking about all the things I could have done for her. The strangest thing was that I was not able to shed any tears like I had when I'd been on the airplane to my father's funeral. It was a deeper hurt this time. My face must have been distorted by my sadness. The unusual silence I exhibited in the lab caused John Cronan's concern. One day he patted me on my back and said softly, "I know how sad you are for your loss, but death is inevitable at the end of life's journey." Then the tears *really* gushed out from my eyes.

Iris also knew how sad I was, and she sent an e-mail and asked: "How are you feeling these days? I hope you haven't been too depressed over Grandma's death. I know you were very close to her (like I am to you), and the death of a mother is always worse than the death of a grandma." She continued: "We were fortunate to have her as long as we did. When I was in grad school, most of my classmates had already attended at least one of their grandmothers' funerals."

It was kind of her to be so in tune with my grief, as Iris faced her own crisis now that Basic Books was gone. Because of the sudden change staff of Basic Books, Iris was working extremely hard to finish the book as soon as possible. On June 6, she wrote:

> Dear Mom,
>
> You have no idea how hard I've been working since I've returned! Earlier this week I stayed up 30 hours straight (I was so intensely focused I couldn't fall asleep). I hope to be finished by this weekend. . . . Every minute of this week has been devoted to the book (copyright issues, captions, photo layout, Susan's comments, etc.) but I'm thrilled to say that everything is coming together rapidly. Thanks to you, I've been able to secure most of the names in Chinese characters. People have also been faxing me their cards with Chinese names all week, and now I seem to have everything I need in Chinese. . . .
>
> Love, Iris

The Commonwealth Publishing Group in Taiwan, the same publisher that had translated Iris's first book, *Thread of the Silkworm*, obtained the translation rights to *The Rape of Nanking* and intended to publish a Chinese version of the book in 1997, at the same time it was published in America. That was why Iris had asked me to fax her the Chinese characters of the names of the people and places that appeared in her book.

On June 16, 1997, Iris wrote to me:

> Dear Mom,
>
> Happy birthday! I've been so absorbed in my work I almost forgot . . . I'll definitely call you tonight, after your celebration with Dad.

Today, I've been trying to find all the names and addresses of all my blurb contacts. Last night I talked with Dale Maharidge, who said he would be delighted to give me a blurb. He was shocked to hear the news about Susan [Rabiner, leaving Basic], and told me more depressing news:

Two famous writers—Anthony Lukas (author of Common Ground*) and Michael Dorris, husband of the novelist Louise Erdrich (her sister Heidi was in my class at Hopkins) both committed suicide recently. Lukas killed himself because he just finished a book and thought it was terrible (his editor, however, exclaimed it was fantastic) and Dorris did it because his marriage was breaking up and his wife had accused him of molesting one of his daughters (a charge he denied in his suicide note).*

Compared to most writers, Dale and I are relatively well-grounded. . . .

Love, Iris

Iris always thought suicide was horrible and incomprehensible.

Iris told us that her new editor, Paul Golob, had informed her that her book's publication date had been pushed back to November 7. I reminded Iris that the book must be published on or before December 13, the sixtieth anniversary of the massacre, to maximize the publicity of the book, and she should not let Basic push the date back any further. Iris also said that the cover had been redesigned and Golob thought it looked much better now and would fax it to her. Iris promised to send a copy to us as soon as she got it, because back in April, she'd said that she was very disappointed with the original book cover design, and it had stimulated many discussions among us and her activist friends. Many of her friends had volunteered to design her book cover or at least offer up new ideas that Iris could relay on to Basic.

On June 25, we received a photocopy of the new cover, and it was much more in line with what everyone thought best fit the book: the background was a photo of bodies from the massacre littered at the bank of the Yangtze River. A big Japanese flag and a Japanese imperial soldier were at the front. We felt the design was the best among all the possible ones we had seen so far. I told Iris that it was very conspicuous and attracted attention. The cover really captured the essence and passion of the subject matter because, when it was displayed in bookstores months later, the bloody crimson and the Japanese flag stood out on the shelf and outshone all the books around it.

Several days later, a thick copy of the final version of the manuscript arrived. I had lost count of how many versions she had sent to us for our comments. Shau-Jin and I used our July 4 holiday weekend to read it carefully and gave her a list of any errors we spotted plus our questions, but at this stage most were just typos. I wrote her: "I love the final version and no doubt this is much better than the first or the second version. I like the Introduction and the Epilogue the best. You summarize it very well; very strong and eloquent. I wonder what the other people think. Have you gotten any feedback from other reviewers yet?"

Indeed, she had. Iris had sent her final version of the manuscript to many of her friends and reviewers for comments and feedback. She told me that in April she had had a good conversation with history professor William Kirby of Harvard, who was impressed with the manuscript and agreed to write a foreword for the book. A number of well-known historians and writers to whom the manuscript was sent responded favorably, such as Richard Rhodes, Nien Cheng, Ross Terrill, and Frederic Wakeman. They all agreed to write blurbs for the book. Iris also told us she had met an Oxford historian, Rana Mitter, on a plane when she was returning to the U.S. in 1995, and Mitter was also happy to write a blurb for her. Among the writers she and Basic had contacted, Nien Cheng was particularly impressed by Iris's book. Nien Cheng, the author of the book *Life and Death in Shanghai*, told Iris that she was eighty-two years old and it gave her great joy to see a young, talented woman write such a book.

That summer, Iris was also looking for work on the side, and she was very pleasantly surprised that she was hired right on the spot when she was interviewed by the Lloyd-Ritter consulting firm. She told us that the interviewers had been very impressed by her résumé and her ability to answer their questions. She started a nine-to-five work schedule in their Sunnyvale office at the beginning of July. After several days working in an office, she complained that she was very tired, as she was essentially working two jobs: the office job, and the final phase of her book. She would get up 6 A.M. to call Basic Books for a number of things related to her book's publication such as footnotes, book jacket, and blurbs. Then, after eight hours in the office working and answering phones for the firm, she worked for hours proofreading and checking footnotes and so forth for the book. It was a chaotic time to be publishing a book for Basic, which essentially did not exist anymore. By July, her editor and almost all the assistants originally at Basic were gone, and Iris was doing many things related to the publication which usually would be done by the publisher.

She only worked for the consulting firm for a month and then resigned when she could not find time to get enough sleep. Luckily, the company head was very sympathetic and liked Iris very much and told Iris she could come back to work any time she wanted.

Another reason Iris was so busy was that she was aggressively planning a book tour to promote *The Rape of Nanking*. Many Chinese-American and Chinese-Canadian communities alongside major universities wanted her to give speeches. Basic Books could only afford to support Iris on a two-city book tour, one city on the East Coast and one on the West, so Iris took the lead and coordinated the whole tour by herself. She essentially depended on relatives, friends, and non-profit organizations in most of the cities she planned to visit by arranging to stay in their homes. The cost of transportation was partially supported by the organizations that invited her, but the planning and coordinating of the tour took much of her time during that period.

On July 7, 1997, the sixtieth anniversary of Japan's all-out invasion of China, Iris forwarded several articles to us that reported protesters demonstrating in Hong Kong and Taiwan in front of the Japanese embassy. They demanded a formal apology and war reparations from Japan. A statement released from the PRC also indicated that the Chinese government maintained a stronger stand on the issue than in previous years, warning against resurgent Japanese nationalism and militarism. Apparently, the rise of China as one of the world powers gave it some leeway to sort out its past issues, which it had never been able to do before while it was still struggling with internal political conflicts. This was excellent news for Iris's book, as China and its history were on many people's minds.

On November 3, 1997, Iris told us she had finally received two copies of the published *Rape of Nanking*. Her hands were shaking when she tore open the brown shipping box. She said she was looking at and flipping through the book for a long time, soaking it all in. I could not blame her for being so intoxicated and exhilarated!

One of the most exciting bits of news in 1997 was on July 28: Harper-Collins sold the first serial rights of *The Rape of Nanking* to *Newsweek* magazine, and an excerpt of the book would be published in their November 17 issue, which would coincide with the time the book hit the bookstores. *Newsweek* was a very popular magazine worldwide, and the excerpt would surely have a tremendous impact on the sale of the book. After we heard the news, we were exuberant. Besides, we have continuously subscribed to *Newsweek* since before Iris was born and had been loyal readers the whole time. Iris had worked as an intern at *Newsweek* back in the summer of 1988, so all of us had special feelings about the magazine.

Our waiting for the *Newsweek* issue carrying her book excerpt was just like waiting for a grandchild to be born. My anxiety got higher and higher as the date gradually approached.

While Iris was arranging the month-long itinerary of her book tour from November 14 to December 19, 1997, including multiple stops in the U.S. and Canada, she learned that the contract with *Newsweek* prevented her from disclosing the contents of her book until *Newsweek*'s excerpt was published. However, once the excerpt was published, she could speak out and discuss the book's contents at the first stop on her book tour on November 14 without any reservations.

Publishing the excerpt in *Newsweek* turned out to be quite dramatic, with many twists and turns. When *Newsweek* delayed publishing the excerpt, Iris sent us a day-to-day summary of the events as they unfolded. She asked us to keep the information in case she later needed written evidence to show how things had developed.

According to Iris, on July 28, 1997, a staffer at HarperCollins e-mailed Iris that she had sold first serial rights to *Newsweek*, and that the excerpt would be published in the November 17 issue (thus the magazine would be on newsstands or in bookstores on November 10 or 11).

On Thursday, November 6, 1997, an editor at *Newsweek* sent Iris a first draft of the excerpt and asked her for suggestions on how to include certain parts of the book. The editor also asked for permission to print certain photos.

On November 7, Friday morning, the editor e-mailed Iris the preliminary layout, with the captions, headline, and deck text. The headline read "Exposing the Rape of Nanking"; the subtitle was "Exclusive excerpts from a Chinese-American author's unflinching re-examination of one of the most horrifying chapters of the Second World War." Iris spent all day e-mailing versions of the text back and forth. Iris asked the editor if there was any chance that the excerpt would get bumped if tensions escalated between the U.S. and Iraq, which was a distinct possibility that week. She told her no, the schedule was set and it would take something *really* big to bump her story.

However, suddenly, that evening at 10:00 P.M., when Iris and Brett got back from a concert in San Jose, she had a phone message from *Newsweek* that had been left at 7:29 P.M.: "Iris, it's Tom Maslin at *Newsweek*. I'm sorry to tell you that we've had to hold the excerpt because the magazine has . . . shrunk by four pages, which is what we had for it. We'll be back in touch with you next week; if you want to speak to me further, please give me a call at. . . ."

The next morning, Iris called us and informed us of the delay. We were all stunned, to say the least. Iris told us Tom's voice in the phone message had sounded strained and uncomfortable.

Iris called *Newsweek* immediately and asked them why this had happened. They told her that four major ads had been pulled from the magazine at the last minute on Friday evening. They explained to Iris that *Newsweek* had to have a certain ratio of advertising pages to editorial pages, and that sometimes stories got cut because of lost advertising. They admitted that such incidents were rare and said that the staff had worked all evening to redesign the magazine because of the lost advertisements, but there was very little they could do.

Iris made a series of phone calls to *Newsweek*, and one of the senior staff told her that one of the major ads that had pulled out was a Toyota ad. But later he called back and said that the delay had nothing to do with the pull-out. I was not so convinced.

My analysis, as I told Iris over the phone, was that the news of Iris's book excerpt had leaked out and somebody was trying to stop it from being published.

I pointed out to Iris that the leak might have been an interview published in the November issue of the Johns Hopkins alumni magazine. The editor of the magazine, Sue DePasquale, had come to Sunnyvale that summer and met Iris in person for the interview. DePasquale had written an excellent and long article about Iris and her book. The article, *Nightmare in Nanking*, as published in the November issue occupied five full pages. Not only that, a photo of Iris with a bloodstained Japanese flag in the background was on the front cover of the magazine. Inside, the article was accompanied by several historic photos of the massacre with the title, subtitles, and captions prominently printed. In the article, Iris disclosed to DePasquale that *Newsweek* had promised that they would run a lengthy excerpt from the book in their November 17 issue.

The Johns Hopkins magazine was one of the first groups of magazines to be online at the time. One of the readers of the magazine wrote to DePasquale (who later shared this with me via Iris) and indicated that the article had instantly attracted many overseas alumni. One reader wrote:

> *Dear JHU Magazine,*
>
> *Kudos for putting the magazine online. It's great for the overseas JHU alumni who have to wait so long to get the paper editions. The article on the Rape of Nanking and Iris Chang was poignant, well-written, and informative. It was particularly interesting since I am now living in Japan and am all too aware of what Iris described, the Japanese unwillingness to confront the more unpleasant aspects of their history. I have taken the liberty of forwarding it to a number of my friends in Japan, both foreigner and Japanese, for discussion and to get the debate started. I hope this will be part of the process that Iris has begun. A small step, but an important one nonetheless.*

Newsweek's delay, I told Iris, might be due to pressure from Japan once they heard about the excerpt. I reminded Iris that the article in the Johns Hopkins magazine had circulated in Japan in the beginning of November.

Iris said that HarperCollins and *Newsweek* had a contract, and if *Newsweek* was not going to publish the excerpt, they needed to give her better answers. Iris had called a number of her friends in New York. All comforted her, assured her that her excerpt would certainly be published, and promised that they would make phone calls to find the reasons for the delay.

On the evening of November 10, we received our usual subscription copy of *Newsweek* and found that that week's issue was unusually thick and had exactly twice as many Japanese advertisements as a typical *Newsweek* issue. By this time, Shau-Jin and I had made a systematic analysis of the advertisements in the magazine. We and Iris all agreed that it was a good sign, because it meant that *Newsweek* had likely worked out a compromise with their advertisers to make sure that next week's Japanese ads had been transferred to this issue to avoid obliging those advertisers to sponsor an issue containing an excerpt of *The Rape of Nanking*.

On November 11, Iris received an e-mail from a head researcher in the foreign department at *Newsweek*, telling her that they were not planning to run the excerpt in the November 24 issue either. Iris immediately called Tom Maslin, but he was in Jerusalem. When she reached him and asked him why her excerpt was not going to run, he said that he did not make the decisions and only accepted orders. Right now her excerpt was not slated for the schedule, and they hadn't told him why either.

Iris called HarperCollins again to look into her rights. The head of the rights department at HarperCollins made phone calls to *Newsweek* and was informed by them that the delay had nothing to do with Japanese advertisers; rather, it was because Seymour Hersh's book *The Dark Side of Camelot* had bumped every book excerpt back a week, and that another excerpt had to run in the magazine on the 17th.

Everyone in Iris's camp thought the story about Seymour Hersh did not make sense. Iris said if it *was* true, why had *Newsweek* not told her on Friday, November 8 in the first place?

In the meantime, Iris told us that if *Newsweek* would yield to pressure from Japan and kill the excerpt, she would immediately hold a press conference. She was sure that the news would fall on friendly ears all over the world, and the Chinese-American community and many human rights organizations would support her one hundred percent.

Iris also told HarperCollins that they should call *Newsweek* and ask them what she should tell reporters if the excerpt did not run on the 17th or the 24th. Iris also asked for a contract amendment to give her permission to give interviews on the 17th, because she had already booked speeches and interviews for her book tour, and it was not her fault that the except had not published as planned.

On November 12, the HarperCollins rights department e-mailed Iris that they had received a written confirmation from *Newsweek* that the excerpt would hit the newsstands on November 24 (in the December 1 issue) and that any publicity she did before then would not affect the excerpt.

Iris flew to Norfolk, Virginia, the first stop of her book tour, on November 14. In the subsequent days, she was busy with public speeches, interviews, and book signings in several cities, but she was still not sure whether *Newsweek* would fulfill their promise.

Although I was in Urbana while Iris was on the road, she always called to inform me that she had arrived at a new place safely. If she was too busy to call, she would write a brief message at the hotel's Internet center when she routinely checked her e-mails. She told me she had been welcomed at every stop on the tour and that huge crowds had shown up at her lectures and her book signings. Her books sold out immediately on every occasion. I kept in touch with Iris and read all the news available about her. I was very happy to learn that her book was having such a strong start.

On Sunday, November 16, *Baltimore Sun* reporter Cheryl Tan called us at home and interviewed us over the phone; she was the first news reporter to do so. She told us that she had interviewed Iris and seen her at the book signing at the Trover Bookstore near the Capitol in Washington. She asked us how we had told Iris about the Nanjing Massacre when she was a little girl and how we felt about her book. When the article appeared in the *Sun* on November 18, I was thrilled. Deep in my heart, I silently told my parents that finally their granddaughter had told the world what happened in Nanjing in 1937. I prayed that the suffering of the Chinese people during the war would never be forgotten.

On November 18, Barbara Culliton (Iris's former professor at Johns Hopkins) picked Iris up in Washington. Culliton had invited Iris to give a lecture and book signing at the Johns Hopkins University campus. She told Iris that she was very proud of her and her book.

When they met, Iris told Culliton what had happened with *Newsweek* and her worry that they might yet yield to the pressure from Japan and kill the excerpt. Culliton said to Iris, "This is terrific news! If they actually *do* cancel your excerpt, your book will be on the *New York Times* 'Best Sellers' list in ten minutes!"

Culliton had read the book before its publication and liked it very much. She told Iris that she personally had an interest in the book, not just because Iris was one of her former students, but because of its historical importance. She also said that she had tremendously strong feelings about journalistic integrity and wanted Iris to keep her posted as to what happened with the excerpt.

In the meantime, Shau-Jin and I continued systematically analyzing the advertisements in *Newsweek*'s past several issues. We counted an average of four to five Japanese ads a week including companies such as Canon, Isuzu, Hitachi, Sony, Toyota, Toshiba, Mitsubishi, Sharp, and Epson.

I was wondering whether Iris's book excerpt would be published at all in the next issue of *Newsweek*. I did not trust anyone's words anymore unless I personally saw it in print!

I knew the December 1 issue of *Newsweek* would be on the news-stands on November 24 or 25. Several days before that date, I was already starting my countdown. When Monday, November 24 finally arrived, I was so jumpy in the lab that I could not concentrate on my work. In the afternoon, around 1:00 P.M., I started making phone calls to the newsstand of the Illini Union student center on campus and asked them if the December 1 issue of the magazine had arrived. They told me it wasn't there yet. I asked when it would arrive. They said it was hard to say; sometimes it arrived on Monday and sometimes on Tuesday. They said if it did arrive that day, it should be in the late afternoon or evening.

I could not sit down. I was pacing back and forth in the lab, wondering whether the excerpt had been published or not. Iris was in New York City at the time, and she had not told me whether there was any news, good or bad. I firmly believed that the excerpt in *Newsweek* would be a major step in determining her book's success.

I was so anxious that I don't know how many phone calls I made to the newsstand to inquire about the arrival of the magazine. The girl at the newsstand must have felt my anxiety and felt sorry for me when I called again and again.

Finally, at 5:00 P.M., the girl at the newsstand told me that the magazine was there! I ran over to the Illini Union. I could hardly breathe as I frantically flipped through the pages. There it was! I stood there and read through the whole excerpt carefully. It was a total of three pages, with the front page titled "Exposing the Rape of Nanking."

I was thrilled. I read the excerpt twice while I was still standing there, just to make sure it was real. I ran back to the lab and called Shau-Jin and told him the good news.

When we finally got home that evening and examined the magazine carefully, we noticed that there was not a single Japanese ad in this issue. Additionally, there was no special headline on the cover to advertise the excerpt, nor in the "Top of the Week" section inside. The three pages of the excerpt were buried in the middle of the big news of that week: the amazing septuplets who had been born to a family named McCaughey! Obviously, the magazine did not want to make a big deal of this excerpt.

Looking back, if Iris had not pressed *Newsweek* to give a reason for the delay, could they have caved in to the pressure of the Japanese companies and killed the excerpt entirely? Was the magazine "terrified" when they heard that Iris would go public about the story if they killed it? Although *Newsweek* denied that the pullout of the Japanese ads was the reason for the delay, no one could explain why the December 1 issue had not had a single Japanese ad, whereas the November 17 issue had carried double the usual number of such ads.

One of Iris's friends told her that it seemed like there were two set of rules in the media—one for Asians, and one for everyone else. Would

Mercedes-Benz dare challenge *Newsweek* if they printed a book excerpt on the Holocaust written by a Jew? Never!

In spite of the fact that the excerpt in *Newsweek* was not prominently advertised on the cover of that issue and that the two-week delay might have missed the ideal timing for book reviews, it still made a tremendous contribution to getting the word out about the book—the first step to making *The Rape of Nanking* a best seller!

⚬⚬⚬

Iris had to overcome many external obstacles before *The Rape of Nanking* was finally published, from the dissolution of Basic Books to the *Newsweek* incident, but she had also faced some internal issues as well. In April, Iris had phoned and had a long discussion with us. She was at a crossroads. The book was in its final production stages and would be published soon, but she had not landed an advance for a next book. Brett urged her to find a nine-to-five regular job to bring in some steady income. Up to that time, her book advances, the NSF grant, and other grants had not sufficiently supported her living and research expenses without Brett's subsidizing. Brett said that her writing profession had been a money-losing business up to that moment.

She said that she could either continue writing book proposals, or she could look for other jobs such as technical writing or a faculty teaching position, and then she could return to her book proposals once things had stabilized. Shau-Jin and I, as well as Brett, encouraged her to get a teaching job. Shau-Jin and I were against the technical writing job. We felt that she had a talent for creative writing, and a teaching job actually was best for her, as it would give her a chance to also pursue independent projects that interested her, as well as work with and meet other people, something she always liked doing. Plus, many teachers wrote books on the side, as the greater flexibility of the teaching schedule was a perfect fit for an author.

In this discussion, we expressed our views on her book and the issue of money. Of course, we said that everyone needed some money to support his/her basic living, but not all contributions to society could be measured by money. We told Iris that even though her book-writing career up to that moment had not made much money, what she was doing was *very* important for society. Her books had intrinsic value in a way that many other books did not, and we were very proud of her.

During the long discussions we had over the phone, Iris poured her dreams and ambitions out to us. Iris told me that recently she had had a chat with one of her girlfriends in Chicago. Her friend asked Iris what her ultimate goal was in her life. Iris told her friend her ambition was to leave her mark in the literary world and to become a world-famous writer. The friend criticized Iris for being too individualistic. She didn't understand why people wanted to be stars, or to be famous. Iris said to me, "What's wrong with dreaming of the Olympic gold, or the Nobel Prize?" She continued, "What's wrong with pushing myself to achieve my full potential?"

After her failure to find a publisher for her book proposal on the biological clock, Iris never stopped thinking about her next project. When she talked about her book ideas, she was filled with enthusiasm. She described a number of possible topics—an epic novel of espionage, inter-racial marriage in the U.S., a historical novel of Chinese building a transcontinental railroad in the American West. She told me that she was constantly studying the best writing in world literature and hoped one day she could be considered on the same level as those authors. When she thought about that, she was so thrilled that she almost wanted to scream. She told me that she wanted to dream big and said that her dad and I were the only ones who would not criticize her as being "megalomaniac" or too "individualistic"!

Many times Iris told us about how she admired Scarlett O'Hara, the main character in one of her favorite books, *Gone with the Wind*. She said that O'Hara's appeal was her passion and determination. Triumph over adversity was one of the most enduring themes in literature, and that was what she wanted to pursue.

Iris also told me that one of her male friends had confided to her that he liked to hire women because a) they worked hard, b) they worked for less money, and c) they had no ambition, so they wouldn't try to steal his contracts. Iris was furious when she heard that. She vowed that she would never fall into that trap. She wanted to find the traits of successful women and write a book on that. She also confided to me that she wanted to have three children in the next few years, but she would plunge back into her writing career after her children left for college. Then, she said, she would have at least twenty years of a writing career without interruption. She wanted both: family *and* career.

Iris was quite sentimental and told me that life was so short. She wanted to accomplish a lot in a short time; yet she never felt she had enough of it. She said she had to seize the moment, right this second! Life would vanish one day, she said, but books and words would be left behind, just like those masterpieces of literature she was reading. She said "Words are eternal." She told me she had to work harder to achieve everything she wanted. Why she was so driven in a way rarely seen in other people? I cannot answer that. Sometimes I was just amazed and inspired by her determination to achieve the best. It inspired me to want to be my best as well.

14

Becoming a Celebrity

Although *The Rape of Nanking* was Iris's second book, this was the first time she had been on a long book-signing tour. Iris kept us informed along the way by calling and e-mailing us about her activities.

The news of her discovery of John Rabe's diary had broken a year before, and Chinese-Americans in this country and in Canada were electrified by the news of both the diary and Iris's forthcoming book. She received many invitations from university student organizations and Chinese communities in the U.S. and Canada who were eager to hear her story. She had carefully planned her itinerary to make every possible stop and fulfill all her invitation requests. At Virginia Beach, her first stop for the book tour, she told me she had received the warmest welcome, and her book had sold out in just a few minutes. Many people bought multiple copies and said that they wanted to give the book to their children to read.

After Virginia Beach, Iris flew to Washington. Her longtime friend Marian Smith, a historian at the Immigration and Naturalization Service, kindly hosted her in her house. Iris went to a book signing at Trover's bookstore near the Capitol. She was telling me that she hoped Illinois congressman William Lipinski or one of his aides would show up, since the bookstore was right on Capitol Hill. That summer, Lipinski was sponsoring a bill demanding that the Japanese apologize and pay reparations for the World War II atrocities they had committed, much like the other Axis powers did immediately following World War II. The bill was a result of the efforts of many Chinese-American activists and human rights groups. Iris was also wondering whether the Japanese embassy in D.C. would send someone to the store to gather information on her book. However, none appeared.

Iris continued on to Johns Hopkins University, Harvard University Law School, and Princeton University. Every event was packed, and Iris continued to be well-received. Shau-Jin's brother Shau-Yen, who lived in New Jersey, saw Iris at Princeton and said that her book was the most popular book among all the books on display during the signing.

Some controversy erupted at the Princeton University conference when the well-known revisionist Japanese historian Ikuhiko Hata spoke and asserted that the death toll in Nanking claimed by the Chinese could not be trusted. Many people in the audience loudly protested. The conference almost spiraled out of control several times, according to the *World Journal* (a major Chinese-language U.S. newspaper), but, in the end, decorum prevailed and overall it was a huge success and a testament to how passionate people were about Nanking.

Shau-Yen, who had been in the audience, called us that night to describe the excitement. In response to Hata, Iris had given her reasons why using burial records to estimate the death toll was the best way, under the circumstances, to estimate the numbers. The estimated number of people killed in the Nanking Massacre ranged from 260,000 to 350,000, based on all the sources Iris had collected. Every time Iris spoke, her eloquence and tenacity won loud applause from the audience.

Uncle Shau-Yen was very proud of Iris. After the conference, he gave her a ride to the Princeton train station where Iris would go on to New York, her next stop. On the train station platform, Iris interviewed Shau-Yen about his experiences when he escaped from Communist China in 1949. Shau-Yen later told us he was quite impressed by the hard-working style of his niece. He said that Iris had taken out a reporter's pad and a pen from her bag and, right there on the bench of the Princeton train station, began to record the adventures of her uncle and her grandpa in 1949! Because she wanted to finish the interview, she decided to skip the train she was supposed to get on and take the next one.

Iris spent Thanksgiving in New York City with her friends—one of a few times that she was not with her family on the holidays. She called from New York on Thanksgiving Day, and we talked for a long time. She was so excited about the fact that *Newsweek* finally had published her book excerpt. She also told us that ABC's *Good Morning America* had asked her to fly to New York on December 7 for an interview.

After returning home from the East Coast, Iris had a signing in the San Francisco area. Then she had to fly back to New York for her *Good Morning America* interview. December 7, 1997 was the fifty-sixth anniversary of the Japanese bombing of Pearl Harbor, which is why ABC wanted to interview Iris and introduce her book on that date. Although we were told we could see her on *Good Morning America* on the morning of December 7, New York time, the program was mainly broadcast on the East Coast. Besides, we did not subscribe to cable TV. All we could do was to ask my sister Ling-Ling in New York City, my brother Bing in New Jersey, and my sister Ging-Ging in Maryland to watch and record it for us. When the time came and Iris was on the program talking, Bing called and put his telephone receiver near the TV screen so we could hear.

We finally got to see the ABC *Good Morning America* interview a week later when Bing mailed the tape to us. Iris did extremely well on the show. We were surprised to see her answering questions in a very professional way, thinking back to when she'd been a shy little girl. She looked so young and fresh, and with the help of TV studio makeup, she looked like a rising star!

Next, Iris flew to Vancouver by the invitation of BC-ALPHA (British Columbia Association for Learning and Preserving the History of WWII in Asia) president Thekla Lit, who organized many events to publicize her book. After several well-received events in Vancouver (a city with a huge Chinese-Canadian population; wherever Iris went, she was mobbed by fans), Iris flew to Toronto, where Joseph Wong, the president of the Toronto chapter of ALPHA, picked her up. Dr. Wong, whom I had never met, called me and said Iris wanted me to know that she had arrived safely. He added that he would take good care of her—he was a medical doctor and Iris should be safe with him. I was very grateful for someone who really understood a mother's concern. Iris always kept her promise to let us know she had arrived safely in a new place.

On December 11, the day Iris arrived in Toronto, she called us late in the night from a restaurant bar and told us that Ted Koppel's *Nightline* program would show "The Good Nazi," the story of John Rabe, that night, and she was in it. We quickly turned on the TV and waited for the program to begin. Sure enough, there was Iris on the screen with William Kirby, the Harvard history professor, and Ursula Reinhardt, the granddaughter of John Rabe, and others.

On December 13, the sixtieth anniversary of the beginning of the Nanjing Massacre, Chinese organizations in Toronto held a big memorial service for the victims of the Massacre. Iris was the keynote speaker of the event, and there was a choir from China specifically for the occasion. A music program was composed and dedicated to the memory of the victims and their suffering. After the event, Iris called me from her room in Toronto. She said, "Mom, you can not believe how many people were in the auditorium, my guess is six to eight hundred people! At the end of my speech, people gave me such long applause . . . I could not hold my tears back when the choir was singing." I could not hold my tears back either, on the other end of the telephone.

That night, I wrote down my emotions and described what a mental journey it had been for me over the past two years with my daughter working on this book. I recounted beginning with the conversation we'd had, encouraging her to write *The Rape of Nanking* at my parents' New York apartment the night of May 18, 1992, more than five years before, to the research trip she'd taken to the East Coast in 1995; from the incredible train ride to Nankng interviewing survivors, to the sudden change of hands of Basic Books in 1997. I dedicated the article to my parents in Heaven; I wanted them to know that their granddaughter had written a book exposing the Rape of Nanking, the epicenter of the forgotten, atrocious war crime, to the whole world, and displayed great courage fighting for justice on behalf of those voiceless victims. I submitted the article to the weekly magazine of the *World Journal* Chinese newspaper. That article was finished in a few hours, the fastest I have ever written in my life.

The Rape of Nanking: The Forgotten Holocaust of World War II became a *New York Times* best seller in January 1998, a fact that many people thought unthinkable. A dark horse, you may say. Yes, it wasn't in our wildest dreams (or Iris's either)! But it happened!

It was originally Iris's idea to publish the book on the sixtieth anniversary of the Nanking Massacre, and that idea really paid off. A couple of months before the book's official release, the publicity of the new book had already started, and it was due completely to Iris's efforts. From the November issue of the Johns Hopkins alumni magazine's lengthy article with her photo on the cover, to her self-planned book tour in coordination with the conferences organized by university students and grassroots Chinese organizations in the big cities of the East Coast, Canada, and the West Coast, and, later, to the Chinese and English newspapers and magazines and the national TV and radio interviews that followed: there was a perfect storm around the book. I faithfully kept track of the public responses and collected all the media coverage about her. Our friends all over the U.S. also sent many local newspapers with coverage of her. I can't describe how excited we were. It seemed that at the time, our life's main interest was following her in the news. Iris was also in close contact with us to let us know what exciting things were happening each day.

After the December 1 issue of *Newsweek* excerpt, several major English newspapers had reviewed her book, including the *Washington Post* and the *New York Times*. In his moving article on December 11, 1997, Ken Ringle of the *Post* wrote: "Few knew what took place in 1937 Nanking, but it's blazed in one woman's soul." The article showed a picture of Iris holding her book during the interview. The article also ran a photo of Japanese soldiers using Chinese prisoners for bayonet practice, plus another photo of a Japanese soldier executing a Chinese captive while other Japanese soldiers stood by, laughing.

On December 14, the day after the sixtieth anniversary of the Nanjing Massacre, in the *New York Times Book Review*, Orville Schell, University of California professor at Berkeley and an expert on East Asian studies, wrote a lengthy and positive review of Iris's book. He wrote: "In her important new book, *The Rape of Nanking*, Iris Chang, whose own grandparents were survivors, recounts the grisly massacre with understandable outrage." Again, the article was accompanied by the big photo of Japanese soldiers using Chinese prisoners for targets at bayonet drill, an image that is difficult to erase from one's memory and still shocks and sickens, no matter how many times one sees it.

On the Chinese media side, North American Chinese newspapers reported on Iris's new book that December. Across the Pacific Ocean, in China, Hong Kong, and Taiwan, all newspapers prominently reported the book too, including Hong Kong's influential English newspaper *South China Morning Post*, the PRC's *People's Daily*, and Taiwan's major newspapers. The book was translated into Chinese by Commonwealth Publishing in Taiwan and released in January 1998, but book excerpts were published in nine segments in a newspaper in Taiwan, from December 2 to 9, 1997.

With all this great publicity, the book sold out quickly across the country. All the bookstores where Iris appeared had shortages, and it was difficult to fulfill demand. When Iris arrived in Toronto in December, Toronto ALPHA president Joseph Wong suggested that his organization raise funds to buy a thousand of her books to donate to Canada's high schools and public libraries, making the book a rare commodity indeed in the stores. Iris complained to us on the phone that it was a shame, she was seeing so many people who came to her signings and found there were no books available, and she had to sign only bookplates for them while they were waiting for their order. She had complained about this to the publisher many times along the book tour. The publisher told her the book was in its fifth printing two weeks after its publication. They were already printing as fast as they could, but still in only a thousand copies per printing. They had no idea that her book was on the way to the best-seller list!

With her book in such high demand, we started to pay attention to the *New York Times* "Best Sellers" list. On December 21, we found that Iris's book was listed in the "And Bear in Mind" section at the bottom of the *New York Times* "Best Sellers" list. Those books listed in "And Bear in Mind" are editors' choices of other recent books of particular interest, in addition to the best sellers. We were very happy. It meant that Iris's book was on the rise and had the potential to make the list.

We were in a very impatient mood over the Christmas holidays of that year. We understood that during the holiday season many people would be busy traveling or celebrating and perhaps no one would pay attention to book reviews or worry about buying books. But even during the holiday rush, several newspapers, such as the *San Jose Mercury News, St. Louis Post-Dispatch, Wall Street Journal,* and *Los Angeles Times* published favorable reviews of her book.

Finally, the Christmas holidays were over, and Iris resumed her book tour. First she went to southern California, Los Angeles and San

Diego. On January 14, she flew to Washington for a TV interview with PBS. At the San Francisco airport, she left a telephone message for us and said that she'd gotten a call from her publisher that her book was number 15 on the *New York Times* "Best Sellers" list! Her voice told us she was weeping—I'm sure they were tears of joy! Shau-Jin and I were jubilant; we could not contain our excitement for many days. In the next phone call, we said "Iris, you've made it!"

We learned that her book had actually reached the list on January 14, but it took almost two weeks for that to show up in the newspaper. We don't know exactly why it's like this. Maybe publishers like to delay the information for two weeks so that they can make sure they have enough stock for potential buyers. On January 25, we went to a Barnes & Noble to buy a copy of the *New York Times* to see with our own eyes that her book was really there.

From that day on, Shau-Jin and I faithfully checked the list every week. Since we could find the list on the *New York Times* Web site, we printed out the list each time Iris's book appeared. The book became number 14, up from number 15, the next week, and number 11 for the following three weeks. It remained in the top fifteen for ten straight weeks. At the time, Iris was only twenty-nine years old. Her editor told her that she was the first Chinese-American to become a best-selling author on the *New York Times* list at such a young age—and for such an unprecedented length of time!

Why did Iris's book become a best seller? In retrospect, I have my own conclusions. First, the Rape of Nanking was not known in the West, even though it had been front-page news in the *New York Times* in 1937. This was partly because the West emphasized the European theater of the war and largely ignored the Asian-Pacific side of World War II, and partly because of the Japanese government's deliberate cover-up of their World War II crimes after the war ended. The Rape of Nanking was forgotten by the outside world until Iris exposed it.

Second, China became an increasingly important and powerful geopolitical player in the 1990s; that gave China a strong position to sort out the past neglected history such as the Rape of Nanking which had never been properly addressed before. Third, Chinese people born in the 1930s who had gone through World War II had now reached retirement and had the time and resources to reflect on their lives, and they wanted to preserve their war memories. That included Chinese-Americans and Chinese-Canadians.

Fourth, in the 1990s, Americans were prosperous, so they had the resources to pay attention to history and culture events that did not necessarily immediately affect their day-to-day lives. And fifth, Chinese activists of grassroots organizations in the U.S. and Canada, having been in the redress movement regarding the Sino-Japanese War for many years, had strongly supported Iris's book as the consummation of years of hard work trying to bring exposure to this period of history.

In short, Iris was very lucky to be writing at the right time and in the right place! But the most important of all, from numerous articles and reviews about her book, almost everyone agreed that it was the massive materials that she had unearthed from archives that made the difference; also, her eloquence and passion for historical truth and social justice expressed in the book reverberated with and impressed readers.

15

A Roller-Coaster Life

O nce Iris's book was on the *Times* "Best Sellers" list, her publisher's goal was to keep it there as long as possible, which was also the goal for grassroots Chinese-American organizations such as the Global Alliance for Preserving the History of World War II in Asia, based in Cupertino, California. To maintain the momentum of the book sales, Ignatius Ding, the Executive VP of the Global Alliance, in January of 1998 sent out thousands of e-mails via his vast e-mail address list to ask every member to support Iris's book and encouraged them to forward the message to their friends via their own address lists.

We too forwarded his message to friends and students via our e-mail connections. Ding's e-mail must have traveled back and forth across the U.S. many times since I got the same message from students and faculty from other parts of the country long after I read his original e-mail to me. Iris's book generated enormous interest and awareness among Chinese-Americans as well as interest from the general public for this forgotten history of World War II in Asia, and it looked as if people had finally realized that there was a chapter in history that needed to be re-addressed, the history of World War II to be rewritten and reconsidered.

In the meantime, in response to the Toronto ALPHA chapter's movement to donate Iris's book to public libraries, organizations in the U.S. did the same thing. Many people bought multiple copies of the book in response to the call. Chinese newspapers also urged readers to send Iris's book to members of congress, senators, and local government officials to help push for political action and a formal apology from Japan.

In January 1998, Iris went to Los Angeles and San Diego for more book signings. When she was signing in Los Angeles and its suburban towns like Monterey Park (where many Chinese-Americans lived), more than a hundred people showed up at the bookstore. Iris told us that many bookstore owners told her that they had never seen a scene like it before!

On January 8, Ye-Ye, Shau-Jin's father, suddenly died at the age of ninety-three. He lived in Santa Monica, California, and had been sick with a serious case of the flu for a week. He collapsed one evening and died shortly thereafter. We were shocked and went to Santa Monica for the funeral a week later. Iris had a tight schedule at the time. She was at a book signing in southern California but was scheduled to fly east for a number of TV and radio interviews, including one by PBS's Jim Lehrer for his *News Hour*. However, she said she wanted to fly back to California on January 16 for the funeral and would scramble to make the proper arrangements.

After the book hit the *New York Times* "Best Sellers" list, the Perseus Book Group, which owned Basic, began seriously putting some effort into promoting the book and gave her financial and material support. They promised that they would provide Iris escorted transportation services and hotel accommodations in each city. I had always worried that her tight schedule of book signings and media interviews would wear her out. I had written to her former book editor, Susan Rabiner, and voiced my concern. Before the change, during the book tour Iris was living in her friends' houses at night at almost every stop, and driving a rental car to the stores by herself. Now with her publisher committed to help her with transportation and accommodations, she could concentrate on preparing her talks and reaching out to more media.

Iris usually gave a half-hour speech before each signing. Her speeches were always stimulating and forceful, according to newspaper reports and our friends who attended the book signing. Iris told us that at the end of her speeches, many people asked her questions. Furthermore, in each book signing someone invariably would come up to her and tell her their personal stories about the atrocities they had experienced or witnessed during the war. Those who had gone through it were eager to share their emotions and their frustrations. Perhaps that's another reason why so many people wanted to show up to her signings: to finally open up about their own past. However, Iris told us that while she liked listening to those stories and supporting those people, she was emotionally exhausted afterward.

On January 16, Iris flew to L.A. from D.C., where she had just been interviewed by David Gergen for the PBS *MacNeil-Lehrer News Hour*. She immediately rented a car at LAX and drove to the funeral home just in time for the ceremony for her grandpa. Everyone was delighted to see her, especially me. It was a big relief to see her arrive safely.

After the funeral, when we returned to the hotel with Iris, a huge bouquet of flowers was waiting in her room. The bouquet had been sent by her publisher to congratulate her making the *New York Times* "Best Sellers" list and to express their sympathy for the recent loss to our family.

I had to go back to Urbana to work right after the funeral. Shau-Jin stayed one more day with Iris and accompanied her to a signing at Borders Books in Thousand Oaks, California. Shau-Jin described to me what he saw at Borders. He said there was a big crowd of people coming in; about half were Asian-American. At the end of the book signing, when the crowd was gone, the owner of the bookstore realized Iris had not had lunch and ordered a sandwich for her. That was almost 4:00 P.M. Iris was eating her sandwich while she continued signing the bookplates for the store, so they could stick them on the books in the next shipment and be sold as author-signed books.

On January 28, Iris called us with excitement and said that Laurel Cook, her Perseus publicist, and Jack McKeown, the CEO of Perseus, had called her in the afternoon to tell her that her book was up to #11 on the *New York Times* list! Her highest spot yet, only two weeks after first making the list. When they called, she could hear wild cheering, whistling, and clapping in the background! She was overjoyed!

Now that the publisher realized her book's market potential, they made arrangements with all the possible bookstores and TV and radio stations in the country for her to do signings and interviews. Her itinerary from January 18 to March 13 was something like stops in Santa Barbara, Los Angeles, San Jose, Oakland, Portland, Seattle, Houston, Austin, San Francisco, Washington, and so on. To follow her, I asked Iris to give me a copy of her itinerary. Although the schedule of the book tour was hectic, Iris always maintained her high spirits and worked very hard.

One thing that pleased Iris was an article written by George Will, who was also a native of Champaign-Urbana and a graduate of Uni High School in Urbana. He is a renowned national columnist, and his articles are syndicated to almost every big and small newspaper in the country. One day Iris got a call from his aide, who told her that Will wanted to write an article about her book and wished to interview her. On February 19, his article "Breaking a Sinister Silence" was published in his column of the *Washington Post*. At the beginning of the article, he wrote: "Something beautiful, an act of justice, is occurring in America today concerning something ugly that happened long ago and far away. The story speaks well of the author of the just act, and of the constituencies of conscience that leaven this nation of immigrants." At the end, he wrote: "Justice delayed is not necessarily justice denied . . .

Elie Wiesel, Auschwitz survivor and Nobel laureate, says that to forget
a holocaust is to kill twice. Because of Chang's book, the second rape
of Nanking is ending." Iris considered this column one of the highest
points of her life, an eloquent summation of all that she had worked
for over the past several years.

That same evening, Iris was invited to the San Francisco Commonwealth Club to speak. Iris told us it was a very prestigious forum and
she considered it quite an honor to be able to speak there. The previous
guest speakers were highly regarded world leaders like FDR, Ronald
Reagan, and Nobel laureates in peace, literature or sciences.

On March 15 and 17, Iris was invited to the U.S. Holocaust Memorial Museum in Washington to give two talks. By this point, I had seen
her on TV but had never listened to her speak live, so I decided to go.
I was very glad that I did.

I flew to Washington, and on March 15 my sister Ging-Ging and I
arrived at the Holocaust Memorial Museum auditorium. I looked at
the seats behind my reserved one; my guess was that it would hold five
or six hundred people. Iris was scheduled to speak at 3:30 P.M. Several
minutes before that time, the whole auditorium was completely full.
Although so many people were there, the room was very quiet. Many
people held Iris's book and were reading it while waiting. The atmosphere was reverently silent mixed with a heavy mood. Around 3:30,
Iris had still not arrived. I started to wonder why, and looked up her
schedule. She was coming from Palm Beach, Florida, where she had
been attending a book festival the day before. She should have arrived
in D.C. at 1:30 P.M., and from 2:00 to 3:00 she should have been in a
Borders bookstore for a TV interview and book signing. While I was
wondering, Iris and Lydia Perry, the organizer for the talk, appeared.
Iris sat down right next to me and said hello to her aunt. I immediately
asked her why she was late. She said quickly that the whole schedule
was running somewhat late. She handed me a copy of March 12th's
Palm Beach Post, with a full-page report on her book. On the top of the
article, titled "The Forgotten Holocaust and One Woman's Obsession

to Remember," was a big black-and-white photo of her. This photo was the one that now almost every newspaper and magazine was using: her clear black-and-white eyes looked straight toward you, with her long straight black hair covering her shoulder. She was dressed in a flowered sleeveless mandarin-collared jacket over a black sweater. She looked solemn, yet sincere and thoughtful. She looked stunningly beautiful, as some of my friends and even strangers expressed to me. Indeed, this particular black-and-white photo (taken by her friend Jimmy Estimada) is my favorite one of her and the one that graces the cover of this book.

After the organizers each gave a short introduction, Iris walked onto the stage. The whole auditorium erupted in hearty loud welcome applause. Iris spoke in a clear voice as she told the audience of this forgotten holocaust. The speech lasted almost an hour. At the end of the talk, many people came to the microphone to ask her questions. From the questioners, you could tell the talk had been well received. Near the end of the Q&A session, one middle-aged Jewish woman stood up and said "We should give Iris Chang a big round of applause for her courage in exposing this atrocity. . . ." The whole auditorium vibrated with thunderous applause. I was quite moved.

After the speech, Iris signed books. There was a long line, and many newspaper and TV reporters were there. Then one of the reporters came up to inform Iris that Nien Cheng was there. Nien Cheng was the famous Chinese-American author of *Life and Death in Shanghai*. Iris was shocked—in a good way, of course—to see her. The photo of Cheng and Iris shaking hands, with Iris's surprised but delighted expression, was published in almost every Chinese newspaper that day. Later, Iris told me she felt greatly honored that Nien Cheng would come to greet her, especially considering that Cheng was so old (though she was beautiful and looked much younger than her age). After then, they were good friends for the rest of Iris's life. (Unfortunately, Cheng died in November 2009 at the age of ninety-four.) Iris said Cheng gave her a lot of useful advice and became a sort of mentor to her. Nien Cheng was a very strong woman. She had gone through the devastating Cultural Revolution in China, in which she lost her daughter.

The evening after the Holocaust Museum talk, Iris was greeted by five hundred people at a Chinese-American-organized banquet in a Chinese restaurant in Washington. I was also invited, so I witnessed this unforgettable evening. During the dinner, Iris was introduced, and she gave a short speech thanking the local Chinese-American community for supporting her. Iris recounted her early days in 1995, three years before, when she had come to Washington to do research on the Nanking Massacre in the Library of Congress archives and had lived in Dr. S. Y. Lee's home. Dr. Lee also spoke and told everyone that when Iris had stayed in his home, he would pick her up at the Metro station after a long day at the archives. Dr. Lee said he always asked her what materials she had found that day, and she would describe the numerous records of the atrocities that she had discovered. She had cried when she described what she had read and the photos she had seen. It was a very touching moment when the banquet hall, with hundreds of people filling it, became silent while listening to the story.

Another memorable event in D.C. was my surprise in seeing that the article that *I* had submitted to the Chinese newspaper *World Journal Weekly Magazine* had been published on March 15, the day Iris had delivered her speech at the Holocaust Museum. I also remember that on that day, my sister and I toured the Museum just before Iris's talk. I was terribly impressed by the Museum's having preserved the Jewish Holocaust memories, and I wished that one day a similar museum, dedicated to the memory of the victims of the Asian Holocaust of World War II, could be built in Washington too.

Iris continued her book tour. She had asked the publisher not to schedule anything for the week of March 23–27, when she planned to return home to celebrate her thirtieth birthday with Brett and friends. This was the peak of her career—her book had been on the *New York Times* list for ten weeks, all before she reached the age of thirty.

Near her birthday, on March 21, I carefully selected a beautiful birthday card and mailed it to Iris for her birthday. The words in the card were exactly what I wanted to transmit to her (which I recorded in my diary):

Life holds so much beauty, but none more glorious than the beauty of a daughter's smile.
Life holds bright moments, but none more rewarding than that of raising a daughter.
Life holds many gifts, but none more precious than the wonderful gift of having a daughter like you to love.

Shau-Jin was taking advantage of the university spring break from March 21 to 29 to go to Taiwan. The Taiwan National Science Council had invited him to evaluate several proposals on their science projects. When he returned from Taiwan, he told me Iris's book was well known in Taiwan and was also on the best-seller lists there too. When the head of the National Science Council met Shau-Jin, he jokingly said "I'd prefer to see your daughter rather than you!"

On April 10, Iris arrived in Urbana, her hometown, for a book signing as part of her Midwest book tour. She went to the local bookstore, Pages for All Ages, the same bookstore that had sponsored her first book signing in 1995 for *Thread of the Silkworm* less than three years before. This time the bookstore really did a lot of publicity surrounding the event, including a big ad in the *News-Gazette*. On that day, many of our friends showed up at the bookstore. Many of our friends' children had grown up with Iris and were asking to take a picture with her. One of the staff at the store told us that she had never seen so many people lined up for the signing of a book, except maybe for a football player who had stopped by many years before.

After the Midwest book tour, Iris returned to California, and on April 16 she gave a speech at Stanford. The best news, she told us, was that her book had been adopted by the graduate program of the Stanford Psychology Department and would be taught in the classroom.

Then Iris attended a conference at UC Berkeley and wrote me a letter on April 20 to describe it:

Dear Mom:

The Berkeley conference went beautifully. None of the Japanese participants gave me a hard time (they were all liberal minded); rather, I was treated like a celebrity. I gave lengthy interviews to reporters from the San Francisco Chronicle *and the* Daily Cal *(the student newspaper), and gave an informal talk before Orville Schell and a group of graduate journalism students a few hours before the conference. For two solid days, I was besieged by scholars, students and members of the community who wanted my autograph. The lecture hall in the Man's Faculty Club buzzed with excitement every time I stepped in ("Iris Zhang is here!" people would exclaim), and I hardly had a moment to myself.*

I was amazed by the response to my speech, which was the keynote address for the conference. The room was packed when I walked in: more than a hundred people had reserved tickets for the lecture, and those who did not had to stand in the back or on the balcony. Afterwards, Wakeman and Irwin Scheiner of the Institute of East Asian studies and other scholars had nothing but the highest praise for my talk.

When I have more time, I'll call you and tell all the stories (there are many): how the crowd reacted with thunderous applause when I criticized the title of the conference (it was called the conference on the Nanking Incident, rather than the conference on the Nanking Massacre. Even the murder of a few hundred Vietnamese at My Lai was termed a "massacre." How could the Rape of Nanking be reduced to an "incident"?); how I ran out of the dining room and up to my room to fetch photocopies of IMTPE estimates of 260,000 people killed in Nanking when a Japanese textbook author (not a conference panelist but a member of the audience) insisted over lunch that there was no evidence on the number of deaths in the city (This man hastily bolted from the dining room after

*I showed him the hard evidence); how Frederic Wakeman regaled me
with stories of his wild adventures in Hollywood (his father was a famous
film maker) and in China (he broke his hand in a fight during a money
changing incident and is now working on a biography of Dai Lai).*

Love, Iris

This multiple-city book tour continued for another two months before
Iris returned to Urbana again in June 1998 to accept Uni High School's
Max Beberman Distinguished Alumni Award at their graduation ceremony. The *News-Gazette*'s staff writer, Huey Freeman, interviewed Iris
for several hours. He described her book tour in an article published
in the paper: "For Chang, getting mobbed is becoming commonplace.
. . . 'I don't have the freedom to go into a city and be undisturbed as
I was in the past'. . . . Chang is recognized by strangers in airports,
restaurants and even in a police station.

"Iris said, 'I went into a Houston police station next to a Chinese
restaurant because there were no phones in the restaurant. Two of
the three police officers recognized me,' she recalled, laughing. 'They
congratulated me.'"

Freeman asked Iris's feelings about the attention she had received,
especially after the emotional turmoil she had gone through while
researching the atrocities.

"'I guess I've gone from hell to heaven, haven't I?' she said. 'But
that's not an entirely correct analogy. It's more like being strapped to
a roller coaster and not being able to get off.'"

Back in March 1998, we received a letter from the principal of Uni
High, Shelley Roberts. Roberts was a new principal who wrote us a
congratulatory letter on Iris's achievement of becoming a *New York
Times* best-selling author. She was very impressed and proud. In the
letter, she enclosed the November issue of *Johns Hopkins Magazine*, in
which a big front cover article was written on Iris's book, *The Rape of*

Nanking. It turns out Roberts herself was an alumnus of Johns Hopkins University, too. In the letter, she said that Iris had already been nominated as the recipient of the Max Beberman Distinguished Alumni Award, the highest award Uni High gave to its alumni. The recipients of the Alumni Award had included several Nobel laureates. Roberts extended her invitation to Iris to be the keynote speaker for that year's graduation ceremony for the class of 1998 in June.

In reply to Roberts, we told her that Iris would be back home for a book signing in April, and suggested that she could ask Iris in person.

In private, after I'd told her about the upcoming invitation, Iris told me that she had already committed to come back home in April; and, in addition, the University of Illinois Journalism Department and other organizations on campus were also planning to invite her to come back in the fall for a campus-wide talk. She said that with the tight schedule of her book tour, she did not feel that she should come back again in June for the high-school graduation ceremony. She said, "Why don't you and Dad represent me to accept the award!"

But during Iris's April book signing at Champaign's Pages for All Ages bookstore, Shelley Roberts, as I had suggested, did ask Iris to come back in June to receive the award in person. She was so sincere and charming that Iris said she just couldn't say no right there, and told her that she would give her an answer after checking her schedule.

In the meantime, I reminded Iris of all the years in high school when she'd felt that she was unrecognized; now it was time for her to come back to show everyone how her belief in herself had made a difference. I told her it was her responsibility to come back to encourage the newly graduated students to use her journey as an example. Finally, Iris wrote to Roberts that she accepted the invitation and would join the class of 1998 for their graduation ceremony on June 6.

At the time, Iris had been touring across the nation. Close to Mother's Day, on May 3, she was named Woman of the Year by the

Organization of Chinese-Americans in Washington. I called her on the night of May 4, when she was staying with her friend Marian Smith in D.C. She spoke with me for only a couple minutes, but told me that she had thanked me in her acceptance speech at the Woman of the Year Award banquet for raising her to be what she was. I was quite moved and almost cried to hear that she had said that about me at such a huge moment.

In her May 5 e-mail to me, she wrote:

> *Dear Mom,*
>
> *I'm sorry that I sounded so rushed when you called me at Marian's home. Sometimes I wonder if I've offended a lot of old friends in the last few months by not returning emails, phone calls and letters. Perhaps many people believe I've been corrupted already. . . .*
>
> *It's true that I've neglected my loved ones for the last few months. I feel ashamed that I have not yet bought you a Mother's Day gift, or even a card—only this note that I am hastily writing from my laptop computer, perched upon a bed in Diana Zuckerman's home. How I wish you could have been there during the Woman of the Year ceremony. I told the audience how you inspired me over the years, how you served as my first role model.*
>
> *Please forgive me. I love you dearly, even though I haven't found the time to talk to you in the last few weeks. And in a few weeks, we'll all be reunited—and the book tour will finally be over. I feel like a soldier returning from a six-month war!*
>
> *Love, Iris*

According to Iris, Diana Zuckerman was a former White House staffer who had invited Iris to stay in her home in Washington. Diane would accompany her to the congressional briefing in the Capitol on May 8. The briefing was for members of Congress and their aides to understand the Japanese atrocities committed in Asia during World War II, including the Rape of Nanking, Unit 731 biological warfare, chemical warfare, and the sex slavery (Comfort Woman) issue. She was also trying to arrange a meeting for Iris with Hillary Clinton.

Although Iris seemed to be enjoying the success of her book in this country, the right-wing ultranationalists in Japan had begun to criticize the book. Worse yet, in April, the Japanese ambassador had openly criticized her book as "one-sided and erroneous" in a press conference. Iris began furiously and courageously defending herself in the press immediately afterward. We were constantly on the phone, and although we could not speak extensively, we did our best to give her the support she needed. Her decision to return home for the Uni High graduation ceremony was timely; it enabled her to get a short rest.

She arrived for the Uni High graduation on June 5. On Saturday, June 6, Roberts invited Iris and us to a pre-ceremony luncheon with her former English teachers, Charlene Tibbetts and Adele Suslick, who had helped Iris tremendously in her high-school years. It was a wonderful reunion.

When we stepped into the Tryon Festival Theatre of Krannert Center for the Performing Arts on the U of I campus for the graduation ceremony, we saw that several hundred people were already sitting there waiting for the ceremony to begin. After several speakers delivered their congratulations to the class of 1998, Iris was introduced as the recipient of the Max Beberman Distinguished Alumni Award. They showed several slides of Iris in her Uni years. One slide showed her with a group of her classmates, with her head circled in the photo. The picture reminded me of all the things that had happened during that period. Since then, how much had changed!

While those memories ran through my mind, I saw that Iris had already stepped up to the podium on the stage and accepted the award plaque. Now she was starting to give advice to the graduating class of 1998. My mind could not quite concentrate on her speech. My thoughts were racing back and forth between the past and the present. It seemed like I was in a dream. I could not believe that in the past thirteen years, she had changed from an unrecognized high-school student to the author of a *New York Times* best seller. I knew some people might think she was just plain lucky, but I knew what a journey she had gone through. Every bit of her success was due to her hard work, her determination, and her conviction, all of which she delivered in her speech that day.

She said, in a beautiful clear voice, ". . . First of all, please, please, PLEASE believe in THE POWER OF ONE. One person can make an enormous difference in the world. One person—actually, one IDEA— can start a war, or end one, or subvert an entire power structure. One discovery can cure a disease or spawn new technology to benefit or annihilate the human race. You are ONE individual and can change millions of lives. Think big. Do not limit your vision and do not EVER compromise your dreams or ideals. . . ."

I could not hold back my tears when she said "I must thank my parents, who are in the audience today and who have always believed in me from Day One. They were the ones who inspired me to never set limits for myself in my dreams and who have served over the last few years as my greatest mentors, confidants, and friends. Mom, Dad—I love you and I thank you from the bottom of my heart." My eyes were wet with tears throughout her speech.

On April 22, 1998, when Iris was in Salt Lake City on her book tour, she had called to inform us that during the signing in one of the bookstores in Salt Lake, a Korean reporter had asked her how she reacted to the criticism of the Japanese ambassador who said that her book was inaccurate and biased. Iris was shocked to hear the accusation and she said she could not believe that an ambassador could make such comments on a book in public! We told her she should not jump to that conclusion and asked her to look into what exactly the ambassador had said and deal with it accordingly.

Later, Iris found out that on April 21, the Japanese ambassador to the U.S., Kunihiko Saito, in a press conference in Washington, D.C., had indeed openly criticized her book as "contain(ing) many extremely inaccurate descriptions and one-sided views. . . ." Iris was outraged and asked us "Can you imagine what would happen if a *German* ambassador to the U.S. made a parallel statement about a book on the Holocaust?"

"There is definitely different treatment of World War II in Asia and in Europe in this country," she also said. She was preparing a rebuttal. Of course, we told her we were behind her one hundred percent. Like her, I just could not believe a Japanese ambassador would openly attack a book.

On April 24, the Global Alliance for Preserving the History of World War II in Asia issued a strong statement denouncing the Japanese ambassador to the U.S., and urged the American and Chinese governments to ask Japan to immediately dismiss Saito for making such a distorting statement.

On the same day, Basic Books also released a strong statement against the Japanese ambassador. In the statement, Jack McKeown, President and CEO of Basic, said: "Iris Chang has performed a vital service in turning a spotlight on the tragedy of sixty years ago in Nanking. As publishers, we will continue to strive to bring the book's message to the widest possible audience. Many eminent scholars and historians have reviewed this book in glowing terms. . . ." The statement also said that the book was now in its seventeenth printing with over 130,000 books in print. "It remained on the *New York Times* 'Best Sellers' list for thirteen weeks, and foreign rights have been sold in Germany, Spain, Taiwan, China, Czechoslovakia, and Italy." The statement also announced that "The book will be published in Japan, despite negative publicity in Japan, by publisher Kashiwashobo."

In a press release, Iris asked the ambassador to name the "erroneous facts" and challenged him to a public debate on national television.

The news of the criticism of the book by the Japanese ambassador and the challenge for a debate from Iris had been reported in newspapers and media widely in this country and overseas. However,

Saito declined to cite any specific inaccuracies in the book and did not respond to her challenge for a public debate.

Rabbi Abraham Cooper of the Simon Wiesenthal Center at the Museum of Tolerance in Los Angeles gave Iris tremendous support. Rabbi Cooper told her that he had sent his protest letter to the Japanese embassy and to all news media outlets. He said, "Can you imagine a German ambassador making a similar statement?" He told Iris "We'll be there for you!"

Early in April, the Associated Press reported that a monthly magazine in Japan, *Shokun*, had featured an article that criticized the Foreign Ministry of the Japanese government for being silent about "anti-Japanese" books such as *The Rape of Nanking*. Iris and Shau-Jin and I speculated that the Japanese government must be under pressure from the ultranationalists to do something about it.

The news of Iris's challenge to the Japanese ambassador for a public TV debate was also in *Time* magazine's May 11, 1998 issue. The news said, ". . . Saito's attack on Chang has so far drawn fire from only a few organizations, but Tokyo is less concerned about Saito than about the damage the book may be doing to Japan's image in the U.S."

It was not true that Saito's criticism had "drawn fire from only a few organizations." Actually, as far as I knew, Saito's remarks on Iris's book had triggered strong reactions in the U.S., and especially from Chinese-Americans and overseas Chinese communities. Many readers wrote letters of protest to newspapers. A number of Chinese newspapers' editorials supported Iris. The Chinese consulate general in San Francisco on May 6 had issued a statement in support of Iris's book and criticizing the Japanese ambassador for being extremely irresponsible by making a public announcement distorting history. The statement said that the Nanking massacre was one of numerous atrocities committed by Japan's militarists during its war of aggression against China. "It's an undeniable history," said the Chinese consulate general, and he demanded Japan respect the truth.

On May 8, a spokesman from the Chinese embassy in Washington also issued a strong statement refuting Saito's criticism of Iris's book and asking the Japanese government to face their past war crimes with honesty. To my knowledge, it's quite rare that a book could generate so much international attention and cause the attack and counter-attack of governments of two countries.

Because the Chinese embassy and the Chinese consulate in the U.S. issued statements in support of Iris's book, Japanese right-wing Web sites claimed that the Chinese government was behind Iris's book. This was absurd. Iris had never contacted the Chinese government while researching her book. Besides, Iris's first book, *Thread of the Silkworm*, criticized Chinese Communism.

In the meantime, a Japanese movie called *Pride* glorified World War II Japanese class-A war criminal General Hideki Tojo as a hero. The movie had a preview in April and was shown in Japanese theaters in May. Showing the movie in Japan coincided chronologically with Saito's criticism of Iris's book. This movie triggered another wave of media coverage on Iris's book and its historical context.

On May 15, Iris e-mailed me and said that a reporter from *Time* in Tokyo had asked about her reaction to the film *Pride*. Her response was: "This film is yet another example of Japanese right-wing denial of the Rape of Nanking and other Japanese war atrocities. But no movie can suppress the basic facts of World War II.

"This film will do more damage to Japan than good, because it has already enraged opinion-makers and politicians all over Asia and the U.S. If Japanese society embraces *Pride*, it will send a clear signal to the international community that the present generation of Japanese endorses the behavior of the wartime government.

"In the end, the truth will prevail. I fervently hope and believe that time will allow more people in Japan to find the courage to say 'This is not the truth about ourselves. This movie is a dishonest depiction of our past.'"

In Japan, it was reported that Tojo's granddaughter, Yuko Tojo, was the force behind the movie, which was rumored to be based on a book she had written. She was trying to whitewash her grandpa's war-crime image. General Hideki Tojo, Japan's wartime prime minister, was executed as Japan's top war criminal in 1948, but was portrayed in the movie as a patriot and gentle family man. A *Washington Post* article on May 25 read: "Fifty years after the war, a remarkable perception gap still exists between Japan and the rest of world. . . . Many in those neighboring countries are still deeply angry at what they see as Japan's lack of remorse, and *Pride* is certain to inflame those bad feelings."

One scene in the movie, according to one report, was that Tojo refused to believe that Japanese soldiers had carried out the Nanking Massacre in China. After I read the report, I told Iris what a good thing it was that her book had just come out! I said to Iris that Tojo had a granddaughter who tried to cover up her grandfather's hideous war acts, but that thankfully *my* father had a granddaughter who told the world what had *really* happened in 1937. It's really a shame that up to this day, Japan as a nation has not been able to face up to its war crimes, and no written official apology has ever been issued.

Iris's book was praised by American historians and respected by Chinese communities internationally, but Japanese ultranationalists tried to discredit her by any means possible. On June 12, according to AP news, a group of Japanese "academics" in a conference in Tokyo accused Iris's book of being misleading and exaggerating the Nanking Massacre. They blamed the killings on the Chinese themselves. They denied the size of the death toll in the massacre. They also questioned the photos in her book. When the AP reporter tracked Iris down and asked her reaction to the Japanese accusation, Iris was in Lake Placid, New York to give a speech to the Cato Institute. Iris refuted the accusations with dignity and eloquence, one by one, over the phone. She told the reporter that the Japanese revisionists' denials ultimately only hurt Japan itself.

When the AFP reporter, Karen Lowe, telephone-interviewed Iris about the accusations of these six Japanese "academics," Iris replied: "These revisionists are engaged in a second rape of Nanking—the rape of history." In the AFP report of June 22, William Kirby, the Harvard University history professor and chairman (who wrote the Foreword for Iris's Nanking book), told Lowe, "This business of the body count is really a gruesome exercise in historical revisionism. If 100,000, 300,000, or 50,000 were killed, is it morally any different?"

"There really isn't any question that it was a policy of terror and murder," Kirby added. "Anyone who suggests that the Rape of Nanking never happened is in historical Never-Never Land."

Rabbi Abraham Cooper of the Simon Wiesenthal Center also commented: "Japan cannot be trusted as a member of the community of nations until it once and for all, sincerely and genuinely, apologizes for its deeds during World War II—beginning with Nanking."

I would be lying if I said that these accusations about her book had no impact on Iris's feelings. Even though we knew, and Iris knew, that the criticisms had no basis, it still affected her life in one way or another. It was very stressful for her that her book was under constant questioning and scrutiny. Worse yet, at this time she was also engaging in an exchange of opinions with her Japanese publisher, Kashiwashobo. The publisher, translating her book into Japanese, confessed to her that it was under the threats of ultranationalists in Japan. Consequently, Iris was bombarded with e-mails from the publisher with all sorts of questions and some unreasonable requests, indicating that Kashiwashobo was under tremendous pressure from the right-wingers in Japan.

In spite of all this, the summer of 1998 still had something that made Iris very happy. On June 24, 1998, she sent me an e-mail:

Dear Mom:

Your darling daughter is typing this email from the Miramar Hotel in Montecito right now, after delivering a one-hour speech at the Santa Barbara Writer's Conference to an audience of 150-200 people. The topic? My transformation from struggling author to bestselling author. Some women were so moved by the lecture that they broke down in tears! Indeed, it was an exhilarating evening for me, because so many old friends came to congratulate me, weep over me, to hug and kiss me. "Iris, you've gone away and come back a star!" The whole evening was one long joyous reunion, and afterwards I went out to the Montecito Inn with Barbara Masin to enjoy some cheesecake dessert.

Santa Barbara really is like a second home to me—after Champaign-Urbana.

I'm ecstatic that my speech in Santa Barbara was so well-received because I hardly had time to prepare my notes. You see, yesterday I really pushed myself write an op-ed article for the New York Times *(both the* Times *and the international edition of* Newsweek *want articles from me about the Japanese revisionists) and didn't have the energy to think about the Santa Barbara speech. Yet the audience loved it. Barbara Masin thought the speech was brilliant—a perfect balance of humor, history and personal narrative—and marveled at the improvement in my lecture style. She remembers how nervous I was during my first book signing in Santa Barbara at Barnes and Noble, which just was only two years ago. . . .*

Love, Iris

Another happy thing for Iris in June was that *Reader's Digest* chose her for the cover of their September issue. A couple of months earlier, she had been interviewed by Ralph Kinney Bennett, a writer from the magazine, and they were going to publish a big article on her and *The Rape of Nanking*. For the cover photo, she went to a beauty salon that was recommended by a friend for a makeover. The magazine photographer came to her place and took many photos of her. When the September issue came out in the middle of August, she immediately mailed us a copy. She was quite satisfied with the cover photo. We enlarged and framed it, and it has been on our wall ever since.

The September issue of *Reader's Digest* stirred up another round of media coverage. *Reader's Digest* has fifty million readers and is published in nineteen different languages worldwide. Iris had collected and showed us the issues with her on the cover in different languages. She got many compliments from readers and friends on her look for the cover photo, but I think the cover story really did a great service to get the story of the Rape of Nanking known to the world.

In October, Iris was invited back to the University of Illinois to give the prestigious MillerComm Lecture to an audience of eight hundred in the huge auditorium on campus; it was a very successful event indeed. On October 10, Iris was also invited to be one of the panelists of the conference on "War Crime of the East" at the UI campus, one of several events scheduled for her visit back to campus.

During the conference, one of the University of Illinois history professors attacked Iris's book, which was a complete surprise to all of us. However, I saw that Iris was very calm and presented her argument in a professional way. By this time, she had already written a number of articles to refute the attacks on her book and had answered numerous questions posed by many American and Japanese reporters concerning the Japanese ambassador's remarks and other Japanese revisionists' charges. I admired the way she handled the situation, and I realized that Iris had grown and matured into an experienced debater! But I also realized that not only did right-wing forces exist in Japan, but that some of Japan's right-wing sympathizers in this country could not be ignored either.

When we drove Iris to the Champaign airport and saw her off for the next stop of her book tour, none of us said very much on the way. I noticed that she was still preoccupied with the incident that had happened at the conference the day before—a surprise ambush by a history professor at her own alma mater. Finally, when she was stepping into the flight gate area, she said to us that a public debate seemed inevitable. She said that only through debating could she answer those criticisms of her book. "Starting with the Japanese ambassador!" she said.

In November, Iris was invited by the University of Hawaii to give a speech and sign some books. Since the date was close to Thanksgiving, she decided to take a vacation with Brett on a Hawaiian island afterward. This was the first time in a long time that she was taking a vacation. Two days after she returned from Hawaii, on December 1, she called us suddenly and told us that she would appear on the PBS *MacNeil-Lehrer News Hour* to face the Japanese ambassador to the U.S., Kunihiko Saito!

We immediately turned on the TV and waited for the 6 P.M. PBS News Hour. After Jim Lehrer reported that day's major news stories, Elizabeth Farnsworth began mediating the dialogue between Iris and Saito on the current issue of an apology. Iris was at the San Francisco TV station studio, whereas Saito was in Washington, D.C. The issue had arisen in October, when the South Korean president visited Japan, where Japan's Prime Minister Obuchi did offer a written apology for Japan's actions during the time it had colonized Korea. Then, several weeks later, when President Jiang Zemin of China visited Japan (the first-ever visit to that country by a Chinese leader), the Japanese prime minister had offered a verbal apology of Japanese wartime aggression against China, but no written statement of apology, infuriating Chinese people worldwide.

Now Farnsworth was asking Ambassador Saito to explain the difference in treatment for these two countries. Saito answered and said he did not see that there was any difference. He played down any difference and insisted that a written and verbal apology were the same. Then Farnsworth turned to Iris and asked why a written apology was so important. Iris replied that if a written apology was the same as a verbal apology, as Saito insisted, then she could not understand why Japan would not issue one to China.

Iris continued: ". . .the Japanese government had delivered an apology to the South Korean government, a written apology, and the Chinese government had expected the same a few weeks ago. And I think that the reason why it became an issue was because that expectation was pretty much dashed during Jiang Zemin's visit, which was, I think, certainly a loss of a golden opportunity for Japan to properly show its repentance for the crimes committed by the Japanese Imperial Army across Asia. . . ."

Saito stated that he thought that Prime Minister Tomiichi Murayama's statement in 1995 had already expressed his deep sense of remorse and had offered sincere apologies to the people of Asian countries.

Farnsworth then turned to Iris. "What would be enough?"

Iris replied: ". . . First of all, for Japan to honestly acknowledge some of the basic facts of these kinds of atrocities, which many revisionists refuse to do; and definitely a written apology, reparation made to the victims . . . inclusion of Japan's wartime aggression in school textbooks in Japan. . . ."

Iris continued: "And I think that people don't believe that Japan has properly apologized or atoned for what happened because these apologies don't come spontaneously and naturally. . . ."

Then she challenged the ambassador. "What I'm curious to know is: can the ambassador, himself, say today on national TV live that he personally is profoundly sorry for the rape of Nanking and other war crimes against China and the Japanese responsibility for it?"

Saito was responding with the usual words that the Japanese government always used: ". . . to the incident in Nanking, we do recognize that really unfortunate things happened, acts of violence were committed by members of the Japanese military. . . ."

Farnsworth wanted to conclude the interview and said "We have time only for a brief response from you."

Iris started to say that what Saito said was not entirely correct, but she was interrupted by Farnsworth asking her: "The apology?"

Iris at first was not quite sure she'd understood the question and repeated back, "The apology."

"Did you hear an apology?" Farnsworth asked.

"I don't know. Did YOU hear an apology? I did not really hear the word 'apology' that was made. And I think that if he had said genuinely, I personally am sorry for what the Japanese military had done during World War II, I would have considered that an apology. I think that would have been a great step in the right direction. . . ."

Shau-Jin and I, after watching the program, felt very worried and frightened. On the one hand we were very proud of Iris that she had the courage to ask the ambassador to apologize to the Chinese people on live TV, but on the other hand we felt that the right-wing nationalists in Japan would be angry if they saw it. I could not fall asleep that night. The next day, one of Shau-Jin's physics colleagues told him that he admired Iris for her courage, but at the end he added that Iris should hire a bodyguard. That comment fed our worries even more.

Right after the PBS appearance that night, Iris was in San Francisco engaging in a public interview with Professor Orville Schell of UC-Berkeley at Herbst Theatre. We did not get her call until later. She called after midnight and told us how successful the San Francisco event had been.

"There were more than eight hundred people in the audience, and most of them had to pay to get in," she said.

She also told us that everyone she met at the theatre congratulated her and said she had done a fabulous job on TV debating the Japanese ambassador. She seemed not worried about it at all. Actually, she was unhappy when we mentioned that she should be more careful about her personal safety. She said our worry was a burden to her and that we should relax. Then, a few days later, we received a big bouquet of fresh flowers from her with a thank-you card. I think she wanted to comfort our frightened souls.

When Iris's book became an international best seller, she reached a status most writers can only dream of: she became a celebrity. But she also paid a price for it. In February 1998, after a long book tour, she had already told us that once she came home, she did not want to go out anymore. All she wanted was to stay home with Brett and have a good sleep. After several weeks of continuous book signings, public speeches, and traveling, she said, her life was a nonstop blur of airport—lecture hall—hotel, airport—lecture hall—hotel. The responses to her speeches were overwhelming. Wherever she went, people besieged her after every speech. When she came home, she inevitably came down with a cold or the flu, only to recover just in time for the next book tour. She was physically exhausted.

Not only that, she said, but during the book signings, many old Asian people came up to her: Chinese, Korean, Filipino, Singaporean, Indian—they poured out their personal stories of suffering during World War II in Asia to her. Some of them wept and thanked her profusely for writing such a book. They said "It's so frustrating to see that Japan to this day hasn't formally acknowledged their war crimes!" They exclaimed "It's about time!" Iris said that on the one hand she felt rewarded that she was sought out and greatly respected by many people, but on the other hand she was mentally and emotionally drained after hearing those stories.

On June 29, 1998, Iris wrote:

> *Dear Mom,*
>
> *I arrived safely in New York today, after giving a well-received speech in Baltimore to the women doctors. Actually, it was very depressing—during the Q and A, a Pakistani doctor told the audience about the atrocities against Bengali women in 1971, a Filipino doctor described how she escaped the Rape of Manila when she was 12, an Indian doctor discussed the Indian tradition of suttee (burning widows alive), etc. Others talked about the international sex slave industry, the trafficking for women and children, female genital mutilation in Africa—you get the idea.*

It seemed that there were endless gruesome stories that people were eager to share with her.

When she was book-signing in one bookstore in San Francisco at the end of March 1998, the store was packed, all seats taken. One woman shouted out at the end of her speech that Iris deserved a Pulitzer and a Nobel Prize! She certainly felt flattered. In another bookstore in San Francisco in April, Iris said one man stood up and said "You've got guts!" There was long applause, and then he said, "Do you think the Japanese have a contract on your head?" At another speech on the East Coast, one person wrote a comment: "Brilliant to tell such a powerful story! I fear for your life." Iris said she was very disturbed by these comments, and they did nothing to quell my own worry either.

Some people told her that she was a Chinese Joan of Arc. Some Chinese people told her that she was Mulan, the legendary Chinese woman warrior who dressed in men's clothes and pretended to be her aged father's son, going into wars. Still another called her Qiu Jin, the turn-of-the-century Chinese revolutionary woman martyr who led an uprising against Manchus. The success of *The Rape of Nanking* now was not just a publishing phenomenon, but the beginning of a political movement. Iris found that people perceived her as some kind of crusader and activist, and that worried her. Michael, her brother, told her that many of his friends, mostly young Asian Americans, were urging her to go into politics. Michael said to his sister, "All Chinese-Americans look up to you to lead!" But in her heart, she said, she considered herself just a writer and a historian who merely wanted to right some wrongs.

But it was not all stress and politics—Iris had good times on her book tours, too. On November 4, 1998, Iris e-mailed me that she'd been able to meet three descendants of Nanking Safety Zone committee members at Ann Arbor, Michigan and received a priceless gift—the original Nanking Safety Zone Red Cross flag:

Dear Mom:

I just had a fabulous event at Shaman Drum bookstore in Ann Arbor, as well as a "hou gou" dinner with Harriet Mills, her sister Angie Mills (who came from Chicago to see me), Neal Brady, son of Richard Brady (a surgeon who worked for the safety zone committee after the worst of the massacre was over) and Rob Gray. Neal Brady (who is a doctor, like

his father) gave me one of the original Nanking safety zone Red Cross
flags, which I showed to an awestruck audience at Shaman Drum this
evening. (It was truly exciting for them to meet with three descendants
of the safety zone committee—two of whom are daughters of the founder
of the zone committee itself. And it was exciting for Harriet, Angie and
Richard Brady as well. . . . Harriet had not seen Brady since he was eight
years old!!)
    Love, Iris

Harriet Mills and Angie Mills are daughters of Wilson Plumer Mills, who was the Presbyterian missionary in Nanking in 1937 and who first suggested that the Nanking Safety Zone be created, according to Iris's book *The Rape of Nanking*, which cites a letter from Mills's daughter Angie to Iris; the letter cites a speech given by John Rabe wherein he says that "Mr. Mills is the man who originally had the idea of creating the Safety Zone." Later, Iris donated the Red Cross flag used at the Safety Zone to the Hoover Institution at Stanford.

On the book tour, Iris met many of our old friends and was also reunited with college and high-school friends. Iris told me that various of her friends reacted to her fame and celebrity status differently. Most of her friends were really happy for her; those she considered her true friends. A few, however, were threatened by her success and turned frosty and unhappy when Iris mentioned her book. But I suppose such things are to be expected from human nature.

She was also amazed that some former authors whom she had worshiped in college now treated her like their peer. Even more surprising was when she got requests from people thirty or forty years older, asking for blurbs and letters of reference. All this had happened in seven years. She said that she still couldn't quite believe it—it had all happened so fast!

But Iris said her major concern was her loss of time to read. One day, she called me after she'd read an excellent article in the *New Yorker* and felt bad. She asked herself how many hours she'd been able to spend reading new books over the past few months. She hadn't had time to read for pleasure in a long time. She said she should get back to reading and writing, and recalled the days when she'd been able to read as many books as she wanted. We laughed when we recalled how we'd caught her reading secretly after her light was supposed to be out, so Shau-Jin had to go down to the basement and unplug the electric circuit breaker. She was quite nostalgic about the years when she'd had plenty of time to read. She really felt this loss and supposed that this was a price she had to pay for her new celebrity status.

On top of her busy schedule of book tours, outside people might not realize that besides her traveling, signings and speeches, she was constantly bombarded with additional e-mail requests from news reporters for written interviews. Sometimes there were ten or fifteen written questions for her to answer, so the reporters could write a news article or a profile. Iris still could find time to answer those questions accordingly. She would always mail me a copy to "preserve" in case her computer for some unforeseen cause erased her files. In addition, in the summer of 1998, she had a heavy correspondence with the Japanese publisher Kashiwashobo, who was supposed to translate her book into Japanese, in working out the differences in historical interpretations, which took a lot of time to answer.

From March to July 1998, especially with the heat of the attack from the Japanese ambassador and the Japanese revisionists still sizzling, Iris received many requests from Japanese news reporters for an interview. Reporters from Japanese magazines such as *Bungei Shuju* and some freelance Japanese reporters asked Iris a number of questions, from why she wanted to write this book to questions on the controversy over the death toll in the Nanking Massacre. Some reporters even went into such details as the legal issue of reparation and the words of apology used by the former Japanese prime minister. She patiently repeated her argument, one point after another, never losing her head to pettiness or emotion.

In July 1998, Iris was invited to write for both the Asian and International editions of *Newsweek* to refute the criticisms raised by Japanese revisionists. Her article, titled "It's history, not a lie," was intended to set the record straight.

In the article, she wrote:

> *The revisionists are fighting an ultimately futile battle if they hope to erase the Rape of Nanking from history. Thousands of pages of primary source documents on the subject must be explained away. These documents are available in archives across the globe. They include American missionary diaries, U.S. Naval Intelligence reports, Japanese military diaries, letters and reports produced by the German embassy and the Nazi party in Nanking, declassified American intercepts of Japanese official communications, war-crimes transcripts, 1,700 testimonials from Chinese survivors, and news reports, including front page coverage of the massacre in the New York Times. In addition, photographs and newsreel film footage still exist.*

In the summer of 1998, Kinue Tokudome, a Japanese reporter who lived in Los Angeles, conducted an interview with Iris via e-mail. Iris took a great deal of time answering her, and Kinue translated the Q&A into Japanese and published it in the October 1998 issue of the Japanese magazine *Ronza*. Among the fifteen questions Kinue posted, the most-asked questions were about the death toll in the massacre, the authenticity of the photos used in the book, and the reparation issue. Iris answered those questions clearly, as she had answered them every other time she'd been asked them before.

Kinue Tokudome asked, "Some said that Japan already had apologized and the issue of compensation had been settled. How do you respond?" Iris replied:

> *"There have been vague apologies made but there has never been, to my knowledge, a specific apology issued by the Japanese government to the*

*victims of the Rape of Nanking. And the issue of compensation is far
from being settled. If you look at the 1951 San Francisco peace treaty you
will find that the treaty explicitly states that the issue of compensation
is to be postponed until Japan has financial means. I have contacts with
many international human rights lawyers and they all tell me that the
issue of compensation is far from being settled."*

Back in February 1998, Iris had been invited by the New York newspaper *Newsday* to write an Op-Ed article, which was published on
February 19, 1998. She specifically wrote about the reparation issue.
Her article was titled "Japan Must Pay for Its War Crimes." In the
article, Iris wrote:

> *Japan has argued that all matters related to reparations were settled in
> the 1951 San Francisco Peace Treaty. But a close reading of the treaty
> shows that the issue was merely postponed until the Japanese economy,
> still devastated by war, had the ability to make good on any restitution
> assigned them. Such an excuse is laughable today. The current financial
> crisis in Asia notwithstanding, Japan ranks as one of the world's wealth-
> iest countries.*
>
> > *If Germany can apologize and pay reparations, why can't Japan? The
> Germans have paid the equivalent of $60 billion to their victims and
> they will continue to pay several more billions by the year 2005. Earlier
> this year they agreed to pay additional billions to victims in Eastern Bloc
> countries. Indeed, in an era when even the Swiss have pledged billions to
> pay for the money stolen from Jewish bank accounts, allowing Japan to
> continue to evade its responsibilities becomes a new assault on the sen-
> sibilities of the victims of Nanking—let alone the conscience of humanity.*

Iris was one of the first few people to press the issue of monetary
reparation from Japan. I could see why the revisionists and the Japanese government were earnestly trying to discredit her and her book,
and had even invented the myth that the Rape of Nanking was a

"fabrication" or a "lie." Iris may not have known it, but her quest to force Japan to pay compensation for the war had caused others to perceive her as an activist.

The last question Kinue Tokudome asked Iris was: "Are you planning to go to Japan when your book comes out there?" Iris's answer showed her sincerity and support for those in Japan who wanted to reconcile the past and present. Iris replied:

> I don't know. All I do know is that I recognize that there are many sincere, wonderful and courageous people in Japan who want nothing more than to promote the truth, and these kinds of people—though in small numbers—can be found worldwide. This is a human quality that transcends ethnicity and nationality. Such people recognize that what happened in Nanking and in other regions of China is a human rights issue, and that patriotism or nationality or ethnicity has no bearing on human rights issues. They see the larger picture. I am one hundred percent behind those people in Japan, and I certainly hope to meet them one day.

One of the most time-consuming e-mail exchanges Iris engaged in at that time was with Charles Burress, a news reporter with the *San Francisco Chronicle*. In the summer of 1998, Burress wrote to Iris and asked her a number of questions about her book. Iris patiently replied, giving him her point of view. On July 26, 1998, Burress's article "Wars of Memory" was published. In the article, Burress mentioned that the Japanese "academics" and the Japanese conservatives had criticized Iris's book, but omitted mentioning Iris's responses to those unfounded accusations. Iris had explained these responses to him in a long course of communications between them. Iris felt that his article was unbalanced. She wrote a letter to the editor in response to Burress's article, but the *Chronicle* did not publish it.

In this new Internet era, newspapers were no longer the exclusive news outlet. Iris posted her long letter in response to Burress's article on the Web and promised to give a copy of the letter to any journalist who asked about Burress's article.

Iris's e-mail address was open to the public. Whenever she was on a book tour and too busy to check her e-mail on the road, her AOL inbox maxed out quite quickly. Even my e-mails bounced and did not reach her. She had so many fans! In addition to e-mails, she received a huge amount of postal mail from her fans. Whenever she came back from a book tour, her mail was piled up high. At the end, she had several boxes of mail from her fans, not only from the U.S., but from other parts of the world as well. I could not forget how she told me about a young man paralyzed from the neck down due to a motorcycle accident. He saw Iris on TV and listened to her speech and managed to write a moving letter to her, with a request for an autographed copy of *The Rape of Nanking*. Iris was very touched and sent him an autographed book along with copies of magazines carrying her picture on the cover and featuring the book.

Some people sent poems and music to her composed specifically for the victims of the Nanking Massacre. One World War II veteran wanted to give her his Purple Heart decoration, and many asked for her picture. All these things surely made her very happy, made her feel like it was all worthwhile.

Iris usually was good about replying to her fans if they wrote her e-mails; but when she got home from book tours tired and emotionally spent, she was overwhelmed by the mountains of mail. She told me she felt very guilty that she was not able to reply to all of it. She was the kind of person who had always graciously replied to her mail before she became a bestselling author. It took almost two years, but with a helper she finally replied to all those accumulated admiration letters from her fans; she said she had sent out a postcard bearing her photo on one side and a "thank you" with her signature on the other side.

She received some hate mail, too. She did not tell us right away, because she did not want us to worry. When we asked her for details, she said the hate mail was very limited, compared with the huge amount of positive mail she received. She seemed not to worry about it. Only after we moved to California to be near her did we realize that she had received an envelope containing two bullets.

Regarding Iris's family life, she did not have a whole lot of time with Brett that year; most of her time was spent on the road, promoting her book. In July 1998, Brett's parents came to California for a visit; they were hoping that Iris would accompany them and Brett to Tahoe and Yosemite for a vacation. Iris was in the middle of the battle defending her book against those Japanese revisionists, and she was also writing her next book proposal, so she had no interest in leaving home once she returned from book tours. In an e-mail of July 18, 1998, she wrote to me: "I think I've outraged countless old friends and acquaintances by now . . . simply by being busy. The truth is, interaction with people— even loved ones—can be draining, and I only have so much physical energy these days. After weeks in front of audiences and cameras, I relish being totally alone."

In January 1998, Susan Rabiner, Iris's former editor at Basic Books, became Iris's agent. After Susan left Basic Books, she had established her own book agency in New York. She sold the paperback rights for *The Rape of Nanking* to Viking Penguin in January 1998. Then Susan encouraged Iris to think about her next book project.

With careful consideration, Iris decided to next write on the Chinese immigration experience in this country. She was able to write the book proposal in between tours. At the end of the summer of 1998, she had already handed her book proposal, "Chinese in America," to Susan. Sometimes I wondered how she could manage to do so many things in such a short time. Her work ability and energy were amazing.

On October 22, 1998, Professor John Cronan handed me a letter and informed me that he had previously recommended that the Department of Microbiology appoint me a Research Associate Professor. Just that day, the department had confirmed my appointment. (Probably because he didn't want me to be disappointed, he had not let me know of his recommendation until the department passed the confirmation.) I was overjoyed, to say the least. Although I had decided that I was going to retire in 2000, to receive this title was still very gratifying. I wrote an e-mail to tell Shau-Jin, Iris, and Michael the good news immediately. Iris returned my e-mail right way with exciting—and even better—news of her own. She wrote:

> *Dear Mom,*
>
> *Congratulations!!!! You certainly deserve this title—especially after all these years of hard work and research. I'm so proud of you. And so happy that John Cronan spoke up on your behalf to get you this title.*
>
> *Your email came through just as I was checking my messages from the Radisson Empire hotel—how fortuitous.*
>
> *This afternoon, I had a wonderful lunch at the Savore restaurant with the top brass of Viking Penguin, and then signed the contract for the third book in my editor Caroline White's office. (Susan Rabiner even took a picture of me signing the contract because of the huge sums involved! We joked about this being "a historic moment.") So this has definitely been a marvelous day . . . for both mother and daughter!!!*
>
> *In a few minutes, I have to get ready to go to a New Yorker party. If I'm not too exhausted, I'll call you tonight and tell you all the exciting things that have been happening in my life in Manhattan!*
>
> *Love you, Iris*

Iris called from New York later to talk about all the wonderful news. The most exciting news was that she'd gotten a huge advance for her third book, *The Chinese in America,* from Viking Penguin—an amount so large that she did not want to disclose the exact amount to us yet. She was on another month-long book-signing and speech tour and was now in New York on the way to Boston. She said as soon as she finished this tour, she would start working on her next book and keep the momentum going.

The fact that *The Rape of Nanking* had hit the *New York Times* "Best Sellers" list fulfilled Iris's prediction for herself that one day she would become a best-selling book author; and, because she *had* made the list, she got a huge advance for her next book, which finally would alleviate some of the financial stresses that had still been weighing on her. It turned out that her writing profession was not necessarily a money-losing business after all; but it had certainly not been without a hard journey and many struggles along the way. I still have to give her a big round of applause for her belief in herself, even when things seemed bleakest.

Now, with the advance for her third book, Iris would be able to write for the next ten to twenty years without worrying about having to take extra jobs to support herself. I am saddened whenever I think about how her own life was cut short and that she was not able to enjoy the fruits of her own achievements and hard work.

After the excitement of the debate with the Japanese ambassador on December 1 was over, I thought there would be no more public appearances for Iris for the year. But I was wrong. Iris told me that the San Francisco-based organization on preserving the truth of the Sino-Japanese War and the UN Northern California Chapter had invited her to appear on December 9, 1998 to mark the fiftieth anniversary of the United Nations' Universal Declaration of Human Rights. She appeared with Martin Luther King III, the son of civil rights leader Martin Luther King, Jr., and Arun Gandhi, grandson of the legendary Indian leader Mohandas K. Gandhi, at the San Francisco Masonic Center in front of five hundred people. Iris told the audience that truth is one antidote to genocide, and that she believed "crimes against humanity must never be forgotten or denied."

When Christmas 1998 was approaching, Iris told us that she and Brett had been invited to Hilton Head Island, South Carolina, for a Renaissance Weekend retreat at the end of December. Iris explained to us that Renaissance Weekend was an annual event hosted by Linda LeSourd Lader and her husband Philip Lader, former U.S. Ambassador to the Court of St. James's. Renaissance Weekend is a family retreat for innovative leaders from diversified fields across the nation. They come to the retreat to exchange views in lectures, seminars, panel discussions, and workshops. Iris was very excited about it because she could meet many intellectuals and the brightest minds in the nation. And she also told us that President Clinton and Hillary Clinton came to the retreat every year, so she had the chance to meet them, too.

After Iris came home from the Renaissance Weekend, she wrote us a fifteen-page, single-spaced letter to describe her adventure at the retreat. She told us that we could not disclose any of her writing about the Renaissance Week to others, as it could result her in never being invited to Hilton Head again. (It's a rule.) Iris was surprised that some of the attendants recognized her immediately, because these people themselves were celebrities. Since I cannot disclose any details of what Iris wrote to us, here I will only say that she met many interesting celebrities such as Betty Friedan, the feminist and the author of *The Feminine Mystique*; Peter Arnett, the CNN correspondent; Peter Benchley, the author of *Jaws*; Amy Tan, the author of *The Joy Luck Club*; and a number of other famous people. But the most prominent ones were President Bill Clinton and First Lady Hillary Clinton. Iris said that at the New Year's Eve event, they did show up and gave a talk to the crowd. She had the chance to take photos with President Clinton and Hillary, respectively. She also gave a copy of her book *The Rape of Nanking*, and of the September issue of *Reader's Digest* with her on the cover, to the Clintons. She even managed to have a short talk with both Bill and Hillary Clinton at the party. The talk was brief because they were surrounded by other people who also wished to talk to the Clintons. Several months later, Iris received a personally signed thank-you note from President Clinton on his official Presidential stationery to acknowledge that he had received the book. Although Iris was critical of President Clinton regarding some current events, she admitted that she had been overwhelmed with emotion when she was able to be so close to power!

After Kashiwashobo acquired the rights for the Japanese translation of Iris's book in the spring of 1998, Iris did not hear anything regarding the actual translations until July. Iris told us she had heard that several Japanese historians and professors had turned down Kashiwashobo's requests to review the translation, and at least one of them admitted to backing out of the project due to pressure on his family from an "unknown organization." Iris said this was not a good sign. Around the same time, rumors circulated that Kashiwashobo had received death threats as the news leaked out that they had acquired the rights to *The Rape of Nanking*.

Both Shau-Jin and I were quite concerned about the development of the Japanese translation project of her book, so Iris was feeding us the news as soon as she heard anything from Basic and from the publishing house in Japan. Iris mailed copies of most important correspondence with Kashiwashobo to us. At the time, because of the unusual situation surrounding Kashiwashobo, Iris had already expressed that one day when she got old, the publication of the Japanese translation of her book by Kashiwashobo would be one important chapter in her memoir.

I have combed through the copies of notes and e-mails Iris gave us about the Japanese translation of her book. There are numerous details and twists of the event worth describing, since this will give a glimpse of how strong the pressure of the right wing in Japan is—so much so that it eventually thwarted the Japanese translation of her book such that there was no Japanese edition published for another ten years.

The first indication that Kashiwashobo wanted to change the contents of her book came in August 1998. That month, Kashiwashobo announced to Basic Books that a "Nanking Incident Research Committee" had undertaken the responsibility of fact-checking her book. Hiraku Haga, the editor-in-chief of Kashiwashobo, wrote to Iris to explain that there were conservative groups in Japan who insisted that the Nanking massacre had never happened. Their strategy was to "pick out detailed, minute mistakes in writers' comments" and "point out how the errors are an indication of a lack of research . . . the errors are then twisted around to prove that the argument has no validity at all." Therefore, Haga wanted all errors to be addressed in the Japanese edition before publication. In October, Iris received a long list of annotations to what Kashiwashobo and the Nanking Incident Research Committee considered to be errors in the book. The publisher requested permission to insert these annotations into her book as a separate appendix or between brackets alongside the original text.

Iris gave the annotations a thorough examination. She found in a few cases that the Committee had indeed found some minor errors in the book, such as misspelled names, and she agreed to let those changes (about ten of them) be corrected. But the vast majority of the annotations were not corrections of errors, but merely additional details of existing facts. Worst of all, according to Iris, many of these annotations were factually incorrect and contradicted several well-established historical accounts of World War II history, such as the Japanese role in the Marco Polo Bridge incident. After reading these annotations, it became clear to Iris that the Nanking Incident Research Committee's true intent was not to correct her mistakes, but to reinterpret entire sections of her book. Therefore, Iris did not permit Kashiwashobo to make the changes. I remember Iris spending long hours in her busy schedule going through the annotations point by point. In the end, she wrote Kashiwashobo a lengthy, three-part memorandum to explain why most of their annotations were not corrections of her errors after all.

After Iris e-mailed them, she thought the whole issue would be resolved. However, Haga wrote back that they had asked a history professor to write an Afterword to the Japanese edition of the book. Iris found that they had inserted some of the Nanking Incident Research Committee's subjective (and erroneous) commentary back into the Afterword. Iris did not want to permit them to do that either.

Meanwhile, Kashiwashobo voiced their concern about the photographs in the book. They said the Committee could not verify the authenticity of some of the photos. They wanted to delete them or put in a disclaimer to avoid the criticism from the right-wing conservatives. After Iris refused, then they wrote back to her and said they wanted to replace the map of Nanking in her book with a more accurate one. Upon carefully examining the new "accurate" map they provided, Iris found that the execution sites where the massacres occurred were missing from the map. She asked why. They replied, "because authorities cannot prove exact locations."

Iris asked us what their exact motives were. Iris felt that Kashiwashobo was cracking under the pressure of right-wing ultranationalists. At a very early phase, Iris said that they had received death threats, and these threats were not to be taken lightly. In January of that year, a right-wing extremist armed with a baseball bat had wrecked the offices of a Tokyo publisher who had published a book, *My Nanking Platoon*, a diary of a repentant Japanese soldier who had committed atrocities at Nanking. A year earlier, a fanatic had slashed a movie screen with his knife as audiences watched the Chinese-made film *Don't Cry Nanking*.

After Iris rejected all their requests for changes, she did not hear any more from Kashiwashobo for a while. Then, in February 1999, Iris began to receive calls from the Japanese media. Reporters were asking her to comment on a "supplement" of "errors" that the Kashiwashobo planned to release with the Japanese edition of *The Rape of Nanking*. Iris was shocked to hear such news—she did not know anything about it. Iris immediately asked the Basic Books foreign-rights department to inquire about the situation.

Iris was stunned when Basic Books learned that Kashiwashobo was planning to release another volume, called *The Nanking Massacre and the Japanese: How to Read The Rape of Nanking*—a book filled with negative reviews of her book and essays from the Nanking Incident Research Committee that challenged her book. The drama soon escalated: when Basic asked for information about the "other" book, Kashiwashobo immediately suspended the publication of both books. To Iris's dismay, Kashiwashobo told news reporters that Iris had demanded the cancellation of the other book. The fact was that Iris did not even *know* the other book *existed* until Basic Books started to inquire.

Iris told the news reporters that she did not give permission to have a "supplement" or "supplementary volume" attached to the Japanese edition of her book. If Kashiwashobo wanted to publish a separate book about her book, that was none of her business—as long as it was not *part* of *her* book.

Kashiwashobo then made confusing and contradictory statements to the Associated Press in a story released on February 24, 1999. Haga told the AP that Kashiwashobo had "no obligation to consult with her about the other book because it is a different project," yet insisted that they would cancel Iris's book if she did not agree to allow the simultaneous release of *The Nanking Massacre and the Japanese*. "We will not publish her book alone," Haga said.

Iris also told us that she had proof that Haga's original plan was to sell the other book as a supplement—indeed, a "supplement that points out errors in the original." In February, a press release was posted on the Internet to announce a professional luncheon that would be hosted by Hiraku Haga and professor Akira Fujiwara on February 24 at the Foreign Correspondents' Club in Tokyo. (The luncheon was later cancelled when Kashiwashobo postponed publication of both books.) The title of the lunch discussion was to be "Nanking 1937? What Really Happened?" In the announcement, it stated ". . . The publisher picked a highly unusual—and arguably unprecedented—path, combining a faithful, completely word-for-word translation and a separate supplement that points out errors in the original and contains essays on the event. . . ."

Iris felt that this was a complete breach of contract. For translation, the publishing house only had the right to faithfully translate the original content of a book into a foreign language, and there was nothing in the contract that said that the publisher had the right to reinterpret the book's contents.

In a sense we all agreed, and we felt relief when Kashiwashobo stopped the publication of the Japanese edition of Iris's book. We were glad it was over. We told Iris it seemed it was not the right time for her book to be published in Japan, although the Japanese people deserved to know their own history better. "Like it or not," Iris said, "it's their history!"

16

Research on Chinese in America

I ris's idea to write about the Chinese in America as her next book's topic came from her many tours for *The Rape of Nanking*. In her introduction to *The Chinese in America*, published in 2003, she wrote, "As I toured the United States and Canada giving talks on the subject [the Rape of Nanking], I encountered vibrant Chinese American communities that I had not even known existed. The people I met ranged from descendants of transcontinental railroad workers to new immigrants studying here on scholarships, from illiterate factory workers to Nobel laureates at leading universities, from elderly survivors of Japanese wartime atrocities to baby girls adopted by white parents."

She continued: "At first, I feared the subject might [be] too broad, but I couldn't let go of the idea of exploring the history of my people. Moreover, I believed I had a personal obligation to write an honest history of Chinese America, to dispel the offensive stereotypes that had long permeated the U.S. news and entertainment media." This was a project she was passionate about, and she devoted four years to writing it.

As promised, when Iris returned from Renaissance Weekend at the beginning of 1999, she began actively working on *The Chinese in America*. The plan for the book, she said, was to collect as many materials as possible and then to write a detailed outline. She had been contacting many of her friends and asking them to give her leads on how to find source materials. Her friends in immigration research suggested several places to look for the records of Chinese immigrants. Iris planned to visit the U.S. National Archives, Bay area archives in California, and museums such as the Chinese Historical Society in San Francisco, Angel Island, and the San Bruno branch of the Immigration and Naturalization Service. She also told us she was going to the UC-Berkeley East Asian library to do research.

Iris spent one week at UC-Berkeley in January 1999, intensively copying source materials from Berkeley's vast Ethnic Studies library. By the invitation of Him Mark Lai, the authoritative historian on Chinese-Americans, she attended the Chinese Historical Society meeting in San Francisco and met many authors who had written Chinese-American histories or stories. She bought $300 worth of books on Chinese-American history at the Society. She said that when she returned home, her car was filled with boxes of books and related materials. I also forwarded her any articles related to Chinese immigration that I found in Chinese or English newspapers and magazines.

Iris was awarded the San Francisco Chinatown Community Children's Center (CCCC) Role Model Award in March 1999. She went to San Francisco for the occasion and took the opportunity to talk to Him Mark Lai at his home. On March 19, she wrote:

> Dear Mom,
>   I just got home tonight, after spending the last few days in San Francisco. It's been a busy last few days.

On Tuesday afternoon, at 3 p.m., I visited Him Mark Lai at his home
in San Francisco. He lives on a hill on Union Street, . . . they are really
wonderful, generous people. Him Mark is also a walking encyclopedia
of Chinese American history. . . . He is well educated (he studied at UC
Berkeley and used to work as an engineer). . . . He is constantly writing
scholarly articles about Chinese American history, yet he toils outside of
the world of academe, without much concern for title or recognition. He
and his wife probably don't have much money.

I spent a few hours talking to him, jotting down notes, browsing
through his library, and then I drove to the gala fundraiser at the Asian
Art Museum. Because of my tight schedule, I actually changed into my
black evening gown in Him Mark Lai's tiny bathroom.

At the museum, I gave my ten-minute speech and received the Chinatown Community Children's Center Role Model award. Fred H. Lau,
chief of the San Francisco Police Department, received the Community
Service award. Lau is the highest ranking Chinese American police
officer in the country. . . .

The gala organizers had actually assigned escorts for us. Lau was
flanked by two Miss Chinatowns: Miss Chinatown USA and Miss Chinatown San Francisco. They looked pretty conspicuous in their tight satin
chipaos and sparkling rhinestone crowns. I was to be escorted by "Mr.
Asia," but somehow he couldn't make it, so the CCCC hastily brought
in another handsome young man to replace him. Predictably, the press
showed up to take pictures. (Him Mark Lai told me later that the Chinese newspapers raved about the elegance of my gown. I wonder if they
actually reported anything that I SAID.)

I have to admit that I was delighted with the free hotel accommodations that I received as a result of accepting this award. Weeks ago, I told
the CCCC that I needed to stay in a hotel in SF so I wouldn't have to
drive back to Sunnyvale late at night, when I was tired. Also, I wanted
to take the opportunity to do some research around Chinatown. A board
member of the CCCC saw to it that the Renaissance Parc 55 would
donate a room for me for two nights. This room—#3164—turned out to

be one of their luxurious, VIP corner suites. The place was bigger than my apartment in Sunnyvale!

On Wednesday, I slept late, and then visited the Gum Moon Woman's Residence and Cameron House. Both were rescue missions during the early part of the century for Chinese women and children. Before, Gum Moon served primarily as an orphanage for young girls; today, Gum Moon operates as a Chinese boarding house with very reasonable rates (about $90 a week). Cameron House, which used to shelter girls who had been sold into prostitution, has become something of a YMCA-style center for Chinese youth.

The people at Gum Moon were kind to open their files for me. I spent the afternoon poring over the journal of the missionary Carrie Davis, written around the turn of the century, and leafing through the personal files on some of the former tenants at Gum Moon. (The stories broke my heart—stories of battered wives, women sold into prostitution, abandoned and neglected babies, little girls who had been raped or who themselves had been the product of rape, etc.) Just a few blocks away was Cameron House, and the staff there showed me the entrance of one of the underground tunnels that used to hide Chinese women from the tongs.

I spent the rest of Thursday back at Him Mark Lai's home, where I asked him a million questions and took notes. He and his wife then invited me to dinner at Mon Kiang, a Hakka cuisine restaurant. I insisted on paying the bill because Him Mark had been so generous with his time. He told me that he was eager to help me because he knows I will do an excellent job, judging from my track record with THREAD OF THE SILKWORM and THE RAPE OF NANKING. Moreover, general histories on the Chinese in America are rare, he said. They place too much emphasis on the Cantonese-speaking Chinatown populations, and neglect to describe the migration of the Mandarin-speaking Taiwanese. In fact, not much has been written about the lives of the Chinese during the last 50 years, he told me.

Him told me that for years he had considered writing a general history of the Chinese. But now, in his 70s, he feels that his time would be better spent writing journal articles on more specialized topics—ones that other historians tend to ignore because of language barriers. His research requires intensive use of Chinese primary source materials, which many scholars cannot read. He genuinely believes that if he does not write these articles before his death, no one ever will.

As I write this I am suddenly moved—almost to tears—by the image of Him Mark Lai working alone, in relative obscurity, in his cramped little house filled with books and papers . . . an old man who has selflessly, tirelessly devoted most of his life to laying down the foundation for Chinese American history, so that other scholars might reap the rewards.

He said to me: "Your book is the book I should write, but never will."

Love, Iris

Iris had used all her public appearances to appeal to the Chinese communities to give her any information or materials related to their family immigration experiences, such as personal stories and letters. She wanted to collect as many materials as possible for her book.

In the beginning of April 1999, Iris was going to the East Coast for a month, for a speaking engagement and to do research in the National Archives and Library of Congress in Washington. She wrote me on April 20, 1999:

Dear Mom,

Sometimes I forget how miserable research can be. I spent hours at the National Archives, opening dozens of boxes and flipping through thousands of documents. By the end of the process, my cuticles were bloody (from paper cuts) and my fingertips black with ink. Even now, I have a throbbing headache from the smell of rotting paper. Many of those boxes haven't been opened for more than a century! Back in the late 1880s, the immigration officials stored documents by folding them into thirds (as you would fold a letter) and then bundling them together with red string. I'm sure the filing system worked well at the time, but it's disastrous for historians and archivists. Some of the pages were so brittle that the pages

*would have snapped in two if I had tried to open them! (A couple docu-
ments were in such horrible condition they would have crumbled away
into confetti.) I alerted the archivists to the problem, and they thanked
me and said that the preservationists would work on the documents
immediately. Apparently they use humidity or chemicals to relax the
pages, and then protect them in transparent sleeves. . . .*

    Much love, Iris

Then, on April 22, 1999, while she was in D.C., she told us, in an
e-mail, "Believe it or not, today Diana Zuckerman and I had a meeting
with Hillary Clinton at the White House! More details to come. . . ."

It turned out, on very short notice, that Diana Zuckerman had
arranged a private meeting between Iris and the First Lady for that
day. Later, Iris told us that she briefed Mrs. Clinton on the Japanese
war crimes during World War II and asked her support for a proposed
bill on declassified documents on Unit 731. Iris promised to send her
more materials to keep her informed. Mrs. Clinton also said to Iris that
she'd love to see her next time Iris visited Washington.

After leaving D.C., Iris went to New York, where she attended the
Committee of 100 meeting. She had been invited to be a member of
the Committee of 100 when she hit the *New York Times* "Best Sellers"
list. The Committee of 100 (or C-100 for short) is a Chinese-American
organization established by prominent Chinese-American elites in
1990 (such as world-famous architect I. M. Pei and musician Yo-Yo
Ma). In the meeting, Iris was chosen to be on the Role Model panel
discussion with several famous Chinese-Americans such as David
Ho, the biochemist who discovered the "cocktail" drug recipe for
AIDS patients. In the panel discussion, Iris told the audience about
her journey to become a writer and why she had wanted to write *The
Rape of Nanking.*

While Iris was trying to concentrate on her research for her next
book, she still could not get away from the distraction generated by
the translation of *The Rape of Nanking* in Japan. The whole thing finally

ended in the middle of May when her publisher announced in a press release, "Basic Books and Japanese publisher Kashiwashobo have agreed to terminate their contract for the Japanese edition of *The Rape of Nanking*." In the statement, John Donatich, the representative of the Perseus Books group, said: "The contract between us stipulated very clearly that no modifications to the text or artwork of Basic's edition be made without the author's consent. We believe a publisher to be neither advocate for nor critic of the book, but an entity that makes the book available for judgment by its public." The statement also said, "Basic Books regrets that Kashiwashobo will not be publishing *The Rape of Nanking* and will begin seeking another Japanese publisher for the work. *The Rape of Nanking* is a fine book with important research and impassioned conviction, deserving publication in Japan."

At this period of time, besides her research on her next book and the speech engagement, much of Iris's precious time was spent in dealing with this matter, and we were all glad it was finally over. (Note: It took ten years, until November 2007, the tenth anniversary of the publication of Iris's book in the U.S. and the seventieth anniversary of the Nanking Massacre, for the Japanese translation of her book to finally be published in Japan.)

There was an unexpected result of the translation dispute. The abrupt halt of the Japanese translation resulted in a boost in paperback sales of the book in the U.S. and even in Japan, though it was only available in English. Caroline White, the book editor of Viking Penguin, told Iris that in March, after the news came out, sales had shot up.

When the Japanese translation issue ended, next came the Cox report—another thing that occupied some of Iris's time during this period. The Cox report was the January 3, 1999 product of a special committee on U.S. National Security and Military/Commercial Concerns with the People's Republic of China. The report alleged that the PRC had stolen some secrets of U.S. nuclear-weapon designs. The redacted report was declassified in May 1999. Iris got a copy of it and found out that her book on Dr. Tsien, *Thread of the Silkworm*, was cited in the footnotes of the Cox report as a reference nine times. To her dismay, it seemed that her book on Dr. Tsien had been used to indicate that Dr. Tsien was a Communist. They also believed that he was a Chinese spy, and had deported him back to China (in the 1950s). Later, an article in *Time* magazine about Chinese espionage also implied Dr. Tsien was a spy, using the Cox report as a source. Worse yet, in a similar article in the *Washington Times*, it simply asserted that Dr. Tsien *was* a spy. This infuriated Iris and she immediately sought to clarify it in a statement, saying that in her three years of research, Dr. Tsien was *never* officially charged by the U.S. government with spying. In the 1950s, the U.S. government had not found any evidence that he was a spy. Iris said that instead, he was accused of being a "potential" Communist; however, the U.S. government could not find any concrete proof of that, either. Therefore, Iris said that unless there was new evidence indicating that he was a Communist, the accusation in the Cox report was irresponsible. Iris asked the staff of the Cox report committee for more information proving that Dr. Tsien was a spy, but they said they could not release anything was not in the published report for reasons of national security.

This was during the tense period that Chinese spying and espionage was front-page news in this country almost every week. On March 6, 1999, the *New York Times* printed a front-page story about a security breach at the Los Alamos National Laboratory involving one of the United States' most advanced thermonuclear warheads, the W-88. Two days after the March 6 article, Dr. Wen Ho Lee, a Chinese-American nuclear physicist working at Los Alamos, was fired and his named leaked to the press as the man under FBI investigation for espionage. The case was compounded by the release of the Cox report.

At this time it seemed that all Chinese-American scientists working on weapons research in this country were Chinese spies, reminiscent of the 1950s McCarthy era's witch-hunt for Communists! Many Chinese-American organizations and minority groups joined together to protest about the U.S. government for its racial profiling and stereotyping. Iris was particularly unhappy about it, and the Wen Ho Lee case was one of the subjects in her speech and in *The Chinese in America.*

Eventually, as we later learned, Dr. Lee was charged with only one count of improperly downloading classified (later labeled "restricted") data. After eight months in solitary confinement in handcuffs and shackles, Dr. Lee was released by Judge James Parker, who offered an apology to Lee for what he called "abuse of power" by the federal government in its prosecution of the case.

In the spring of 1999, Iris told us that she had been invited to give a keynote speech at a conference organized by Bay area Asian-Americans called Aspire 1999. We were already planning to visit her around that time, so she invited all of us to the conference evening gala event.

On May 29, we flew to San Francisco and arrived at the Hyatt near the airport in time for the dinner and the speech. We sat at a table of several distinguished guests to whom Iris had introduced to us: California House Representative Michael Honda, Oregon State House Representative David Wu, entrepreneur John Chen, and others. When we finished the dinner before the dessert, the MC introduced Iris to the podium and Iris delivered her keynote speech.

The title of her speech was "The Human Right to Historical Honesty." Her powerful and clear voice attracted the attention of all five hundred people in the ballroom. I observed that during her speech no one left their table and only her words filled the air. She touched on the current issue of the Cox report and the ongoing racial profiling of the Chinese for espionage. She said "I am not here to defend or accuse Tsien. I'm not even ruling out the possibility that he was a spy. . . . But if the U.S. government is going to make serious accusations against a man who isn't here to defend himself, then they should be prepared to back up their accusations with evidence. There's a big difference between accusation and actual proof!"

She also gave her reason why historical honesty was important; it had direct bearing on our future as an ethnic minority in this country. "As Asian-Americans," she said, "we have the right to see our people included—both honestly and accurately—in the pantheon of American history." She continued: "Unfortunately, to this day, there are still few films or books about Asians that are historically honest. We still have images of Asian women as prostitutes or sex slaves, and Asian men as drug lords or spies—or just plain geeks." She told the audience, "One way to dispel prejudice is to write a book. I'm trying to combat stereotypes with my current work in progress—a narrative history of the Chinese in America."

She strongly criticized the Cox report and the *Washington Times*, saying, "Their story reminds me of the kind of irresponsible journalism that marred the Tsien case during the McCarthy era." She said, "I think the Asian-American community is entitled to historical accuracy and honesty from the U.S. government. If they're going to call Tsien a spy, then they should open up the records and prove it, especially on a subject that happened fifty years ago. You can't have a government arbitrarily labeling people as Communists or spies. And you can't engage in a fair discussion with the U.S. government if they are withholding evidence, or jumping to conclusions without evidence and then insisting, when questioned, that their facts are classified. As U.S. citizens, we have the right to know. At this moment, more is at stake than whether Tsien was a spy or not. If we don't press our own government for accountability, they may come to believe that they can rewrite history at whim."

This led to the reason why she had wanted to write *The Rape of Nanking*. She told the audience, "History is one way to maintain checks and balances to power. . . Historical amnesia only increases the possibility of human-rights abuse and genocide. For it emboldens those who think they could get away with murder, and not be judged for their actions by future generations." Iris continued: "We have a moral responsibility to speak out against injustice. . . . It was this sense of moral responsibility—and moral outrage—that goaded me to write my second book, *The Rape of Nanking*."

I was certainly very moved by her speech. After the party, she was surrounded by young Asian-Americans who asked her questions and started taking photos with her. Her speech impressed many people, and one representative of a famous speakers' agency came up to her and tried to recruit her as a client.

Besides travel, speech engagements, and research for her next book, she was also writing Op-Ed pieces to newspaper editors whenever she saw fit because at this time, almost two years after the publication of *The Rape of Nanking*, the book was still subjected to discussion in the media and people still could not stop talking about it. Iris was not scared to fight back when she felt a criticism of her book was unfair.

In a letter to the editor of the *Los Angeles Times* on October 17, 1999, she referred back to Joshua Fogel, who had criticized Harriet Mills's book review of the book *The Good Man of Nanking: The Diaries of John Rabe*. In Fogel's letter, he wrote that "Iris's book *The Rape of Nanking* was not only based on 'flimsy' evidence, but roundly criticized by historians who have investigated the topic. . . ." Iris asked in her letter, "Exactly which parts of my research did he find 'flimsy'? The Rabe diary? The thousands of records kept by American missionaries who witnessed the massacre? The firsthand accounts of both Chinese survivors and Japanese participants? The contemporaneous press coverage?" Iris continued, "Fair disclosure would require Fogel to mention that almost all the historians critical of *The Rape of Nanking* are Japanese. . . . Outside of Japan, however, the response to my book has been overwhelmingly favorable. . . ."

I don't think Iris was exaggerating. J. G. Ballard in England had written an excellent review of Iris's book that was published on February 21, 1999 in London's *Sunday Times*. After the review, Iris's book was on the best-seller list in London. Ballard praised the book highly, saying "I shuddered over each page of this heart-rending book, but strongly urge everyone to read it." Iris was thrilled, especially because Ballard himself was a respected author and critic whom Iris truly admired. Iris had read his book *The Empire of the Sun*, which described his childhood war experience in the 1940s, when he and his parents were in Shanghai during the Sino-Japanese War.

Later, in the 1980s, our family had watched the movie of the same name, based on his book. After the book review, Iris was able to correspond with him. Ballard was very kind and mailed an autographed bookplate specifically for us. Iris pasted the autographed bookplate into his book and gave it to us as a gift. On the bookplate, he signed "For Shau-Jin and Ying-Ying Chang, Survivors of the Pacific War. Best wishes, J G Ballard." We were as excited as Iris was!

Iris told us that it was not uncommon for a book to be criticized when it was first published. As she wrote to us on November 4, 1999, John Steinbeck's book *The Grapes of Wrath* had also been attacked at the time it was published:

> *Dear Mom:*
>
> *Tonight I read an article about John Steinbeck's life in the Los Gatos mountains area, and learned that the reaction to THE GRAPES OF WRATH mirrored that of THE RAPE OF NANKING. In a letter to a friend Steinbeck wrote: "The vilification of me out here from the large landowners and bankers is pretty bad. The latest is a rumor started by them that the Okies hate me for lying about them. So I'm frightened at the rolling might of this thing. It is completely out of hand. I mean a kind of hysteria about the book is growing that is not healthy."*
>
> *Love, Iris*

One of Iris's friends told her, "The root of the hostility in some criticism toward you lies in the fact that you got so much fame and attention for *The Rape of Nanking*. A backlash is inevitable."

On the other hand, Iris was happy that so many people supported her. In August 1999, Lou Reda's documentary *The Rape of Nanking*, in which Iris was interviewed, was shown on the History Channel. The documentary gave a boost to the sales of Iris's book. Iris said she could see the ranking of the paperback on Amazon.com soar immediately after the documentary aired.

But the most gratifying thing was that the Rape of Nanking has now earned its place in world history because of her tireless efforts. On September 22, 1999, she wrote:

> *Dear Mom,*
>
> *Now, a piece of good news: the Rape of Nanking has earned its place in world history. When I visited the local SuperCrown in Sunnyvale last week, I found the Nanking massacre included in several recently published histories of the 20th century. For instance, author Martin Gilbert devotes pages 161 to 165 of his massive "A History of the Twentieth Century, volume 2: 1933-1951" to the Rape of Nanking, and even quotes me directly on page 162. (His information on Nanking is derived almost exclusively from my book, with the exception of a few quotes gleaned from other works.) The Rape of Nanking also appears in "The Complete Idiot's Guide to 20th Century History" (p. 232), and Peter Jennings's "The Century," and Steven Ambrose's "American Heritage New History of World War II."*
>
> *Remember how I agonized about RON missing the 50th anniversary of World War II? In the end, it didn't make a difference. In fact, now in retrospect, I believe the timing of THE RAPE OF NANKING was perfect. It appeared in print only three years before the close of the millennium, giving other historians time to include this atrocity in world history epics slated for publication in 1999 or 2000.*
>
> *Much love, Iris*

Starting in August of 1999, Iris had spent her time reading all the books and thesis papers she had collected on the Chinese in America. After finishing each book, she typed the major themes, and the most intriguing facts, into her computer databases in preparation for her writing. Her neck and wrists were sore from the long hours of typing. Finally, she hired a student researcher to help her type the information into the computer. The materials she collected were vast. In February, Iris and Brett moved to a new apartment down the street in hopes of being able to cure Brett's allergies; they suspected the old apartment might have mold problems. Their new apartment was not big, so she hired a carpenter to install shelves on the walls to hold her boxes of books and research materials. When we came to visit them at the end of May, I was impressed to see two walls of shelves full of books and papers.

Iris said that the more she read, the sharper the picture she had in her mind of individuals, and of the progress of the Chinese as a group. And she said she was no longer threatened by the boxes of books and materials, like she had been at the beginning of this project, but actually looked forward to writing it.

Iris used to tell me that writing was a lonely journey. She was constantly encouraging and driving herself by words such as "I shall write the book as if I only had one year to live. Write as if I am under a death sentence."

Iris reminded herself to continue writing to preserve history. "People die twice—once as mortals, and once in memory. I weep when stories are lost."

That was why Iris wanted to preserve the Chinese immigration experience in America. She also wanted to preserve our family history as part of her book. In the spring of 1999, she gave us a list of questions to answer in writing, such as how we'd escaped the Communists and moved to Taiwan, how we'd gotten to the U.S., and what our feelings had been when we'd first reached the U.S. She also videotaped us during interviews when she came home in the summer. She used to say, "The spoken word vanished with the wind. Likewise, the unrecorded life disappears as if it never existed." But unfortunately, at end, due to limited space, Iris told us that she was not able to include our own family stories in *The Chinese in America*, which was already five hundred pages thick!

In the summer of 1999, PBS aired a program on Chinese-Americans. It was a perfect time for such a program to educate the public about this ethnic minority, especially when the Cox report and Dr. Wen Ho

Lee's case were still in the air. We told Iris that her book on Chinese-Americans, just like the Rape of Nanking, would be right on target yet again!

Near the end of 1999, Iris told us that she had been chosen as one of the top hundred most influential Asian-Americans of the decade for a millennium issue of a magazine called *A Magazine* for Asian-Americans. But she declined their invitation to a celebration gala in Los Angeles because she wanted to concentrate on writing. Since August 1999, Iris had declined many invitations for public appearances; some people might be offended, Iris said, but her main goal for the next couple years was writing the next book and finishing it on time. In an e-mail on November 12, 1999, she wrote, "During the last few days I've been busy reading, reading, reading . . . highlighting sections from books and giving them to my typist." And she did exactly that for many months.

Even in such a time-conscious period, Iris had been unselfishly spending her precious free time helping young students. I recall she told me that while screening to find a student to help her type her research materials into databases, one candidate was a Stanford student who told Iris that she wanted to write about the Rape of Manila and wanted to meet her to seek her advice. Iris made an appointment to meet the student at the Stanford campus near the Thanksgiving holidays. Iris was never stingy to anyone who showed a willingness to learn or who asked her for advice. This was also true for scholars or writers who might be her competitors in the book market; she never hesitated in giving out advice to help their research. For example, Iris told James Bradley, the author of *Flyboys*, to contact the key person, Bill Doran, for the bulk of the narrative. Iris was always unselfishly helping others—at the root of this was her strong belief that truth should be told and justice restored.

Iris's personal life was quite eventful that year as well. In January, she called me to say that she was going to the UC-Berkeley library to do research for her next book and would stay in a hotel for a week.

This was only about a month after she had debated the Japanese ambassador on national TV. Because of the political sensitivity of the debate, I was worried about her physical safety. On the phone, I told her that she should be careful and not travel alone. Iris was upset and lashed out when she heard my words. She thought I was a worrywart, but I considered it ordinary mother-to-daughter advice. After all, what mother isn't a worrywart to some degree? Immediately, I apologized to her and admitted that I should not be so protective of her. Indeed, she was thirty-one years old and married. But somehow I still felt that she was my little beloved daughter and that I would do anything to protect her, especially since I'd had such an eerie feeling after her debate with the ambassador and still had not been able to shake it.

Apparently, Iris felt sorry after our phone conversation. On January 18, 1999, right after the call, she sent me an e-mail:

> *Dear Mom,*
>
> *About last night: there is no need to apologize for anything. I felt terrible about losing my temper. It wouldn't have happened if I wasn't feeling so stressed out.*
>
> *I thought about you today as I drove through town. I thought about how you and Dad had shaped me during the last 30 years. Both of you loved me and believed in me at a time when everyone else in town seemed intent on deriding me.*
>
> *Did you recall how, as a teenager and college student, I used to confide my ambitions to you—as well as my darkest fears that I might never fulfill them? But you always said, "Don't worry Iris, you WILL succeed. I KNOW you will. Because there is something unique about you, something special that set you apart from all the other children as you were growing up. I saw this in you, almost from the moment you were born."*
>
> *Those words would sustain me for years—through years of risks, failures and bouts of depression. You may not have realized it at the time, but those words had power. Those words changed my life.*

That's why we should expect the best for each other, not fear the worst.
People tend to move, subconsciously, in the direction of other people's
expectations.

Love, Iris

Her e-mail made me cry right there in my office. We knew each other
so well. She was my daughter and also my best friend—we never
had any hesitation about expressing our innermost feelings. It was
gratifying that she still remembered my encouraging words from the
unhappy days of her teenage years.

In January 1999, Diana Zuckerman, Iris's friend and also the director
of the Institute for Women's Policy Research at the time, interviewed
Iris about her personal life and her view on women's roles in family
and society. Iris talked about both her father and me. "Both my mother
and my father always felt that we children could succeed in anything
that we put our minds to. And my father never treated me differently
because I was a girl. He encouraged me to study math and science,
and I'm tremendously grateful to him for that, because it's helped
me to become a better thinker, more logical and analytical. Both my
parents encouraged me to read widely. I never really got a sense that
my options were limited just because I was female."

One time when Iris was in college, Shau-Jin told her, "Your intelligence is easily in the top one percent of the world's population. Just
remember, you are smarter than at least ninety-nine percent of the
men on this planet." I don't know where Shau-Jin got that statistic, but
I think he must have felt that way after he talked with Iris about some
math puzzles or science problems. Iris told me our confidence in her
certainly built her self-esteem when she was growing up.

In February 1999, Iris and Brett moved to a new apartment on
Old San Francisco Road in Sunnyvale, several blocks from their old
apartment. The apartment they were going to move into was newly
constructed and was just down the street. When we visited this new
apartment at the end of May, we saw that there was a high-power line

near the building, which Iris had not noticed before they signed the contract. About this time, Iris was seriously thinking about having a baby, and after she noticed it, the power line made her worried because there was some speculation in various news reports that close proximity to high-power lines might be linked to cancer. They only lived there for a year before they moved again.

Brett also changed jobs around this time. He was planning to leave his technology management position at Applied Signal Technology and look for employment as a quantitative analyst at a hedge fund. However, after Brett and Iris attended their first Renaissance Weekend, they felt how fortunate they were to be right in the center of the broadband revolution. They said that many people they met from New York City were considering leaving their jobs and moving to Silicon Valley. So they made a decision to stay in Silicon Valley. Brett accepted a technology-development position at Cisco Systems.

Besides focusing on her writing, Iris was thinking about having a baby at this time. In January, she told me that she'd had a physical checkup with her OB-GYN, and the result was normal and healthy. She had expressed the desire to have a baby soon. We were very happy to hear that, and gave her all the encouragement we could. I had always told her about the joy of having children. Although raising children might somewhat delay her career, I assured her that the experience was absolutely worthwhile. In a conversation in March 1999, we told Iris that Shau-Jin was going to retire in the coming fall (after thirty years of teaching) and that I planned to retire in 2000. If she had a baby in the next year, we would be glad to come to California to help her. I told her that if that became true, then it would be exactly sixty years between me and the baby!

In February and March 1999, when the Japanese translation of Iris's book was a big issue in the news, she noticed that her phone line had some background static noise. One time when she talked to her editor about the Japanese translation issue on the phone, both of them heard the background noise and even heard vague far-away voices. After that, Iris always noticed a clicking sound whenever she made a phone call. She expressed concern that her phone line might be bugged. She reported this to the phone company, and they did an on-site check but could not find anything unusual. She told us she would use more e-mails rather than the phone to communicate with us and with her friends.

Around this time, Iris and Brett were eager to buy a house and start a family, but Iris was in the middle of a multi-city book tour. Finally in the fall of 1999, Iris finished her travels, and they agreed to start house-hunting. They worked with a realtor based in the Los Gatos Mountains, and soon they made an offer on a house in the mountains of Los Gatos, near Bear Creek. Iris loved the house and described to us the magnificent view from the wide ceiling-to-floor windows. But the house was up on a mountain and was quite isolated. It would take Brett at least a half hour to drive to his office, and the traffic on Highway 17 was usually heavy at rush hour. They realized that living on a mountain was impractical for their lifestyle. Both of them had adapted to an urban way of life. Fortunately, the seller did not accept their offer, and they were both secretly relieved.

With Thanksgiving approaching, our original plan was to visit our children in California, but the trip was unexpectedly canceled because Shau-Jin was not feeling well the day before. To be on the safe side, we canceled the trip, and, in the end, it was for the best. Though Shau-Jin soon felt better, it turned out that our 21-year-old cat, Iris's beloved Cat, was seriously ill.

For several months, Cat had been sick and in bad condition, and soon after Thanksgiving, on Saturday, November 27, we took her to see a vet, and the doctor told us that she was at the end of her life and that he recommended putting her to sleep. Shau-Jin was against the idea, and so was Iris: we wanted Cat to die naturally. So we took her home. Two days later, on November 29, she died. Cat was Shau-Jin's beloved pet, and her death hit him hard. He wrote to Iris and Michael:

Dear Iris and Michael:

The cat died this morning (Nov. 29) during her sleep. She was still alive last night around 12 pm, and was dead when we checked on her this morning at 7 am. We buried her in our back yard, and planted a persimmon tree at the same spot. It was painful to see her suffer in the past week. Your mom and I are both sad and relieved that she died swiftly and peacefully.

Love, Dad

Iris replied that she was glad Cat had died peacefully and that we didn't have to put her to sleep. She reminisced about the days when she and Cat were young. Iris concluded that Cat had had a long and good life.

Iris was invited to return to Renaissance Weekend at the end of 1999 for the big celebration of the new millennium. She invited Shau-Jin, me, and Michael to join her and Brett for a family reunion there. We declined, due to scheduling reasons, but we encouraged Michael to join Iris and Brett. Iris bought an elegant purple evening gown from Bloomingdale's specifically for the occasion. From the photos she took at the Renaissance Weekend, I saw that Iris, Brett, and Michael were enjoying the new millennium eve party immensely.

On October 27, 1999, Iris wrote me an e-mail to reflect on our mood after a long phone chat. Indeed, we knew that we should feel lucky:

Dear Mom,

It was wonderful talking to you and Dad a few nights ago. Few people achieve the level of intimacy and love that we enjoy, as parent and daughter, on an almost nightly basis. As a family, we are blessed, truly blessed, and we must remind ourselves of this every day. Many of my friends don't feel comfortable talking to their parents—ever. Some people literally CAN'T. In his memoir, THE RICE ROOM, Ben Fong-Torres said that a language barrier divided him from his parents like the Great Wall of China. "This is one of the great sadnesses of my life," he wrote.

"I'm a journalist and a broadcaster—my JOB is to communicate—and I can't with the two people with whom I want to most." And then there are those who never knew their mothers. A few nights ago, I leafed through Richard Rhodes' autobiography, A HOLE IN THE WORLD, after our lunch together. As you know, Rhodes was starved, beaten and psychologically abused as a child by his stepmother (his mother had committed suicide by shooting herself, and his father degenerated into an alcoholic, leaving him virtually incapable of protecting his family). Every time I reread his book, I'm convinced that Richard Rhodes is lucky to be alive. He was a genuine victim (as opposed to, say, Adeline Mah, author of FALLING LEAVES). But even his experience pales in comparison to the stories of abandoned children in PRC orphanages. I don't even want to get into that right now.

Delving into history, into other people's stories, places all our problems into perspective. Time and again we have to remind ourselves how extraordinarily lucky we are.

Much love, Iris

17

Struggles for a Baby and a Movie

After the big celebration at Renaissance Weekend in Hilton Head, South Carolina, Iris told me that the year 2000 would be a year to write and finish the first draft of her next book and, most importantly, to get pregnant. Iris and Brett had wished to start a family in the previous year, but without success.

That January, she told me that she was reading a number of books and articles on pregnancy, and that she needed to adjust her diet. She also bought a shield for her computer monitor screen. She had been in front of the computer for very long hours and she was worried that the radiation from the computer screen might cause miscarriages, as some sources claimed. She was eating nutritious food and getting enough exercise to make sure she was healthy.

On February 9, 2000, Iris informed us that she and Brett had moved to a townhouse in North San Jose. She had finally found this townhouse for rent when her boxes of research materials almost occupied their whole apartment. Iris said this house was a twenty-minute drive from the previous apartment and that it had more than double the space of the previous one, with a double-car garage attached. Besides, it was a five-minute walk to Cisco, where Brett worked. Iris felt very lucky because the owner of the house was very nice and the rent was reasonable. It took them about two weeks to move, unpack, and settle in. During the process, Iris organized her books, research materials, manuscripts, records, letters, etc. She could not believe that she could accumulate so many materials and almost filled the space again in the new house and in the garage.

On February 14, hearing that "Peanuts" cartoonist Charles Schulz had died, Iris was quite sentimental and wrote me a letter:

Dear Mom:

I have a favor to ask of you. Can you save the last Peanuts comic strip that appeared yesterday (Sunday), and mail it to me? I'm still reeling from the news of Charles Schulz's death. It's the end of an era.

I still remember all the hours I spent reading Peanuts books as a child. Do you recall the time we went together to a garage sale in Champaign, and you bought me my first Snoopy cartoon book—a used paperback, already yellow with age? That's when I first fell in love with the Peanuts comic strip. You and Dad grew up with Peanuts cartoons as well, in Chinese newspapers in Taiwan, making both of you part of the Peanuts era as well.

Years later, in Santa Barbara, I met Charles Schulz in person at the SB Writer's conference (the summer of 1991, I believe). During his lecture, however, I was surprised by his demeanor, which was bitter, gloomy, and depressed—almost nasty!

After his lecture, I stood in a long line, waiting for Schulz to autograph a copy of his book for me. When I finally stood in front of him, I asked Schulz if I could write a profile about him for the New Yorker *or some other major magazine. "Why is a young person like you interested in an old man like me?" was his response. (At the time, I thought he was being sarcastic.) But later I learned that Schulz—like Charlie*

Brown—is a terribly insecure person, fundamentally convinced of his own unworthiness.

That was the last time I ever saw Schulz. But last year, I had one more opportunity to see him. To make a long story short, I didn't have time to make the long, two-hour drive to Santa Rosa, and I figured that I would see Schulz at the next Santa Barbara Writer's Conference. I never expected that Schulz would pass away only a few months later.

Do you think Charles Schulz committed suicide? Don't you find it odd that he died the night before his final strip ran in the Sunday newspapers? As you know, Peanuts ran from 1950 to 2000—a perfect 50 years. And he died right when the strip ended. But life is seldom as neat and tidy as a cartoon box. It's almost as if he timed his dramatic exit from this world . . . achieving his final deadline.

Love, Iris

It seemed like Iris could not get the death of Charles Schulz off of her mind. The next day, she wrote to me again about him:

Dear Mom,

I think it was Charles Schulz's pessimism—as well as his ability to understand human failure, insecurity, heartbreak—that made millions love Peanuts.

You're absolutely right. Schulz had no reason whatsoever to be depressed, after achieving wealth and fame at such an early age. But depression is not rational. Perhaps he did have a mental problem, or some chemically induced condition. But whatever it was, it prevented him from losing touch with the underdogs of the world.

It's strange, but I still feel a void in my heart after Schulz's death— even though I never knew him, and didn't particularly like him after our meeting in person. It made me wonder, what is the secret to Schulz's magical appeal?

The answer, I believe, is simple. Schulz understands the heart of a loser. He captures those moments in life when we feel utterly unloved,

unwanted, and alone. And all of us—no matter how successful—have
felt like losers at some point in life.

   Love, Iris

I had a feeling that at this time in her life, Iris felt that she could understand how Charles Schulz felt at the end of his.

Shau-Jin retired from the University of Illinois after thirty years of teaching and research in physics just before the new year, and I was planning to retire from the Department of Microbiology in May 2000. Our friends wanted to give Shau-Jin, and several other Chinese faculty members at the UI who also retired at about the same time, a retirement party. The organizers invited Iris and Michael to come for this occasion, but both of them were busy working. So I asked both of them to write a few words for their father's retirement. Iris, as usual, wrote a long, loving, and moving statement, which was read on March 2, 2000 at the party. She knew I was going to retire in May, which was only two months away, so in the statement she also gave her loving thoughts about me. Needless to say, I was so touched.

Date: March 2, 2000
IRIS CHANG'S MESSAGE FOR HER DAD'S RETIREMENT PARTY
   My parents have spent half their lives at the University of Illinois.
It's hard to believe they are now retiring from academic life. After three
decades, the two of them have left behind a legacy of research and educa-
tion for which they should be proud.
   My mother was my first role model, and remains one of my great
heroes. For as long as I could remember, she would strive to balance
career with family. As a child, I saw her rush home from the labora-
tory to cook for us. These meals, both healthy and exquisite (worthy of
a Chinese gourmet restaurant) would take hours to prepare, and as she
labored over a countertop or steaming stove the two of us would dis-
cuss our dreams, our insecurities, our relationships with others. These
kitchen talks helped forge who I am, enlightening me about the range of

opportunities—and difficulties—that faced professional women of her time. After dinner, Mother often went back to the university at night to continue her research. Time and again, always by example, she demonstrated her sincere dedication to her work.

It was only much later in my life, after I married and launched my own career, that I began to truly appreciate her struggle to live three roles: that of wife, mother and scientist. But she performed beautifully in all three. It is a great privilege for me to call myself her daughter. Nothing could make me prouder.

My father, too, represented an ideal for me to aspire to. He is, perhaps, one of the most idealistic people I know—one of the rare individuals on this earth motivated solely by the pursuit of knowledge, rather than personal ambition. Years ago, I was astounded to learn that, despite his obvious talent and brilliance, in his youth he never craved, or even dreamt that he would achieve a position higher than that of high school teacher. Money, power, social status—all of these things meant nothing to him unless he could enjoy a quiet intellectual life, doing the two things he loved most: physics, and the nurturing of young minds. I consider him blessed because he found that life at the University of Illinois.

Father also possessed a strong sense of justice. I always believed that had he not become a physicist that he would have made an excellent judge. He had a keen sense of what was fair, as well as the uncanny ability to perceive an issue from all different points of view. But he also had a deep compassion for others, an intuitive understanding of human weakness, and a genuine sympathy for the underdog, a feeling that extended even to animals—such as cats, baby birds and insects. Nothing distressed him more than to see a helpless creature hurt, just as nothing infuriated him more than to see a blatant abuse of power.

Perhaps what I admire most about my father is that he never lost that childlike wonder for the world. Rare in a world of cynics, Father has retained his fascination for the universe, and for all the mysteries that lie within. For him, education is a lifelong endeavor. He devours books like a student, reading biology, computer science, literature, history,

*astronomy, psychology—to name just a few subjects that interest him. He
is what Einstein would have considered the quintessential intellectual—
the person who learns for the same reasons a child wants to learn . . . for
love, curiosity, and the sheer thrill of discovery.*

*He found joy in the smallest things in life. One time, when taking
a walk with my father in Crystal Lake Park, we passed an oil slick
gleaming on the water. Pointing to that iridescent patch, Father mentioned that a similar slick once inspired a genius to calculate the size of
an atom—because he possessed the ability to grasp the universe within a
drop of oil. What I learned from my father that day is that the power of
truth lies within us all—but truth reveals itself only to those [who] know
how to see.*

*For my parents' retirement, I give them my love and deepest congratu-
lations. Of course, their retirement signifies not just an ending, but an
exciting new beginning. They used to tell me that in life, it is the journey,
not the final destination, that counts. For life is not a race, but a quest.
May these thoughts be with them, and inspire them, as they embark on
the next stage of their journey together.*

If Iris had not mentioned the walk we took at Crystal Lake in Urbana
when she was in high school, I would have forgotten it. I remember
it was a perfect October fall day; the red sugar maple leaves were glittering, and the copper brown oak trees were lining the lake under
the golden sunshine as we walked along the park path. Shau-Jin was
talking to Iris about how he looked into the beauty of nature. He
pointed to a little puddle on the path on which a rainbow of oil was
reflected under the sun. That sight inspired Shau-Jin to talk about the
ingenious experiment designed by past scientists using oil films on
water to estimate the size of molecules. I was amazed that Iris could
remember it so clearly.

After my retirement, I focused on repairing our house and cleaning
the clutter that had accumulated during so many years. I should have
done these chores a long time before, but had never been able to find

the time, and I finally had it. Shau-Jin was busy engaging with a number of Chinese-American professors to form an organization called the Chinese-American Association of Central Illinois (CAACI) at the end of 1999, and he was elected the first president. CAACI was originally created to push for a legislative bill (H.R. 126) initiated by Illinois House Representative William O. Lipinski. Lipinski initiated the bill to express the sentiments of Congress concerning the war crimes committed by the Japanese military during World War II. And later, with the news of the unfair treatment of Dr. Wen Ho Lee, Chinese-Americans realized that we should band together to voice our concerns on the issue of human rights, including racial profiling and discrimination. Since then, Shau-Jin and I had been actively involved in promoting awareness of human-rights issues in Central Illinois. Because of Iris, we had hooked up with the Global Alliance for Preserving the History of World War II in Asia in California and a number of similar organizations across the U.S., Canada, and Asia.

Iris called routinely to update us on her progress in writing her book. When her thirty-second birthday arrived on March 28, 2000, she wrote me that she did not want to celebrate it. In the letter, Iris said she was very health-oriented these days, and she didn't even like the idea of stepping into an airplane! She wrote, "It could be a reaction to the year-long tour for THE RAPE OF NANKING in 1998, or simply my unwillingness to be interrupted as I write the third book." She had taken every step to ensure that she was physically healthy in preparation for her pregnancy.

In April, she said she had finally finished all the entries in her database. From these entries, she would write the outline and then the first draft of the manuscript. During this period, she complained that progress was slow and that she was not very productive. There were two major factors that interfered with her writing. One was her struggle to have a baby, and the other was to get a movie made from *The Rape of Nanking.* Whenever she watched a good movie or heard a bestselling book had gotten contracted to make into a movie, she would be depressed and ask why her own book had not.

On May 3, 2000, she went to Los Angeles for the Committee of 100 meeting and met several people in the movie industry. It made her realize that her movie sub-agent had not been capable of getting her a movie deal for over a year due to a faulty plan. Iris called us to complain that a year had been wasted and she needed to ask her movie agent and sub-agent to revert the movie rights back to her. She confessed to us that she was devastated to find out that she had lost more than a year of time, a prime time at that, when her book was still on the best-seller list. She became extremely depressed over this movie issue and almost got sick thinking of the lost time. We told her that she should not blame herself, and we reminded her that she'd been extremely busy at the time traveling to promote her book, and had had no time to think about the movie project. We said to her that lessons are learned by going through failures, after all.

Iris was determined, however, to make a movie happen and spent June actively looking for a new movie agent and finding possible producers and directors for the movie version of her book. She updated us from time to time that she had met several potential movie producers and directors; but by the end of the year, she still had not gotten a concrete result. She admitted that the movie industry was quite different from the publishing business.

Watching movies was still a major pastime for Iris whenever she wanted to relax and take her mind off writing. She not only went to see movies in the theater with Brett and friends, but she often rented videos to watch at home. Because she was obsessed with making her Nanking book into a movie, our conversation turned to movies most of the time. Sometimes she was devastated to have to tell me that some of the books on the *New York Times* "Best Sellers" list at the time as hers—for example, *The Perfect Storm* and *Into Thin Air*—had already been made into movies.

When she saw movies such as *Braveheart* and *Gladiator*, she was very impressed. On the other hand, after she saw a movie called *Romeo Must Die*, she told me it was one of the most offensive movies she had ever seen. According to Iris, the Chinese-Americans in the movie were portrayed as foreigners, not Americans. And worse yet, almost all the Chinese in the movie were brutal, cruel, and evil. This led her to reiterate her conviction that more Asian-Americans needed to enter the field of entertainment.

Iris told me that her friend, a Chinese-American actress who appeared in the movie *The Joy Luck Club*, complained to her that there were not many opportunities for Asian actors in Hollywood. Iris expressed her opinions on the issue in an e-mail:

> . . . about Asian actors in Hollywood, I'm convinced that this situation will not change until (a) we get more Asians in those key "money" positions in the industry and (b) Asians THEMSELVES support films that portray them with dignity. Perhaps the Chinese community itself is to be blamed for not encouraging their sons and daughters to pursue careers in show business. We need not only more Asian actors, screenwriters, and directors, but more Asian producers, distributors and studio heads. Also, we need [a] loyal constituency of viewers—Asian or otherwise—who are willing to go out, in droves, to support a movie with multi-dimensional Asian characters. Only when Hollywood sees hard evidence, in cash, that this viewership exists (and I believe it does!) will Hollywood change.

Iris's interest in film and scriptwriting never wavered, and she continued to hone her screenwriting skills. Back in October 1999, she had flown to Burbank to take David Freeman's screenwriting class over the weekend. I admired her passion in pursuing her interests; she was a person who never passed up a chance to learn and was never afraid to meet a challenge.

We visited Iris and Michael at the end of June and liked Iris and Brett's townhouse very much. The townhouse complex was located in quiet North San Jose and was surrounded by white pines, sweet gums, and pear and cherry trees. I particularly liked the location because it was not far from a major Chinese grocery shop, in a shopping center with many Chinese restaurants. Iris entertained us by taking us to the Santa Cruz beach. It was the July Fourth weekend, and everywhere we went was full of people. On the way to Santa Cruz, she drove us to see the house in the Los Gatos Mountains where they had made an offer the year before that did not go through. The road to the house was winding and narrow. I told Iris that it would have been very inconvenient to live there, and they were fortunate that they did not end up buying it.

In the meantime, Iris was disappointed to find that she had not gotten pregnant. She was visiting her OB-GYN doctors and doing various physical tests to find out why. All the tests showed that everything appeared to be normal for her and Brett. By this time, she was really getting discouraged and growing increasingly puzzled. Her inability to get pregnant was compounded by her frustration in the movie project. I had offered my motherly soothing words to her as much as I could. I told her that to be unable to have a baby was not the end of the world, and I asked her to relax.

With all the discouraging events—no pregnancy, and no movie deal—at the end of 2000, Iris was still able to steadily write several pages a day of her book. At the end of the year, she said she had finished about half of the book's first draft, far from her original plan to finish the first draft of the whole book by then. She admitted that she had a mental block and couldn't write as fast as she had hoped. She also complained that the topic of the book, "Chinese in America," was too broad, and she was finding it more difficult to write on a broad subject than on a single specific event like Nanking.

However, I felt that her inability to proceed with her writing plan as scheduled was caused by a number of other distractions too, such as going to conferences and joining human-rights activities, not just the movie and pregnancy. She was invited to many conferences across the country. She had declined many of them, but in some cases she just could not avoid it, such as when the conference was right in California.

In the year 2000, Iris spent a lot of time pushing Senator Dianne Feinstein's Japanese Imperial Army Disclosure Act, or Senate Resolution S. 1902. She personally wrote to Feinstein, mailed a copy of her Nanking book to her, and telephoned her aides. She spent many hours sending e-mails and her endorsement letters to senators and representatives asking them to support both this bill and a similar one in the House. Iris saw this as her duty, regardless of how busy she was.

On August 3, Iris attended a press conference in Los Angeles and gave a speech urging every Chinese-American to support Feinstein's bill, S. 1902, the Japanese Imperial Army Disclosure Act, which sought to mandate the declassification of all remaining documents about the Japanese Imperial Army in U.S. government archives.

Iris told media that "history is based on documents! I could not have written *The Rape of Nanking* without access to primary source documents!" She said, "The historical truth, once released, has a way of changing history on its own. The ugliness of a nation's wartime record might stimulate a future government to think twice about committing atrocities, especially if that government realizes that these actions might haunt them down the road. If we the people do not insist on the disclosure of historical records, then we are acting as silent accomplices to those in power, and those would prefer that their crimes remain secret forever."

She reminded people "that the essence of American democracy comes from our ability to question and challenge those in power, and to make them absolutely accountable to the people. It is our duty as American citizens to hold our elected officials responsible. We should be keeping a tally on which politicians support important legislation, and which merely give us lip service. We don't work for them . . . they work for us."

Right around this time, Representative Tom Lantos also initiated a similar bill, H.R. 5056, in the House. In a press conference, Lantos announced: "The Imperial Japanese government was involved in heinous war crimes during the World War II era, and it is extremely important that we do all we can to bring those crimes to light. Iris Chang, in her brilliant book *The Rape of Nanking*, gives an outstanding account of just one instance of these atrocities. We have made great progress in declassifying documents relating to Nazi Germany, but now we need to take major steps to assure that documents in American archives relating to Japanese atrocities are also made public." Iris was quite happy about it and informed us as soon as she heard the news.

With help from all sides and the "pushing team" of Chinese-American activists, the Disclosure Act finally passed in both Senate and the House in October 2000. On December 26, President Clinton signed it into law. This indeed was a major victory for Chinese-Americans.

Another thing that consumed some of her time was the fact that publishers constantly asked Iris to write blurbs for upcoming books. She could read a book very quickly, but it still used up her time. She insisted on reading the whole book before she would write an endorsement, rather than simply glance through it as most people did.

Iris was sought out to write blurbs for new books not only on Asian history, but also on human-rights violations, and sometimes even fiction books. It gave her the chance to read different kinds of books, but was still a distraction, albeit a pleasant one. Iris was thrilled when the editor of Jim Lehrer's fiction book *The Special Prisoner* at Random House asked her to write a blurb for the book. Iris had grown up with the PBS six o'clock evening news with Jim Lehrer, and she felt it an honor to be considered for writing an endorsement for the book.

At the time she was having difficulty conceiving, she was asked to write a blurb for a book called *The Lost Daughters of China*, by Karin Evans. She was disheartened by the book's description of Chinese orphanages and the Chinese government's one-child-per-family policy. Millions of infants, almost all of them female, were abandoned due to

Chinese culture's gender discrimination against females. She said she wept as she read the book. She had expressed a lot of her sentiments and felt the injustice and discrimination against women in some cultures and religions. We had talked about adopting a child from China if she could not get pregnant for whatever reason, but she always felt that to produce a child of her own was one of her utmost wishes.

On the subject of blurbs, there was an unfortunate episode that hurt Iris very much at the time. In March 2000, Iris was asked to write a blurb for a book on Japan's imperial family. The author had actually been introduced to the publisher by Iris, and the book was based on solid research and well written. Iris wrote a very favorable blurb to endorse the book, but in the end she found out that the publisher did not dare use her blurb due to a protest from an established scholar in the field. A professor at a famous university on the East Coast threatened the publisher that if they used Iris's blurb, he was going to withdraw his own blurb from the book. Not only that, he threatened that he would ask all others withdraw theirs as well. This professor was powerful enough to make the poor author beg the publisher to pull out Iris's blurb, regardless of the fact that Iris was the one who had helped him and recommended him to the publisher in the first place.

Iris was furious when she learned of this. She told us that although she was disappointed about the author's collapse under pressure, she had sympathy for him. She could understand that the author had to compromise in order to preserve his academic career in Japanese history. On the other hand, with regard to the other professor, she said that she had never seen a professor stoop so low as to organize a conspiracy among his peers to sabotage a book—merely because the book contained one endorsement by an author he did not like. Iris felt this kind of abuse of academic power was unacceptable and should not be tolerated by publishers. I remember Iris vowing that she would expose this incident in her memoir someday.

Since the publication of the Nanking book, in spite of overwhelmingly excellent and positive reviews endorsing the book, there were still a few attacks. In one instance, Iris told us about Honda Katsuichi's fine book (English translation) *The Nanjing Massacre: A Japanese Journalist Confronts Japan's National Shame.* In the introduction of the book, editor Frank Gibney made an incredible claim and wrote that Iris Chang "hopelessly exaggerates an 'atmosphere of intimidation' in Japan." Then, a few pages later in the book, Mr. Honda wrote: ". . .my 1971 book of reportage, *Journey to China*, in which I traced the path of the Japanese Army through China . . . I was targeted by Japan's extreme right-wing forces and received a number of threats which prompted me to move out of my home and keep my address and telephone number a secret, a policy that I have continued to this day. *Bungei Shunju* and other magazines put out by conservative publishers have continued their attacks on me for more than twenty years." It was well known that Mr. Honda usually wore a wig and dark sunglasses to conceal his identity from Japanese right-wing politicians and activists. Iris wondered why Gibney would criticize her in such manner.

Some of Iris's friends felt that a few academic "scholars" in Asian studies in this country, particularly in Japanese studies, either out of jealousy or because their research funding came from Japan, might be conspiring in a smear campaign designed to discredit Iris and her book. Indeed, the vicious, although relatively few, attacks on her book made Iris feel there might be a smear campaign to discredit her.

This tumultuous, trying year passed very quickly. For Iris, the year was full of disappointment—failure to produce a baby, no movie deal, and only a half-finished book draft—but she did at least succeed in helping pass the Japanese Imperial Army Disclosure Act and to continue fighting for the cause she cherished.

After Shau-Jin and I retired in 1999 and 2000, Shau-Jin was invited to teach at the Department of Physics and Material Sciences at the City University of Hong Kong as a visiting professor for half a year. Both of us were delighted to go to Hong Kong, because we had lived there briefly from 1950 to 1951. We were eager to visit the place again and renew our memories and travel a bit.

On January 13, 2001, we arrived in Hong Kong and lived in City University's guesthouse, which was located in the center of the busy district of the city. Shau-Jin was teaching physics at City University and I was learning how to get around the city via public transportation, but most of my time was spent on the computer. I was in constant touch with Iris, Michael, and all my friends in Champaign-Urbana.

On February 11, Iris called us from California and gave us some bad news. As we knew, she had had problems getting pregnant for the past two years. She was determined to find the root of the problem. She was investigating and had done a lot of research. She also saw a number of doctors and ordered many tests. Finally, she found a world-renowned fertility doctor in Chicago who also came to the Bay area once a month. She told us she was fortunate to be able to consult with this doctor and to finally find the root of her infertility problem. It turned out that she and Brett were immunity-incompatible. Her blood test showed she had had miscarriages at least four times without knowing it. And she might have activated Nature Killer (NK) cells, too. All these medical terms were new to me, and it threw me into a research spell. I was constantly on the computer, searching and understanding the problem of infertility and how to resolve it. From what I understood at the time, Brett and Iris had, unfortunately, a mismatch in their immune systems. When the fertilized egg or the embryo was formed, Iris's body rejected it and saw the embryo as a foreign entity. The result was a miscarriage. The doctor told Iris that her body had a normal and healthy fertility apparatus in every aspect, but the immunity incompatibility with Brett threw them into a two-percent category that meant she had to either receive an immunity treatment or do in-vitro fertilization (IVF) and hire a surrogate mother to bear a baby for them.

This news saddened Iris and us immensely. On the phone, I immediately told her my thoughts about going to adoption rather than fiddling either with immunity treatment or surrogacy. We talked almost two hours and ended up using up the time limit on the phone card. The talk was very emotional. After the phone call, I felt I might have voiced my opinions about adoption too strongly, so I wrote an e-mail to apologize and told her I respected her decision, whatever it would be.

On February 13, Iris wrote back:

> *Dear Mom,*
>
> *Please don't apologize for your reaction over the phone—I know you spoke out of love and concern for me. I appreciate your taking the time to search for information on the Web, but I could save you the time by mailing you copies of my files. In the past few weeks, I have amassed literally hundreds of pages of data. . . .*
>
> *The doctor's assistant told me that in the Bay area office, every single one of his patients who chose the gestational surrogate route ended up having children—healthy children. (Most women, however, prefer to use the experimental drugs or IVIG therapy instead of hiring a surrogate. About eighty percent achieve successful pregnancies through immunological treatment.) . . .*
>
> *Love, Iris*

She told us that after hearing this bad news, she could not help but cry quietly by herself, even though Brett continually reassured her that eventually they would have a baby. The doctor told her there were two ways to have a baby in her case: to use IVIG (intravenous immune globulin) therapy together with an experimental drug, Enbrel, or to hire a surrogate mother to carry the baby. The former treatment involved blood products and had some risks and side effects; it could also depend on some other factors since the procedure was still experimental, in the early stages of its use.

In addition to this sad news, at that time stocks had plunged in the U.S. market and the economy seemed to be heading toward a recession. That news made everyone moody, and we were not exceptions;

but in such a depressing atmosphere, Iris was still very positive and optimistic. She was trying to comfort me.

On March 15, 2001, she wrote:

> Dear Mom,
>
> I thought about our conversation yesterday. Oh, I know you are terribly upset about the stock market plunge. But don't agonize over anything beyond your control. . . . In Chinese, the character for "crisis" is the same one for "opportunity." Just remain calm, gather information, and follow a careful strategy.
>
> We have much to be grateful for: our health, our success, our savings and debt-free finances. I have been reading books about Chinese families who had made the fateful—and often fatal—decision to stay in the PRC in 1949. The suffering they endured under the Cultural Revolution is almost as horrific as the history of those who survived the Rape of Nanking. What problems do we have, compared to those people?
>
> Love, Iris

In the meantime, Iris continued to search for ways to overcome the infertility problem. She had also explored alternative medicine such as Chinese acupuncture and Chinese herbs, which also claimed they could overcome infertility. She was visiting a good Chinese acupuncturist who indeed helped her deal with her stress and insomnia, if not the infertility.

Iris also contacted the local supporting group for infertility, called Resolve, and met many couples with similar infertility conditions as hers. In those meetings, she learned that she was not alone, and she obtained much information concerning the pros and cons of each route to fertility. It just felt good to talk to people sharing the same fears and concerns.

On the outside, Iris was very efficient at finding solutions to her problems and stayed relatively upbeat, but that didn't mean she wasn't going through emotional ups and downs inside. One day she described to me that when she was sitting in a Chinese restaurant waiting for her order, she watched all the tables around her. She saw a mother whose child was sitting next to her, eating joyfully. She saw another mother holding her baby on her lap while eating. She felt a sting behind her nose and eyes and her tears started flowing silently down her cheeks. She felt very sad as she thought about how she could not bear a child of her own. I listened to her with great sympathy. I could not say very much, because my heart went out to her, and I could not think of the right words of comfort. I wished I were not in Hong Kong. I wanted to embrace her and to give her support not only mentally, but physically.

Not all the things that happened at this time were bad, though. Iris reported to us that some movie producers in Hollywood were interested in buying the movie rights to *The Rape of Nanking* and adapting it into a movie at long last. On February 24, 2001, Iris wrote:

Dear Mom,

As I mentioned earlier, I met with several famous Hollywood producers last Wednesday at the Mayflower restaurant near Ranch 99. (For security purposes, I will keep their names confidential for now.) They flew up to San Jose to see me, and one was literally taken aback by my age and appearance. (He was astounded—or pretended to be—to meet "such a beautiful author," and later, in a phone conversation, said he had expected me to be older, scholarly-looking, with glasses: "Instead, in walks this lithe, willowy beauty!" he exclaimed.) Anyhow, they were absolutely passionate about my book, and believe that the film version could be an epic of the same caliber as THE LAST EMPEROR and SCHINDLER'S LIST. They are now prepared to top any offer that my agent at CAA has received so far. By next week, we should have not just one, but two bids for the motion picture rights to THE RAPE OF NANKING.

My work has also inspired a poem, written by one of my fans in New York City, who has developed some kind of obsession for me. He keeps sending letters to my PO box (by the way, I am so glad that he doesn't have my actual physical home address—I stopped responding to his correspondence years ago). Ever since the publication of THE RAPE OF NANKING, he's mailed me samples of his writing, cartoons, heart-shaped boxes of chocolates, cards, small gifts like pens, and photographs of himself. Now he's giving me CDs of his poetry. . . . Do you think I should be concerned? I have to admit I was a little troubled by his obsession at first, but I don't believe he has either the imagination or the resources to track me down. Judging from his picture, he doesn't seem particularly dangerous or threatening—just a simple, ordinary man with literary ambitions. Still, I'm relieved that I have a PO box to handle my mail. The US postal system has only my last home address, not my current one.

Love, Iris

Over the phone, Iris told me about her conversation with the Hollywood producers and their ideas about the movie, but she also stressed her own vision of it. She said if she was going to be the one to write the script, she wanted it to contain several major characters: Frank Tillman Durdin, Minnie Vautrin, John Rabe, Robert Wilson, Tang Sheng-chih, Li Xiuying, and a Japanese soldier or a Japanese news reporter.

Iris wanted the movie to include sets of characters from each different ethnic group (American, German, Chinese and Japanese), and to show the changing of characters as well as the contrast exposed during wartime. She wanted to show how a person would make decisions under pressure in the darkest, most difficult times—the conflict between self-interest and humanity. For example, Frank Tillman Durdin was a foreign correspondent for the *New York Times* in 1937. Iris said, "He was my age when he covered the Rape of Nanking. He was twenty-nine when he broke his first big story, the Rape of Nanking, and I was twenty-nine when my book was published and hit the *New York Times* 'Best Sellers' list. For that reason, I felt a special link with him."

In Durdin's obituary, published in the *New York Times* in 1998, Iris was quoted as saying: "Tillman Durdin was not only writing the pages of history under pressure, but tried to save Chinese lives in Nanking. He should be remembered as an exemplar of humanity and courage in the darkest of times." Iris said that Durdin had had to decide whether he wanted to be an impartial observer, exploiting the suffering of others for the front-page news, or to step in and help the war victims.

Minnie Vautrin, the American missionary educator, was in Nanking in 1937 when the Japanese soldiers invaded and occupied the city. She saved thousands of men, women, and children in the Safety Zone. However, when the Japanese soldiers came to the Safety Zone demanding women, she believed their claim that some prostitutes were in the Zone. She handed over the "bad" women so the "good" women in the zone could be saved. Later, Vautrin realized that some of the "bad" women had voluntarily given themselves up as "prostitutes," sacrificing their lives to save others. She had fought fearlessly against the Japanese soldiers, but in the end she couldn't sustain the mental sufferings and some of the decisions she'd made. After she returned to the U.S. in 1940, she committed suicide.

John Rabe, a German businessman and a Nazi, who chose to stay in Nanking to protect his employees and thousands of Nanking civilians in the Safety Zone by using his Nazi armband, was caught in his ideals of socialism and the brutal reality of Nazism after he returned to Berlin. Iris said that Rabe changed from an ordinary German citizen to a hero in China— and then to an outcast in Germany.

Dr. Robert Wilson was the only surgeon in Nanking during the Nanking Massacre. He worked extremely hard and sacrificed his own health to save the lives of others.

General Tang, who vowed to Chiang Kai-shek that he would fight to the death to defend the city of Nanking, abandoned the city and fled before the fall of Nanking. (However, he was following the orders of Chiang. It was not completely Tang's fault.) He eventually became a high-ranking Communist after previously having been a Nationalist. Iris said the story of General Tang was a good contrast to an ordinary Chinese pregnant woman, Li Xiuying, who fought with her bare hands against two Japanese soldiers trying to rape her. She miraculously survived thirty-seven bayonet wounds.

Iris said the movie should include a Japanese character: a soldier or a news reporter who was torn between stopping the violence and obeying authority. The character needed to be sacrificed to illustrate what happened to Japanese people who defied the system. It could be a Japanese soldier who disobeyed his orders and was executed, or a news reporter who rebelled, seeking the truth, and lost his status but gained his soul.

Iris passionately described her vision of the movie to anyone who was interested in adapting her book into a movie. Finally, in March, Iris told us that a Hollywood production firm had made an offer for the movie rights to her book, but it took another several months before the formal contract was signed. She had been working on this project for so long, and finally her hard work had borne some results!

In spite of her fertility problems and the movie project, which sometimes distracted her from her writing, Iris had been working steadily on *The Chinese in America*. She mailed us a copy of the manuscript all the way to Hong Kong, about two thirds of the book, and wanted us to give her our comments. Shau-Jin and I read her manuscript carefully and gave her a list of errors we'd found, along with our thoughts, without any reservation.

On April 1, 2001, a U.S. Navy surveillance plane collided over the South China Sea with a Chinese fighter jet sent to intercept it, and the surveillance plane made an emergency landing on Chinese territory, Hainan Island. We watched the news attentively in Hong Kong, which was not very far from Hainan Island. We were sensitive to any news related to China-U.S. relations because we would be affected by it. Originally we had planned to visit Guangzhou while we were there, but we decided to cancel the trip because of the high tension between China and the U.S. After a ten-day standoff between the U.S. and China, on April 11 the crew was allowed to return to the U.S. without the plane.

On April 20, Shau-Jin read a *New York Times* article reporting that the U.S. State Department had warned Americans of Chinese origin that they could be detained in China for spying if they had ever written critically about the Beijing regime or had contacts with rival Taiwan. Shau-Jin and I immediately wrote to both Iris and Michael about the news. It was especially relevant to Iris, as we knew she was always outspoken—and her previous and current books were related to China.

Iris replied to us:

> Dear Mom,
>
> I think you're being very wise.
>
> The detention of these Chinese Americans reveals the precarious nature of our status as an ethnic minority. When Sino-American relations are excellent, Chinese-Americans benefit by serving as visible role models and goodwill ambassadors between the two countries. But when Sino-American relations are tense, Chinese-Americans can suffer reprisals from both white Americans and native Chinese.
>
> Remember when I mentioned that the Chinese-Americans are often perceived as foreigners in the US—even if they make enormous contributions as US citizens? The same applies to the PRC. I can tell you horror stories about Chinese Americans who moved to mainland China after World War II, with idealistic hopes of rebuilding the country, only to lose their businesses, their savings and even their lives during the Cultural Revolution. They were not embraced by the PRC simply because they were racially Chinese.
>
> Perhaps that is the real story of the Chinese in America—we are "strangers" and "foreigners" on both shores.
>
> Love, Iris

At the end of our stay in Hong Kong, in June, Shau-Jin and I visited Xian, the ancient city of China. We had a wonderful time seeing the Terra-Cotta Warriors of the First Emperor of the Qin Dynasty near his mausoleum, with many other tombs nearby. While we were in Xian, Iris was taking a break from her writing with Brett in Lake Tahoe. They visited Carson City and Virginia City and took a gondola ski-lift ride to the peak of a mountain. She said it was a relaxing vacation, and she felt rejuvenated when she returned home.

On July 15, when we returned to our Urbana home from Hong Kong, Iris wrote:

> *Dear Dad,*
>
> *It was wonderful to talk with you and Mom the other day. You mentioned you might be interested in doing some research on the Chinese in America at the U of I library. If you have time, please let me know if the library has copies of the Statistical Yearbook of the INS. Mainly, I need the annual data, since 1949. Here are the questions that I had submitted to the INS history office, followed by the table with the information (they have not yet responded.). . . .*
>
> *Love, Iris*

For the next several weeks I helped Iris, reviewing the INS Statistical Yearbook borrowed from the U of I main library and doing research for her.

Besides writing her book, Iris seemingly could not sit silently without voicing her concern about a series of reports of Japan trying to whitewash its war-crime history. The year 2001 was full of reports on the rise of Japanese revisionism of its war history and emerging nationalism. In one report, South Korea and China were angry over a new textbook which toned down or eliminated the war crimes Japan committed during World War II in Asia such as the Nanking Massacre, the sex slavery system (Comfort Women), and the Unit 731 chemical and biological experiments on live POWs. In the meantime,

American veterans forced into slave labor for Japanese companies (such as Mitsui & Co., Nippon S Corps) while captive during World War II were pushing for compensation in court.

On July 21, 2001, Iris and Barry A. Fisher, a Los Angeles international human-rights lawyer, representing slave labor and Comfort Women victims, co-authored a commentary published in the *Los Angeles Times*. In the article, they criticized the U.S. government not only for not helping the ex-Comfort Women and former American veterans in pursuing justice in court, but, also, because "the American government in April filed a formal 'Statement of Interest of the United States of America,' asking that the case be dismissed."

The article also stated that "The U.S. government's stance also reveals a racist double standard. In the recent series of cases against German, Swiss, and Austrian banks and industries that enslaved Jews and Slavs, the U.S. championed the rights of the European victims and eventually helped them achieve multi-billion dollar settlements. But when it came to the Asian victims, the U.S. not only refused to help but actively thwarted efforts to seek justice."

Because of the wide media coverage on forced labor and "Comfort Women" compensation lawsuits against Japan, on August 15, 2001, Iris informed us that she had been invited to appear on a panel on Ted Koppel's *Nightline* program. After the program, we congratulated her, and Iris forwarded a number of e-mails she had received reflecting the same sentiment. One e-mail wrote: "Your point that Japan, in the past, was never forced to deal with its past, in WWII, hit home." Another e-mail: "Ted Koppel asked the panel members why it is so difficult for the Japanese to apologize for their wartime atrocities. He did not get a direct answer from the Japanese on the panel. The only person who gave a reasonable answer was Iris Chang. She said it is because Japan was not required to be apologetic."

On the personal side, in August 2001, viewing the risks and the side effects of IVIG therapy and experimental drugs, Iris finally decided, for safety's sake, to go with the surrogacy route. She had been busy investigating the surrogate-mother service and interviewing candidates. Close to their tenth wedding anniversary, Iris and Brett went to Yosemite National Park for a break; and on the way there, they went to meet the future surrogate mother and her husband. Iris told us she found the surrogate mother and her family satisfactory. She had followed all the proper procedures with the service and her doctor in preparation for having a baby by surrogacy.

Over Labor Day weekend, 2001, Iris went to Chicago as a bridesmaid for her friend Carolyn Wu's wedding. She did not have time to drive home to see us, so we drove to the hotel in Chicago to meet her on September 1. Although we had had e-mail and telephone exchanges throughout the year, to see her in person after all this time was still exciting. We only stayed one night with her, but she updated us on all the things happening around her: her new book, for which she would finish the first draft very soon, and her movie project, for which she was awaiting the final written contract. She said she wanted to delegate chores to others once she had a baby. She and Brett also intended to buy a house when the baby arrived. I told her we were thinking about moving to California, near her, so we could help her out. She was very happy to hear that.

In September 2001, there was a big conference in San Francisco organized by U.S. and Japanese officials in celebration of the fiftieth anniversary of the San Francisco Peace Treaty. Japan insisted that all matters related to wartime reparations to its victims had been settled by the San Francisco Peace Treaty. In reality, Iris said, a close reading of the actual treaty revealed that the reparations matter was merely postponed until Japan had the financial means to pay. The entire issue had been left hanging for more than half a century and still had never been resolved.

To protest and counteract the official commemoration of the fiftieth anniversary of the San Francisco Peace Treaty, the Bay area activist groups, Global Alliance and the Rape of Nanking Redress Coalition (RNRC) and University of California at Berkeley Ethnic Studies, jointly held a big three-day conference and a rally from September 7 to 9. The conference coincided with the official one, at the same time and in the same city. The conference was named "Fifty Years of Denial: Japan and its Wartime Responsibilities." Iris was invited to be the keynote speaker on the first day of the conference.

On September 8, 2001, Iris wrote to us to report on the event:

> *Dear Mom and Dad,*
>
> *I just wanted to let you know that I returned from SF safely tonight! The conference was incredible—it was almost as if the entire event was designed to honor me. Congressman Mike Honda, a member of Sen. Feinstein's staff and several luminaries heaped lavish praise on me during their dinner speeches—how this book changed their lives, made world history and launched an international movement. And the crowd went wild over my opening lecture this afternoon—Washingtonians wanted to have it introduced in the Congressional Record, the director of the Nanking massacre museum asked for a copy so he could translate it into Chinese, reporters asked if they could publish it. My lecture was interrupted constantly by rousing applause and cheers; at the very end, everyone gave me a standing ovation. Amazing, considering that I wrote the speech at midnight yesterday, and had no time to rehearse. Anyhow, I will give you more details later.*
>
> *Much love, Iris*

Iris said that Article 26 of the San Francisco Peace Treaty stated, "Should Japan make a peace settlement or war claims settlement with any State granting that State greater advantages than those provided by the present Treaty, those same advantages shall be extended to the parties to the present Treaty." According to Iris, the latest declassified State Department records showed that the U.S. held secret negotiations with Japan and helped wartime victims in several countries, such as the Netherlands, receive compensation from Japan. But the U.S. chose to ignore Article 26 of the treaty and sold out its own veterans by waiving their claims to reparations. Iris called the San Francisco Peace Treaty a travesty of justice, a betrayal to our own American veterans.

Just two days after the conference, on September 11, 2001, the whole world watched in horror as terrorists destroyed the Twin Towers in New York. My brother Bing, working in New York's Wall Street financial center, escaped the catastrophe as he luckily had passed through the World Trade Center an hour before it collapsed!

In this chaotic time, we knew that Iris was busy speaking out about her concern for civil liberties of individual citizens.

In an e-mail on September 18, Iris wrote:

Dear Mom and Dad,

On Sunday night, Brett and I went out to dinner with Mike. We are all deeply concerned about the hate crimes committed against Arab Americans in our area. Just today I learned of a man of Indian ancestry, mistaken for an Arab, who was stabbed in San Francisco. The blind patriotism and religious fervor sweeping the United States is, to say the least, disturbing— and even the network broadcasts, such as this evening's Nightline, *sound like wartime propaganda. (Meanwhile, news coverage of the harassment of Islamics in America has been minimal.) A few days ago, the* San Francisco Chronicle *interviewed me along with several other Bay area luminaries about our reaction to the terrorism. I warned that the US government may use this crisis to erode individual freedom and American civil liberties. They ran my statement and photo in this Sunday's* Chronicle, *and I can show you the article when you visit us in November.*

Events are unfolding faster than I can react to them: first the WTC and Pentagon tragedies, then the Japanese prime minister's unexpected apology to the comfort women, and now, a major court victory of a former Korean slave laborer against a Japanese corporation. This week, I tried to work on my book and recover from general exhaustion and a mild case of flu, but I have to admit that it's hard to stay focused. I plan to do nothing more than write, exercise and rest for the next few weeks.

Love, Iris

Iris was concerned about all kinds of human-rights issues at home and abroad, not just for Asian-Americans. On October 10, Iris said that she'd been invited to participate in a live televised panel discussion on racism, along with Jewish and Arabic activists. Iris spoke out, for the latest racism against Islamics sprang from the September 11 terrorist attack. Because of the 9/11 tragedy, Muslims in this country were singled out and discriminated against. Iris fully understood this kind of racial discrimination, which every ethnic minority had gone through in time of crisis, such as Japanese-Americans during World War II and Chinese-Americans during Wen Ho Lee's spying case. She said the best solution to combat racism was education. Through honest literature and films, we should show and proclaim the common humanity of all cultures, races, and religions that could bind us all together in a harmonious world.

At the end of September, Iris joyfully told us that she had finished the first draft of her book on the Chinese in America. In October, she said her editor at Viking was very impressed with her writing, praised her lavishly, and had started to edit it.

On November 10 of that year, Shau-Jin's mother died. She lived to ninety-seven, but in the last few years she had lost her memory, and it was hard on Shau-Jin to watch his mom decline. The funeral in Los Angeles was arranged for December 1. After the funeral, we took a ride with Iris and Brett back to San Jose and lived in their town home for a month. Iris wanted us at her side during her medical procedure.

Iris was scheduled to have her egg retrieval in December; after the IVF, the embryos would be transferred to her surrogate mother. We were glad that we could help and give her the support she needed. In the meantime, I was also looking into the real estate market in the Bay area to find an apartment to rent or a townhouse to buy.

In the last two weeks of December, while we were living at their home, Iris finished the necessary medical procedures to complete the surrogacy. She felt happy that it was painless and her worry had been unnecessary.

During this time, Iris was also writing an Op-Ed for the *New York Times* on the slave-labor issue, and now the Bush administration betrayed the American POWs of World War II by not pursuing justice and compensation from Japan. I watched her toiling over the draft of her article in front of the computer because the Op-Ed had a word limitation. She was trying to reduce the number of words to the specification without losing the content. After each modification, she would show us the draft for our comments. I admired her hard-working habits and her determined spirit. Finally, the article was submitted and published in the *New York Times* on December 24, titled "Betrayed by White House." The subtitle was "Japan's former prisoners deserve compensation." Iris was always speaking out on behalf of those who had been unfairly treated; she was unflinching in fighting for justice and human rights.

On December 30, 2001, Iris got a call from her fertility clinic informing her that her surrogate mother was pregnant! Both Shau-Jin and I were downstairs in the house and heard her yell when she heard the good news. I immediately ran upstairs to hug her, and Shau-Jin did too. We both embraced her. Tears were streaming down Iris's face. We congratulated her that she would be a mother soon, and she said, "You are going to be grandparents!" Brett was out of town in Illinois with his parents, and they were ecstatic too when they heard the good news. We knew how hard she had been working to solve her infertility problem, and all our tears were joyful.

In front of the TV, when Iris and Shau-Jin and I watched the ball drop in Times Square on the eve of 2002, all of us felt that the year of 2001 had not been so bad after all! Iris had solved her infertility problem through surrogacy, the movie rights of her book had been sold, and she had finished and handed in her first draft of the book *The Chinese in America* before the deadline. I'm sure she was proud of herself too. Once she set a goal, she worked hard to achieve it without any hesitation, and persevered despite obstacles along the way.

18

A New Book and a Son

Even though Iris had hired a surrogate mother, she was still very involved in the pregnancy. In fact, it seemed she was even *more* involved than if she had actually been bearing the child herself. She constantly updated us on what was happening with her surrogate. She maintained a very close relationship with the surrogate and her family, both over the phone and via e-mails. She did everything to make the surrogate happy, and encouraged her to exercise and eat healthful food. When the surrogate complained of the heat and the burden of the weight on her belly during the last several months of pregnancy, it meant that Iris could not sleep either. When the surrogate told Iris that she could feel the kick of the fetus, Iris was as excited as if she had felt the kick in her own belly. It was a very intense emotional journey for both of them.

Iris had handed in the first draft of her book to Viking Penguin, but the manuscript still needed to be edited and revised. On February 16, 2002, Iris wrote to me:

Dear Mom,

The reason you haven't heard from me is because I'e been working hard on the revisions of the book. . . . Today I woke up at 6 am and I've been writing continuously since then, stopping only to eat or to walk along the creek. Every phone in the house has been unplugged so I won't be disturbed. Perhaps we can talk on Sunday.

When I'm not working I'm researching subjects like real estate, nannies and prenatal childcare. (To a certain degree I feel as if I'm writing several books at once.) . . .

Love, Iris

Iris and Brett were actively looking for a house to buy before the baby arrived. Besides the fact that they had wanted to buy a house for quite some time, the owner of the townhouse they were renting wanted the house back, so they had no choice but to move. Every weekend they went with realtors to see open houses in Fremont, Cupertino, and nearby areas. After several months of house-hunting, they finally bought a nice townhouse just across the street from their rental. On April 26, 2002, Iris happily informed us that they had moved into their first house. The townhouse was relatively new and the interior had been kept meticulously clean by the last owner. They were very happy about the price because at the time the housing costs in the Bay area had dropped due to the dot-com bubble's bursting.

Not only was Iris busy with house-hunting, she was also looking for a nanny who could help her when the baby arrived. She told me that she felt she was racing against the clock and wondered which one would come first, the baby or finishing the revision of the book.

On our side, since we had returned home from California in January 2002, we were actively cleaning our house in preparation to sell it and move to California. It was a long and painful process, because I had to decide which items to save and which to throw away. I threw away literally truckloads of forty years of stuff from the basement and closets.

I wrote to Iris that sorting out our mail from the past twenty years was a time-consuming process because I was reading some old letters along the way. Iris wrote back: "It's important to keep these old letters, as they have historical value. Letters and photographs—our last links to the past—are the two things that I would never throw away. Better to donate extra items to the UI archives than to toss them." So I saved all the letters and brought them with us to California, and they certainly came in handy when I began writing this memoir.

On May 4, 2002, we got an excited call from Iris: the ultrasound result showed that the baby was a boy! Iris announced that they had already decided on the name of their son: Christopher Joseph Chang Douglas. Iris said their son was the product of four people: Iris, Brett, the fertility doctor, and the surrogate mother. She said she had named her son Christopher after her fertility doctor. Iris wanted to honor this doctor; without him, she would not have known the cause of her infertility problems and would never have had the baby.

Iris planned to visit us in May, as Wooster College in Ohio had decided to award Iris an honorary degree of Doctor of Humane Letters. She was scheduled to accept the degree at the commencement on May 13, 2002. After the ceremony, she wanted to pay us a visit. She knew we were sorting out stuff in the house and pretty soon the house would be on the market for sale. She wanted to come home to take one last look at the house we lived in for twenty-four years. She had been ten years old, in the fifth grade, when we moved into the house, and there were many memories within those walls.

Iris spent a week with us, looking over her childhood belongings in her bedroom. In the basement, several boxes holding her grade-school and high-school papers and schoolwork were still there. Sitting on the carpet in the basement and on the bed in her room, she spent hours going through her writing, letters, artwork, and so forth. She cherished every piece. Perhaps behind every one of her papers, there was a story taking her back in time. She had a strong memory; she could describe to you every detail of what had happened in those days. She was not very organized with other stuff like clothes or other knick-knacks, but for her papers and files, she had always organized them meticulously.

That week, in May 2002, we took an after-dinner walk with Iris around the pond across from our house. She talked to us endlessly while we strolled in the woods. This was the same woods and pond where she had spent years playing as a little girl. She was in a mood to reminisce: recalling her childhood dreams, her fears, her frustrations, and finally overcoming her obstacles. Now she was looking into the future with a son on the horizon. Again, there was uncertainty ahead, but her eyes sparkled with hope. Just as we were walking toward our house, the last rays of the spring sunset fell on everyone's cheerful face.

Back at home, Iris was constantly in contact with her surrogate mother, and she was doing very well. Two months later, on August 10, Iris told us that she and the surrogate had started packing their suitcases in preparation for the delivery, even though the due-date was still weeks away. She wanted to be ready just in case. Meanwhile, she was very busy and made good progress on the rewrite of the final chapter of her book, so that the bulk of the work would be done in time.

Then, ten days later, on August 20, after a trip with Brett to Carmel to celebrate their eleventh wedding anniversary, Iris reported that the surrogate was entering her thirty-eighth week of pregnancy, and everything was still going well. About her book, she said that "all that is left is the epilogue, introduction, and footnotes. I should be done with the epilogue within a week or two." It seemed like it was a race between the arrival of her baby and the finishing of her book.

The next day, August 21, Iris informed us that the surrogate mother had told her that Christopher had begun to "drop." She said that typically, once the baby started his descent, delivery was about two weeks later. She predicted that Christopher would arrive at the end of the month.

She was right. As predicted, Christopher Joseph Chang Douglas was born on the evening of August 31, almost exactly two weeks from when she first felt the "drop."

We flew to Iris's home on August 29, just in the nick of time. Iris and Brett drove immediately to the hospital when they got the call on August 31 that the surrogate had started to go into labor. Three days later, Iris and Brett brought the tiny Christopher home, tightly wrapped in his receiving blanket. Iris was exhausted, due to the emotional drain, yet it was such a joyous occasion. For the next several days, all of us, plus Ping, the nanny they had recently hired, surrounded Christopher day and night, feeding, changing diapers, burping, but still loving every minute of it.

On September 4, I started sending e-mails to all our close relatives about the arrival of Christopher. In the announcement, I had to explain the fertility problems Iris had faced and how Christopher had been born by IVF and surrogacy. Many relatives asked a lot of questions, and some were quite bewildered and surprised at this news, as Iris had not wanted us to disclose her complicated pregnancy before this. However, all our relatives seemed understanding and respected Iris's wish for privacy, and were just happy that everything had worked out so beautifully. Iris told us later, after she'd watched a Charlie Rose interview of Michael J. Fox, talking about his Parkinson's with courage, she'd decided she wanted to write a book about her emotional journey in struggling to conceive and have a child. She wanted to help others and to tell those in similar situations that they were not alone.

We stayed with Iris for three weeks after Christopher was born. We took care of the baby while Ping was busy with other chores. Ping not only took care of Christopher when Iris was working or running errands, but she also cooked dinner for them. Iris took the night shift with the baby once Ping went home. One day, at the dinner table, Iris expressed to us that she had fears that she would not be able to accomplish all her life goals, such as the books she wished to write, the oral history project she had initiated with the Asian-American activists, the film project, and so much more. She must have been overwhelmed with finishing her book, the baby, and the family chores. We told her she should not put so much pressure on herself. Shau-Jin said to her, "Do your best, and don't try to be a perfect mother!"

Earlier, in May, I had gotten some bad news from my sister Ling-Ling in New York. She had been diagnosed with colon cancer. The news upset all my siblings. My brothers, my younger sister, and I decided to visit Ling-Ling in July to support her. She had been living alone since my parents died in 1994 and 1997. While all my siblings and I gathered in New York City, we recalled emotionally our innocent childhood with our parents. We also resolved some of the misunderstandings among ourselves over the years, and really came together as siblings. It was so sad that our parents had passed on not very long ago—and now cancer cells were spreading to Ling-Ling's vital organs. Shortly after I returned from New York, our house was sold after less than a month on the market. Facing leaving our house of twenty-four years along with Ling-Ling's illness, I felt the heavy weight of sadness bear down on me even harder.

The buyer of our house allowed us to stay there until November so we would have some time to clean up our belongings and move out to California. Nonetheless, we only had two months to sell all the furniture and items that we did not want to take to California. Thankfully, once I determined which items we should take with us and found a mover, things moved quickly. On November 18, 2002, we handed over the house keys, said good-bye to the house, and flew to San Jose. I was eager to join Iris, Michael, and our new grandson. Leaving Illinois was difficult for Shau-Jin. He gave up his office in the Physics Department on campus and left his physics colleagues with whom he was quite close. The most difficult part was that we would miss our old friends whom we had known for the past thirty years.

We first rented a small apartment in Cupertino for two months and looked for a house. Just at this time, a townhouse similar to Iris's, in the same neighborhood where Iris and Brett lived, came on the market. It was only a two-minute walk from our house to theirs. We immediately bought it.

Because we were so busy, first looking for a house and then moving, during the first several months after we moved to California we did not have time to help Iris as much as we wanted. Worse yet, Ling-Ling's cancer had become terminal and she was near the end of her life. Shau-Jin and I flew to New York and took care of her for the final two weeks of her life. Ling-Ling died on March 18, 2003.

Life with a baby surely was very different from life before. Although Iris's nanny helped a great deal during the day, sometimes she still felt exhausted with all the chores related to the baby. However, she told us that when Christopher threw a broad smile to her or stared at her with his beautiful big eyes after he was fed, burped, and changed, she thought of her struggle with infertility and how she had dreamed of this day. She cried and laughed at the same time.

On March 22, 2003, Iris received the first copy of her newly published book, *The Chinese in America*, which she showed to us with pride. Although this was the third book she had published, I could still see her joy and emotion when she held that thick hardcover. The jacket was beautifully designed, with a bright red background throughout. On the front was a photo of a three-generation Chinese-American immigrant family, the old dressed in ancient Chinese costumes and the young in modern Western clothes. It was a thick book of 500 pages, the product of four years of hard work!

Once the book was published, Viking Penguin arranged a multi-city book-signing tour for Iris to promote the book; it was one solid month on the road, from April 24 to May 24, 2003. While Iris was on the road, Ping took care of Christopher during the day and we took over after Ping left at 5 P.M. until Brett came home around 7 P.M. By this time, at the age of about eight months, Christopher could sleep through the night, which helped Brett a great deal overnight. We had promised Iris that if Ping needed our help during the day, we were nearby and would pitch in, and this gave Iris much peace of mind while she was out on the book tour.

Iris sent us e-mails and called frequently when she was on the tour. Her book signings, speeches, and media interviews were tightly packed from city to city. She called to ask about Christopher whenever she got a chance. She traveled to the East Coast first, and we followed her news through New York, Princeton, Philadelphia, Washington, Durham (North Carolina), then Chicago, Denver, on and on. Whenever a newspaper had published a review of her latest book, she would e-mail us the article. Most reviews were good and positive. She told us that she was welcomed at every stop, and her speech was always well-received.

In an e-mail on April 30, 2003, Iris wrote:

> Hi Mom and Dad! I'm typing this from a computer in the Nassau Inn at Princeton. Hope all is well with you, Brett and Christopher. The Yale event was extremely well received, with all books sold, and C-span will cover my lecture tonight at Princeton. I'm going to take a nap now before the event. Love, Iris

I knew she was concerned about Christopher, so I usually described how he was doing and asked her not to worry. Shau-Jin and I went to visit him quite often to see whether Ping needed our help. Iris was very happy that we lived so close to her.

On May 12, 2003, Iris wrote:

> Thank you, Mom! Give Christopher a big kiss for me!
>
> Everything went beautifully in Chicago today. First, I gave a long interview with Patrick Reardon at the Chicago Tribune this morning, who identified all of the important themes of my book. Then I posed for a photo shoot with a freelance photographer who turned out to be a U of I graduate. She spent hours taking countless portrait pictures of me for the Tempo section of the Tribune, some of

which I can later use for publicity purposes after the Tribune *selects and runs one image.*

Next, I signed copies of THE CHINESE IN AMERICA *at local bookstores . . . one young woman approached me, saying she was a graduate of Uni High in 1993 and that I was an inspiration for her.*

Afterwards, I delivered a lecture at the Chicago Public Library, which was well-attended and praised (every seat was taken), with people in the audience fighting to ask questions afterwards. . . .

Finally, I had a relaxed and enjoyable interview with Milton Rosenberg, a radio talk show host in the Tribune *building. He had interviewed me for* THE RAPE OF NANKING *and called* THE CHINESE IN AMERICA *"a spectacular book."*

In many ways, I felt I had returned "home"—embraced not only by old friends and acquaintances, but by strangers who knew of my reputation through Uni High, the U of I, the Chicago Tribune *or my previous books. This was certainly one of the best days of my tour.*

Much love, Iris

In her later life, Iris told us that she certainly never forgot the day in 1989 when she'd called us, crying, from a public telephone booth in the *Chicago Tribune*'s building. Sometimes, Iris felt that the fact that the *Chicago Tribune* had not hired her was the best thing they could have done for her career!

On May 21, 2003, an Op-Ed Iris wrote for the *New York Times* titled "Fear of SARS, Fear of Strangers" was published while she was in Denver on her book tour. We wrote to her that we liked the article. It was a proper time to voice the Chinese-American community's concern that the ban of Asian students coming from China, Hong Kong, and Taiwan to the summer school of UC-Berkeley was not fair. The SARS epidemic cases were found not only in Asia, but in other places globally as well. Iris wrote in the Op-Ed, "As long as any university maintains criteria for exclusion based on nationality, not sound medical diagnosis, it will face charges of prejudice. After all, SARS is a global disease. A blanket ban on Asians isn't protection against the virus—it is simply discrimination under a different name." In the article, Iris listed all the health-related discriminations Chinese-Americans had faced in the past 150 years. It was a proper article for her to write at the time she had just freshly finished the book *The Chinese in America*.

On May 24, Iris returned home after a month on the road non-stop without a chance to see Christopher and the rest of her family. I thought she could rest a while at home after the tour, but it was not very long before she was traveling again. This time the book tour was on the West Coast—mainly in California. On June 4, Shaun-Jin and I, as well as Michael and almost all of Iris's cousins and relatives in California, were present when she was book-signing at one of the San Jose Barnes & Noble bookstores. We witnessed the huge crowds at the book signing and confirmed, as she had told us, that it seemed like people were still more interested in her previous book, *The Rape of Nanking*, than her current book. Many of the questions from the crowd and media still pertained to Nanking.

Once Iris came home, she faced millions of things waiting for her, not to mention a huge pile of mail that had accumulated on her desk. She found that Christopher was looking older and was surprised to see that he could push himself in his walker, skating wildly on the surface of their garage at high speed. She might have felt a little guilty that she had not been able to be with him for that month when he was growing so rapidly.

In the summer of 2003, besides the book activities, Iris was actively redecorating her house. Not only cleaning and throwing away boxes of junk; she was also rearranging the furniture in the living room.

Christopher started walking when he was almost a year old. His curiosity got him into everything and gave everyone in the family a headache. We had to keep our eyes on him every minute so he wouldn't get into too much mischief!

On July 30, 2003, Iris described Christopher's power:

Dear Mom,

We have a little Hercules on our hands. Yesterday, Christopher did a pull up on the changing cart, crawled down the equivalent of ten flights of stairs, partially pried open the sliding kitchen door and broke one of the shutters. He can rip off his bib with one fell swoop and even dismantle the tray from the high chair.

On August 31, 2003, Christopher's first birthday, Iris not only ordered a big ice cream cake for the occasion, she also bought a bunch of colorful balloons. Ken and Luann came from Illinois for the big event. Michael came, too. Iris and Brett were busy opening gifts for Christopher. I don't think Christopher understood why so many people were in the house and why he was asked to pose in front of the camera for so many shots. The house was filled with laughter, and Christopher was the star. One of the best shots was a family picture of all of us surrounding the handsome Christopher with his beautiful smile and startling eyes. It was printed on our New Year's, 2004 greeting card and mailed to all our friends.

Iris continued to engage in many book activities, such as September's San Francisco Litquake, which invited her, as well as many Bay area authors, for a reading of their works. Iris realized that she was lucky that we lived nearby. On July 29, 2003, she wrote, "We are blessed in so many ways, especially by having you and Dad so close by. . . . I'm grateful that I have many people around me who love Christopher and are willing to help."

On October 3, 2003, in an e-mail, I asked Iris whether she was putting too much emphasis on her career, placing her career before her family. She replied:

That is not true. It's just that I believe that I have some power to shape my destiny and I want Christopher to have in his mother a strong role model, a person who is his own individual, impervious to the whims of others.

I cannot teach Christopher to be an intellectual and a socially respon-sible person unless I demonstrate to him, through my actions, that I myself am such a person.

I want to teach Christopher that it is far better to belong the critical minority than the unquestioning majority. I want to teach him the ability to think independently, to evaluate ideas and information on his own—without the official sanction of the authorities—and, if possible, to create.

These qualities are not universally popular in our society. My tendency to stand alone, apart from the crowd, has caused me great pain and suffering throughout my life, but in the end, I am a stronger and better person because of it.

In the fall of 2003, I enrolled in a class of *Ikebana*, Japanese flower arrangement, at the Cupertino Senior Center. This was something I had always wanted to learn. In addition, Shau-Jin and I were taking painting classes and hiking frequently with groups from the Sunnyvale Community Center. Both of us were enjoying these classes and had a good time. Later, I also found a clay art class that I really enjoyed and devoted many hours to making vases, plates, flowerpots, and so forth. I was absorbed in my own hobbies and all the perks of the retirement lifestyle and did not realize until later that Iris was suffering a major setback in her quest for her movie project. The company that had optioned the film rights to *The Rape of Nanking* could not find investors to make the film. They did not renew their option after the end of a year.

So in the spring of 2003, Iris was back to square one. Of course, she was a person who would not take "no" for an answer. She was taking a different approach this time. She enrolled in a special workshop called the A-Team, in which the participants met once every two weeks. The leader of the A-Team would coach her and others in a strategy to achieve individual goals. She flew to Burbank every two weeks and spent two days over a weekend attending the fast-paced meeting to learn from her mentor and to get connected to movie industry people. She ended up in collaboration with an Asian-American movie producer. After half a year and long hours of discussion and negotiation and much effort, Iris still had not gotten anywhere. The major problem was finding investors. Even though she had a sound visionary script and business plan, people with capital were just not willing to make that final leap of commitment.

Often when we met up, Iris expressed her disappointment and frustration over the movie project. Her frustration stemmed from the fact that she felt a movie would reach out to an even wider audience than the book and further educate people about Nanking and the history of Chinese-Americans. She had delivered those sentiments in a speech at the Committee of 100 in June, in front of many influential Chinese-Americans, by asking: "Have we, as Chinese-Americans, done enough to educate our children about our heritage and our contributions to this country? If the answer is no, we have to ask ourselves why. If even we Chinese-Americans don't care about our own history, why should anyone else?"

Iris continued: "It's disgraceful that there is still not a major feature film on the subject of the Rape of Nanking, or on the subject of the Comfort Women, or on the subject of Unit 731. We have to ask ourselves some hard-hitting questions. Like, why isn't there a Chinese-owned studio. Certainly the talent, passion, and intelligence are there. Is it that we simply don't care? Or are we not able to work together effectively to bring about change?

"There is only one group of people who can really prevent this project from happening, and it isn't the Japanese or the Hollywood system: it is ourselves. We are the ones who get to decide whether it happens or not."

On October 5, 2003, Iris asked us to watch over Christopher so she, Brett, and Michael could go to the Asian Business League banquet in San Francisco where Iris was going to receive an award. She delivered a short speech in accepting the award. The speech was in the same tone, telling Asian-American business elites that "First, we need to support each other. . . . Secondly, and even more importantly, we have to create our own power. We should stop asking others for permission. Rather than beg for entree into non-Asian organizations, we must create our own. It is high time that we stopped banging our heads against the glass ceiling and started using our own capital resources and entrepreneurial drive, to build more of own hospitals and companies and law firms and media empires and venture capital funds. . . ."

She advised the audience that "If there is one thing I have learned from my career as a writer, it is that the surest path to success is to listen to your heart, your own inner passion, while striving to create something of enduring value. Quite often this means standing alone and forging one's own path. To quote Sigmund Freud: 'I became aware of my destiny: to belong to the critical minority as opposed to the unquestioning majority.'"

At this time, she was turning her attention to her next book project. Iris had proposed several ideas to her book agent, and the story of American POWs in the Philippines struck a chord. In early November 2003, with the help of a military historian, Iris was preparing a trip to Ohio. She asked us to help Ping and Christopher while she spent a week in November in interviewing a group of surviving American veterans who had been captured in the Philippines by the Japanese Imperial Army during World War II. Again, she returned to the profession and topic she knew best: writer, investigative journalist, and historian, working to dig and expose a forgotten historical event of World War II in Asia.

19

The Breakdown

To understand what transpired during the last leg of Iris's lifetime journey, it would require a day-by-day, even hour-by-hour, account of the twists and turns and many of the inconceivable struggles with her demon. This chapter will present the chronological events as they took place; they are quite dramatic, but very real, to anyone who seeks a clue as to what exactly developed during those pivotal months:

In 2004, Iris focused her research on a group of American World War II POWs in preparation for the proposal for her next book. This was the story of the American 192nd tank battalion from the Midwest states of Wisconsin, Illinois, Ohio, and Kentucky. The 192nd was deployed to the Philippines in 1941. They fought the Japanese and were subsequently captured by the Japanese Army. This tank battalion unit went through hell in the Philippines. There were some survivors, but many died from starvation, disease, and torture. In November 2003, Iris had visited and interviewed several of the battalion survivors in those states. Now she systematically interviewed and tape-recorded each one of them over the phone. This involved many hours of Q&A and was a long and tedious process. The stories of these surviving POWs were horrendous and excruciating beyond words. Iris said even her typist could not stop her tears while she was transcribing the recorded tapes. This book project was certainly a dark subject and not good for her mental health, but Iris said she just could not turn her back on those veterans and let their stories be forgotten.

Right after the publication of *The Rape of Nanking*, we strongly suggested to Iris that she should not write on such a gruesome subject for her next book. That was how she decided to write about the Chinese in America. As soon as we heard she was going to write the following book about the American POWs in the Philippines, we expressed our concern, but Iris said she could not forsake them.

After the arrival of Christopher, Iris slept with him in the bedroom on the top floor of their townhouse. During the day, Christopher was taken care of by Ping while Iris worked in her home office. Brett was taking care of Christopher in the evenings, whereas Iris was taking care of him at night. Around this time, as Christopher moved from a crib to a toddler bed, he learned he could get out of that bed and jump into bed with Iris, which disrupted her sleep. Sometimes she worked late into the night. By the time she went to bed, it was almost time for the baby to wake up. It seemed that Iris was continuing to push herself to maintain the same productivity she'd had before Christopher was born. She did not realize that she was suffering constant sleep deprivation.

In March 2004, when Christopher was over a year and a half old, Iris decided that he should start playing with other children of his age. Besides, Brett's mom Luann often called from Illinois to remind both of them that they should spend more time with Christopher and find a place for him to interact with other children. So Iris changed Ping's schedule and put Christopher in the Cisco Day Care Center two or three afternoons a week.

In the meantime, we had made a plan for a trip to Italy for about three weeks, from April 2 to April 23. The trip unfortunately coincided with Iris's book tour for the paperback edition of *The Chinese in America*. Fortunately, on March 31, Luann and Ken came from Illinois to help watch Christopher while we were away.

Before Iris left for the month-long book tour, she showed me the itinerary. I was shocked and said to her, "How can you travel to so many cities in such a short time?"

"I told them. That's the best they can do," Iris replied, slightly annoyed.

Iris had made numerous prior book-signing trips for *The Rape of Nanking*. Now that she was an old hand at book tours, I thought she knew what she was capable of managing. Therefore, I felt that I should just let her be, even though I was uncomfortable with the itinerary. Due to our forthcoming Italy trip, I had no time to think about it further.

After Iris left us in November 2004, I went back and traced what she had done during the last few months of her life. I rechecked the itinerary of her paperback book tour in 2004. The book tour was from March 31 through May 6, during which time she traveled to some twenty cities for thirty-five events. The most strenuous part of the trip was her zigzagging across the continent almost four times. Even a person in top physical and mental condition would have found this schedule highly stressful.

On March 31, Iris attended a function at San Francisco Public Library in the evening. The next day, she flew to Dallas on an early flight and started her month-long tour.

On April 2, we departed for Italy. Whenever possible, when we arrived at a different city, we would find an Internet cafe to check our e-mail and to inform Iris and Michael where we were. We were also happy to receive e-mails from Iris, who told us her book tour was going very well.

On April 4, when we were in Rome, Iris sent an e-mail saying she'd had a terrific time in Chicago. She also attached a letter from Professor

Da-Hsuan Feng, the Vice President for Research at the University of Texas at Dallas. The letter was the introduction speech to her lecture in Dallas. In the speech, Professor Feng gave glorious praise of Iris's book *The Rape of Nanking*. Although Iris was on a book tour for her book *The Chinese in America*, people were still talking about her Nanking book.

On April 11, 2004, Iris wrote a short note saying she was at Colgate University, and on April 16, in reply to our e-mail, she said she was at the Baltimore airport and about to leave for Boston. These e-mails were short and revealed nothing unusual.

Shau-Jin and I returned home on April 23. Immediately we went to see Christopher, Luann, and Ken. Christopher was very happy to see us. We brought a gift for Christopher, a wooden replica of Pinocchio that we'd bought in Montecatini.

When Iris was on the road, she usually called home whenever possible to check on Christopher. On Monday, April 26, Iris arrived home in the late afternoon from San Diego, after almost four weeks on the road. This was the first chance she'd had to be home. She missed Christopher tremendously and wanted to see him.

The next day, she was scheduled to give a speech at the San Francisco Commonwealth Club. Iris felt that the speech was very important because the Club had a prestigious reputation. For this important occasion, Iris expressed her need for peace and quiet to prepare her speech, so she was scheduled to stay in a hotel in San Francisco. I saw her for only several minutes at the door that evening when she rushed out of the house to drive to San Francisco. She saw Christopher very briefly before she left. She looked extremely exhausted.

I knew Iris very well. She had already felt guilty that she could not spend more time with Christopher, just like any other working mother. She tried her best to be a good mother to her child, but her time and energy were limited. She was under tremendous pressure to be a good mother in a conventional sense, to conform to traditional family values. I sympathized with her because I myself was a professional woman. I could feel the pressure society in general puts on working mothers, something that many women surely still feel even today.

In retrospect, Shau-Jin and I felt that Iris had become preoccupied and somewhat absent-minded right after the April book tour. She looked tired and seemed to have lost her energy. This could have been due to the five-week, non-stop travel on the road, but she became exceedingly moody, more quiet and apprehensive than expected. I have mulled it over and tried to figure out what factors caused such a change. Finally, there was one thing in particular that bothered me and stood out in my mind.

On one occasion after the April paperback book tour, Iris disclosed to me that she had been threatened on the tour, but she did not specify where and at which event. She just said, "One person came and approached me after the talk and said in a threatening tone, 'You would be safer if you joined our organization.' I was stunned and did not know what to say, and I just quickly walked away. Did I do something wrong?" she asked me.

At the time, I assured her that she had done nothing wrong and she should not worry about it. I even suggested, in order to put her mind at ease, that she might have misinterpreted his words.

But she said, "I don't think I should have just run away immediately . . . I don't think I handled it right. . . ."

She mentioned the incident again on October 5, 2004, to both Shau-Jin and me when we took her for a walk in the Hakone Garden just a month before her suicide. Again, we did not know who this person was and where and when this incident had happened, or whether the person was really threatening her. We usually listened and tried not to press for more details when Iris was reluctant to tell us. That had been our habit over the years.

Up to this day, I believe something must have happened during the April book tour that made her very fearful. In the past, she'd known how we would worry about her safety, so she usually hesitated to disclose to us the details of anything unpleasant that had happened to her. She believed that on that tour, someone had threatened her and she hadn't handled it well. As a result, she felt like someone was after her. Was this true? I don't know. I guess I will never know. But we do know that she became increasingly fearful.

At the beginning of May, Iris was finishing up her public appearances. Around this time, Brett went to his hometown in Illinois to attend his high-school class reunion. For Mother's Day, with Brett not being home, Iris said she wanted to invite me to a Mother's Day concert at the Mountain View Center for the Performing Arts. I told her, "You are a mother too. Why don't we celebrate together?"

On Saturday, May 8, the day before Mother's Day, Iris came to our townhouse holding a dozen red roses and a dozen purple irises in one hand. In the other hand, she held a lovely white basket that contained a beautiful purple flowered plant. She was determined to celebrate Mother's Day with me and to forget about her recent unhappiness. I was deeply touched, but at the same time I felt that something was missing.

On Mother's Day, Iris drove me to the concert hall in Mountain View. At the concert, she sat beside me. When the lights dimmed, I could see that her facial expression was unsettled. She was also quiet in the car while we were driving to the concert. This was unusual, quite unlike her usual talkative self. I wondered what was going through her mind.

When the choir sang Handel's *Silent Worship*, my eyes welled with tears. I was thinking of my mother. I wondered what Iris was thinking about. Was it about her book tour? Was she thinking about being a good mother? I looked at her sitting next to me, but could not figure it out; I could only see that she was sad, feeling a sense of loss.

Around this time, Iris was looking into daycare facilities for Christopher. She was also earnestly engaged in talking to her neighbors who had children of Christopher's age, hoping to organize a playgroup. When both Iris and Michael were young, I had organized a playgroup with my friends in Champaign-Urbana. Once a week, the mothers took turns hosting and watching over the children, so that not only could the kids play with each other, but the mothers could get a little break. Iris liked this idea.

One day, Iris was happy to report to us by e-mail that "Christopher now knows his numbers! Yesterday, he laid out before me three wooden numbers—1, 2, 3—in a neat row, and this evening, he handed Brett, one after another, a perfect sequence of numbers from a jumbled pile of numbers (1-2-3-4-5-6-7-8-9-0). Isn't that amazing?"

On June 9, Iris called me because she had a phone interview over the phone at 6:00 A.M. with a radio station in Boston. She asked Ping to come earlier that day to take care of Christopher. She said she would like me to come to watch Christopher at 4 P.M. when Ping left. When I went to her house at 4 P.M., I noticed that Iris's face looked gray and very tired. She said that she had just finished the phone interviews with the tank battalion survivors and she wanted to take a nap. I was heartbroken. It was obvious that she had not gotten enough sleep.

On Saturday, June 12, Iris was awarded an honorable degree from the California State University at Hayward. Iris had told us several months before that the university president had informed her that she was the 2004 recipient of an honorary degree. She would be the keynote speaker at the graduation ceremony that day. Shau-Jin and I were very happy for her and told her we would be there. In 2002, when Iris had been awarded the honorary degree from Wooster College in Ohio, we were not able to go. Now we lived in the Bay area, and we certainly were honored to be there to observe the ceremony and see Iris honored.

The president of the university, Norma Rees, invited Iris and us for an early breakfast before the ceremony. At the end of the ceremony, Iris came over to us with the president and asked us to join them to take several pictures. Iris was dressed in a cap and gown, holding her honorary degree certificate in her hands. She was very happy and had a big smile. This was one of the happiest moments of her life and it was also, as far as I ever saw, the last one.

In June, without any other public engagements, I noticed that Iris was spending more time with Christopher, and she was also starting to observe Christopher's behavior and his speech very closely. She took an interest in watching the other kids of his age and compared him to them. Christopher's second birthday was only three months away. Iris was starting to wonder why Christopher had not yet spoken in complete sentences.

I told her that children developed at different speeds. I told her it was very normal for some children to speak later than average that she should not be concerned about it. Indeed, Shau-Jin, Luann, Ken, Brett, and Ping all agreed that Christopher was quite a handsome and intelligent boy. He had learned how to walk at about one year old and was very active. There was no sign indicating anything out of the ordinary, except that he was overactive and full of energy. His excess energy sometimes caused headaches for everyone. He was just like a little "curious George" in the house. We needed to pay extra attention in watching over him.

For some reason, Iris did not agree with all of us and kept telling me that she was worried about Christopher. She then began actively doing research on child development. I cannot remember the exact date, but it was around this time in June that she started to tell me that she suspected that Christopher had signs of autism.

Because Iris was talking about autism, I started to do some research on it too. There was a group of activists in the U.S., particularly in California, who claimed that a preservative, a mercury-containing chemical used in vaccines, could cause autism in children. This controversial theory had been debated in the media for a long time. On one hand, the government health officials and many other scientists claimed that the mercury in the vaccines was in such small amounts as to be insignificant, and that further studies did not show any strong link between the mercury in vaccines and autism in children. On the other hand, the activists claimed, the government study designs had flaws, and they did not believe the results reported by government health officials. Iris sided with this group of activists and believed that the government's results could not be trusted.

My birthday was very close to Father's Day. We usually celebrated the two occasions together. On Saturday, June 19, I made lots of Chinese dishes and invited everyone in the family to come to celebrate Father's Day. Iris gave us a beautifully framed picture of Christopher with his handprint next to the photo. Iris specially framed it for us as a gift for this special occasion. Again, like Mother's Day, this was the last Father's Day Iris celebrated with us. Although on the surface she looked fine, I could see that she was quieter and seemed preoccupied, almost obsessed, with something. That night, Iris wrote me a thank-you e-mail:

> *Dear Mom,*
>
> *I'm glad you like the framed picture of Christopher with his gold handprint. And thank you for fixing such a splendid dinner tonight, and for helping Brett watch Christopher when I was away in Texas!*
>
> *Christopher clearly understands many more words than he can vocalize. This evening, we read a book on colors, and he astounded me by the size of his vocabulary. When I asked him questions (like "Where is the frog?" "Where is the sheep?" "Where are the slippers?" "Where is the glass of orange juice?" "Where is the tiger?") he pointed accurately to all the pictures. I was so impressed!*
>
> *Much love, Iris*

On June 30, I bumped into Iris on the path in our housing complex. She said she was on her way home after taking a walk on the levee in the back of our townhouses. She looked tired and unhappy. I told her she looked sick and asked what was the matter. She told me that she just had a conversation with Susan Rabiner in New York. Susan told her she was editing a book about the Gulf War Syndrome. The book described that the sickness of those Gulf War soldiers, which was diagnosed when they came home, was actually caused by the vaccine injected in them before they went. Iris was quite upset about this. She said that the author of the book did research and found out that the vaccine given to the soldiers was tainted with experimental chemicals. Iris said, "The government wanted to do tests on the vaccine and used the soldiers as guinea pigs." After Iris died, I found out the book is called *Vaccine A: The Covert Government Experiment that's Killing Our Soldiers—And Why GI's Are Only the First Victims*, by Gary Matsumoto. The existence of this book made Iris further believe that the autism in children was caused by the vaccines they received. Furthermore, she did not trust the health institution of our government and regretted that she'd let Christopher receive so many vaccinations as an infant.

On Wednesday, July 14, I went to see Iris and found no one home. I saw that the flowers she had planted in the big pots in front of their house had withered. She had forgotten to water the plants, I thought, as I knocked on her door. It turned out that Iris and Ping had taken Christopher to Fremont to see a doctor. She had Christopher's hair, urine, and blood tested for any toxins, such as mercury.

Iris took Christopher to see many more doctors. She started to investigate the cause of autism and do whatever she could to help Christopher, who she presumed was autistic. This was very natural for a mother who loves her child so much under such circumstances. She would explore all kinds of remedies to help her child, and yet the rest of the family regarded her concern as excessive. Later I learned that Iris had already read many books and done extensive research on autism. As a writer, she was very sensitive and keen in her observations. She might have already detected some subtle clues indicating autism in Christopher while the rest of us did not.

On Wednesday afternoon, August 11, Ping called us and told us Iris was sick and had asked us to come. Shau-Jin and I immediately went to see her and found her in an exhausted and devastated state. We did not realize the seriousness of her health situation until then. We learned that she had not been eating well and had hardly slept for several days. We found that she had been browsing for hours on the

Internet, reading many books and working incessantly in her home office. We knew she was going to Kentucky to interview the tank battalion veterans the next day. Ping was the first one who suggested that Iris should not go on the trip. After seeing her current state, we also tried to persuade her not to go. For the next hour while we were there, Iris seemed to feel better. She told us that she would be all right. She asked us all to go back home so she could rest and take a nap.

Early in the morning of the next day, I got up and immediately went to see Iris. She was up already, and she told me that she was fine. She said she had managed to fall asleep for a couple of hours. She was busy packing and preparing for the trip. Ping had not yet arrived. Christopher and Brett were still asleep inside.

I asked Iris, "Are you sure you want to go today?"

"Yes, Mom, I think I'll be fine," she replied.

It seemed to me that she was strengthened and determined, unlike the day before. She told me that she had spent a long time arranging the interview with those veterans in Kentucky and other Midwest states, and that she could not just cancel the trip at the last minute. I figured she was old enough to make her own decisions, and I reluctantly let go of my maternal instincts to prevent her from going. This is, of course, my biggest regret.

After I saw Iris get into the cab and leave for the airport on her way to Louisville, Kentucky, I waited until Ping came over and then headed home. I comforted myself while walking home by recalling that Iris had told me that she'd slept a couple of hours and felt fine. On top of that, I reassured myself that she could take a nap and rest on the airplane.

Luann arrived in the afternoon of the same day. She had come to help while Iris was out of town, as prearranged. That night, I received a call from Iris in a Louisville hotel room, informing us that she had arrived safely. This was her usual routine when she was traveling. I had been anxiously waiting for her call all day. On the phone, she said she was very tired and had a headache. I told her she should immediately lie down and go to sleep. When she called, it was almost midnight in Kentucky, since there was a three-hour time difference. She said she had not eaten yet but was too tired to go out. I suggested that she call room service, but she said she was staying in a hotel where there was no restaurant in the hotel. I told her to call a nearby restaurant for take-out, and she promised she would.

That night, we went to sleep and assumed that Iris would be all right. But at about 2 A.M. California time, in the early morning of Friday, August 13, we were awakened by a phone call. I picked up the phone, and it was Iris. Her voice was shaking, and told me she had seen some frightening pictures on the TV in her hotel room. Iris and I then had a conversation about this. Apparently she could not fall asleep, so she turned the TV on. I asked her what kind of pictures were on the TV screen. She said it showed some horrible atrocities and ugly images of children torn apart by wars. She said that the TV was showing something similar to scenes from hell, like an imagined World War III.

She had then turned off her TV, waited a while, and then turned it on again, to find that the ugly images had disappeared. I responded that maybe the TV had been showing a war movie. It's very possible, I said, that during the wee hours of the night, TV stations would show such a genre of horror films.

Then Iris told me she did not feel things had been quite right from the very moment she'd arrived at the hotel. The clerk at the front desk looked suspicious to her, and spoke to a person who later kept looking at the window of her room. While Iris was talking with me on the phone, she told me that she could still see that person standing outside on the lawn not far from her room. He looked at her window as she peered through her curtain. She told me she suspected her room was wired and that what she had seen on the TV was real and intentionally shown to threaten her.

It was past 5 A.M. in Kentucky. I asked her, had she gotten any sleep at all? She said she couldn't fall asleep, and she was exhausted and had a terrible headache. She was sick, I could tell. She had to be ill, because she had not been able to sleep for the three or four days prior to the trip.

She had also not eaten enough, nor had she drunk any liquid for some time. She said she had ordered some take-out dinner that was delivered to her room, but she did not have any appetite and hadn't eaten anything. She didn't want to drink anything either, afraid that someone might poison her. I knew that under severe sleep deprivation, people could have delusions. Under this circumstance, all I could think of at the time was to have some friends nearby to help her. We did not call Brett because we didn't want to wake up Christopher or Luann at such an early hour.

I asked Iris whether she knew anyone in Louisville. I reminded her about the people she had made contact with for this trip. She said she knew a retired former Army officer, a veteran, living near Louisville, but she said he was very old. I told her that at least he lived nearby, and maybe he could come to help her. It would be comforting for her just to have someone else with her. I didn't want her to be alone.

Iris waited until after 6 A.M. in Louisville before she finally called this kind veteran. Subsequently, he and his wife came to see Iris in the hotel room. The wife was a retired nurse and, after observing Iris for a bit, recommended that she go to a hospital. Iris was soon in an ambulance on the way to a hospital.

After Iris left for the hospital, I called the ER unit of the hospital. They informed me that Iris had arrived and was waiting in the ER ward for a doctor to examine her.

In the meantime, Brett was informed of what had happened, and he called the hospital and answered all the questions that were necessary for admitting Iris into the hospital. Brett continued to call her to monitor her condition. Michael was calling constantly, to monitor both us and his sister's situation. I was busy on the phone all day long. I was also frantically trying to get airplane reservations to fly to Louisville right away. The earliest available flight was the next day. On

August 14, Shau-Jin and I took a 6:20 A.M. American Airlines flight and arrived in Louisville at 5:25 P.M. after a three-hour layover at Chicago's O'Hare airport. My heart was pumping hard all the way. I could not wait to see Iris.

As soon as we arrived in Louisville, we immediately went to the hotel where Iris had stayed. The hotel let us into her room, which we had had them lock up for us before we arrived and was reserved for our stay. We found that her two suitcases were there, safe and sound. We immediately took a taxi to the hospital. In the hospital, we were told that Iris was in the Psychiatric Unit.

When we arrived at Iris's room, she was sound asleep. Her room was a standard hospital room with a bathroom, very similar to the maternity ward I had stayed in when I gave birth to both children. We realized that she had been given shots that made her sleepy. We patiently waited for her to wake up.

Then, suddenly, she turned and opened her eyes and spotted us. She screamed out "Mom!" as she sat up abruptly and burst into tears. I came forward and embraced her tightly. After she cried for a while, she seemed to feel much better and I could see she was somewhat relieved. She started to describe to us what had happened, from the hotel to the hospital. She told us that in the Emergency Unit, they'd done a lot of medical tests on her. She was sent to the Psychiatric Unit because they had not found anything wrong with her physically.

Obviously, she was still under the influence of the medication the hospital had given her. She was very fragile and emotional at that moment. We comforted her and explained to her that she was overly exhausted because of lack of food and rest. She was in good hands and would be better soon.

A couple of nurses came to the room and checked on us from time to time. Later, all the nurses told us that they were very glad that we had come. We stayed with Iris in her hospital room until 9 P.M., leaving when visiting hours were over, and we assured her that we would come back to see her first thing in the morning.

We stayed in the same room of the hotel Iris had stayed in. The hotel was very close to the airport. The takeoffs and landings of the airplanes were so noisy that it was impossible for us to fall asleep. No wonder Iris could not sleep, I thought. I turned on the TV and checked all the channels and could not see anything unusual on the screen. It was a very standard hotel room: a queen-size bed, a round table, two chairs, and a TV on a dresser. I imagined that the veteran and his wife must have been sitting on the chairs beside the bed when they'd communicated with me on his cell phone the whole morning the day before.

I was exhausted by the trip and by visiting Iris in the hospital, but I could not fall asleep like Shau-Jin—he could sleep easily under any condition. I could not sleep. There were many questions haunting me: Could this hotel room be wired? Could the pictures she saw on the TV screen have been set up by someone to threaten her, as she suspected? Could someone really be after her, as Iris thought? Why was a person looking at her window in the middle of the night? Was it her imagination, or was it real? I could not answer those questions that night, and I cannot answer them today. It's still a big question mark in my mind.

Although her concerns might seem unfounded, I can't dismiss them because I know that Iris was a very sensitive person and very observant in every situation. She could detect many subtle signals or messages that most people would miss. One fact to illustrate how brilliant her instinct was: she was able to detect that her son, Christopher, had autism when he was only twenty-two months old, whereas no one else, not her husband or her relatives, nor even Shau-Jin and I, were able to detect any issues at that time. Now we know indeed Christopher has a mild to moderate autism disorder, which the doctor diagnosed when he was over three years old. Therefore, I cannot easily disregard Iris's complaints or suspicions of some of the situations she described to me.

Early on Sunday, August 15, I was awakened by the thunder of airplanes as they flew in and out of the Louisville airport. It seemed the hotel had been built directly under the flight path of the runway. The sound made my heart pump faster, and Shau-Jin and I got up quickly and took a taxi straight to the hospital to see Iris.

As soon as we reached the hospital, I made it very clear to the nurses that we needed to take Iris home as soon as possible, preferably the next day. The nurses agreed that it seemed there was no reason they should keep her there. They could see how Iris trusted us and how she felt comforted when we were around. The head nurse paged the doctor to get a consent form. Since I'd told them that I had to change the return airline ticket for Iris and confirm our reservation, we needed to know for sure that the doctor would allow her to go home. The doctor finally said yes, and then the nurses began to write reports and summaries for us to bring home.

It was a hectic day. I was on the phone a lot to make all the travel arrangements. At the same time, Shau-Jin and I spent the whole day with Iris in the Psychiatric Unit. Brett called to check on her. Michael also called and asked what he could do. I told him he could pick us up at the airport when we arrived in San Jose the next day.

In the evening, the doctor finally came and met with us. He briefed us on Iris's condition in front of us all. He believed Iris had experienced a so-called "brief reactive psychosis" due to stress conditions such as lack of sleep and food. He added that her condition could also be a possible onset of a bipolar disorder and recommended that Iris see a doctor for followup after her return home.

When we told him we lived in the San Francisco Bay area of California, his eyes lit up and he stated that the Stanford Medical Center had a doctor who was the world's leading expert and the best psychiatrist for treatment for bipolar disorder. He gave us a reference. He also prescribed an antipsychotic drug, Risperdal (risperidone, from Janssen Pharmaceutica), 2 mg a day, for Iris to take for at least a year.

This was the first time we had ever heard of bipolar disorder, and worried about the side effects of the drug, but he assured us that the medicine was safe and had been in use for over ten years. Iris asked the doctor many questions, as she was not at all certain that she wanted to take the drug. We told her that we would also consult another doctor after returning home.

At the time, we didn't have a chance to tell the doctor of Iris's recent history of worry about her son's possible autism and its contribution to Iris's sleep deprivation and toll on her energy just prior to this trip to Kentucky. Without knowing this history, it is understandable why the doctor would have speculated about the possible onset of bipolar disorder. We, as well as Iris, never believed that bipolar disorder was the correct diagnosis.

The next morning, Monday, August 16, we finished the discharge procedure in the hospital and took Iris back to the hotel. As we rode in the taxi, Iris made some strange remarks about the advertisements on the billboards along the side of the road, which we did not understand.

When we reached the hotel room, it was near noon, and the August sunshine was very bright. We unlocked the room and went in. Iris sat down on the bed and surveyed the whole room with her wary eyes slowly and silently. She also turned on the TV and checked all the channels. We did not see anything abnormal. Iris did not say a word and just sat there. When it was time to leave, she took her suitcases and gave a last uncertain glance at the room. We left for the airport.

We had a layover at O'Hare. During the waiting period, Iris wanted to go to a bookstore, so I went with her. While she was looking at all the magazine covers in the airport bookstore, she again made some comments that I didn't understand. She was absorbed with her own thoughts. She seemed absent-minded and sometimes a little confused.

When we finally landed at the San Jose airport, we called Michael to come pick us up. While we were waiting for Michael, Iris said that she felt dizzy and had a headache. She told me that things seemed distorted to her and that the expressions of people around her were strange.

At the time, we did not know how powerful psychiatric drugs were and thought that Iris's behavior was strange. I later realized that while in the hospital, Iris had been given heavy doses of Risperdal and a tranquilizer to calm her down. The side effects of psychiatric drugs could be severe; that explained why she felt dizzy and had a headache and distortion of her visual perception.

Finally, we spotted Michael's car, and he drove all of us to Iris's home. As soon as we walked into her house, we found Brett, Luann, and Christopher about to have dinner. Ping had prepared many dishes for them. It was obvious that the dinner table was too small for four extra people. The four of us stood there, appearing very awkward. I could see that Iris was not very happy with this scene, and she told us she wanted to go to our house to rest. Brett came over soon after and spent the evening with her until she was ready to rest.

An Untimely Death

After returning from Louisville, Iris stayed with us in our home. With Luann watching over Christopher and our house being much quieter, Iris chose to stay with us in the hope that she could sleep better. After the trauma she'd suffered in Louisville, we also wanted her with us, so we could watch over her to make sure she would be fully recovered. Brett was very busy with his work, and therefore Shau-Jin and I were helping him to find a psychiatrist for Iris. In my search for a psychiatrist, I discovered that the famous doctor at Stanford whom the psychiatrist in Louisville had recommended was not accepting any new patients. In addition, almost none of the psychiatrists listed on Brett's Cisco health insurance plan were available. There apparently was a shortage of psychiatrists in the Bay area.

Tuesday, August 17, the day after Iris returned home, was Iris and Brett's thirteenth wedding anniversary. While I was frantically trying to find a psychiatrist for Iris, she was only interested in shopping. I sent Shau-Jin to accompany her because she was still moody and had been instructed not to drive while taking Risperdal. Iris had started to take 2 mg of Risperdal per day since her hospitalization in Louisville.

When Iris came home from the shopping mall, she looked exceptionally beautiful. As it turned out, she had gone to a cosmetic shop and asked a cosmetician to give her a makeover. She looked like a movie star! That night, Brett came to take her out to dinner to celebrate their anniversary. For some reason, I could see that Iris was still unhappy even though we all complimented her. Her breakdown in Louisville must have had a profound impact on her.

Iris continued to take 2 mg of Risperdal every day, as the doctor in Louisville had prescribed. The medicine made her sleepy and less energetic. In our family and among our relatives, no one had ever had the experience of seeing a psychiatrist or taking antipsychotic drugs. Therefore, we had no idea of the effects of the drug. On the surface, Iris looked normal; but none of us knew, at the time, the strong adverse side effects of a drug such as Risperdal. I drove Iris everywhere, anywhere she wanted to go, because it was unsafe for her to drive while she was on the medication. Family members who didn't realize this got the wrong impression: that I was overly protective.

On Monday, August 23, Iris finally had an appointment with Dr. A, a psychiatrist from Brett's health plan. Brett came to pick her up, and we went with them. I presented to Dr. A a detailed medical note I had written about what happened in Louisville, and a copy of the hospital report.

Dr. A listened to us. He was quite laid-back and did not make any comments. Then he said he was about to take off for a month's vacation and would follow up with Iris only upon his return. He did not say anything concerning Iris's mental condition. Iris did ask him about stopping the medication, but he persuaded her to continue taking it until he came back.

In the meantime, I found out that Dr. A was not a board-certified psychiatrist. I began desperately looking for a board-certified psychiatrist for Iris; additionally, I didn't want to wait for Dr. A to return from his vacation. Finally, after an intensive search, I found Dr. B, who had graduated from a reputable university. I highly recommended Dr. B to Brett, but Dr. B was not on the list of Brett's medical insurance plan. That meant Brett and Iris would have to pay extra medical expenses out of their own pockets if Iris went to see him, but we all agreed that Iris should see Dr. B until she could get in to see a qualified psychiatrist from Brett's health plan.

On Wednesday, August 25, Iris, Brett, Shau-Jin, and I went to see Dr. B. I handed him the summary I'd written about Iris's situation in Louisville. We also told him about her worries over her son's autism. Dr. B did not say very much, but comforted Iris. He said he would see her the next week to follow up.

In the meantime, Iris was still worried about Christopher. Although I was actively looking into the literature about autism and also closely observing Christopher's behavior, I could not decisively say either way. Indeed, Christopher would turn two in a few days, and it was too early to come to any conclusions. In my mind, children's development varied tremendously from one individual to the other. We comforted Iris and told her she should wait and continue to watch his development.

Both Brett's and Christopher's birthdays were near the end of August. To celebrate their birthdays, Ken also flew in from Illinois. Iris wanted to get a birthday gift for Brett. I drove her to Westfield Shopping Mall. We wandered in the mall for two hours before she finally decided on a gift for him. Then she began looking for a birthday gift for Christopher, who would turn two on August 31. In retrospect, she had just come back home from her breakdown less than two weeks before, and she was already resuming her duties as a wife and mother. Even though she was moody and unhappy, she seemed to be functioning well.

Sunday, August 29 was our fortieth wedding anniversary. The invitations for about fifty people had been sent out before Iris's breakdown. Now that the time was approaching, my mind was so occupied with Iris and her recent breakdown that I was really not in the mood for a celebration. I almost wanted to cancel the whole event, but it was too late. No one could imagine my suffering at the time.

On the day of our anniversary, Iris said that she and Luann had taken Christopher to a party sponsored by the fertility clinic where Christopher was born. After she returned, she told me that she'd enjoyed talking to all the parents who, just like her, had had their children through the same method. She looked very tired when I saw her that evening.

Our fortieth anniversary party was in the evening at a Chinese restaurant. Iris was dressed beautifully. However, I could see that she was tired and looked very sleepy. It could have been due to all the activities on that day, or to the Risperdal. At the party, after several relatives spoke, everyone expected Iris to say a few words. After all, she was such a seasoned public speaker. I was very anxious and worried that people might notice that something was wrong. Up to that moment, no one knew; even our close relatives did not know what had recently happened. Iris didn't want us to tell anyone. We understood that she was a very private person and honored her wish. With everyone's eyes turned toward Iris, she stood up with her glass of red wine and said, "I'd like to make a toast to my parents for making it to their fortieth anniversary; I don't know if I will be that lucky. . . ." Her words were very soft and slow, in contrast to her usual style. Some relatives noticed the unusual way Iris behaved on that day because they had known Iris for a long time. After she passed away, they told us that they had detected something strange about her on that day.

Two days later, August 31, was Christopher's second birthday. In the morning, Iris and I took him to the Gymboree in the Westgate Mall. After that, she shopped in a party store and bought a dozen variously colored and shaped argon-filled balloons. We had a hard time squeezing the balloons into the car. Christopher sat in his rear car seat and was very happy, screaming "balloon, balloon." Iris also ordered a big ice cream birthday cake.

In the evening, we all gathered in Iris's town house, including Ken, Luann, and Michael. In spite of the house being filled with brightly colored balloons and gifts, there seemed a lack of celebratory atmosphere. Iris took many pictures of Christopher. It was a briefly happy occasion, but there was a sense of uncertainty in the air. This was the last birthday party Iris spent with Christopher. The next day, Ken and Luann left for Illinois.

Once Ken and Luann left, Iris went back to her own house to sleep. She said she had many things to do. She needed to find a preschool for Christopher right away, so he could play with other kids. Therefore, I devoted myself to helping her with that project. Finally, we found one located in the heart of a quiet residential area of Santa Clara, about a twenty-minute drive from home. Later, we took Iris and Christopher to visit the school; and on September 13, Iris enrolled Christopher in the preschool.

Iris was now seeing Dr. B once a week, and she persuaded him to reduce her dosage of Risperdal by half (1 mg from 2). From the very beginning, Iris did not like to take any drugs, and she kept trying to reduce the dosage or stop it entirely. The rest of the family was hoping that with the Risperdal, Iris would be less depressed, but to no avail: there was no difference.

On Wednesday, September 9, Iris took Christopher to see his doctor in Palo Alto, and I went along to help her. Christopher's pediatrician was a woman doctor who had been seeing him since he was born. The doctor maintained that she did not think Christopher had autism, or at least she could not see it at this stage. She found that Christopher was physically healthy, except for an allergy problem. But she suggested that Iris consult an autism specialist, and gave her a number of names in an effort to ease her worry.

In the meantime, Iris could not sleep at night again in her house with Christopher next to her bedroom. Since Risperdal has a sedative effect, her sleep problems might have also been due to her decreased dosage. In any case, we suggested that she sleep in our house. Ping could come to work late in the afternoon and stay overnight to take care of Christopher. Ping said she would give it a try.

The next time Dr. B saw Iris, he learned that her condition had not improved and that her problem with insomnia had resumed with the reduced 1-mg dosage of Risperdal. He wanted to change the drug and prescribed a similar antipsychotic drug called Abilify (aripiprazole, from Bristol-Myers Squibb). I immediately searched for information about this drug on the Internet and found that it was a relatively new drug. Some users called it a wonder drug; others said it had serious side effects on them. Without knowing anything about antipsychotic drugs, we listened to the doctor. As soon as Iris took the Abilify, 10 mg, she became excessively sleepy. She could sleep for twelve hours or more straight. Iris now essentially lived with us in our house, so I carefully recorded the kind of drugs and the dosage she took and the effect of the drug on her. Later, I gave a copy of her medical chart to Brett so we both could monitor her medicine intake.

Iris was so sleepy on Abilify that she was not able to get up in the morning to take Christopher to preschool. So Shau-Jin and I took him to the preschool in the morning and picked him up in the afternoon. Iris yawned all the time and did not have any energy to work.

Then Ping said that she could not stay overnight five times a week. At best, she said, she could only work three nights a week. Shau-Jin and I also felt physically and mentally drained from taking care of Iris. Therefore, Brett called Luann in Illinois, and she agreed to come to help. Iris felt that her illness and inability to take care of Christopher was a burden to everyone, something she hated. I could see that she was very sad and that she felt helpless.

On Saturday, September 18, because Iris's condition was not improving, Brett and I both called Dr. B to express our concerns. He immediately arranged a meeting that afternoon and asked all of us to come. That afternoon, since Luann had arrived from Illinois and could watch Christopher, we went with Iris and Brett to Dr. B's office. He heard our briefing on Iris. We described that Iris could not get rid of her worries and her excessive drowsiness and lack of energy since she started taking the drug Abilify. Dr. B stunned us all with what he said next—in a very serious tone, he said he thought Iris's condition was very grave, and he suggested that Iris check into a recovery facility. He said the facility was in Sausalito near the beach; it was quiet and ideal for mental patients to recuperate. As soon as Iris heard this, she immediately showed her disapproval. I could understand her suspicion of any facility designed for so-called "mental patients." She had learned many historical instances of government persecution of political dissidents. One way was to put those dissidents into mental institutions and abuse them, sometimes leading to death. I did not blame her for her suspicions. She was already suspecting that evil forces were at work against her for what she had written and done in the name of justice.

She told Dr. B that she did not think her mental state was that bad and that she didn't need to go to a recovery facility. Actually, I saw that Dr. B was fully aware of Iris's sensitivity. He was very careful and had already avoided using the word "hospital" or "institution." He pointed out that the facility was like a resort or a residential facility, except that there were supervisors overseeing the residents.

I was interested in finding some specialists in the psychiatric field who he could recommend to help Iris in her situation. Dr. B mentioned two psychiatrists at a local medical clinic.

The discussion in Dr. B's office lasted nearly an hour and did not really get anywhere. When we all left the office, I saw that Iris was very alert and displeased. After we reached home, Iris told me that on the way home, she and Brett had already decided that Dr. B was too old and that they did not believe what he said. She was going to discontinue seeing him.

I was astounded to learn that she had made this decision just because he mentioned that she should check into a recovery facility. In spite of that, I told her that I thought Dr. B was quite kind to arrange a special meeting immediately on a Saturday afternoon and to voice his concern. However, Brett said he had lost confidence in Dr. B when Dr. B said "To be honest, I've never treated a patient like you before."

I got busy looking into the background of two psychiatry specialists that Dr. B had recommended. It was a surprise to find that these two doctors specialized in electroconvulsive therapy (ECT), which was commonly known as electroshock treatment. My God, I said to myself, if I told this to Iris, it would further confirm her decision that she would never go to Dr. B again. Iris had told me a long time ago about how cruel it had been to use electroshock therapy to treat mental patients in the past.

Indeed, when I told her about what I had found out about the doctors, she was very upset and said, "Do you know this is a very old method for treating mental patients? There is tons of scientific evidence that has proved it's ineffective. I could not imagine he would suggest that I go to see doctors using this kind of method. . . ."

Dr. B's recommendation was only making her feel worse.

Dr. B was going to take a week-long vacation and, before he left, he asked Iris to see him after he came back from the trip. This gave Iris an excuse to avoid making a followup appointment with him, and she switched to another doctor.

In the September 18 meeting, to help Iris's condition, Dr. B had prescribed the antidepressant drug Celexa (citalopram, from Forest Pharmaceuticals). He prescribed 5 mg of Celexa for Iris to take for four days, then increasing the dosage to 10 mg. This was in addition to the 10 mg of Abilify.

At this time, Iris was already experiencing the strong side effects of Abilify. Most obvious were her lack of energy and the fact that she was drowsy all the time. In addition, when she woke up from her daily nap, she complained that her shoulder and leg joints were sore, which were new symptoms that she thought likely to have been caused by the drug. I was quite worried about the side effects of Abilify and voiced my concern to Dr. B. He said the dosage was the lowest possible and that the side effects would gradually disappear. In retrospect, it appears to us that Abilify had a big impact on Iris's mental state; it was a turning point in that her condition became worse after she started taking Abilify, and then later worsened even more with Celexa.

After Iris decided she was not going to see Dr. B anymore, Dr. A came back from his month-long vacation. Brett made an appointment for Iris to see him because we had not found another doctor yet. The appointment was on the evening of September 20. Since Brett would be out of town on that day, he asked us to take Iris to the appointment, which was at 8:15 P.M. It was probably Dr. A's last appointment for the day.

Dr. A let us all into his office, and he looked very tired. Perhaps that was why we felt that he was not very interested in hearing about Iris's condition. Iris told him that she had seen Dr. B, but was not going to see him anymore and wanted to continue with *him*, Dr. A. Dr. A did not like the drug Abilify that Dr. B had prescribed, and said he would change Iris back to Risperdal, but he did not insist on changing back right away.

When the session was about to end after only ten or fifteen minutes, he reminded Iris to make the co-payment right there, just as before. This distressed us all, and we could not help getting the impression that he was more interested in the co-payment than anything else. When we walked out the office, we felt very disappointed because he had not been helpful at all.

After this meeting, I told Brett, who agreed with me, that we needed to find a board-certified, better, more concerned psychiatrist immediately.

Tuesday, September 21, was a day I would never forget. In the morning, after Luann and I took Christopher to the preschool, I went home; by this time Iris had gotten up, and she said she wanted to go to the post office and then the library. I wanted to go with her as usual, but she refused. I did not like her to drive by herself. The sedating side effect of the drugs was quite serious, making driving dangerous. However, she was upset because I was accompanying her everywhere and she felt I was following her too closely. She insisted on driving by herself to the library. I acquiesced and told her she needed to get home before 6 P.M. She agreed.

I was uneasy all afternoon. Near 6 P.M., I called Luann and learned that Iris had not returned home. Brett was in Ohio. I was so worried, I went to the entrance of our housing complex and stood at the side of the street and waited. I watched every passing car, hoping to see Iris's car. I waited and waited and the day became dark, and I still had not seen Iris's white Oldsmobile. I was almost going crazy with not knowing where she was.

At this point, I also called Brett in Ohio and told him what had happened and asked him what was the license number of Iris's car. About 7 P.M., we called the police and reported that Iris was missing and told them the car model and license number. Then at 7:30 P.M., Iris called me. She sounded a little confused. She said that she had gone shopping and become tired, so she'd checked into a hotel to sleep. She said she had just woken up and realized that it was already evening. Her voice was soft and sounded a little guilty.

I comforted her and said it was all right. I asked whether she needed me to pick her up. She said she was in the nearby shopping square and would drive back home right away. We waited another half hour before she showed up. She was all right, but she looked very confused. Several minutes later, two police officers arrived at her home. We explained to them that Iris had just returned and we were so sorry to have bothered them. The police did ask Iris a number of questions before they left.

During the police questioning, Iris told them that she was fine without giving any details. After they left, Iris told us that she had checked into a hotel, and she thought she had swallowed some sleeping pills, and she wanted to go to the hospital for a checkup. We were very confused and wondered whether what she was saying was true or not. Shau-Jin and I asked her many questions, and she said she had indeed taken sleeping pills in the hotel.

By this time, Michael had arrived; we had told him about Iris being missing. We decided that what Iris had told us was true, so Michael drove us all to a local hospital's emergency room. On the way, Iris told us that she was really not sure whether she had taken the sleeping pills or not. From her appearance, she seemed normal and sober and not under any influence of any drugs. At the ER, while waiting in the doctor's office, she told me again that she could not remember whether she had taken the sleeping pills or not. When the doctor finally came, he examined her and asked a few questions. The doctor concluded that she had not taken any sleeping pills and said that if she had, she would not have been as sober as she was. I was puzzled as to what had really happened while she was in the hotel.

Several days later, we found a big unopened bottle of vodka in her kitchen cabinet. Later, we realized that she had indeed made her first suicide attempt in the hotel. She'd bought the vodka and sleeping pills and checked into a hotel, but then she must have fallen asleep in the hotel, perhaps due to her prescription medications. In the end, she did not take the sleeping pills nor the vodka. When she woke up, she was not sure herself whether she had taken the pills. At the time, we still had not realized the strong side effects psychiatric drugs could have on a person's mental function, nor the possibility that they could cause or amplify thoughts of suicide. We now know that the Abilify Web site warns that the drug "can affect your judgment, thinking, or motor skills," as well as the side effects of increasing the risk of suicide, drowsiness, anxiety, and muscle stiffness, and the Celexa Web site warns about suicide, anxiety, and akathesia (a dangerous agitation associated with self-destructive or aggressive impulses).

It is my firm opinion that the side effects of the medication had altered Iris in a big way. In all the years we have known each other, as mother and daughter, Iris has always been strong, resilient, and undaunted and had never considered suicide as a way out. She often expressed that she could not understand how people would commit suicide. Her first attempted suicide occurred when she was on 10 mg of an antipsychotic drug, Abilify, for nine days, and on 5 mg of an antidepressant, Celexa, for two days.

I have since learned from all the sources (see Epilogue) that antidepressant drugs like Celexa belong in the class of medications called SSRIs (Selective Serotonin Reuptake Inhibitors) which includes Prozac, Paxil, and Zoloft. These medications can paradoxically have the side effects of making a depressed patient even more anxious and suicidal. It could make people confused and alter their personalities. In some patients, SSRIs can induce suicide ideation and behavior; these serious side effects of SSRIs have been well documented in recent years, but we were not aware of it at the time. And perhaps even more importantly, research has revealed that the first few days on an antidepressant SSRI, and any time that a dose was changed, were the times of greatest risk.

What happened on September 21 was very scary for all of us. The incident indicated that Iris was considering committing suicide, and now my deepest fear became a reality and I knew I had to watch her even more closely.

The next day, she got up early and seemed alert. She told me she was going to her home office to clean up and work. I went to see her in the afternoon; she was working hard in her office sorting out her papers. This was the first time since she'd come back from Louisville that I saw her as the old Iris—hard at work.

"You look good today," I said to her.

She said, sounding like her old self, "Because I don't want to die."

I was overjoyed to hear her say that and stayed in her office for a while. I helped her a little before I went to pick up Christopher from preschool. Once Christopher got home, Iris played with him, and she also tried to help Luann with the household chores. But after several days, Iris became depressed again.

On Friday, September 24, Brett told us that Luann had suggested that she would like to take Christopher with her to Illinois in light of the current situation. After we heard the news, both Shau-Jin and I felt uneasy about the suggestion; but when we told Iris about it, to our surprise, she agreed. She expressed that she felt it was best for Christopher to move to Illinois. Her reason was that she believed someone was going to hurt her immediate family members, and Christopher would be safer if he lived away from her.

Once Iris and Brett agreed, it was no use for us to show our disapproval. The date for the move was October 9. Ken would come to California on October 1; then Ken and Luann and Brett would travel together to take Christopher to Illinois.

On Wednesday, September 29, Brett accompanied Iris to see Dr. A because we still had not yet found another psychiatrist for her. She complained to Dr. A that she was too sleepy with the Abilify, so Dr. A asked her to discontinue Abilify and go back to Risperdal.

On Saturday, October 2, there was only one week left for Christopher in California. It was sad for us to think that he would separate from his mother soon. Iris was very sad too, but I could see that she truly believed someone might want to harm him. Now that Christopher was going to live with Luann and Ken, she seemed calmer, even though it was such a sad situation. Needless to say, Shau-Jin and I were heartbroken that we would not be able to see our grandson every day like we had for the past two years.

At this time, we tried to cheer Iris up by encouraging her to call her close friends, such as Barbara Masin. Barbara drove up from Santa Barbara and visited Iris for a weekend. They went out hiking and saw a movie together. It seemed that Iris's spirits were lifted somewhat when Barbara was with her. But as soon as she left, Iris was depressed again.

Iris switched back to Risperdal 1 mg and Celexa 10 mg each day after she saw Dr. A on September 29. We had been very concerned about whether the medication was right for her. It seemed like it did not help her much with her depression but just made her sleepy and agitated. We were desperate and felt that she needed a good doctor to follow her progress. Shau-Jin and I went to the San Jose State University library to do a background search on each doctor on the list provided by Brett's health plan. It turned out that most of the doctors were either child psychiatrists, or their office location was too far away, or the specialty was not listed.

Shau-Jin and I wanted desperately to lift Iris's spirits. We were alone in this struggle, because Iris did not want us to disclose her condition to anyone outside of her very closest family members: Brett, his parents, her parents, and her brother. We respected Iris's wishes. We did not dare to ask other friends of ours or hers for help or advice, for fear that she would think we'd betrayed her, which would mean we would lose her trust in us.

Almost every day, we asked Iris to take a walk with us on the levee in the back of our housing complex. We knew that the exercise was good for her, and we hoped the walking outside in the sunshine would dispel her depressive thoughts.

On Tuesday, October 5, it was partly cloudy, a typical northern California autumn day. I could not sleep the night before. Christopher was going back to Illinois with Luann and Ken that coming Saturday, only four days away. The thought haunted me. We went to Iris's house that afternoon and asked her to take a walk with us. For a change, instead of walking on the levee near our house, Shau-Jin suggested that we go to Hakone Garden, a Japanese garden, located in the Saratoga Mountains, a twenty-minute drive from our home.

When we arrived at Hakone Garden, which was up on a hill, there was not a single person in the garden, and the surrounding area was very tranquil and peaceful. We passed a small arched wooden bridge and walked up the path leading to a bamboo garden. The silence gave me an unspoken anxiety. Finally, we reached a small resting place where we could sit down. It was a wisteria vine-covered shelter surrounded by oaks and pines. It was unbelievably quiet; I could only hear the wind as it blew through the woods and the rustling sound of leaves. Suddenly, Iris said to us, "They tried to recruit me."

"Who?" Shau-Jin asked, surprised.

Iris sat down on the wooden bench, her body against a vine-covered post.

"During the book tour. There was a person who came up and talked to me in a threatening tone, 'You will be safer to join us.'"

"What did you say to this person?" Shau-Jin asked.

"I was scared and did not know what to do, so I just ran away and did not say a word," Iris replied. "Dad, do you think it's safer to join an organization or not to join? I'm worried about the safety of our family."

"Iris, you are fine." Shau-Jin tried to calm her down. "In my opinion, not to join any organization was the safest way. You see, if you want to maintain the freedom of speech, stay where you are now, an independent writer and author. That is the best."

Shau-Jin continued, "You may join an organization if you want to, but not because someone is threatening you to do so."

Then I also told Iris that that was why Shau-Jin and I liked to work in an academic institution. We could have the freedom to voice our opinions at any time. We also assured her that she had done nothing wrong, and that everything would be all right. She was safe with us.

We spent about an hour discussing the issue. It seemed Iris did not feel she'd handled the situation well; said she should not have just run away from that person. I could see she was not convinced about what we told her. This was the second time she had mentioned this incident to us. The first time was right after she'd come back from the extended five-week-long book tour in April and May. She wanted us to keep it confidential.

In that garden on that day, she reiterated her fear that someone was trying to harm her and her immediate family. Now the sun peeked out of the clouds and the autumn colors of trees were so bright that it hurt my eyes. The seeming tranquility of the garden could not give me any peace. My heart was heavier than before we'd come.

It seemed that the drugs Iris was taking were not helping her at all. I started wondering about the side effects of the drugs. I had read the warnings of those medicines in fine print, stating that SSRIs such as Celexa could have a suicidal risk in children and adolescents, but Iris was thirty-six years old. At the time, I did not realize that SSRIs could induce suicide ideation and behavior in adults too. Nevertheless, the warning about suicide gave me an eerie feeling.

The doctor in Louisville had described Iris's breakdown as a brief reactive psychosis. He also added that it could be a possible bipolar disorder onset. But Iris had no history of bipolar disorder. I had ordered a number of books on the topic and had started to read them. She did not have many of the symptoms of bipolar disorder. She had anxieties and worries about Christopher, which was natural for a mother.

In my reading research about mental illness, one book specifically mentioned that a mood stabilizer such as lithium or Depakote should be added and taken together with antidepressants. I had wondered why the doctor had not prescribed a mood stabilizer for Iris when she was taking Celexa. Several days before Iris's suicide, the last doctor she saw finally did prescribe Depakote in addition to Celexa, but it was too late.

Because Iris did not want us to disclose her condition to our relatives and friends, I began actively looking into the national and local support groups for mental illness. I immediately joined the local chapter of NAMI (National Alliance for the Mentally Ill) of Santa Clara County. I also learned that there was a local support group for bipolar disorder that met regularly at the Stanford Psychology Department building. Even though I did not believe Iris was so-called "bipolar," I was eager to learn what bipolar disorder was and how it could be treated and cured, as I did not want to rule out any possibility of helping her.

I told Iris about the support group with high hopes and asked her to come to the meeting with me. At first she refused, but after much urging she finally agreed. That was on Wednesday, October 6. We drove to Palo Alto and found the Stanford Psychology building in front of the fashionable Stanford Shopping Center. It turned out the group was a self-help organization, formed entirely of bipolar patients, and had nothing to do with Stanford University or its clinic. The organization borrowed the room from Stanford. The only connection to Stanford was the organizer, who was being treated by the famous bipolar expert at Stanford, the psychiatrist who had been recommended by the doctor in Louisville.

It was not a pleasant experience. First of all, the organizer and another co-organizer described that they both had bipolar disorder. They were being treated with numerous psychiatric drugs, a total of six or seven at a time, and finally they'd had to stop all medication "cold-turkey" in a hospital under supervision and start all over again. This was definitely sending a chill down our spines. Then the other patients, one by one, described their symptoms and the drugs they were taking. Essentially they were comparing notes, but they were prohibited from quoting or commenting on their doctors. My original intention in going to this meeting was to get a possible idea of how to cope with Iris's depression. But what we got were horror stories from each patient. It seemed that every one of them took several different drugs simultaneously on a trial basis, and the conclusion was that none of them worked very well. It was a totally disappointing meeting.

At the meeting, even though Iris was depressed, she was the most alert among all the people in the room, and she asked a lot of very logical questions. When we came out from the meeting, Iris told me that she felt bad that all of the people there were like "zombies," and she was appalled to learn that a doctor would prescribe so many drugs which did not help them in any concrete way. She vowed to me on the way to the parking lot that she would never come to this kind of group meeting again and she was going to stop taking her medication from that moment on.

I was very much regretting taking her to this support group meeting, and the result was completely the opposite of what I had anticipated. That night, I was very agitated and depressed myself. I felt a melting-down sensation from my shoulders on down, and I could barely breathe. I thought maybe I was in the throes of an anxiety attack. I felt fearful and hopeless because I couldn't help Iris.

Iris tried to spend as much time as possible with Christopher because he would be leaving for Illinois soon. She pushed him in the stroller and walked with us on the levee. I could see that her heart was struggling with so much emotion.

On Saturday, October 9, we got up at 5 A.M. and went to see Christopher off for the early flight to Illinois. The taxi van was waiting in front of their house. It was still dark. Christopher was pulled out of his warm bed and was half awake and did not know what was going to happen. Iris got up early and stood there watching as Brett moved suitcase after suitcase and handed them to the taxi driver to load into the van. Luann and Ken packed most of Christopher's clothes, toys, books, his favorite blanket, and so forth in several big bags. The luggage completely filled the back part of the van. Iris stood there without any expression. She seemed to be trying to insulate herself from the sorrow of the scene. Finally, after Brett put Christopher in the car seat in the back with Luann, he got into the front seat next to the driver. Iris walked around the van to the other side where Christopher was sitting. She gave Christopher a big hug and then she gently touched his face with her soft hands. She stroked his face up and down a few times. She did not cry; neither did Christopher. Finally, the car engine started and the van disappeared in the dark morning mist.

We returned home and tried to get some sleep, but I could not. I went to see Iris in her house. With all the people suddenly gone, she was the only one in the house, and I felt I needed to be with her.

The next day was Sunday, and with Christopher and everyone gone, Iris and I were taking a walk on the levee. It was a bright, sunny day. She was quiet as we walked. While we walked, I stared at our two shadows projected on the trail, moving right along with our steps. There was no other sound, just that from our footsteps. She did not want to talk; she was silent, immersed in her own thoughts.

Several days earlier, Brett had found a psychiatrist, Dr. C, referred by one of their friends. At first, Dr. C did not want to accept Iris as a patient right way. After I learned that from Brett, I immediately called Dr. C and told him that Iris was the author of *The Rape of Nanking;* that impressed him; he promised to see her right away. On Monday, October 11, Iris was going to see Dr. C for the first time. Brett asked us to take Iris to see the doctor since he would still be in Illinois and could not make it, so Shau-Jin and I accompanied her to Dr. C's office.

In the office, I handed to Dr. C my summary report of Iris in Louisville and the current update on Iris. This was the third time in two months that I had handed this report to a psychiatrist. Dr. C told us very frankly that his policy with patients and their family members was complete openness. He stressed that any discussion should be in front of patients. If we sent him e-mails, copies should be addressed to the patient too. I could sense that Dr. C wanted to win his patient's trust by using this open policy. Looking back, I doubt that this open policy was good in Iris's case, because we could not discuss and tell Dr. C privately information about Iris that was vital for her mental health. Dr. C did not know that Iris did not trust doctors in general and was not willing to disclose her innermost thoughts to them, rendering him unable to properly treat or diagnose her.

I was living with Iris until Brett got back from Illinois on Tuesday evening, October 12. On that day, I walked with Iris to her mailbox in her nearby post office, which only took twenty minutes. On the way there and back, I tried to get her mind off her worries. I asked her about the *Lord of the Rings,* the series of books that she and Michael had read and enjoyed when they were in high school, as a way of distracting her and perhaps taking her back to happy memories about her favorite pastime in the world, reading books. Iris was able to describe the complicated stories of the Hobbit and The Ring in great detail, including the names of the characters and the places and the plots. I was amazed that her mind was so clear.

After seeing Dr. C, Iris still maintained that she wanted to stop all the medications. Iris stopped taking Celexa on October 7, after the support group meeting. She told Dr. C on the phone that she would discontinue seeing him if he insisted on her taking medicine. As a compromise, Dr. C persuaded her to continue seeing him and then he would decide whether she could gradually decrease the dosage of Risperdal. All of us told Iris that both the medication and the psychotherapy sessions were needed for a rapid recovery. If she didn't want to take medication, then at least she should have psychotherapy sessions with a doctor. She agreed to continue seeing Dr. C. Looking back at what ended up happening, it was so ironic: Iris was the one who did not want to take the medication, whereas the rest of the family believed in doctors and thought the medication would help her.

Iris called Luann to ask about Christopher every day, sometimes twice a day. She talked to Luann for a long time on the phone, asking details of Christopher's activities. She missed him greatly.

I was actively looking into exercise programs in a community center for Iris and myself, so we could go together every morning to exercise. I was told that the central San Jose YMCA had a good exercise program. On Friday, October 15, I asked Iris to go with me to check it out. At the beginning, she hesitated, but with my encouragement she went along with me. From our house to the YMCA was not far, about a twenty-minute drive. When we arrived at the YMCA, we went into the lobby. The clerk showed us their programs and allowed us to go in to check out the facility.

When we came out to the lobby, it was about noon and we were quite hungry. We found a tall, thin African man who was busy setting up food on a long table in the hallway. On the table was a sign which read "Free Food Tasting," and on the other end another sign which read "Queen of Sheba Restaurant welcomes you." We went up to the man and asked what that meant. He said he was the owner of the restaurant, which was just across the street from the YMCA. He came from Ethiopia, and the food on display was typical Ethiopian food, and it was free.

We could not believe our luck. This was the first time I could remember having a free lunch ever in my life. The food had just been cooked in the restaurant and brought in on the table. The steam with its distinct aroma from the exotic food made both Iris and myself salivate. We each took a plate and dished some food onto our plates. There was injera bread (similar to the Middle Eastern pita bread), black and red bean casseroles or stews, hard-boiled eggs in a special sauce, and some meat dishes and white rice. All the dishes were delicious. We could not believe the owner of the restaurant was so generous. Iris and I sat down at the small table and chairs they set up for the event and enjoyed the meal. I had never had Ethiopian food in my whole life. I found the food delicious and could not believe such exquisite food came from a country so torn by conflict and war.

I saw the satisfactory expression on Iris's face also. This was the first time she had enjoyed food wholeheartedly since she had returned from Louisville. When we finished the meal and went out to the parking lot, we looked at each other and burst out laughing. This was our usual behavior when we came across unexpected good luck. This kind of facial expression only occurred when both of us were completely happy and satisfied.

This was the last—and one of the most memorable—moment we had together in the final period of her life. I knew she enjoyed life, she loved life. Here was the daughter I knew. Unfortunately, she did not get the chance to experience more of this joy in her life. I am saddened whenever I think about her laughter on that day.

When we came home, I helped Iris sort her papers for donation to the Hoover Archives and other institutes. In the process, Iris told me that I was the best mom in the world. I could not stop my tears whenever she said that to me!

That day was a remarkable, memorable day, but then things deteriorated rapidly.

On Monday, October 18, Iris saw Dr. C, and later we learned from Iris that Dr. C agreed with her: she could decrease the Risperdal to 0.8 mg from 1 mg, and the dosage would be decreased gradually over a period of time. That meant that Dr. C thought Iris was getting better. We did not know what Iris told Dr. C in the psychotherapy sessions twice a week. We learned later, after she died, that Iris had never disclosed her innermost thoughts to Dr. C, who told us at the funeral that Iris had misled him.

Every day, Shau-Jin and I had a routine walk with Iris on the levee. She always told us that she had much unbearable pain, which I assumed was mental pain but not physical pain. I just could not envision it while she described it to us with such anguish. I wished so much that I could relieve her pains by sharing them with her. She also told me that sometimes she felt she was being smothered, as if she was drowning in the ocean. Only later, I realized that the excruciating pain she described could have been induced by the medication she was taking—a serious side effect of the antidepressant after its withdrawal (see Epilogue).

The morning of Thursday, October 21, when I went to see her, she was very unhappy and complained that I was following her too closely. I found she had not eaten well the night before, so I suggested going out for lunch. We drove to a nearby restaurant. In the parking lot, when she stopped the car, she sat there and told me without any expression that she wanted to cry but had no tears. Her face was greenish and in a horrible depressed state. At this time, she had already mentioned that she did not want to live anymore. I also noticed that her arm and leg movements and facial expression were rigid. And it seemed even worse that she wanted to cry but had no tears. Back then, I did not suspect that all these symptoms could be the serious side effects of the medication.

In the afternoon, she came to ask her dad to make a series of duplications of her photos on DVD on his computer. She said she wanted to send them to the archives. We did not suspect at the time, but in retrospect she might have already prepared for her final destiny.

Shau-Jin and I were quite worried that day, so we called Brett and went over to their house. The four of us talked. We told Iris that she should not harm herself. We tried not to use the word "suicide" for fear it would give her the idea or confirm her already-dark thoughts. She did not answer. That night I knew it was a very dangerous and critical time, but I was in despair and did not know what to do. I wanted to write to Dr. C and tell him about Iris's suicidal thoughts, but I was afraid that he would insist that I send a copy of my e-mail to Iris as he believed in a policy of openness with his patients. I hesitated and did not e-mail him.

Over the weekend I called Iris and Brett, but they weren't home. I didn't know what Iris was doing. Out of desperation, finally on Sunday evening, October 24, I gathered my courage and mailed my e-mail to Dr. C. I told Dr. C that Iris had told us that part of her wanted to live, but another part of her wanted to die. She said this occasionally, but on Thursday she mentioned it several times, and I had to do something.

Then Dr. C noticed that my e-mail did not have Iris's e-mail address and returned it to me. He lectured me that he did not wish to communicate without Iris's knowledge and wanted me to re-send my e-mail to him and a copy to Iris. I had no choice and did so accordingly.

Brett also wrote to Dr. C the next morning and told him that Iris had been off the Celexa for more than two weeks now and only on Risperdal 0.8 mg and had become increasingly depressed. In the evening, Brett sent another e-mail to Dr. C, sending a copy to Iris and us, and said that Iris had been visiting Web sites like thefinalexit.org and other suicide and euthanasia Web sites. This really alarmed us a great deal.

In the evening, Dr. C called Iris at home and got no response, so he called us. We immediately went to their house and found that Iris and Brett had just come home from a walk. We told them that Dr. C had called and was quite concerned with Brett's e-mail about Iris's browsing some suicide Web sites, and he wanted to talk to Iris. Iris returned the call. On the telephone, Dr. C told Iris that she had two choices: either take the antidepressant Celexa or go to a hospital. Iris was stunned. She agreed to take the medication. But after she hung up the phone, she was very angry and told us we had betrayed her by reporting this to Dr. C.

Two days after she took 1 mg Risperdal and 5 mg of Celexa on Thursday, October 28, I took a walk with her in the morning and had lunch with her in her house. I tried to be with her all the time. I came home to rest for a while that afternoon. At 3:30 P.M., I called to check on her, and there was no answer. I knew she should be alone at home and wondered why she was not answering, so I went to her house. She was not there, and her car was gone. I went upstairs to her office and found that the computer was on. I saw that she had last been browsing a Yahoo map, and that there was an address on the map. I immediately called Shau-Jin and asked him to search for that address. Shau-Jin called me back and said it was Reed's Sporting Goods and the shop sold hunting equipment. I was alarmed and waited anxiously in Iris's house for her to come home.

Finally, an hour later, she came home, looking somewhat uneasy. While she was making an excuse about cleaning the garage, I checked her purse in the living room. In her purse I found a safety manual for using a gun and a sheet on how to apply for a license to own a gun. I was terribly scared and went to the garage and confronted her about the gun safety manual. I asked her why she needed a gun. She was stunned and became very unnatural and said that she needed it to defend herself. In the meantime, Brett came home from work and Shau-Jin came to the house too. I told them about the incident. Brett calmly asked her why she needed a gun. We all told Iris that she was safe—she did not need a gun. Then Brett asked Iris to go outside for a walk.

I was very scared that night, but I still did not know the proper way to deal with the situation. Everyone thought I was always overly worried, but the fact that Iris was going to a gun shop was unthinkable! Nobody in our family had ever even *handled* a gun in our entire lives, not to mention *owning* a gun. This was completely out of character for Iris.

It should be noted that the day Iris visited a gun shop was the third day she had resumed taking Celexa, and September 21, when she'd made her first suicide attempt, was two days after she first took Celexa. I cannot help but thinking that there is a strong correlation between her taking the antidepressant Celexa and her suicide attempts.

The next day was Friday, October 29. In the morning when I went to see Iris, she did not want to see me. She apparently knew that I was checking on her very closely, and she wanted to distance herself from me.

Iris had an appointment to see Dr. C that afternoon. Since Iris refused to let us accompany her, I e-mailed Brett that he should take Iris to see the doctor and tell Dr. C that Iris intended to buy a gun. I was glad when Brett told me later that he'd made an appointment to see Dr. C that afternoon. It turned out, however, that the meeting with Dr. C was quite short and Brett did not have a chance to mention the gun to him. In September, Brett had criticized me for worrying too much about Iris. Now he apologized to me because he realized that Iris indeed had suicidal tendencies.

After October 28, the day I found out she had gone to a gun shop, Iris avoided me. On Sunday, October 31, I went to a farmer's market in the early morning and bought some fresh flowers. I made a flower arrangement to send to her, plus some healthful food I'd bought from the farmer's market. In the evening, I invited Brett and Iris to have dinner with us. This was the last evening we were ever with Iris. It was Halloween night, but it did not have the flavor of Halloween; I might have totally forgotten that that night was supposed to be a holiday. The four of us ate the meal quietly. No one seemed to want to talk. It was strange, but Iris was very calm and peaceful. She told me "thanks" and "the dishes were delicious." I had the illusion that we were at our Urbana home. She was a little girl and was happy and content. When she finished the meal and told me how delicious the dishes I'd cooked had been, suddenly I felt very comforted and relaxed, a feeling I had not had for a long time. I was overjoyed.

After dinner, I asked them whether they wanted to watch the tape of the "Three Tenors" I'd recorded from PBS TV programs years ago. Iris loved opera, so we watched it. Again, it seemed that we had returned to the time that was twenty-some years ago—we were in our Urbana family room, in front of the fireplace, watching a TV program. I hoped that moment would stay forever.

Tuesday, November 2, was the presidential election. The day before, Iris had told us that someone had e-mailed her and predicted that John Kerry would win. She felt relief when she heard the prediction. The next day, as we know, Kerry lost to Bush. We knew that Iris was against Bush's foreign policy at the time and supported Kerry strongly. Besides, she'd written several articles which were highly critical of the Bush administration. The prospect of enduring four more years of the Bush administration was too much for her. The election results could make her even more depressed.

Iris began to feel hopeless, I later realized. She wanted to carry out her plan, and she did not want us to find out. In the last week of her life, she prohibited me from visiting her. She did not even want me to call her, and did not return my calls or my e-mails. In that final week, Shau-Jin and I took a walk ourselves to ease our worries. I went to a Palo Alto support group on Wednesday, November 3. Shau-Jin and I went to another support group in San Jose on Friday, November 5. We tried to gather information on how to deal with depression in loved ones who were possibly suicidal. For all this time, she was actively planning her final exit, while we tried to find a way to rescue her. We raced against each other, and we did not realize that she would carry out her plan so quickly. One week later, on November 9, she was gone.

It was an untimely death. Over the years, Iris had always commented that life was too short for her to finish the things she wanted to accomplish. She said many times that she wanted to write more books, to make films, and to record more oral histories. It was so painful to realize that many of her dreams were not fulfilled. Yet, it is not how she died, but rather how she lived that will be her legacy. Whenever I think of Iris, the memories of a loving daughter and a beautiful soul always remain with me. In her short thirty-six years, she had inspired many, many people in the world with her noble spirit—her passion, dedication, sincerity, and determination—in preserving historical truth and in pursuing justice for the voiceless victims. Iris was a woman whose heart beat passionately for those who suffered. She was a woman who could not forget—she could not forget their agony, and she refused to let their stories go untold.

Iris's life was short but brilliant, like a splendid rainbow across the sky, one that the goddess she was named after would be proud of. Iris's rainbow was magnificent, vanishing quickly. What she left behind is a legacy of a life full of courage and conviction, and a life's work that will continue to illuminate and inspire.

EPILOGUE

From the day Iris died, the question of why she would take her own life has haunted me. I still cannot believe that a person like Iris, who was so enthusiastic about life, would kill herself. Whenever she heard about someone committing suicide, she would tell us that it was unfathomable to her. It seemed that suicide would never, ever be an option to Iris.

The tragedy of her death was so overwhelming at the beginning that I was numb. I was confused. I was not able to comprehend it fully. In the next few years, I started to recall every detail of her life in its last several months. Writing this memoir has helped me sort out many things.

We all felt that the first time we'd seen the change in Iris was when she returned home after her month-long book tour in April 2004. Before the tour, she'd seemed all right. Something must have happened on the tour to make her so afraid.

As most people know, her book *The Rape of Nanking* had caused a firestorm in Japan. Immediately after her death, people speculated that she might have been murdered by the Japanese right-wing groups. I initially excluded this possibility when news reporters raised the question right after her death. However, with time and a careful recall of the events that happened in the last period of her life, I need to reevaluate the small possibility that such groups played a role in her death. Iris was moody and paranoid after her book tour. If we believe what she told us—that someone on the book tour had threatened her—then her sudden change of behavior after the tour made more sense. We may never know what really happened.

In the last six months of her life, Iris constantly referred to an "evil force of conspiracy" attempting to prosecute her because what she had written. Family members always brushed these claims aside, attributing them to her imagination. However, after I read several political commentaries on Iris's death—for example, Steven Clemons's eulogy of Iris (located in the appendix)—the aura of conspiracy will always stay with me no matter how unlikely it may sound.

On top of everything else, Iris started to suspect her son of having autism. Over the ensuing two months, with interview-trip preparations added to her intense investigations about autism, she experienced penultimate physical and mental exhaustion, resulting in her breakdown in Louisville. Treatment with antipsychotic and antidepressant drugs did not improve her condition; instead, it worsened. During that time, I had already suspected that the antipsychotic and antidepressant drugs her doctors were prescribing might exacerbate her condition. I was not so sure about it until 2009, when detailed studies finally emerged to discuss the adverse effects of psychiatric medications.

In 2009, I incidentally saw an on-line comment about Iris's death. The writer hypothesized that Iris's death could likely be a case of medication-induced suicide. In the note, the name of a psychiatrist, Dr. Teicher, was mentioned. Later, I realized that Dr. Martin Teicher is a well-established clinical psychiatrist at the Harvard Medical School. I immediately contacted him. In October 2009, I had the chance to meet him in person at McLean Hospital while I was in Boston attending my PhD thesis adviser Professor Eugene P. Kennedy's ninetieth birthday reunion at Harvard Medical School.

To make a long story short, Teicher gave me several of his published research papers on the emergence of intense suicidal ideation and behavior of patients on the psychiatric drug fluoxetine (such as Prozac, from Eli Lilly). Dr. Teicher's findings on the antidepression and antianxiety drug fluoxetine were alarming and scary. In the 1990 paper [reference 1, see Notes and References section], he and his co-workers found that patients free of recent serious suicidal ideation developed intense, violent suicidal preoccupation after two to seven weeks of fluoxetine treatment. The suicidal ideation state persisted for as little as three days to as long as three months after discontinuation of fluoxetine. He and his co-workers [1] also found that a number of antidepressants, including SSRIs (of which Celexa is one), could induce and exacerbate suicidal tendencies in some patients. It's important to note that the antidepressants paradoxically could worsen depression and induce akathisia, anxiety, and mania.

Dr. Teicher also presented me with a paper published in 2004 [2], in which the researchers found that the current suicide rate for schizophrenia and other psychoses was twenty-fold higher than the rate at the time before the advent of psychiatric drugs. Dr. Teicher told me that when he practiced as a young psychiatrist, he had been more optimistic about the benefit of these "new" psychiatric medications. He has since found that these medications seem to have more serious adverse side effects than previously thought.

I asked Dr. Teicher about the possibility of racial and gender differences in reaction to the psychiatric drugs prescribed for Iris. I had speculated that perhaps the psychiatric drugs Iris took had had stronger adverse side effects to her due to her Asian roots and her gender. It is scientifically established that certain variations in genes, called polymorphisms, tend to vary by ethnicity and can affect the safety and effectiveness of drugs by affecting how they are metabolized [3]. In answering my questions about racial and gender differences in response to psychiatric drugs, Dr. Teicher showed me in several papers [4] that indeed there were racial, ethnic, and gender differences. Asians seem to have a lower threshold for both the therapeutic *and* adverse effects of antipsychotic drugs than Caucasians.

This made me wonder if Iris had been overmedicated because her dosages were calculated based on studies on Caucasian patients. Dr.

Teicher explained his usual protocol for starting a patient on a medication such as Risperdal at a starting dose of 0.25 mg. Iris's initial prescription was 8 times this dose.

In the meeting, I was surprised to learn that although himself a psychiatrist, Dr. Teicher had serious reservations about using psychiatric drugs to treat his patients. He also introduced a book to me: *Side Effects: A Prosecutor, a Whistleblower, and a Bestselling Antidepressant on Trial*, written by Alison Bass [5], a health reporter for the *Boston Globe*. When I returned home from Boston, I read Bass's book and realized that there were a number of other similar books on the subject. It opened my eyes about the lesser-known negative effects of psychiatric medications, especially the associations with suicidal ideations.

From Bass's book *Side Effects*, I realized that not only Prozac, but another similar SSRI antidepressant, paroxetine (Paxil), also caused suicides among users. The book revealed that there was no hard proof that Paxil performed any better than sugar pills in children and adolescents. The company that produced Paxil, GlaxoSmithKline, withheld the unfavorable data from the drug trials and the suicide risk of the drug from the public, and misled physicians and consumers about its safety.

I also learned that the medical researchers who conduct drug trials that are submitted to FDA for approval are financially supported by the pharmaceutical companies to test their products. There are no real protections to make sure that the studies are unbiased. Bass's book forced the government to start protecting its citizens.

Dr. Peter Breggin is another author who has written extensively on the adverse effects of psychiatric medications [6]. Dr. Breggin was one of the early whistle-blowers who promoted extreme caution in the use of psychiatric drugs to treat patients. His work was considered very controversial and was ignored by the medical profession when first published. This was partly due to the lack of disclosure of the pharmaceutical companies and the lack of oversight of federal government agencies and research institutes. Many of Dr. Breggin's findings are now widely accepted, and the new "atypical antipsychotic" drugs such as Risperdal and Abilify are now known to have most of the same risks as the older drugs they replaced [3]. The FDA and the National Institutes of Mental Health now carry warnings on their Web sites that antidepressant medication can double the risk of suicide, compared to placebo [7]. A very recent study [8] found that risks of suicidal thoughts or committing suicide were similar for patients starting any kind of antidepressant. In addition to the risks assumed by taking these drugs, there are also risks when a patient stops taking them.

In the recent book *Anatomy of an Epidemic: Magic Bullets, Psychiatric Drugs, and the Astonishing Rise of Mental Illness in America* [9], author Robert Whitaker, a health science investigative reporter, found that taking psychiatric drugs long-term actually did more harm to the brain than good. The drugs often created more mental problems than benefits in patients. The excessive and abusive consumption of psychiatric drugs resulted in a drastic increase of disabled mentally ill in this country to an epidemic level—the number of mentally ill in the U.S. tripled over the past two decades!

I wish I had learned of the risks of antidepressants and antipsychotic drugs sooner, before Iris was treated with them. In 2004, the psychiatrists who treated Iris were unaware of the potential serious toxic side effects of those drugs, and they were also not well educated about racial and ethnic differences in response to those medications. The age affected by these medications is not limited to youth, as the product labels state, but all ages are at risk for the adverse effects, such as suicidal ideation [1].

Iris had never had a serious depressive or a manic episode in her entire life; therefore Shau-Jin and I, as well as Iris, never believed that she had bipolar disorder. And that was why, at the beginning, Iris was the one strongly opposed to taking any of the prescribed drugs. I have to give credit to Iris, who knew herself better than any other member of the family, even at her lowest point. It was the family members who were ignorant about the toxicity and the serious side effects of antipsychotic and antidepressant drugs—our trust in her doctors and our hope that she would become better by taking those medications turned out to have been counterproductive.

Iris was probably much more sensitive to psychiatric drugs than the average person. Dr. Breggin, in his book *Medication Madness: The Role of Psychiatric Drugs in Cases of Violence, Suicide, and Crime* [6], wrote: "It turned out that the first few days are the greatest time of risk. Perhaps in the same way that the first few sips of alcohol or puffs of a cigarette have such strong effects on the previously uninitiated drinker or smoker, so, too, the first few doses of an antidepressant in the uninitiated can have the most overwhelmingly harmful impact." This, to me, is an exact description of what happened to Iris.

Iris was neither a drinker nor a smoker. In her whole life she had never taken anything stronger than coffee, let alone any psychiatric drugs. Her first suicide attempt on September 21, 2004 and her attempt to buy a gun on October 28 were both completely out of character for her. Coincidentally, both these incidents occurred several days after she began to take Celexa.

I believe Iris's suicide was caused by her medications. She represented a classic case in which psychiatric medications change one's personality. I do not need to repeat the huge number of bizarre cases documented [6, 9], in which an originally ordinary mildly depressed patient becomes violent and destructive after taking antidepressants. The time from Iris's breakdown to her suicide was incredibly short, less than three months, and coincided exactly with the time she started taking psychiatric drugs. And the tragic, violent way she ended her life was not characteristic of Iris. The rapidity of the downward spiral and the violent manner ending her life were very likely triggered by the medications she took. I admit that I am not a clinical psychologist or psychiatrist. But, as a research biochemist, this is the best conclusion I can draw from my close observation as Iris's primary caretaker in the last half year of her life and my own independent research.

Observers have argued that other factors might have played a role in her suicide, such as her fertility treatments that might have affected her mood. As far as I know, her fertility treatment length was very limited, only involving several weeks before the egg retrieval in December of 2001. Her emotional spiral began in 2004.

Others blamed the dark nature of her Nanking book as the cause of her suicide and asserted that perhaps no one should write books on a topic so dark. I know Iris had absolutely no regrets that she had been able to write the Nanking book and expose this tragic chapter of history to the world. Shau-Jin and I also believed that the Nanking book was not a real cause for her suicide; after all, the book was written seven years before her death. It was unfortunate that she was going to write about the American POWs' horrible experience in the Philippines in the 1940s for her next book. Even though this last research was also on a hideous subject and it certainly was not good for her mental health, I don't feel it was a major factor in her depression.

Could Iris's suicide have been prevented? I strongly believe that if she had been given a chance to rest, physically and mentally, without psychiatric medications, she would have recovered and would be with us today. Intensive psychotherapy would have been helpful as well, as we all know there is no magic bullet to snap a patient instantly out of depression. With rest and support, she would have been able to manage her problems, personal or professional, in a systematic and logical way. She had dealt with other obstacles in her life successfully. She was always a strong and passionate person with enthusiasm for life. Tragically, Iris was not given a chance to recover from her physical and mental exhaustion. She was immediately given an antipsychotic drug and then an antidepressant with side effects which could exacerbate her anxiety and mild depression.

I hope this book will help people become aware of the possible danger of psychiatric drugs and to think twice before taking them. Even though the statistics show that the percentage of suicide among patients on antidepressants is low, still it is higher than placebo. Every single life is important and valuable. I don't want what happened to us to happen again in anyone's family.

It was frustrating that when the media learned of Iris's nervous breakdown and reported the doctor's diagnosis as bipolar disorder onset (a diagnosis that was never verified or confirmed), people started to speculate about Iris's mental health without having the information they would have needed to understand her in her final six months. One published book even speculated that she was mentally ill as early as 1999. All these speculations are self-serving due to ignorance. Some people have even suggested that Iris's enormous passion and drive might have been a manifestation of the mania phase of bipolar disorder. Friends who knew her and are trained in clinical psychology resoundingly disagree [3]. This kind of generalization implies that any person who is energetic and ambitious or a perfectionist would have or would develop bipolar disorder. I don't think this oversimplified postulation is acceptable at all.

Iris was an extremely private person. She did not want her plight to be known by the public. Another reason that she wanted the whole thing kept private was the stigma against mental patients in our society. Indeed, mental illness in the Asian culture is especially a taboo subject, as it elicits cruel judgments. Out of our respect for her privacy, we complied with Iris's request that her depression be kept secret; but after she died, we decided to accept the invitation of the Asian American Mental Health Network to speak out in public on behalf of the mentally ill. Open discussion of mental issues and support from relatives, friends, and communities are essential steps for recovery from mental illness—this is the lesson we learned.

Life cannot return when it vanishes. My earnest hope is to use this book to help families with mentally ill members. As many mental-health experts [6] now believe, psychotherapy, faith, and the love and support of family are essential for helping a mental patient fully recover. At the present time, antidepressants tend to offer only modest benefits compared to placebo. This shows that it is often hope that helps reduce depression, not the specific medication. We are far from fully understanding the function of the human brain.

Although Iris has been dead for over six years as this book is about to go to press, her image and spirit were always in front of me as I wrote this book. Those images—her innocent smile, her loud laughter, her curious eyes, her endless thought-provoking questions—are constantly with me. But the most significant thing about Iris was her spirit: to strive to be the best and never give up the pursuit of historical truth and social justice. It's precisely this spirit which has inspired people worldwide. *The Rape of Nanking* galvanized the global Chinese communities and vitalized the international redress movement in forcing Japan to reflect on its actions during the Second World War. However, up to this day, Japan still has neither issued a formal apology to the victims nor paid any reparations to the people whose lives were destroyed in the rampage. And worst of all, Japan has failed to educate its own citizens and future generations about the truth of the wartime atrocities Japan perpetrated in Asia during the Second World War.

As a mother facing the tragic death of her daughter, I'm in a unique position: I could mourn the loss of my beloved daughter for the rest of my life, or I could convert my loss into something positive. In *The Rape of Nanking*, Iris quoted George Santayana's immortal warning, "Those who cannot remember the past are condemned to repeat it," to express the reason why she wanted to write the book. It is my mission to continue the unfinished work that Iris initiated—to educate the next generation about the cruel lesson of history in the hope that that history will *not* be repeated.

A year and a half after her death, on Iris's birthday, March 28, 2006, my husband and I, together with many of her supporters, established the Iris Chang Memorial Fund (www.irischangmemorialfund.net) to continue the work she cherished and to pay tribute to her fighting spirit and enduring legacy. In the past several years, alongside the time I spent writing this book, I devoted my time to activities in education— for the next generation—about the Asian Holocaust. This work gave me a reason to live on and the courage to look forward—and the hope for a peaceful and harmonious world in the future.

Iris wanted the world to remember her writing, her words. She always said that life would vanish one day, but books and words would be left behind. In January 1997, in an e-mail to me, she wrote: "Words are the only way to preserve the essence of a soul. What excites me about speeches is that even after the speakers are dead and buried, their spirit lives on. This, to me, is true religion—the best form of life after death. (And, for now, probably the ONLY form of life after death.)" If, as she said, "Words are eternal," and "Books are the ultimate for writers to reach immortality," then she had already reached her life goal—except that she would have achieved even more if she lived longer.

At the end of the writing of this book, I came to this ultimate question, one whose answer I have always been—and continue—searching for: what is the meaning of life? The answer will surely vary with different people. When I thought about Iris's life, her speech and all those letters she wrote to me and her dad, she clearly expressed that she was a person listening to her heart, her own inner passion, while striving to create something of enduring value. That she meant "standing alone and forging one's own path." And she wanted her son Christopher "better to belong to the critical minority than the unquestioning majority."

To know her inner passion, in an interview in June 2003, she told Robert Birnbaum: ". . . it is important for me to write about issues that have universal significance. One of them that has resonated with me all my life has been the theme of injustice . . . for some reason, I seem to be bothered whenever I see acts of injustice and assaults on other people's civil liberties."

In concluding this book, while I was trying to find a quote from someone who had the same philosophy about life as Iris, I accidentally heard a line over the radio that struck me at once as representing Iris's essence: "There are some that live their lives for others."

POSTSCRIPT

C hristopher is a handsome eight-year-old boy at this writing, and
he lives with his paternal grandparents Ken and Luann in central
Illinois near his father Brett's home. Brett remarried in January 2006,
and he and his wife have two children.

Shau-Jin and I still live in the same townhouse in San Jose. Christopher visits us twice a year during his spring break and summer vacation, and he loves to come to California to visit us. Besides managing
the Iris Chang Memorial Fund, Shau-Jin and I are active in Bay area
organizations such as the Global Alliance for Preserving the History
of World War II in Asia. Because of Christopher's autism, we have also
joined the Bay area organization Friends for Children with Special
Needs. When I have time, I hope I can help the national organizations
in preventing suicide.

NOTES AND REFERENCES

1) Teicher, M. H., Glod, C. A., Cole, J. O. (1990). "Emergence of intensive suicidal preoccupation during fluoxetine treatment." Am J Psychiatry 147:207-210.

   Techer, M. H., Clod, C. A., Cole, J. O. (1993). "Antidepressant drugs and the emergence of suicidal tendencies." Drug Safety 8(3):186-212.

2) Healy, D., Harris, M., et al. (2006). "Lifetime suicide rates in treated schizophrenia: 1875-1924 and 1994-1998 cohorts compared." British Journal of Psychiatry 188: 223-228.

3) "It is scientifically established that certain variations in genes, called polymorphisms": Personal communication with Dr. Diana Zucherman, Clinical Psychologist and the President of the National Research Center for Women & Families, http://www.center4research.org. Other information in this book has been also kindly provided by Dr. Diana Zucherman via personal communication.

4) Okuma, T. (1981). "Differential sensitivity to the effects of psychotropic drugs: psychotics vs normals; Asian vs Western populations." Folia Psychiatr Neurol Jpn 35(1): 79-87.

   Bond, W. S. (1991). "Ethnicity and psychotropic drugs." Clin Pharm 10(6): 467-70.

   Lin, K. M., R. E. Poland, et al. (1991). "Pharmacokinetic and other related factors affecting psychotropic responses in Asians." Psychopharmacol Bull 27(4): 427-39.

   Matthews, H. W. (1995). "Racial, ethnic and gender differences in response to medicines." Drug Metabol Drug Interact 12(2): 77-91.

Bakare, M. O. (2008). "Effective therapeutic dosage of antipsychotic medications in patients with psychotic symptoms: Is there a racial difference?" BMC Res Notes 1: 25.

5) Bass, Alison (2008). *Side Effects: a prosecutor, a whistleblower, and a bestselling antidepressant on trial.* Algonquin Books of Chapel Hill, a division of Workman Publishing, N. Y., N. Y.

6) Breggin, Peter R., M.D. (1991). *Toxic Psychiatry.* St. Martin's Press, N. Y.

—— (2001). *The Anti-Depressant Fact Book: What Your Doctor Won't Tell You About Prozac, Zoloft, Paxil, Celexa, and Luvox.* Da Capo Press.

—— (2008). *Medication Madness: The Role of Psychiatric Drugs in Cases of Violence, Suicide, and Crime.* St. Martin's Press, N. Y.

7 "The FDA and the National Institutes of Mental Health now carry warnings on their Web sites that antidepressant medication can double the risk of suicide, compared to placebo": http://www.nimh.nih.gov/health/publications/eating-disorders/fda-warnings-on-antidepressants.shtml.

The Abilify Web site states that antidepressants may increase suicidal thoughts or behaviors: http://www.abilify.com/Default.aspx?sa=t&source=web&cd=3&ved=0CCkQFjAC&url=http%3A%2F%2Fwww.abilify.com%2F&rct=j&q=abilify%20side% 20effects&ei=vDxDTJSBIML98AakspUQ&usg=AFQjCNEmuZnhqoRv2cM0IGq_-bFnCG8QJw

The Celexa web site and label warn that "patients of all ages taking antidepressant therapy should be closely monitored": http://www.celexa.com/

8) A very recent study: Schneeweiss S, et al. "Variation in the risk of suicide attempts and completed suicides by antidepressant agent in adults. A propensity-score adjusted analysis of 9 years' data." Arch Gen Psychiatry 2010; 67: 497-506. http://www.medpagetoday.com/Psychiatry/Depression/19904

9) Whitaker, Robert. (2002). *Mad in America: Bad Science, Bad Medicine, and the Enduring Mistreatment of the Mentally Ill.* Revised paperback, 2010, Basic Books, Perseus Books Group, N. Y.

—— (2010). *Anatomy of an Epidemic: Magic Bullets, Psychiatric Drugs, and the Astonishing Rise of Mental Illness in America.* Crown Publishing Group, N. Y.

APPENDIX

EULOGY DELIVERED BY JAMES BRADLEY
AT LOS ALTOS, CALIFORNIA, ON NOVEMBER 19, 2004

I stand here with a message for two-year-old Christopher.

My name is James Bradley.

My father was John Bradley.

My father was one of the guys who raised the flag on Iwo Jima.

Growing up, I didn't learn much about the famous Iwo Jima flag-raising photo from him, because he couldn't talk about it.

My father died in 1994.

After his death, I went on a quest to learn about that of which he could not speak.

Christopher, your mother was Iris Chang.

She wrote haunting words about difficult historical truths.

Your mother died in 2004.

Later, I imagine you will also go on a quest to learn about that of which your mother could not speak.

In 1997—five years before you were born—I was struggling in my efforts to write a book about the six flag-raisers in the photo.

For two years I had tried to find a publisher.

Twenty-seven publishers wrote me rejection letters.

My spirits were low.

Then one Sunday I felt a beacon of hope.

A book about World War II was on the *New York Times* "Best Sellers" list.

It was *The Rape of Nanking.*

And it was on that day that I first saw those two beautiful words . . . Iris Chang.

Somehow I got up the courage to write a letter to your mother.

She responded with a picture postcard encouraging me.

The picture on the postcard was a photo of her.

I hung the postcard photo of Iris on the wall of my study.

Every day, as I wrote through my fears, I said to myself, "If she can do it, I can do it."

Flags of Our Fathers became a *New York Times* #1 best seller. Twenty-seven publishers had said "no." Your mother had said "Do it."

Then I wanted to write a second book, but I couldn't find a story.

I turned once again to your mother.

She e-mailed me a suggestion that I contact a guy named Bill in Iowa who had some "interesting information."

I phoned Bill, who then gave me the story that became my second book, *Flyboys.* This book, a gift from your mother, became a #2 best seller.

The opening line of *Flyboys* begins with the words, "The e-mail was from Iris Chang. . . ."

At the back of the book is the Acknowledgement—my opportunity to thank those who made *Flyboys* possible.

The Acknowledgment in *Flyboys* begins with those beautiful two words . . .

"Iris Chang."

Christopher, since writing these books, I have addressed hundreds of audiences around the world.

And I have learned that I am just one of thousands who owes thanks to your mother.

In my quest to find out about my father, I learned that in the brutal battle of Iwo Jima, my dad—a medical officer—held over two hundred screaming young boys in his arms as they died.

And in your quest to find out about your mother, you will learn that she held hundreds . . . thousands . . . no, hundreds of thousands—of tortured dead and screaming victims in her mind's eye.

Iris Chang touched millions and will be remembered on all continents in countless ways.

Here is just one of them.

Four years ago, I established the *James Bradley Peace Foundation*.

The foundation sends American high-school students to China and Japan for one year, to live and study.

The goal of the foundation is to create understanding across cultures so that some day, arms like my father's won't hold the dying . . . and minds' eyes like your mother's won't have to hold war's dead.

Two days ago, our board met and decided that from now on, the American students we send to China will do so as recipients of our foundation's new *Iris Chang Memorial Scholarship*.

Christopher, when you are older, I invite you to come and sit on our board. Come help us choose more students worthy of the *Iris Chang Memorial Scholarship*. By then, you'll be able to meet the many students who will have studied in China in your mother's name.

They will tell you what I already know:

About how when they entered China, they saw the beautiful words "Iris Chang" in the airport bookstores . . . city bookstores . . . and libraries across the land.

How Chinese students study your mother's words to learn their country's history.

And how her photo graces museum walls there, motivating others to search for the truth.

Christopher, as you grow older, my hope is that you can experience three things that I have.

Someday you will learn that of which your mother could not speak.

I hope it will help you understand your mother's legacy, as I have come to understand my father's.

I hope you will someday work sitting under a photo of your mother and feel the warm power of her special inspiration felt by so many others and me.

And later—when you make that difficult but rewarding inner journey to discover your unique mission in the universe—when you find your personal truth—I hope you will acknowledge the example of your valiant mother, who once fearlessly told truth to the world.

Perhaps you will write an acknowledgement to her, a thank-you like I once did.

A thank-you that begins with two bright and hopeful words.

Those two beautiful words . . .

. . . Iris Chang.

REQUIEM FOR IRIS CHANG

by *Steven Clemons*

http://www.thewashingtonnote.com/archives/2004/11/requiem_for_
iri/index.php

I HAVE JUST BEEN GUT-PUNCHED BY THE NEWS that a dear friend
and intellectual soul mate over the last several years, Iris Chang, was
found dead in her car near Santa Clara, California.

Iris's book, *The Rape of Nanking: The Forgotten Holocaust of World
War II*, had immeasurable impact on a collective historical amnesia
problem not only in Japan, but also in the United States and around
the world. This brilliant and beautiful writer and thinker was, to me, a
modern Joan of Arc riding into the nastiest of battles calling for honest
and fair reconciliation with the past.

We met via e-mail years ago. She joined a quest I was on some years
ago to try and get people to look seriously at the contemporary legal
consequences of back room deal-making by John Foster Dulles on the
eve of signing the San Francisco Peace Treaty, formally ending Allied
Occupation of Japan on September 8, 1951. I wrote a *New York Times*
piece on this subject, which appeared on 4 September 2001.

Whereas I thought I had found an interesting historical tidbit
that had been neglected by historians and lawyers, Iris Chang knew
that I had just wandered unsuspecting into a raging battle between

Chinese and Japanese warriors over memory and the historical record. She called me, and we had a two-hour phone conversation where she helped prepare me for the onslaught of criticism that would fly my way from those who wanted to preclude any discussion of Japan's wartime responsibilities.

She followed up with her own *New York Times* articles on the debate about Japan, war memory, and what I called—America's complicity in Japan's historical amnesia. Unfortunately, her articles are not available on the Internet.

We met several times in person, once after a talk I gave at De Anza College in Cupertino, California, where she sat anonymously in the back of a room of 500-600 people interested in Japan's war memory debate. This subject is one she owned—and was one that I had just stumbled into—but her brilliance and authority on this subject was tempered by intimidating modesty. She never let anyone know that she was there at De Anza.

We also shared a platform together at a conference organized in April 2002 by the University of San Francico Center for the Pacific Rim.

It would be irresponsible for me to suggest anything more than the authorities are suggesting about her death, but I would only add that I find it distressing and worrisome that two brilliant change-agents, Iris Chang and the late film-maker Juzo Itami, who made us see our worlds differently than we otherwise would—each supposedly committed suicide, after bouts of depression. I have never bought the story about Juzo Itami, whom I also knew and who was at war in his films with Japan's national right wing crowd and yakuza.

I have no choice but to accept what has been reported about Iris's death—but all I can say, and I can barely express anything sensible about this tragedy, is that the world has lost much in her passing.

Iris Chang wrestled with the tensions between conviction, faith, and communal lies. She was attacked from so many corners for her important work that she tried to untangle why truth was so frequently strangled by conviction, faith, and delusion.

We once discussed at length this passage from Friedrich Nietzsche's "The Anti-Christ." I don't believe that Iris was a Nietzsche acolyte, but what follows below captures much of what we were both struggling with at the time:

One step further in the psychology of conviction, of "faith." It is now a good while since I first proposed for consideration the question whether convictions are not even more dangerous enemies to truth than lies. ("Human, All-Too-Human," I, aphorism 483.)

This time I desire to put the question definitely: is there any actual difference between a lie and a conviction?—All the world believes that there is; but what is not believed by all the world!—Every conviction has its history, its primitive forms, its stage of tentativeness and error: it becomes a conviction only after having been, for a long time, not one, and then, for an even longer time, hardly one.

What if falsehood be also one of these embryonic forms of conviction?— Sometimes all that is needed is a change in persons: what was a lie in the father becomes a conviction in the son.—I call it lying to refuse to see what one sees, or to refuse to see it as it is: whether the lie be uttered before witnesses or not before witnesses is of no consequence.

The most common sort of lie is that by which a man deceives himself: the deception of others is a relatively rare offense.—Now, this will not to see what one sees, this will not to see it as it is, is almost the first requisite for all who belong to a party of whatever sort: the party man becomes inevitably a liar. For example, the German historians are convinced that Rome was synonymous with despotism and that the Germanic peoples brought the spirit of liberty into the world: what is the difference between this conviction and a lie?

Is it to be wondered at that all partisans, including the German historians, instinctively roll the fine phrases of morality upon their tongues— that morality almost owes its very survival to the fact that the party man of every sort has need of it every moment?—"This is our conviction: we publish it to the whole world; we live and die for it—let us respect all

who have convictions!"—I have actually heard such sentiments from the
mouths of anti-Semites. On the contrary, gentlemen!

An anti-Semite surely does not become more respectable because he
lies on principle. . . . The priests, who have more finesse in such matters,
and who well understand the objection that lies against the notion of a
conviction, which is to say, of a falsehood that becomes a matter of prin-
ciple because it serves a purpose, have borrowed from the Jews the shrewd
device of sneaking in the concepts, "God," "the will of God" and "the
revelation of God" at this place.

I am too sad to write more about her now.

Arafat's passing has been grabbed by many as an opportunity to move
the sorry state of Israeli-Palestinian conflict in a new direction.

Perhaps those in Japan who reviled Iris Chang's important work
can step down from their strident defense of a white-washed history
and find a course that leads to a more introspective and self-aware
nationalism than is the case today.

ACKNOWLEDGMENTS

There are many people I would like to thank, as without their support, it would not have been possible to complete this book.

First, my deepest gratitude goes to my husband, Shau-Jin, for his patience and love. He encouraged me to write this book from the very beginning, and for five years he has endured the long hours of endless discussion. He was always supportive and gave me tremendous confidence in finishing this book and was my true champion. And to my son, Michael, whose love helped us get through the most difficult period of our lives after Iris died.

I would like to thank Ken McLaughlin, who was very enthusiastic about the book the first time we met during his interview for a *San Jose Mercury News* article. He edited part of the first draft in the early phase of the book. He also helped me connect with his writer friends. His enthusiasm and his confidence in me will be always remembered.

Thanks to Lara Heimert, the editor-in-chief of Basic Books, who took time to meet with me and encourage me, and suggested a number of ways to improve my manuscript.

My gratitude also goes to Peter Li, who patiently edited my book proposal. He also spent hours in reviewing the draft of the book and gave me numerous valuable suggestions.

To Ignatius Ding, who gave his critical opinions in improving my book and generously agreed to write a Forward even though his life is so busy. Without his insight and support, this book would have simply been not possible.

My deepest thanks goes to Richard Rhodes, who agreed to write the Introduction as soon as he finished reading the preliminary manuscript. His advice about the publisher process and suggestions for improving my manuscript were invaluable. Shau-Jin and I cherished the meeting with him and his wife, Ginger, in May 2010 in the San Francisco Bay area, and we had such a good time talking about many common known physicists and the memory of Iris.

Special thanks to Dr. Diana Zuckerman, who gave me her invaluable expertise and insight in psychology and psychiatry after she reviewed the last few chapters of my manuscript. And to Dr. Fidelia Butt and Shushih Butt for their many valuable suggestions, and also to Hann-Shuin Yew, whose comments in improving the final version of the manuscript are precious. Thanks also to my brother Bing Chang and to Brett Douglas for his careful reading of my manuscript before publication.

During the writing of this book, many friends gave me encouragement and support. Special thanks to Hua-ling Hu, who patiently and kindly guided me through the publication business over numerous phone calls. Other friends such as Wena Poon and Teresa Yu-pei Singer gave me their legal advice in negotiating the contract, and particularly to Teresa Yu-pei Singer for answering many questions related to legal issues.

I would also like to thank my brothers Cheng-Cheng Chang and Bing Chang and my sister Ging-Ging Chang and Iris's many cousins who have given me tremendous support after Iris's tragic death.

I must also extend my gratitude to the many individuals and organizations in the Bay area of California and elsewhere who have supported me since Iris died and have encouraged me throughout the entire process of writing this book: Cathy and David Tsang, Charles and Becky Shao, Eugene Wei, Allen Ho, Betty Yuan, Daisy Chu, Kuo-Hou Chang, Christina Leung and members of Bay area Alliance for Preserving the Truth of Sino-Japanese War (ATPSJW); Rodger Scott, Julie Tang, Susan Hsieh, Lillian Sing, Peter Stanek, Jean Chan and members of The Rape of Nanking Redress Coalition (RNRC); members of Global Alliance for Preserving the History of WWII in Asia (GA); Flora Chong, Joseph Wong and members of Canada Toronto Association for Learning and Preserving the History of WWII in Asia (ALPHA); Thekla Lit and members of Canada British Columbia ALPHA; Nancy Lo, Jack Meng, Michael Lee and members of San Diego Association for Preserving Historical Accuracy of Foreign Invasions in China (APHAFIC); Jeannie Liu and members of Los Angeles ALPHA; Victor Yung, Don Tow and members of New Jersey ALPHA; Kaimay Terry and members of Minnesota ALPHA; Sarina Chiang, Albert C. C. Yang, Renne Lu, Agnes Ahn and members of Boston Historical Society; Larry Wu and members of Washington DC Truth Council; Walter Ko, Sherwin Liou and members of St. Louis ALPHA; C. C. Tien, Jack Peng, Kuei-sheng Chang, Jiu-fong Lo, George Koo, Alice Mong, Richard Chu, Cinian Zheng-Dubin, Cindy Chan, Jane Wu, Ping Tcheng, William Jiang, Peter Balakian, Ron Yates, Steve Clemons, Eamonn Fingleton, Victor Fic, James Bradley, John Price, Werner Gruhl, Ted Leonsis, Bill Guttentag, Violet Feng, Richard Sousa, Linda Bernard, Brad Bauer, Elena Danielson, Susan Rabiner, Barbara Masin, James Hong, Sen Luan, Lung-ching Chiao, Isabel Chiu, Duoliang Lin, Amy Hsieh, Xiu-xin Liu, Lucy Yuan, Meihuey Huang, Lisa Chung, Timothy Larson, Bill Spahic, Anne Pick, Bihua Zeng, Connie Wu, Kevin Chiang, Eric Huen, Belinda Zhang, William King, Lolita Chuang, Cynthia Lam, Cynthia Yao and my 1958 high school graduation classmates from Taiwan.

Many thanks also go to Serena Jones who skillfully edited my first draft of the manuscript, and finally, my gratitude to Jessica Case and William Claiborne Hancock of Pegasus Books, who took the risk accepting my book proposal. My special thanks to Jessica Case for her brilliant final editing; her passion and devotion to this project will always be remembered.

Thanks to Boron's Educational Series publisher for the permission to quote Iris's words in *Barron's Top 50, An Inside Look at America's Best Colleges* (Barron's Educational Series, Inc. 1991 edition).

Thanks to the *San Jose Mercury News* for permission to reprint the photo of Iris Chang which was published in the *Mercury News*.

BOOKS DEDICATED TO IRIS CHANG

The Devil of Nanking, a work of fiction by Mo Hayder (a British bestselling novelist), says, on the inside front page, "For Iris Chang, 1968–2004, whose bravery and scholarship first lifted the name of Nanking out of obscurity."

The *New York Times* best-selling author Simon Winchester, in 2005, dedicated his book *A Crack in the Edge of The World* to Iris Chang by saying, on the inside front page, "With this book I both welcome into the world my first grandchild, Coco, and offer an admiring farewell to Iris Chang whose nobility, passion, and courage should serve as a model for all, writers and newborn alike."

In honor of Iris Chang, donations can be sent to the following organizations:

Iris Chang Memorial Fund
Global Alliance for Preserving the History of World War II in Asia
P.O. Box 641324
San Jose, CA 95164
www.irischangmemorialfund.net

The Iris Chang Journalism Award Fund
University of Illinois, Urbana, IL
www.uif.uillinois.edu